Hobbes's Kingdom of Light

Hobbes's Kingdom of Light

A Study of the Foundations of Modern Political Philosophy

DEVIN STAUFFER

The University of Chicago Press
Chicago and London

The University of Chicago Press, Chicago 60637
The University of Chicago Press, Ltd., London
© 2018 by The University of Chicago
All rights reserved. No part of this book may be used or reproduced in any manner
whatsoever without written permission, except in the case of brief quotations in
critical articles and reviews. For more information, contact the University of
Chicago Press, 1427 E. 60th St., Chicago, IL 60637.
Published 2018
Printed in the United States of America

27 26 25 24 23 22 21 20 19 18   1 2 3 4 5

ISBN-13: 978-0-226-55290-3 (cloth)
ISBN-13: 978-0-226-55306-1 (e-book)
DOI: https://doi.org/10.7208/chicago/9780226553061.001.0001

Library of Congress Cataloging-in-Publication Data

Names: Stauffer, Devin, 1970– author.
Title: Hobbes's kingdom of light : a study of the foundations of modern political
   philosophy / Devin Stauffer.
Description: Chicago ; London : The University of Chicago Press, 2018. |
   Includes bibliographical references and index.
Identifiers: LCCN 2017044569 | ISBN 9780226552903 (cloth : alk. paper) |
   ISBN 9780226553061 (e-book)
Subjects: LCSH: Hobbes, Thomas, 1588–1679. | Hobbes, Thomas, 1588–1679—
   Political and social views. | Political science—History—17th century. |
   Church and state.
Classification: LCC B1247 .S73 2018 | DDC 320.01—dc23
LC record available at https://lccn.loc.gov/2017044569

♾ This paper meets the requirements of ANSI/NISO Z39.48-1992 (Permanence of Paper).

Contents

Acknowledgments

Much of the work on this book was done during the academic year of 2013–14, while I was on a fellowship in Munich. I would like to thank the Carl Friedrich von Siemens Foundation for that extraordinary opportunity and its director, Heinrich Meier, for his support and friendship. I would also like to thank David Bolotin, Christopher Bruell, Timothy Burns, Eric Buzzetti, and Hannes Kerber for reading and commenting on my manuscript as it was in the works.

My deepest debt is to my wife, Dana Stauffer, for the many hours she devoted to reading and discussing drafts of chapters, as well as for the love, wisdom, and patience she showed during the years I was working on this book. Diomedes was right when he said that it is better "when two go together."

An earlier version of chapter 1 appeared as " 'Of Darkness from Vain Philosophy': Hobbes's Critique of the Classical Tradition," *American Political Science Review* 110 (August 2016): 481–94, https://doi.org/10.1017/S0003055416000812, © American Political Science Association 2017. A few paragraphs from chapter 2 appeared in earlier form in an essay, "Hobbes on Nature and Its Conquest," in *Mastery of Nature: Promises and Prospects*, edited by Svetozar Y. Minkov and Bernhardt L. Trout (Philadelphia: University of Pennsylvania Press, 2018), © 2018 University of Pennsylvania Press. An earlier version of a part of chapter 3 appeared as " 'Of Religion' in Hobbes's *Leviathan*," *Journal of Politics* 72 (July 2010): 868–79, https://doi.org/10.1017/S0022381610000228, © Southern Political Science Association, 2010. Chapter 4 is a revised version of an essay, "Hobbes's Natural Theology," published in *Political Philosophy Cross-Examined: Perennial Challenges to the Philosophic Life*, edited by Thomas L.

Pangle and J. Harvey Lomax (New York: Palgrave Macmillan, 2013), 137–51, © Thomas L. Pangle and J. Harvey Lomax, 2013, with permission of Springer Nature. The Harry Ransom Center at the University of Texas at Austin provided the photograph of the engraved title page of Hobbes's *Leviathan* that appears in the appendix.

Editions and Abbreviations

Below is a list of the editions of Hobbes's works I cite in my text, beginning in each case with the abbreviation by which the work is cited. If a work contains article numbers within each chapter, that is the form in which I cite it (e.g., *De Cive* 1.7). In the case of *Leviathan* (that is, the English *Leviathan*), I have followed Edwin Curley's creation of a similar system, based on the paragraph divisions in the Molesworth edition, which are almost identical to those in the original Head edition. Although these paragraph numbers are not present in the recently published Clarendon edition of *Leviathan*, which is now the authoritative edition and the source from which I draw direct quotations, I use Curley's chapter and paragraph system rather than the page numbers of the Clarendon edition because the former allows readers to see immediately what chapter is being cited and thus to locate a given passage in one of the numerous other editions of *Leviathan*. For all works besides *Leviathan*, if a work cannot be cited by chapter and article, it is cited either in a specified form (for example, by letter number in the case of Hobbes's *Correspondence*) or, in all unspecified instances, by page number.

Translations from Hobbes's Latin works are my own. In my quotations of Hobbes's English works, I have taken the liberty, where it has not already been done by an editor, of modernizing Hobbes's spelling, punctuation, and capitalization, except where doing so runs the risk of distorting his meaning. Although this modernization sacrifices something of the texture of Hobbes's writing, it makes for greater readability and avoids unnecessary distractions. All remaining instances of emphasis, whether by italics or by capitalization, are from Hobbes himself, unless otherwise noted.

A Dialogue   *A Dialogue between a Philosopher and a Student of the Common*
                    Laws of England. Edited by Joseph Cropsey. Chicago: University
                    of Chicago Press, 1971.

Anti-White   *Critique du De Mundo de Thomas White.* Edited by Jean Jacquot
                    and Harold Whitmore Jones. Paris: J. Vrin, 1973.

Beh.   *Behemoth, or the Long Parliament.* Edited by Ferdinand Tönnies,
                    with an Introduction by Stephen Holmes. Chicago: University of
                    Chicago Press, 1990.

Correspondence   *The Correspondence of Thomas Hobbes.* Edited by Noel Malcolm.
                    2 vols. Oxford: Clarendon Press, 1994.

De Cive   *De Cive The Latin Version.* Edited by Howard Warrender. Ox-
                    ford: Oxford University Press, 1983. I refer in one instance in my
                    notes to the English translation by Michael Silverthorne in *On*
                    the Citizen, edited by Richard Tuck and Michael Silverthorne
                    (Cambridge: Cambridge University Press, 1998). I have also con-
                    sulted that edition when translating passages from *De Cive.*

De Corp.   *De Corpore: Elementorum Philosophiae Sectio Prima.* Edited by
                    Karl Schuhmann. Paris: J. Vrin, 1999.

De Hom.   *De Homine.* In *Thomae Hobbes Malmesburiensis Opera Philo-*
                    sophica quae Latine Scripsit Omnia, Vol. 2, 1–132. Edited by
                    Sir William Molesworth. London: John Bohn, 1839–45.

Elem.   *The Elements of Law, Natural and Politic.* In *Human Nature and*
                    De Corpore Politico. Edited by J. C. A. Gaskin. New York: Oxford
                    University Press, 1994.

EW IV   *The English Works of Thomas Hobbes*, Vol. 4. Edited by Sir Wil-
                    liam Molesworth. London: John Bohn, 1839–45. The relevant
                    contents of *EW* IV are (by page number):
                         229–78: *Of Liberty and Necessity*
                         279–384: *An Answer to a Book Published by Dr. Bramhall,*
                         called the "Catching of the Leviathan"
                         385–408: *An Historical Narration concerning Heresy, and the*
                         Punishment thereof
                         409–40: *Considerations upon the Reputation, Loyalty, Man-*
                         ners, and Religion of Thomas Hobbes

EW V   *The English Works of Thomas Hobbes*, Vol. 5. Edited by Sir William
                    Molesworth. London: John Bohn, 1839–45. *EW* V consists entirely
                    of *The Questions Concerning Liberty, Necessity, and Chance.*

EW VII   *The English Works of Thomas Hobbes*, Vol. 7. Edited by Sir Wil-
                    liam Molesworth. London: John Bohn, 1839–45. The relevant
                    contents of *EW* VII are (by page number):
                         1–68: *Seven Philosophical Problems*
                         69–177: *Decameron Physiologicum, or Ten Dialogues of Natu-*
                         ral Philosophy

	181–356: *Six Lessons to the Savilian Professors of the Mathematics*
	443–48: *Considerations upon the Answer of Dr. Wallis*
Hist. Eccles.	*Historia Ecclesiastica.* Edited by Patricia Springborg, Patricia Stablein, and Paul Wilson. Paris: Honoré Champion, 2008.
Latin *Lev.*	Latin *Leviathan.* In *Leviathan.* Edited by Noel Malcolm. Oxford: Clarendon Press, 2012.
Lev.	[English] *Leviathan.* Edited by Noel Malcolm. Oxford: Clarendon Press, 2012. But see the remarks above regarding my use of the paragraph numbering in the Hackett edition, edited by Edwin Curley (Indianapolis, 1994).
Obj.	*Objectiones ad Cartesii Meditationes.* In *Thomae Hobbes Malmesburiensis Opera Philosophica quae Latine Scripsit Omnia*, Vol. 5, 249–74. Edited by Sir William Molesworth. London: John Bohn, 1839–45.
OL	*Thomae Hobbes Malmesburiensis Opera Philosophica quae Latine Scripsit Omnia.* Edited by Sir William Molesworth. 5 vols. London: John Bohn, 1839–45.
On Thucydides	*On the Life and History of Thucydides.* In *Thucydides, The Complete Hobbes Translation*, 569–86. Edited by David Grene. Chicago: University of Chicago Press, 1989.
Tract. Opt.	*Tractatus Opticus.* Edited by Franco Alessio. *Rivista critica di storia della filosofia* 18 (1963): 147–228.
Vita [prose]	*Thomae Hobbes Malmesburiensis Vita, Authore Seipso.* In *Thomae Hobbes Malmesburiensis Opera Philosophica quae Latine Scripsit Omnia*, Vol. 1, xiii–xxi. Edited by Sir William Molesworth. London: John Bohn, 1839–45.
Vita [verse]	*Thomae Hobbes Malmesburiensis Vita, Carmina Expressa, Authore Seipso.* In *Thomae Hobbes Malmesburiensis Opera Philosophica quae Latine Scripsit Omnia*, Vol. 1, lxxxi–xcix. Edited by Sir William Molesworth. London: John Bohn, 1839–45.

Introduction

For a man who preferred humility to pride and even took a certain pleasure in describing himself as a worm born a twin with fear (*Vita* [verse], lxxxv–lxxxvi), Thomas Hobbes was remarkably bold in proclaiming the groundbreaking significance of his own thought. Hobbes claimed that he had established a new science of morality and politics, the first such science worthy of the name. Although he was well aware that others before him had devoted themselves to political philosophy and that there was an august tradition going back at least to Socrates, Hobbes was convinced that the pretentions of traditional political philosophy concealed an abject failure. Traditional political philosophy, in all its forms, was as unscientific as it was dangerous to peace and civic stability.[1] Thus, while he acknowledged that geometry had an impressive history, and that natural philosophy had begun to flourish with Galileo, Hobbes proclaimed that political philosophy was no older than his own *De Cive* (see *De Corp.*, Ep. Ded.). But what exactly did he mean by this remarkable claim? And why should we take it seriously?

Let me begin with the second of these questions, since the first can be answered only through a detailed interpretation of Hobbes's works. We find ourselves today at the culmination—or at any rate well along the path—of a civilizational development that Hobbes helped to launch. But that civilizational development has resulted in a bewildering predicament that he would not have predicted. On the one hand, what has emerged out of the theoretical revolution that Hobbes and others initiated is now a shining structure: the modern liberal state, dedicated to human rights, equality, and the continual

---

1. See *De Cive*, Ep. Ded., Pref.; *Elem.*, Ep. Ded., 1.1; *De Corp.*, Ep. Ded.; *Lev.* 31.41, 46.6–11, 46.31–37.

progress of humanity toward ever greater security, prosperity, and freedom. Modern liberalism and modern secularism continue to spread and deepen their influence, expanding a victory of already immense scope. Do not most people in the West continue to believe, even if they are sometimes reluctant to say it, that our modern Western civilization is a tremendous advance on the ways of the past and far superior to any living alternative? On the other hand, serious doubts about the goodness of the victorious principles and the way of life produced by them have arisen and are not disappearing. If anything, they seem to be spreading and intensifying. Our sense of superiority as moderns is often accompanied by a sense of loss and by an awareness, perhaps only dim, that for all of our advances, our lives have been somehow diminished and our souls deprived of something essential to their flourishing. The doubts in question, then, can be found not only among those who stand outside the modern West and wish to keep it at bay or yearn for its destruction; they also dwell within. These internal doubts have a long history in the West, going back as far as Rousseau. Almost as soon as the tide was turned, they began to emerge. Their persistence today finds expression in such surprising developments as Jürgen Habermas's recent talk of a "postsecular" culture, not only as something that is upon us, but even as something to be welcomed in our longing to fill a void left by secular liberalism.[2] Or consider the force with which Aleksandr Solzhenitsyn's criticism of the spiritual emptiness of modern humanism struck many of those who first heard it and continues to strike many who read it today.[3] Even the widespread loss of faith in modern rationalism itself—is that not traceable, at least in part, to doubts about the vitality of the civilization that has arisen from it?

This puzzling predicament of continued success combined with lingering discontent gives us reason to go back to the origins of the modern development. Our need is not so much to tell the story of how we got to where we are—although that is important too—as it is to recover and reexamine the original arguments and decisions by which the first modern thinkers broke

2. This is a relatively recent development in Habermas's thought, but it can be found in several of his works. See, for instance, *The Dialectics of Secularization*, 37–38, 45–47, 50–52, *An Awareness of What Is Missing*, 15–19, 74–75, *The Future of Human Nature*, 102–4, 110–11, and *Between Naturalism and Religion*, 1–6, 131, 211–12. On the fragility and crisis of modern secularism, see also Lilla, *The Stillborn God*, Introduction; Pangle, *The Theological Basis of Liberal Modernity in Montesquieu's Spirit of the Laws*, 2–4 and 130–46. For a powerful expression of ambivalence about the "consciousness of being modern" that displays both a sense of superiority to the past and grave reservations about modernity, see Manent, *The City of Man*, Introduction, and *An Intellectual History of Liberalism*, Preface and Conclusion.

3. See Solzhenitsyn, "A World Split Apart."

free from the premodern outlook and established something new. There are two features of nearly all modern thought that make the roots of modernity difficult to see. The first is its progressive character. Each stage of the modern development has been understood by its proponents as an advance on the past and a further step in the process of enlightenment once described, by one of its great heralds, as "man's emergence from his self-incurred immaturity."[4] The second is its hostility to tradition. At each stage, the modern philosophers and their followers have been less inclined to revere or pay homage to their forebears than to disavow or underestimate their dependence on what has come before. These two features of modern thought, combined with the simple passage of time and the natural tendency of those who live in impressive structures to forget how the foundations were laid, obscure from us the original steps that were taken in full awareness of how novel and in need of justification they were. The leading early modern thinkers, precisely because they were breaking new ground, could not take for granted the answers to basic questions that we who live in the civilization they built now unthinkingly accept as our inheritance. But the recovery of their outlook and arguments is essential for our self-understanding as moderns and for a truly radical—in the original sense of going to the roots—assessment of the problems of modernity that have emerged since they did their work. Were the seeds of those problems planted at the beginning? Or have they arisen because originally sound arguments and doctrines have been forgotten? It would perhaps be unnecessary to ask these questions—they might not even arise—if the progress of modernity had proven to be as unquestionable as it was once expected to be. Yet, since we no longer remain so confident of our superiority and ever-increasing maturity, we must look back to the beginning.

But why to Hobbes? In characterizing the civilizational development that Hobbes helped to launch, I have alluded to its most important and distinctive features: liberalism and secularism. Hobbes, however, would seem too ardent a defender of the absolute power of the sovereign to be regarded as a forefather of liberalism, and it would not be conceded by all Hobbes scholars that he should be considered a secularist. Regarding the latter point, while there are those who would disagree, it is hardly novel or shocking to claim that Hobbes played a crucial role in laying the foundations of modern secularism.[5] Of course, the

---

4. Kant, "An Answer to the Question: 'What is Enlightenment?'" 54.

5. Consider, for instance, the key place of Hobbes in Chapter 2 ("The Great Separation") of Mark Lilla's *The Stillborn God*. There Lilla argues that Hobbes was the pivotal figure in breaking with the tradition of Christian political theology and reconceiving of politics in purely human terms, that is, without any dependence on the claims of theology or revelation. According to

proof of the pudding on this disputed question is in the eating. So let me leave it to the study that follows, not only to provide support for the claim in question, but to attempt to show that it is true in a more thorough and radical way than even many of its proponents think. Hobbes himself described the enemy he sought to defeat as the "Kingdom of Darkness," by which he ultimately meant more than that "confederacy of deceivers," spanning from the early Church Fathers to the later scholastics, whose "dark and erroneous doctrines" helped the Roman Catholic Church attain so much power over men in this world (see *Lev.* 44.1). That characterization is only one salvo in a broader struggle against a more deeply entrenched and powerful foe.

As for the question of liberalism, it is certainly true that Hobbes would grant the sovereign far more expansive powers than would anyone we would readily recognize as a liberal. Yet, although Hobbes's absolutism makes it impossible to regard him without qualification as the first liberal thinker, he did prepare the ground for liberalism in certain key respects.[6] Most important, he was the first to argue that a rightful claim of the individual as individual— his right to self-preservation—is prior to any moral law or set of duties. This argument implied a departure from stricter and more hierarchical notions of virtue and obligation, and a movement toward greater freedom, equality, and individualism. This moral reorientation, in turn, carried crucial political implications, the clearest and most important of which is the limited end or purpose of the Hobbesian commonwealth. In conscious opposition to the classical tradition, Hobbes sought to limit the end of the state to the protection of rights through the securing of peace. And this is just one feature, if the central one, of a broader political transformation that he sought to initiate. Since the precise character and full dimensions of the interconnected moral and political changes at which Hobbes aimed will be a major theme of this book, suffice it for now to say that, while it can hardly be denied that

---

Lilla, "Hobbes's great treatise *Leviathan* contains the most devastating attack on Christian political theology ever undertaken and was the means by which later modern thinkers were able to escape from it" (75). Thus, "the way modern liberal democracies approach religion and politics today is unimaginable without the decisive break made by Thomas Hobbes" (88).

6. Among the many sources that take up the question of Hobbes's relationship to liberalism, those that I have found most helpful are, on the side that stresses the link, Owen, "The Tolerant Leviathan"; Manent, *An Intellectual History of Liberalism*, xvii, 26–32 (cf., however, 40); Strauss, *Natural Right and History*, 181–82, "Some Notes on the Political Science of Hobbes," 121–23, "Notes on Carl Schmitt, *The Concept of the Political*," 100–102; Macpherson, *The Political Theory of Possessive Individualism*, 1–3; Flathman, *Willful Liberalism*, 2–5; on the side that stresses the gulf, Jaume, "Hobbes and the Philosophic Sources of Liberalism" (cf., however, 209–13); Wolin, "Hobbes and the Culture of Despotism"; Mitchell, "Religion and the Fable of Liberalism."

the work of later thinkers—Locke, Montesquieu, and others—was needed to turn Hobbesianism into full-fledged modern liberalism, Hobbes put the first shovel in the ground, and he remains the thinker in whose thought the foundational arguments are most fully and decisively expressed.

Now, at this point, some readers, especially those familiar with the work of Leo Strauss, will be looking in the other direction, that is, not forward from Hobbes to thinkers such as Locke, but backward to Machiavelli, and wondering why he is not the subject of this book. Is not Machiavelli, as Strauss has convincingly argued, the founder of modern political philosophy?[7] It is certainly true that, long before Hobbes wrote a word, Machiavelli declared his own break with the classical tradition, which he rejected as hopelessly and dangerously utopian. Machiavelli proclaimed that his new modes and orders would no longer be based, as those of earlier writers had been, on dreams of perfection, but would rest for the first time on the "effectual truth" of our dire situation.[8] Machiavelli compared himself to an explorer of new lands, a comparison endorsed by Strauss in his memorable remark: "It was Machiavelli, that greater Columbus, who had discovered the continent on which Hobbes could erect his structure."[9] Yet, as that formulation itself suggests, while Machiavelli discovered the new world, Hobbes was modernity's first great architect and builder. To put the point less metaphorically, Hobbes developed, in partial but not complete agreement with Machiavelli,[10] a new science of morality and politics, a new doctrine of justice, and a new teaching about the basis of legitimate sovereignty. Whereas Machiavelli left much to the prudence of well advised or properly educated princes, Hobbes attempted to do something more systematic and thus less dependent on chance. In this respect,

7. This was not always Strauss's view. It was not his view, in particular, when he wrote *The Political Philosophy of Hobbes*. But, as he indicated in the preface to the American edition of that work, which he published almost twenty years later, he changed his mind (see xv–xvi). See also *Natural Right and History*, 177–82, "What Is Political Philosophy?" 40–49, *Thoughts on Machiavelli*, 172–73, 295–99. Cf. Mansfield, "Hobbes and the Science of Indirect Government," 97–98; Cropsey, "Hobbes and the Transition to Modernity," 213–14; Saxonhouse, "Hobbes and the Beginnings of Modern Political Thought," 124–25; Hirschman, *The Passions and the Interests*, 12–13, 32–34.

8. See *Discourses On Livy*, Preface to Book I; *The Prince*, Chap. 15.

9. *Natural Right and History*, 177; see the opening line of the preface to Book I of Machiavelli's *Discourses On Livy*.

10. That the agreement was not complete is indicated most clearly by Hobbes's criticism of the predatory politics of republican Rome in the dedicatory letter of *De Cive*. Consider also *Lev.* 15.4–7. See also Malcolm, *Reason of State, Propaganda, and the Thirty Years' War*, 118–19; Skinner, *Hobbes and Republican Liberty*, 66–69; Sullivan, *Machiavelli, Hobbes, and the Formation of a Liberal Republicanism in England*, 81–82, 86.

Hobbes even implicitly raises, whether fully consciously or not, a Machiavellian objection to Machiavelli, who called for the conquering of chance but did not accomplish it. None of these observations are meant to suggest that the study of Machiavelli is not of great importance for understanding the roots of modernity. But they do suggest that it is in Hobbes, not Machiavelli, that one can see most clearly and fully the emergence of the new political science in the form in which it came to transform the world. And finally—to mention here a point the significance of which we will try to grasp later—Hobbes's political science, because it was developed more than a century after Machiavelli wrote, was developed in light of and in relation to the new natural science that emerged in the interim. The study of Hobbes, then, also allows us to consider the important but perplexing question of the relationship between the new political science and the new natural science.

*

In studying Hobbes, one finds oneself cast upon an ever-widening sea of Hobbes scholarship. One of the pleasures of writing this book has been voyaging on that sea, and I have benefited from the work of many Hobbes scholars, even some encountered in distant harbors. But let me briefly describe my own approach to Hobbes, which differs in important ways from those most prevalent in Hobbes scholarship in recent years.

I have taken an approach to Hobbes that is both broad and exploratory. I have not tried to discover the one key that unlocks all of the mysteries of Hobbes's thought, nor have I singled out for exclusive attention one of Hobbes's distinctive doctrines. My aim, instead, has been to take a comprehensive view of Hobbes by examining the main components of his thought and by trying to understand how they fit together and relate to one another. Hobbes is most well known, of course, for his political philosophy, and, like most scholars of Hobbes, I came to him through that aspect of his thought. But I also explore in this book three other essential components of his thought: his critique of the classical tradition, his largely neglected but nevertheless vital natural philosophy, and his critique of religion. I delve into each of these realms of Hobbes's thought in considerable detail before turning to a direct consideration of his political philosophy. By taking such a broad view of Hobbes's attempt to put philosophic rationalism on a new, more stable footing—for no less, I believe, was his ultimate aim—I think it is possible to reveal the full scope of Hobbes's ambitions and to show that Hobbes was a more radical and revolutionary thinker than he is generally taken to have been. In Hobbes's view, I argue, philosophy in its classical and scholastic forms was untenable. It had to be replaced with a new materialistic physics as well as with a political philosophy rebuilt from the ground up, with new doctrines resting on a new foundation. Hobbes was also, I contend, a thoroughgoing critic of traditional Christianity, the political power of which he wanted to weaken and the theoretical claims of which he wanted to refute. Although there is not a single key to Hobbes's thought, there is a thread that runs through and unites the whole: the challenge of overthrowing a set of traditional forces and doctrines—a "Kingdom of Darkness" supported by a corrupted form of philosophy, but at its heart religious—that had long cast a gloom over philosophy and wreaked havoc in politics. The central claim of this book is that Hobbes was offering and trying to promote a new comprehensive outlook—a rational and secular "Kingdom of Light"—that would dispel the reigning darkness, chasten religion, and bring a new dawn of enlightenment. Because Hobbes was engaged in a broad struggle with multiple fronts, the true dimensions of that struggle can be appreciated only if we consider his project in its totality.

If my approach is broad and exploratory, the primary realms of my exploration are Hobbes's own writings. Much outstanding work has been done in recent years on the historical context in which Hobbes wrote and on his relationship to some of his leading contemporaries. There can be no doubt that the political storms of his time, as well as his acquaintance with the likes of Galileo, Gassendi, and Descartes, had a profound impact on Hobbes's thought. Hobbes lived in a time of extraordinary religious, political, and scientific upheaval, and scholars such as Quentin Skinner, Noel Malcolm, and Richard Tuck have illuminated important ways in which Hobbes's thinking was shaped by the complex, fast-flowing currents of his time. New light has been shed, for instance, on Hobbes's ideological congruence with the "*de facto* theorists" who argued for an acceptance of the new Commonwealth in the wake of Charles I's execution,[11] on Hobbes's relationship to the seventeenth-century European "Republic of Letters,"[12] and on Hobbes's contentious but productive interaction with Descartes.[13] These are only a few examples of the contributions that have emerged from the surge in historical studies of Hobbes; all Hobbes scholars, myself included, have benefited from this

---

11. See Skinner, *Visions of Politics*, 3: 238–307. This section of *Visions of Politics* spans three chapters and consists of substantially revised versions of three earlier essays: "History and Ideology in the English Revolution," "The Ideological Context of Hobbes's Political Thought," and "Conquest and Consent." Hoekstra, "The *De Facto* Turn in Hobbes's Political Philosophy," provides helpful explanations of Skinner's revisions of his earlier arguments and offers an alternative account of Hobbes's connections to the *de facto* theorists.

12. See Malcolm, *Aspects of Hobbes*, 457–545.

13. See Tuck, "Hobbes and Descartes," "Optics and Skeptics."

development in Hobbes studies.[14] Nevertheless, there are certain dangers or drawbacks that come with the increased attention to Hobbes's historical context. For the emphasis on such issues runs the risk—and, to some extent, has had the effect—of drawing scholars off the trail of Hobbes's own fundamental reflections, which he himself almost always presents without direct reference either to England's immediate troubles or to other thinkers of his time.[15] Moreover, the contextualizing approach often leads to an underestimation of the possibility of dramatic ruptures, and thus to not taking seriously enough Hobbes's own claim that he was making a radical break and charting a new course. The more pivotal the thinker, the more problematic is the tendency to explain his thought primarily in terms of the historical circumstances in which he wrote.

The alternative to historical contextualization is immersion in Hobbes's own arguments. This approach need not reject the work of the contextualizers wholesale; rather it can complement it—and sometimes challenge it—by digging into the difficulties in Hobbes's texts and addressing questions that it is better suited to address.[16] The first task—hardly an easy one—is simply to try to understand Hobbes's arguments as he presents them. This includes trying to grasp the interconnections between different arguments, distinguishing what is primary for Hobbes from what is secondary, asking what is bedrock and what is more tentative or derivative, and, in general, trying to look at matters *through Hobbes's own eyes*, to see problems as they appeared to him and to grasp why he responded to them as he did. Although this is the first task and the one to which this book is primarily devoted, a serious

14. Two other impressive works in the same vein are Collins, *The Allegiance of* Thomas *Hobbes*, and Sommerville, *Thomas Hobbes: Political Ideas in Historical Context*. Jon Parkin's *Taming the Leviathan* is also noteworthy as the most thorough discussion of the reception of Hobbes's thought in England in the second half of the seventeenth century. For an account of the virtues of the contextualizing approach, especially as practiced by Malcolm, see Springborg, "The Enlightenment of Thomas Hobbes"; for more critical views, see Berkowitz, "*Leviathan*, Then and Now," and Zuckert, *Launching Liberalism*, 43–81.

15. There are a few obvious exceptions: *Behemoth*, Hobbes's critique of Thomas White's *De Mundo* (often referred to as *Anti-White*), and his objections to Descartes's *Meditations*. But these exceptions prove the rule when it comes to the more important works at the center of Hobbes's corpus, including *The Elements of Law, De Cive, Leviathan*, and *De Corpore*.

16. Consider the following admirable remark from Malcolm, one of the masters of historical contextualization: "Investigating the political and biographical context of *Leviathan* may help to explain the timing of its composition, and may also elucidate some of its particular features. At most, then, it may go some way towards explaining why Hobbes wrote the way that he did, and when he did; but it is very far from exhausting the meaning of his work, or from explaining why Hobbes believed that what he wrote was true" (*Leviathan, Vol. 1: Introduction*, 82).

engagement with Hobbes must ultimately involve also questioning the adequacy of his arguments and the solidity of the positions they support. I take that further step in what I regard as the appropriate places, but always with the caution that comes from an awareness of the danger of criticizing what one may not yet adequately understand. That is a danger of which I have tried to stay ever mindful. But it is not one that can be entirely avoided, especially by someone who approaches Hobbes with some skepticism. My own skepticism toward Hobbes arises in large part from my study of and affinity for the classical authors whom he opposes. Still, I have tried at every step of the way to give Hobbes a full hearing, in order to remain open to learning from him, to face squarely the challenges he poses, and to avoid the ridiculous spectacle of whacking a straw man named "Hobbes" who bears little resemblance to the great man himself.

Let me say a final word here about the structure and approach of this book. The book has seven chapters, but, as I have indicated, there are four main themes: Hobbes's critique of the classical tradition, his natural philosophy, his critique of religion, and his political philosophy. Because my approach is so broad, I have been forced to be selective in the passages I have chosen to discuss. I have tried to find a path through Hobbes's works that focuses on his key arguments and reflections, not one that burrows into every nook and cranny. My aim throughout has been to capture the fundamental and decisive, not to achieve the complete or exhaustive. That inevitably means that many questions, themes, and passages have been left out. If a reader familiar with Hobbes thinks that important details or considerations are missing, he or she will likely be right. I have also not tried to write anything like a comprehensive commentary on any single work of Hobbes. Instead, I have drawn from passages in nearly all of Hobbes's works as they have seemed most illuminating to the questions at hand. No single work of Hobbes contains the fullest expression of his deepest thinking on every important matter; Hobbes himself, at any rate, never raised such a claim on behalf of any of his works or set one of them clearly apart from and above the rest. To be sure, *Leviathan* is justly regarded as his masterpiece, and, like most Hobbes scholars, I have drawn from that work more than from any of the others. But on some questions, such as the problems and possibilities of natural philosophy, other works are more revealing of key aspects of Hobbes's thought.

1

"Of Darkness from Vain Philosophy"

To begin to understand Hobbes's claim that he was the first to put political philosophy on a sound and scientific footing, we must first consider his dissatisfaction with the long-standing tradition of political philosophy in place before he began his work. Hobbes was well aware, of course, that there was such a tradition. How could he not have been, when he regarded it as one of the sources of the storms that destroyed the peace in England? By Hobbes's own account of it, the tradition in question began with Socrates, whose turn to political philosophy not only inspired the likes of Plato, Aristotle, and Cicero to direct their attention to "civil science" but also attracted leisured gentlemen, who were enticed by the dignity of politics and the apparent ease of its study (*De Cive*, Pref.; cf. *Hist. Eccles.*, lines 341–73). When Hobbes raised his claim, then, that natural philosophy had begun only with Galileo and that political philosophy was born in his own *De Cive*, he knew all too well the objection that claim would provoke. Rather than leave it to others to raise the objection, he stated it himself: "But what? Were there no philosophers, either natural or civil, among the ancient Greeks?" (*De Corp.*, Ep. Ded.).

Hobbes's response to this objection is not to deny that there were men in the ancient world who went by the name of philosophers. But from the presence of men called philosophers, "it does not necessarily follow that there was philosophy." Instead of genuine philosophy, "there roamed in ancient Greece," according to Hobbes, "a certain phantasm with a superficial gravity (though inside full of fraud and filth) that somewhat resembled philosophy" (*De Corp.*, Ep. Ded.). If true philosophy is "the wisest mistress of human life and the singular glory of human nature," it was not that beauty that was born in ancient Greece, but rather, in her place, "that painted and garrulous harlot" who was "for so long taken for philosophy" (Latin *Lev.*, 1053). Such remarks—to which further examples could easily be added—suffice to provide an initial sense of Hobbes's contempt for classical thought.

We must be careful, however, not to let his vivid expressions of that contempt carry us all the way to the conclusion that his contempt was simple or total. Hobbes's first scholarly work, after all, was a translation of Thucydides. And if his respect for Thucydides could perhaps be attributed to his affinity for a classical historian who displayed the tough realism he found lacking in the more idealistic classical philosophers, Hobbes at times spoke admiringly of Plato as well. Plato was "the best philosopher of the Greeks" (*Lev.* 46.11), and it is with good reason that his thought has always found favor with "the better sort" of men (*A Dialogue*, 124; see also *EW* VII, 346). Hobbes occasionally acknowledges that even Aristotle at least half-deserves his glorious reputation and that he should be regarded as a true philosopher after all, if only because his genuine love of truth and virtue distinguished him from the fawning and ignorant "sectaries" who followed in the wake of the classical masters (Latin *Lev.*, Appendix, 1191; see also *A Dialogue*, 123; *EW* IV, 387; *EW* VII, 72, 76). More important than these occasional expressions of admiration for the classical philosophers, which serve at least to temper the more striking expressions of contempt, is the fact that the influence of Aristotle, in particular, left its mark on Hobbes's own thought. For instance, Hobbes's analysis of the passions, as Strauss has shown in painstaking detail, is modeled on, and in some places repeats almost verbatim, Aristotle's analysis in his *Rhetoric*.[1] And in his presentation of his natural philosophy in *De Corpore*, Hobbes sometimes approves of Aristotle's definitions and relies on his framework—for example, in his discussion of time (see *De Corp.* 7.3), or in his account of the relationship between accidents and their subjects (see *De Corp.* 8.3).[2]

It is likely this last fact—that Hobbes sometimes draws on Aristotle in *De Corpore*—that led Frithiof Brandt to claim, in his classic work *Thomas Hobbes' Mechanical Conception of Nature*, that when Hobbes refers throughout his works to Aristotle, it is "most frequently in agreement" and "always respectfully."[3] But that claim goes much too far. If we must be careful not to overestimate Hobbes's disdain for Aristotle, so too must we avoid an excessive swing back in the other direction. After all, many of Hobbes's harshest remarks about classical philosophy are reserved for Aristotle. Let one example, from

1. See Strauss, *The Political Philosophy of Hobbes*, 35–42. On the importance of Aristotle's *Rhetoric* for Hobbes, see also Evrigenis, *Images of Anarchy*, 46–59.

2. See Spragens, *The Politics of Motion*, 38–47; Leijenhorst, *The Mechanisation of Aristotelianism*, 4–7 et passim, especially 128–37, 155–63.

3. Brandt, 57.

the chapter of *Leviathan* titled "Of Darkness from Vain Philosophy and Fabulous Traditions," suffice: "I believe that scarce anything can be more absurdly said in natural philosophy than that which is now called Aristotle's *Metaphysics*; nor more repugnant to government than much of that which he hath said in his *Politics*; nor more ignorantly than a great part of his *Ethics*" (*Lev.* 46.11).[4]

The important task, however, is not to gauge the precise level of Hobbes's hostility to Aristotle, but to discover the reasons for it. Although the aim of this chapter is to examine Hobbes's critique of the classical tradition as such, the figure who continually comes into view as the primary target of that critique is Aristotle. Why did Hobbes direct so much of his powerful arsenal of rhetoric and argument against Aristotle? A few preliminary considerations can provide some orientation, if not yet a complete answer. As Hobbes emphasizes time and again, Aristotle's thought, more than that of any other classical philosopher, eventually became fused with Christian doctrines. If Aristotle was only one of the Greek philosophers whose thought was influential in the early church, and not the most influential one at that, his influence surpassed all others with the later emergence and development of scholasticism. By the time Hobbes wrote, the "Empusa" of scholasticism—a specter not with one leg of bronze, the other of an ass, but rather with one leg of heathen philosophy, the other of Christian theology (*De Corp.*, Ep. Ded.)— had become so dominant in the European universities that what was studied there, Hobbes says, was "not properly philosophy . . . but Aristotelity" (*Lev.* 46.13; see also *Elem.* 17.1; *EW* VII, 348; *Hist. Eccles.*, lines 381–84). One might presume that the blame for the degeneration of philosophy into dogmatic "Aristotelity" should be laid at the feet of the appropriators, not those of the appropriated; but Hobbes argues that it is not as simple as that, because Aristotle's teaching readily lent itself to such an appropriation. In other words, there was already a problem at the roots, and so it is no surprise that the tree that emerged, albeit after being watered by sources that Aristotle could not

---

4. In his biography of Hobbes, Aubrey reports: "I have heard him say that Aristotle was the worst teacher that ever was, the worst Politician and Ethick—a country fellow that could live in the World would be as good: but his *Rhetorique* and *Discourse of Animals* was rare" (*Aubrey's Brief Lives*, 158). If one is inclined to discount the importance of this remark because it is merely reported and not from a published work of Hobbes, consider Hobbes's own reference in *Behemoth* to "the babbling philosophy of Aristotle and the other Greeks" (95); see also *Lev.* 47.16. Compare Sorell, "Hobbes and Aristotle," 364, 370–71, who suggests, without warrant in my view, that both the remark quoted in the text and Hobbes's remark as reported by Aubrey "can be understood as indirect criticisms of school divines, whom Hobbes undoubtedly detested, rather than Aristotle himself" (371). See also Evrigenis, *Images of Anarchy*, 48–50, 100–101, 109–10; Spragens, *The Politics of Motion*, 38–39.

fully have anticipated, proved to be a tangled growth bearing poisonous fruit. Furthermore, insofar as Hobbes thought that Aristotle's teaching had been corrupted by its appropriation, he must have regarded Aristotle—as indeed he did—as the serious core of the scholastic tradition and the philosophic rival most in need of confrontation.

These preliminary considerations begin to indicate the importance of Aristotle for Hobbes. Let us turn, then, to a closer examination of Hobbes's critique of classical thought in general and of Aristotle and his scholastic followers in particular. In examining the objections and arguments in Hobbes's critique, I will start from those that appear most prominently on the surface of his texts and that speak most directly to moral and political questions. But one cannot leave matters at Hobbes's relatively straightforward moral-political critique of the classical tradition, because he also criticizes what may provisionally be called the "metaphysics" of Aristotle. Moreover, Hobbes's arguments against Aristotle's metaphysics—we will later see why this term should be regarded as merely provisional—prove to have a bearing on politics, because Aristotle's metaphysical framework, Hobbes contends, had problematic political implications, or at least unintended political consequences. The character of this connection between the metaphysical and the political, as well as its entanglement with issues of religion and theology, will emerge in the course of our consideration of Hobbes's critique. We will thus begin to see, albeit in a negative or indirect way initially, since we are starting from Hobbes's rejection of an outlook that is not his own, the breadth of Hobbes's venture and the necessity of allowing the connections between its different aspects to disclose themselves gradually.

The Moral-Political Critique

Hobbes attributes extraordinary power for good as well as for ill to political philosophy or, as he tends to call it, moral philosophy.[5] The extraordinary power for good, however, is described primarily by way of a promise, as it must be, according to Hobbes, since the moral philosophy of the past and the present (Hobbes's present) has been a disaster. By considering the damage and danger of the "false and loquacious semblance" of moral philosophy that has so far prevailed, then, Hobbes seeks to indicate the benefits that will flow from his own revolution in moral philosophy (*De Cive*, Pref.; see

---

5. Hobbes typically speaks of "moral philosophy," "civil philosophy," or "civil science," terms that he uses interchangeably in the passages that will concern us in this chapter. Consider especially *De Cive*, Ep. Ded., Pref.; see also *De Corp.*, Ep. Ded., 1.9.

also *Elem.*, Ep. Ded.; *De Corp.* 1.7). Hobbes's primary charge against all prior moral philosophy—or, at any rate, his most direct and evident charge—is that it has been a source of chaos and conflict in political life. Indeed, according to his most extreme expressions of the charge, moral philosophy has been *the* source of *all* chaos and conflict in political life: "The two-sided dogmas of the moral philosophers, partly correct and attractive, partly irrational and brutish" have been, Hobbes says, "the causes of all quarrels and killings" (*De Cive*, Pref.). Now, Hobbes is surely well aware that this statement is a vast exaggeration. A man whose first publication was a translation of Thucydides' account of the Peloponnesian War, and who is known above all for his teaching that outside of civilization the life of man is "solitary, poor, nasty, brutish, and short," can hardly have seriously thought that the world enjoyed peace and a golden age before the moral philosophers unleashed the forces of destruction. Hobbes exaggerates in order to amplify an accusation that he puts more simply elsewhere: "The sophists of the past"—among whom he identifies by name Plato, Aristotle, Cicero, Seneca, and Plutarch—have been "the champions of anarchy" (*De Cive* 12.3). But what did these philosophers teach that could warrant such a description?

Hobbes assigns this title, "the champions of anarchy," as he is discussing the seditious doctrine that tyrannicide is licit and sometimes even laudable (*De Cive* 12.3). Hobbes repeatedly points to the danger posed by this teaching, as well as by a prior teaching that prepares it as a premise prepares a conclusion. The prior teaching is, in its narrow form, that private men may and even should judge of the justice of the commands of kings or, in its broad form, that private men may claim for themselves a knowledge of good and evil independent of the sovereign's dictates (see *De Cive*, Pref., 12.1–2; *Elem.* 27.4; *Lev.* 29.6). If this teaching is considered in its narrow form, it is not hard to see the danger that concerns Hobbes, or the way in which the conclusion follows from the premise: to teach men to judge the justice of the commands of kings is to lay the basis for the condemnation and the attempted overthrow of kings whose commands are judged to be unjust. Aristotle, for instance, as part of his famous division between correct regimes and their perversions, drew a distinction between kingship and tyranny (see *Politics* 1279a17–b10). Yet is it not but a mere step, Hobbes asks, from that distinction to the belief in a right to revolution and even in the justice of tyrannicide (*De Cive* 12.3; *Elem.* 27.10; *Lev.* 19.2, 29.14)?[6]

That the premise in question has a broader form, however, indicates that Hobbes blames the classical philosophers for more than the dangerous

---

6. See Cropsey, "Hobbes and the Transition to Modernity," 215; Evrigenis, *Images of Anarchy*, 116–17; Skinner, *Reason and Rhetoric in the Philosophy of Hobbes*, 315.

distinction between kingship and tyranny. "The original error," which was the "root" of this particular doctrine, was that the philosophers let themselves be seduced by "the oldest of the Devil's temptations," the prospect of knowing good and evil for oneself (*De Cive* 12.1–3). Moreover, Hobbes criticizes Aristotle directly and by name for teaching that democracy is the only form of government compatible with liberty and thus with justice, and for teaching that rulers ought to be bound, as their subjects are, by the civil laws. Aristotle—Hobbes's Aristotle, at any rate—put the force of his philosophic authority behind the democratic conception of justice and the belief in the sanctity of the rule of law (see, e.g., *De Cive* 12.3–4; *Elem.* 27.2–6; *Lev.* 21.9, 46.35–36; *Beh.*, 43). But these, Hobbes argues, are problematic and dangerous teachings: the former encourages resistance against all nondemocratic governments; the latter ties the hands of the sovereign and puts the power of judgment back in the hands of the subjects, who are taught to see themselves as guardians of the laws against their transgression by the sovereign.

Now, it comes as a surprise to anyone familiar with Aristotle's *Politics* to hear Aristotle criticized for his excessive commitment to democracy and the rule of law. Is it not a central lesson of Aristotle's political science that, as valuable as the rule of law may be as a check on the passions of men, laws are always derivative from the regime that makes them? Does not Aristotle himself thus stress that it is the *regime*, not the laws, that is ultimately authoritative in every city (see *Politics* 1281a34–39, 1282b1–13)? And as for the claim that he regarded democracy as the only just form of government, Aristotle surely indicates that the democratic claim of the many (the poor) to deserve to rule is as problematic as the oligarchic claim of the few (the rich), to say nothing of its merits relative to the claims of the virtuous and the single outstanding individual. Is it not because none of these claims is without problems, both in principle and in practice, that Aristotle argues for a regime that mixes democratic and oligarchic elements while trying to carve out at least some role in ruling for the virtuous (consider *Politics* 1281a11–33, 1281a39–b37, 1293b31–1294b17)?

Hobbes cannot have been unaware that Aristotle was not an unambiguous supporter of democracy who thought that democratic principles require only the check provided by the rule of law. After all, Hobbes criticizes Aristotle elsewhere for his view that some men are by nature superior to others and thus more deserving of rule (see, e.g., *Elem.* 17.1; *De Cive*, 3.6, 3.13; *Lev.* 15.21).[7] When one takes this criticism, too, into consideration, what seems at first to

---

7. See Kraynak, *History and Modernity in the Thought of Thomas Hobbes*, 48–49; Sullivan, *Machiavelli, Hobbes, and the Formation of a Liberal Republicanism in England*, 91–92; Johnson Bagby, *Thomas Hobbes: Turning Point for Honor*, 114.

be a straightforward critique becomes more complicated and even begins to appear contradictory: How can Aristotle be criticized for being at once too democratic and too inegalitarian? Nor is this the only apparent contradiction in Hobbes's critique of Aristotle and the other classical philosophers. Another is that, even as he blames the classical philosophers for spreading the anarchic conviction that men should sit in judgment on the commands of established sovereigns, he also faults them for accepting too uncritically the opinions of their times, that is, for bowing to the authority of the prevailing *nomos* and for cultivating such habits of deference in their disciples and readers (see *De Cive*, Ep. Ded.; *Elem.* 27.13; *Lev.* 4.13, 21.9). So Aristotle is criticized not only as a democratic elitist, but also—and equally paradoxically—as a champion of anarchy who slavishly bowed to the established order. What sense can be made of what looks like a set of contradictory charges?

A partial resolution of the second paradox, which bears at the same time on the first, is possible through the following line of reflection. In deferring to the dominant opinions of their times, the classical philosophers, Aristotle in particular, were deferring to an outlook shaped decisively by the ascendancy of democratic principles. It may well be the case that neither Aristotle's epoch nor his thought was as democratic as Hobbes sometimes leads his readers to believe (see, e.g., *Lev.* 21.8–9, 46.35; *Beh.*, 23, 158). But Hobbes's exaggeration is again in the service of highlighting a problem. The problem is that in the historical circumstances in which the classical authors wrote—and this holds for Roman authors, such as Cicero, as well as for their Greek counterparts— deference to the prevailing opinions had the effect, not of supporting a stable order, but of throwing the weight and authority of philosophy behind turbulent democratic convictions (see *De Cive*, Ep. Ded.; *Elem.* 27.10; *Lev.* 21.8–9, 46.35; *De Hom.* 13.7). Even the "elitist" teaching that some men are by nature superior to others could strengthen democratic tendencies, because all men in their vanity tend to assume that they belong among the naturally superior and thus are encouraged to assert a claim to rule (see *Elem.* 17.1). But as problematic as these dynamics may have been in the ancient world, the problem becomes much worse when the political teachings of the ancients are brought to bear in later ages that are no longer so democratic.[8] This is a crucial element of Hobbes's diagnosis of the ideological roots of the English Civil War. By his account, many men "of the better sort," who were born under the monarchy but educated in the classical authors in the universities, were first seduced by

---

8. See Schuhmann, "Hobbes and the Political Thought of Plato and Aristotle," 216–18; Manent, *An Intellectual History of Liberalism*, 21–22; Kraynak, *History and Modernity in the Thought of Thomas Hobbes*, 49–52.

the eloquence of authors like Aristotle and Cicero, and then "from the love of their eloquence fell in love with their politics" (*Beh.*, 3, 43).[9] A dangerous faction of gentlemen thus arose who regarded the king's rule as a bit in their mouths restraining their legitimate assertion of their liberty. These rebellious men, made more powerful than their numbers by their eloquence and vehemence, eventually came to dominate the stormy House of Commons during the Long Parliament and, in the end, demonstrated the bloody implications of the classical hostility to monarchy transferred to a modern monarchical age (see *Beh.*, 3, 23–24, 43–44, 56–58, 158; Latin *Lev.*, 1095–97, 1131; *Hist. Eccles.*, lines 369–76, 1157–60).[10]

This line of reflection explains the complicated circumstances that account for some of the apparent contradictions in Hobbes's critique of classical political philosophy. But it does not yet bring us to the deepest level of that critique. And if matters were left at this line of reflection, the effect would be to historicize the critique too completely. For, in addition to his arguments shaped by historical circumstances, Hobbes has a more universal criticism—one that is at once simpler and yet more penetrating. Consider, for instance, a passage from Hobbes's denunciation of all prior moral philosophy in the Epistle Dedicatory of *De Cive*. After contrasting the success of the geometers with the failure of the moral philosophers, Hobbes points as evidence of that failure to the endless quarrels that have been intensified by the influence of the moral philosophers. He then makes this remark about the chaotic situation in which "the war of the swords" has long been nourished by "the war of the pens":

> These things are most manifest signs that what moral philosophers have written up to now has contributed nothing to the knowledge of the truth; it has pleased men, not indeed by illuminating the mind, but by strengthening hastily accepted opinions with charming language that flatters the passions. This part of philosophy finds itself in the same state as the public roads, by which all travel and go to and fro, some walking here and there as they wish, others quarreling, but nothing getting accomplished. There seems to be one reason for this situation, namely, that none of those who have treated this matter, have used a suitable starting point [*commodo principio*] for teaching it. (*De Cive*, Ep. Ded.)

The deeper difficulty that, according to Hobbes, beset all prior moral philosophy—and this of course includes classical thought and Aristotle in

---

9. See Skinner, *Hobbes and Republican Liberty*, 66–68, 140–42, "Classical Liberty and the Coming of the English Civil War," 13–15; Sullivan, *Machiavelli, Hobbes, and the Formation of a Liberal Republicanism in England*, 102–3.

10. See Hoekstra, "A Lion in the House," 215–16; Tuck, *Hobbes*, 74–75.

particular—is twofold. The first aspect is conveyed by Hobbes's description of the opinions that have been buttressed by the "charming language" of the moral philosophers as "hastily accepted" (*temerè receptas*). The second aspect is simpler but ultimately more important: the dependence of the moral philosophers *on opinions as such* and their (connected) failure to establish or employ a proper starting point.

Regarding the first point, Hobbes probably has in mind one "hastily accepted" opinion above all: the belief that man is born fit for society or that he is by nature a political animal. Near the beginning of *De Cive*, Hobbes points to this conviction, for which Aristotle is the original spokesman, as the foundation on which "the greatest part of those who have written anything about public affairs" have built their doctrines (*De Cive* 1.2; see Aristotle, *Politics* 1253a1–39). These authors have "either supposed, or claimed, or postulated" that man is naturally social. Yet, although this fundamental conviction or axiom has long been widely accepted, it is, Hobbes declares, "nevertheless false." "The error stems from an overly superficial contemplation of human nature" (*De Cive* 1.2). Aristotle and others, by mistaking a veneer of apparent sociality for man's true nature, have embraced and encouraged an excessively sanguine view of the motivations of men and their natural relations; they have failed to see through the façade of mutual concern among men to the underlying truth that the primary concern of each man is for his own honor and advantage. The danger of such naiveté is that it leads men—writers and readers alike—to underestimate the severity of the steps that must be taken in order to secure peace and order among men (*De Cive* 1.2; see also *Lev.* 17.1–12, 18.20). It is in part to combat this danger that Hobbes is so explicit in his own contrary assertions that society is unnatural for men and that men are not only out for themselves but also driven by nature into conflict (*De Cive*, 1.2; see also Ep. Ded.; *Lev.* 13.6–10; *Elem.* 14.2–6).[11]

Hobbes's critique of the classical view regarding man's natural sociality is well known and relatively straightforward. Let us focus, then, on the second point mentioned above: Hobbes's criticism of the earlier moral philosophers for their reliance on opinions as such and for their lack of a proper starting

---

11. Compare Pettit, *Made with Words*, 99–100; Sorell, "Hobbes and Aristotle," 373–74; Skinner, *Hobbes and Republican Liberty*, 41–42, 94; Herbert, *Thomas Hobbes: The Unity of Scientific and Moral Wisdom*, 11–12. Evrigenis, *Images of Anarchy*, 100–101, 109–10, argues that when Hobbes attacks the view that man is a ζῷον πολιτικόν, he is not criticizing Aristotle himself but directing his fire only at Aristotle's scholastic appropriators (100–101, 109–10). If this were so, however, it would be very strange for Hobbes to use the Greek phrase, as he does at *De Cive* 1.2. Compare also the effort of Craig, *The Platonian Leviathan*, 383–86, to downplay the disagreement between Hobbes and Aristotle regarding man's natural sociality.

point. This aspect of his criticism, too, is not meant to apply only to Aristotle, but it applies especially to him. And we can see in this consideration, even more than in the preceding one, an important reason besides the sheer immensity of Aristotle's influence that Hobbes directs so much of his firepower at him.[12] According to Hobbes, Aristotle and his heirs "take for principles those opinions which are already vulgarly received, whether true or false— being for the most part false" (*Elem.* 13.3). Aristotle and the Aristotelians take their bearings by praise and blame, calling by the names of the virtues those qualities men praise in everyday speech and by the names of the vices those qualities they blame (see *Elem.* 17.14; Latin *Lev.*, 1095–97; *Beh.*, 44). Now, in criticizing Aristotle for this approach, Hobbes cannot be accused of misrepresenting him. Aristotle *does* take his bearings from the opinions expressed in everyday praise and blame.[13] But why does Hobbes regard such an approach as so problematic?

The problem, according to Hobbes, is that everyday opinions do not provide a sufficiently solid basis for either a secure political order or a science of morality worthy of the name. The problem—the problem of opinions—has several levels. Most simply, everyday opinions are "for the most part false." Yet Hobbes tends to focus less on their falsity than on their fluctuation. Opinions are diverse and variable; different men hold different opinions at various times, and even in the same man opinions blow with the winds of circumstance (*De Cive* 3.21–32; *Lev.* 4.24, 15.40; *De Hom.* 13.8). The endless disputes within moral philosophy are reflections, Hobbes argues, of a prior diversity and variability of opinions within practical life. Because the moral philosophers have merely reproduced in exalted philosophic language quarrels that begin on the plane of popular opinion—which is already a battleground of competing claims—it is not surprising that moral philosophy has tended to divide into competing schools or sects, nor that these have reinforced and intensified the quarrels they have absorbed (*De Cive*, Ep. Ded.; *Elem.*, Ep. Ded., 1.1; *Lev.* 46.6–11).[14] This is another—deeper and less historically contingent— meaning of the charge of "anarchism" that Hobbes directs at moral philosophy. And if the dynamic in question is problematic for obvious practical reasons, because moral philosophy has fueled the fires it should be extinguishing, it is

---

12. See Strauss, *The Political Philosophy of Hobbes*, 139–40.

13. See, e.g., *Nicomachean Ethics* 1094b11–1095a4, 1095a30–b14, 1098a26–b8, 1103a9–10, 1119b22–1120a8, 1129a3–31.

14. Compare Bacon, *New Organon* 1.67, 1.71–79; Descartes, *Discourse on Method*, 7. See also Weinberger, "Hobbes's Doctrine of Method," 1337; Hanson, "Science, Prudence, and Folly in Hobbes's Political Theory," 653–54.

problematic for theoretical reasons as well, because opinions that are so variable and contested "can never be true grounds of any ratiocination" (*Lev.* 4.24).
No stable political order and no true science can be established on such a shaky
and ever-shifting foundation.

There is a reason, according to Hobbes, that opinions are so variable, beyond the obvious diversity of men and circumstances—a reason that explains
why that diversity leads to a diversity of opinions. Underneath opinions,
Hobbes argues, lie passions. Passions in all of their turbulent variability are
the wellsprings of opinions, because men call "good" and "bad"—that is, they
praise and blame—that which they desire or detest (see *De Cive* 3.31, 10.11;
Lev. 4.24, 6.6–8, 6.13, 11.19; *Elem.* 5.14, 27.13; *De Hom.* 11.4, 13.8). To take one's
bearings by opinions, then, is unwittingly to defer to and to buttress the passions. This is what Hobbes means when he says that Aristotle and "other heathen philosophers" merely give a description of the passions, calling them by
the names of the virtues (see *Lev.* 46.11, 4.24, 46.32; *Elem.* 27.13; *EW* VII, 75).[15]
Of course, Hobbes knows that Aristotle would have a response to this charge:
Aristotle's famous doctrine of the mean is intended, not to give the stamp
of approval to the passions, but to educate men in the proper stance toward
them (see *Nicomachean Ethics* 1106a25–1109a24). But Hobbes dismisses that
doctrine as woefully inadequate.[16] Although Aristotle sought to teach men to
resist the passions, or at least their extremes, his teaching was too flimsy and
equivocal to be effective. His doctrine remained entangled with the passions,
and he overestimated the power of reason to educate the passions: "As oft as
reason is against a man, so oft will a man be against reason" (*Elem.*, Ep. Ded.;
see also *Lev.* 11.21). Furthermore, Aristotle failed to identify *the end* on which
the virtues depend for their specification. Even if he plausibly enumerated the
virtues, Aristotle, "yet not seeing wherein consisted their goodness," muddied
the waters by speaking of the proper degrees of the passions, rather than of
the end to which the virtues are means; but "it is not the Much or Little that
makes an action virtuous, but the cause" (*Lev.* 15.40; *Beh.*, 44; see also *De Cive*
3.31–32; *Elem.* 17.14).

This last consideration—that Aristotle failed to identify the end to which
the virtues are means—can give us some guidance on a question that necessarily arises at this point: How did Hobbes think that he himself, by his own
approach and doctrine, could avoid the rocks on which Aristotle and others
had foundered? In particular, how did he think that the problem of opinions

---

15. See Strauss, *The Political Philosophy of Hobbes*, 140; Manent, *The City of Man*, 169, 172;
Hirschman, *The Passions and the Interests*, 52; Evrigenis, *Images of Anarchy*, 137.

16. Compare Garsten, *Saving Persuasion*, 38.

could be solved or avoided? This question becomes more complicated when one considers that Hobbes's own approach culminates in a teaching about the "laws of nature" that, by his own acknowledgment, can be regarded as a doctrine of the virtues with considerable overlap with Aristotle's (see *Lev.* 15.40; *De Cive*, 3.31–32). And of course it can hardly be said that Hobbes's doctrine avoids any entanglement with the passions. After all, it is by basing his doctrine on the most powerful passion—the fear of violent death—that Hobbes claims he can lay such a foundation "as passion not mistrusting may not seek to displace" (*Elem.*, Ep. Ded.). Yet Hobbes departs from Aristotle precisely in this way, that is, by basing his doctrine on the foundation of a single passion that can counteract the whims of the other passions. And more important is the difference between Hobbes and Aristotle concerning the end of virtue. For Hobbes's attempt to bring simplicity and clarity to a realm long clouded by complexity and obscurity depends on his specification of a single, clear end from which the virtues may take their bearings: peace. If Aristotle defined the virtues as means in the sense of means between extremes of the various passions, Hobbes presents them as means in the simpler sense of means to an end that they should serve. Thus he faults Aristotle for proceeding, as he puts it, "as if not the cause, but the degree" of the virtues (or of the passions they regulate) made them virtues (*Lev.* 15.40).

Now, as significant as these differences between Hobbes and Aristotle may be, they are in need of elaboration; and, because they depend on features of Hobbes's fully developed doctrine, they do not yet tell us much about the approach by which Hobbes arrives at his conclusions. What is the proper starting point that he claims to have discovered? And what is the "clear and exact method" by which his conclusions are derived from that starting point (see *De Cive*, Ep. Ded. with *De Corp.* 1.7)? This is not the place to pursue these questions, since the task of this chapter is to examine Hobbes's critique of classical thought. We will return to the comparison between Hobbes's moral teaching and Aristotle's in a later chapter. Before moving on to the next stage of our examination of Hobbes's critique of classical thought, however, let us conclude this one by briefly addressing a puzzle that emerges from what we have considered so far.

As we have seen, Hobbes repeatedly highlights, even to the point of vast exaggeration, the terrible damage that has been caused by moral philosophy. One might expect, therefore, that he would be driven to call for the abandonment of such philosophy as a pseudoscience that sows chaos wherever it spreads. But Hobbes, of course, does quite the opposite. Far from calling for the abandonment of moral philosophy, he moves in the other direction by promising to raise it for the first time to the rank of a genuine science and to transform it such that it will at long last be a force for good in human life. Yet, if things were better before the rise of moral philosophy, why not call for a return to that simple, peaceful situation, instead of launching a massive new enterprise in such a dubious and dangerous branch of philosophy?

It is only a partial answer to that question to say that a return to that simple age is no longer possible: once the genie of moral philosophy has been let out of the bottle, it cannot be put back in.[17] And it still does not fully answer the question to add that the simple age was surely never the golden age of peace and harmony that Hobbes sometimes pretends it was. Those answers are only partial because Hobbes clearly believed that he could accomplish something far greater than a return to a primitive, uncorrupted past. Hobbes's claim—and we should never lose sight of how bold it is—is that his own moral philosophy could be as beneficial as Aristotle's was pernicious, and as scientific as his was unscientific. He goes so far as to promise an "incomparable benefit to [the] commonwealth" than which "nothing more useful can be discovered" (*Elem.*, Ep. Ded.; *De Cive*, Pref.). We will return to this extraordinary promise after examining the other major dimension of Hobbes's critique of classical thought.

The "Metaphysical" Critique

The dimension of Hobbes's critique of classical thought to which we now turn is directed even more pointedly against Aristotle than the one just considered. But what is this other dimension? What should it be called? I have so far used the word "metaphysical," in part for lack of a better term, but also for a further reason. It could instead be called Hobbes's critique of the natural philosophy of the classical schools, which he describes as "rather a dream than science" (*Lev.* 46.11; see also *EW* VII, 128). But one of the reasons it was merely a dream, in Hobbes's view, is that it was not kept sufficiently distinct from metaphysics. And more important for present purposes, Hobbes's critique of it focuses not so much on the whole of classical natural philosophy, in all of its various questions and schools, as on a few closely connected issues on which Aristotle's teaching in particular blurs the line between the natural (the physical) and the supernatural (the metaphysical).

Now, Hobbes is aware that in using the term "metaphysical" to refer to the supernatural, or to that which is "beyond the physical," he is following Aristotle's scholastic heirs in taking a questionable step that was not clearly taken by Aristotle himself. If the original meaning of the title of Aristotle's *Metaphysics*

17. See Kraynak, *History and Modernity in the Thought of Thomas Hobbes*, 177–78.

was only that it was written or placed "after the *Physics*"—that is, after Aristotle's articulation of his natural philosophy in his *Physics* and elsewhere—the scholastic schools of Hobbes's time took it in the loftier sense of "beyond the physical" (*Lev.* 46.14).[18] But although it is a mistake, according to Hobbes, to take the title of Aristotle's work in this way, it is an understandable mistake, and not just for the reason Hobbes most immediately gives: "And indeed that which is there written is for the most part so far from the possibility of being understood, and so repugnant to natural reason, that whosoever thinketh there is anything to be understood by it, must needs think it supernatural" (*Lev.* 46.14). To understand the deeper reasons why Hobbes thinks that Aristotle himself allowed or even invited the misunderstanding of his heirs, we need to consider the central questions at issue in Hobbes's critique of Aristotle's "metaphysics."

There is one doctrine, above all, that Hobbes traces back to Aristotle and against which he is unrelenting in his attack: the doctrine of abstract essences. This doctrine, according to which there are in the world certain essences separated from bodies and thus beings with an incorporeal existence, is "built on the vain philosophy of Aristotle" (*Lev.* 46.18; see also Latin *Lev.*, 1079). But in what way does it rest on an Aristotelian foundation? It is not an easy matter—either in considering Hobbes's view of Aristotle or in examining Aristotle's own writings—to discern whether Aristotle accepted the view that essences have an existence separate from bodies.[19] Yet it is sufficient for Hobbes—sufficient for Aristotle's culpability—that Aristotle left his own view so opaque and that he spoke so often of "substances" and "essences" (as his terminology came to be translated). For Aristotle thereby left open a door through which his followers, led already by the natural human propensity to believe in incorporeal spirits, could travel in their search for philosophic support for their religious beliefs. It is perhaps the most unmistakable testimony of his belief that Aristotle made a terrible error that Hobbes chooses the context of his criticism of Aristotle to make his own most uncompromising statements on the question of being and the possibility of incorporeal existence. On the question of being, Hobbes argues that it is a great mistake to think that there is any deep mystery surrounding the word "is" or the notion

18. Compare Leijenhorst, *The Mechanisation of Aristotelianism*, 18–22; Skinner, *Reason and Rhetoric in the Philosophy of Hobbes*, 411.

19. For a preliminary sense of the difficulty of discovering Aristotle's view of the matter, see, e.g., *Metaphysics* 995b13–18, 995b31–36, 997a34–b20, 999a24–b5, 1001a4–24; compare 1033b19–1034a8. On these passages and the questions they raise, see, above all, Bruell, *Aristotle as Teacher*. See also Forde, *Locke, Science and Politics*, 21–23, 28, 33, 52; Herbert, *Thomas Hobbes: The Unity of Scientific and Moral Wisdom*, 12–13; Spragens, *The Politics of Motion*, 85–86.

of existence: we could easily dispense with the word "is" and "be not a jot the less capable of inferring, concluding, and of all kind of reasoning than were the Greeks and Latins." Such an innovation, moreover, would have the benefit of destroying the illusions that there is a genuine need for the terms derivative from the Latin *est*—"these terms of *Entity, Essence, Essential, Essentiality*"— and that such terms name things that exist apart from particular bodies (*Lev.* 46.16–17).[20] As for the question of incorporeal existence, it is on the heels of his statement about Aristotle's role in the emergence of the doctrine of abstract essences that Hobbes delivers the most strident assertion of his own materialism in his entire corpus:

> The world (I mean not the Earth only, that denominates the lovers of it *worldly men*, but the *universe*, that is, the whole mass of all things that are) is corporeal, that is to say, body, and hath the dimensions of magnitude, namely, length, breadth, and depth; also, every part of body is likewise body, and hath the like dimensions; and consequently every part of the universe is body; and that which is not body is no part of the universe. And because the universe is all, that which is no part of it is *nothing*, and consequently *nowhere*. (*Lev.* 46.15)

The danger of failing to be so clear and emphatic, according to Hobbes, is that if one even suggests that the notion of an "essence" can refer to something distinct and separable from a body to which it is tied, one nourishes beliefs in all sorts of incorporeal beings and possibilities that philosophy should instead try to combat. Aristotle's teaching not only allowed the "demonology" of the Greeks to survive; it also fostered the beliefs that a man's soul, as his essence, can subsist apart from his body, that ghost-like beings can travel throughout the world without the restrictions of bodies, and that faith, wisdom, and other virtues can be poured or blown into men from heaven (see *Lev.* 46.18, 45.2–4; Latin *Lev.*, 1071, 1081, Appendix, 1177). Why are such beliefs so dangerous in Hobbes's eyes? The danger of which he complains most loudly, if not the only one with which he is concerned, is the political danger. Hobbes argues that the prevalence of such beliefs strengthens the power of the "ghostly authorities" (clergymen of various sects) and weakens the attachment of subjects to the civil sovereign. The more intense and wide-

---

20. Hobbes pursues this line of argument in many places. In addition to *Lev.* 46.16–17, see Latin *Lev.*, 1081, Appendix, 1144, 1773–79; *De Corp.* 3.4, 5.3–9; *EW* IV, 303–4, 393–94; *EW* VII, 81; *Anti-White* 27.1, 28.4–5; *Obj.*, no. 14. See also the helpful discussions of Paganini, "Hobbes's Critique of the Doctrine of Essences and Its Sources," 342–44, 347–51; Leijenhorst, "Sense and Nonsense about Sense," 100–102, *The Mechanisation of Aristotelianism*, 45–47; Malcolm, *Aspects of Hobbes*, 190–91.

spread such beliefs, the more powerful and plentiful are the weapons, in the form of threats and promises, by which religious authorities can challenge the temporal power in the name of a higher spiritual kingdom. That challenge is like a disease—Hobbes compares it to epilepsy—that corrupts the body politic, causes it to shake and move in unnatural ways, and ultimately threatens to destroy it by oppression or civil war (*Lev.* 29.15, 44.16, 46.18; see also *Beh.*, 41–43).[21]

The danger to which Hobbes points was not merely a hypothetical one in his time. The worst inciters of the English Civil War, by his account, were the Presbyterian ministers, without whose seduction of the people the antimonarchical orators in the House of Commons could not have succeeded (see *Beh.*, 2–3, 20–28, 57, 95, 158–60; *Lev.* 44.17, 47.3–4; Latin *Lev.*, 1097). Hobbes also spares no contempt for the machinations of the Catholic Church, which, like a dark kingdom ruled by a shadowy king and his army of malevolent fairies, had long asserted its power to the detriment of stability, liberty, and science in Europe (see *Lev.* 44.1–3, all of 47). But these, of course, are manifestations of the danger in the context of Christian Europe and thus, it would seem, far removed from the pagan world in which Aristotle wrote. How did it happen that Aristotle came to loom so large and cause such trouble in Christian ages?

As Hobbes tells the story,[22] the philosophic schools first established by the Greek masters persisted until the time of Jesus and the emergence of the primitive church. At that time, philosophy remained relatively harmless and free: "No one was compelled to swear by the words of Aristotle, even though his doctrines were more widely accepted than those of other sects" (Latin *Lev.*, 1059). If philosophy was still relatively harmless and free, it was also prevalent, as was the superstitious belief in incorporeal spirits: "there were many demoniacs in the primitive church" (*Lev.* 45.9). When the philosophers, or those sectarians who fancied themselves philosophers, embraced Christianity, they did so with reservations—they were *semicocti Christiani* (half-baked Christians)—and to reconcile the new faith with their philosophic principles, they interpreted Christian doctrines in light of the dogmas

21. See Hoekstra, "The End of Philosophy (The Case of Hobbes)," 32; Lloyd, *Morality in the Philosophy of Thomas Hobbes*, 392; Shapin and Schaffer, *The Leviathan and the Air-Pump*, 92–98.

22. The following account is drawn primarily from Chapter 46 of the Latin *Leviathan*, which differs substantially from its counterpart chapter in the English *Leviathan*. I have left out corroborating references and provided citations only for quotations, lest each sentence in this paragraph and the next be followed by a long list of references. The main corroborating sources are these: *Hist. Eccles.*, lines 395–2216; Latin *Lev.*, Appendix, Chapters 1 and 2, especially 1195–99; *EW* IV, 387–403; *Lev.* 44.8, 44.11, 45.9; *Beh.*, 16–17, 40–43; *A Dialogue*, 123–26; *EW* VII, 76–78; *EW* V, 64. See also Johnston, *The Rhetoric of Leviathan*, 196–205.

of their philosophic masters (Latin *Lev.*, 1063). Thus philosophy first merged with Christianity. But this combination predictably gave rise to disputes, especially over the doctrine of the Trinity. The attempt to resolve these disputes through a series of synods and councils, including the pivotal Council of Nicaea, eventually cemented the notion of a "catholic" (i.e., universal) faith, but it did not end the dynamic by which the importation of philosophy stirred controversies over the proper interpretation of church doctrine. In fact, the role of philosophy grew only larger as later theologians turned to Aristotle with less restraint. After the Catholic Church had grown more powerful by surviving the collapse of the Roman Empire, upon whose grave it came to sit as its crowned ghost (*Lev.* 47.21), another crucial development came in the time of Charlemagne. Charlemagne joined forces with Pope Leo III, "an old man skilled in worldly affairs," who traded his assistance with the legitimization of Charlemagne's empire for a recognition of the supremacy of papal authority. At Leo's behest, Charlemagne took the fateful step of establishing the first universities, which provided the cradle for scholastic theology, "a mixture of Aristotle's philosophy and sacred Scripture" (Latin *Lev.*, 1075). As the universities spread their influence, Aristotle became at once the dominant intellectual authority in Europe and a kind of high priest: "In the universities, the *Logic*, *Physics*, *Metaphysics*, *Ethics*, and *Politics* of Aristotle were taught as if the entirety of the sciences were in one man—at that time the greatest Church Father—*Aristotle*" (Latin *Lev.*, 1075).

The original purpose of the universities and of the scholastic theology that emerged from them, according to Hobbes, was to defend the dogmas of the Catholic Church and thereby to secure its power and claim to supremacy (see *Hist. Eccles.*, lines 1854–84). By putting philosophy into the service of a politically motivated theology, the universities, far from providing a home for genuine inquiry, completed the destruction of the freedom of philosophy. Although Aristotelian philosophy seemed to reign supreme in the universities, it "had there no otherwise place than as a handmaid to the Roman Religion" (*Lev.* 46.13),[23] and even the weakening of Roman Catholicism meant, not the liberation of philosophy, but only a partial change in the master (see *Lev.* 47.3–4,

---

23. Reading "had there no otherwise place" with the 2nd ("Bear") edition, rather than "hath there no otherwise place" with the 1st ("Head") edition. Malcolm incorporates "had," regarding it as an authorial revision. For Malcolm's case for regarding "had" as an authorial revision, see his *Leviathan, Vol. 1: Introduction*, 316. It is possible, however, that even if Hobbes made the change himself, he did so for reasons of prudence rather than principle—that is, he may have wanted to cover the tracks of a suggestion that the continued presence of scholasticism in the universities went together with a lingering allegiance to the Roman Catholic Church. But consider *EW* VII, 347, where Hobbes himself suggests that "hath" was either a printer's error or a slip of his pen.

47.19–20; *Beh.*, 56–59). We have already considered the political danger that arose from this appropriation of philosophy. But the political danger is not the only problem that concerns Hobbes. Just as problematic—from a certain perspective, even worse—is what the absorption of philosophy by theology meant for philosophy itself. Philosophy was thoroughly corrupted, not only in its aims but also in its character and content, as it was forced to serve a foreign master and to lend its power to the support of its natural enemy (see *Lev.* 46.13, 47.27–28; Latin *Lev.*, 1075–77; *Beh.*, 40–42; *EW* IV, 264; *EW* VII, 77–79, 348).[24]

If Aristotle had possessed a crystal ball in which he could have foreseen these developments, it is not likely that he would have liked what he saw. After all, Aristotle himself, according to Hobbes, may not even have accepted the very doctrines that made the appropriation of his thought attractive to theologians in the first place. I have already alluded to Hobbes's remarks about the meaning of the word "metaphysics" as the title of Aristotle's great work: Does the word refer to that which transcends nature or merely to the fact that Aristotle wrote or placed the work in question after his *Physics*? "The word *metaphysics* will bear both these senses," Hobbes says, and he suggests that the scholastic theologians were wrong, or at any rate departing from Aristotle, in taking it in the more exalted sense (see again *Lev.* 46.14). There may be no such thing, then, as a genuine science of "metaphysics" in Aristotle's authentic teaching, as opposed to its later appropriation (see also *Anti-White* 9.16). Connected to this consideration is Hobbes's uncertainty as to whether Aristotle himself accepted the doctrine of abstract essences. After sketching in Chapter 46 of the *Leviathan* the political problem caused by that doctrine, Hobbes raises the possibility that, when it comes to Aristotle himself (again, in contrast to his later appropriators), "it may be he knew [sc., the doctrine of abstract essences] to be false philosophy, but writ it as a thing consonant to, and corroborative of, their religion, and fearing the fate of Socrates" (*Lev.* 46.18). This suggestion that the doctrine of abstract essences may have been for Aristotle merely an exoteric doctrine born of caution rather than conviction has to be balanced with the numerous instances in which Hobbes writes as if Aristotle himself held the view in question. Nevertheless, it is a striking indication that Hobbes does not simply assume that Aristotle was a thoroughgoing "Aristotelian."[25]

---

24. Compare Bacon, *New Organon* 1.65, 1.77, and 1.89; see also Kennington, *On Modern Origins*, 22.

25. For instances in which Hobbes treats the doctrine of abstract essences as Aristotle's own view, see Latin *Lev.*, 1081, Appendix, 1177; *De Corp.*, Ep. Ded.; consider also Latin *Lev.*, Appendix,

Yet, even if he suspected that Aristotle's own views differed in important ways from those of his scholastic heirs, Hobbes gives no indication that he ever followed the path that such a suspicion could open up, namely, to investigate in a thorough way whether Aristotle's genuine thought is more tenable and genuinely scientific than the outlook his "sectaries" defended in his name. Hobbes's unwillingness to follow that path can be explained only in part by the obscurity of Aristotle's most fundamental works, especially the *Metaphysics*, which Hobbes repeatedly bemoans (see, e.g., *Lev.* 46.14; *Beh.*, 41–42; *Anti-White* 9.16). The more important reason is Hobbes's settled conviction that, even if one labored to penetrate their obscurity, one would not find a clear and solid position behind the fog. It is even fair to say that, from Hobbes's perspective, if Aristotle's thought was indeed distorted as it was coopted—at least in the sense that merely exoteric doctrines were taken as much more than that—Aristotle in a way deserved such a fate, because his thought did not contain the resources to fend off its appropriation and distortion. The problem is not just Aristotle's overly accommodating rhetorical approach; it is also that there was no truly solid ground, no genuine science, there to oppose, in principle as much as in practice, the theological appropriation of his thought.

Two indications that this is Hobbes's view of the matter can be found in his critique of the "vain philosophy" of the classical tradition in Chapter 46 of *Leviathan*. The first is Hobbes's sweeping declaration, already mentioned, that the natural philosophy of the classical schools was "rather a dream than science," a declaration that is surely meant to apply to Aristotle, among others. The second is that, in the wake of his criticism of the doctrine of abstract essences, which falls within the broader purview of his critique of Aristotelian-scholastic metaphysics, Hobbes turns to a brief statement on physics, and here, too, he is critical of both Aristotle and the scholastics, but now without indicating any important divergence between them (46.24–29). His primary example concerns how "the Schools" answer the question of why some bodies sink naturally toward the earth whereas others ascend away from it. The scholastic answer, taken "out of Aristotle," is, in the first instance, "that the bodies that sink downwards are *heavy*, and that this heaviness is it that causes

---

1161, 1167. For other passages that are either ambiguous or indicative of doubts on this or related points, consider, in addition to *Lev.* 46.18 and *Anti-White* 9.16, Latin *Lev.*, 1085; *EW* IV, 394–95, 427; *Beh.*, 41–43. For a contemporary of Hobbes who also suggests that Aristotle may have concealed his true views behind doctrines he did not accept, compare Descartes, Preface to the French Edition of *Principles of Philosophy*, 5–6. See also Paganini, "Hobbes's Critique of the Doctrine of Essences and Its Sources," 339, 350; Pangle and Burns, *The Key Texts of Political Philosophy*, 247–48; Hoekstra, "The End of Philosophy (The Case of Hobbes)," 45.

them to descend." If pushed to clarify this answer, the schoolmen will define heaviness as "an endeavor to go to the center of the Earth," or they will give another answer: "the center of the Earth is the place of rest and conservation for heavy things, and therefore they endeavor to be there" (46.24). Hobbes argues that the first answer amounts to nothing more than an empty description (it is "as much as to say that bodies descend, or ascend, because they do"), and that the second answer is a ridiculous ascription, to inanimate objects, of desires and purposes that makes nature seem more orderly and purposive than it is (46.24; see also 2.1; *EW* VII, 7, 76, 82).

Generalizing from this example, we may say that Hobbes seems to have come to the conclusion that Aristotle's physics—that is, his natural philosophy in the narrower sense of the term, in which it is either subordinate to or independent of metaphysics—offers little more than empty descriptions, on the one hand, or dubious teleological explanations, on the other.[26] We will consider Hobbes's own natural philosophy in the next chapter. Suffice it for now to say that, while he borrows here and there from Aristotle, Hobbes makes it clear from the outset of *De Corpore*, the central work of his natural philosophy, that he regarded himself as following in the footsteps of those who first broke with the Aristotelian tradition in natural philosophy. The towering figure for Hobbes—the man who, as he proclaims in the Epistle Dedicatory of *De Corpore*, was "the first that opened for us the gate of physics as a whole" by unlocking "the nature of motion"—is Galileo, not Aristotle. Galileo was so transformative, according to Hobbes, that "the age of physics" should not be "traced back further than to him" (*De Corp.*, Ep. Ded.; see also *Anti-White* 10.9). Hobbes speaks in the same passage of the tremendous progress in astronomy and natural philosophy made also by Copernicus, Harvey, Kepler, Gassendi, and Mersenne. Aristotle is mentioned in this key passage only as the source of "the many absurd and false assumptions" that the early Church Fathers and later theologians merged with Christian doctrines in the process that ultimately gave rise to the monster of scholasticism.

*

At the end of our consideration of Hobbes's critique of the moral philosophy of the classical tradition, I called attention to the fact that, despite the

---

26. See also Latin *Lev.*, 1059: "The Peripatetic school, which made the others go silent by its loquacity—what does it have, except for clever tricks of dialectic and rhetoric? Has it rendered intelligible the cause of any natural phenomenon (not obvious to all)?" See also *De Corp.*, Ep. Ded.; *Anti-White* 10.9. Compare Bacon, *New Organon* 1.48, 1.63. See Malcolm, *Aspects of Hobbes*, 151; Spragens, *The Politics of Motion*, 87–90.

dangers of moral philosophy, Hobbes does not call for its abandonment, but instead forges ahead and raises a bold claim about what can be accomplished by his radical reforms. In this respect, his critique of the past culminates in an expression of hope for the future. This point can now be expanded, for we are now able to see more fully why Hobbes thought that he was standing at a crucial juncture in the history of philosophy. If we look at this juncture through Hobbes's eyes, we see a powerful philosophic tradition that has long dominated intellectual life in Europe, but has proven to be worse than useless: it has combined an unscientific moral philosophy that has only intensified political conflict with a metaphysical natural philosophy that has fed the same beast and, by its fusion with theology, rendered philosophy servile and corrupt. Even if some parts of Europe have freed themselves from the grip of the Roman Catholic Church, that development has hardly solved the problem. In some ways, it has even made matters worse by preparing new battlefields of doctrinal conflict.[27] The problem, as we have seen, is at once political and theoretical, and if the theoretical problem feeds the political one, the political problem in turn confirms the theoretical one:

> Whence comes it that in Christendom there has been, almost from the time of the apostles, such justling of one another out of their places, both by foreign and civil war; such stumbling at every little asperity of their own fortune and every little eminence of that of other men; and such diversity of ways in running to the same mark, *felicity*, if it be not night amongst us, or at least a mist? We are, therefore, yet in the dark. (*Lev.* 44.2)

Darkness itself, however, can sometimes provide a light to hope, in accordance with a principle that Francis Bacon expresses well: "Every error that has been an obstacle in the past is an argument for hope for the future." The uncovering of errors raises hopes, according to Bacon, because it bolsters the conviction that "the source of the difficulty is not in the things themselves, which are not in our power, but in the human understanding, and its use and application; and that is susceptible of remedy and cure" (*New Organon* 1.94).

Hobbes, who expresses the same principle, if not quite so vividly as Bacon does (see, e.g., *De Cive*, Pref., 13.9; *Lev.* 29.1, 30.14), displays a remarkable—almost stunning—hopefulness about what the future might hold if his principles should prevail. After remarking on the progress made in geometry and the benefits it has bestowed on human life, he writes this about moral philosophy:

> If the moral philosophers had carried out their own task with equal success, I do not see a greater contribution that human industry could make to

27. See Boyd, "Thomas Hobbes and the Perils of Pluralism," 405–7.

happiness in this life. For if the reasons of human action were grasped with the same kind of certainty as the ratios of magnitudes in figures, ambition and avarice, whose power depends on the false opinions of the multitude about right and wrong, would be disarmed, and the human race would enjoy such constant peace that, with the exception of struggles over space as the population of men naturally expanded, it does not seem that it would ever have to fight again. (*De Cive*, Ep. Ded.)

If this is Hobbes's most extreme expression of hope, it is not his only one, and it differs from the many others only by degree (compare, e.g., *De Cive*, Pref.; *Elem.*, Ep. Ded.; *Lev.* 20.19, 29.1, 31.41; *Beh.*, 58–59, 70–71, 159–60). Although Hobbes is generally thought of as a pessimistic thinker because of his famously bleak view of the natural human condition, his pessimism sits side by side with a tremendous optimism.[28] In a sense, these are two sides of the same coin, because it is on the basis of the very fearfulness of small men, shivering at the prospect of violent death, that Hobbes, the "very able architect" (see *Lev.* 29.1), thought that he could design a structure more solid than any built before. The distinctively modern blend of pessimism and optimism that we can see in Hobbes's view of the human condition and the prospects of civilization finds a parallel in his natural philosophy: by rejecting the naïve beliefs of the Aristotelians that nature is orderly, purposive, and readily intelligible—by accepting instead the very great limits on what we can know of an aimless and mysterious nature—Hobbes thought that a genuine and effective science could be established.

To be sure, a number of questions regarding Hobbes's hopes remain. What is the relationship between his optimism about what could be achieved by his new moral or political philosophy and his optimism in the realm of natural philosophy? If the latter is not as boldly expressed, is that only because in natural philosophy Hobbes regarded his own efforts less as a groundbreaking innovation than as a contribution to a broader movement already under way? Or is it also because the prospects of success on the plane of natural philosophy were less clear to him, perhaps both as to what success would entail and as to whether it could be achieved? These are difficult questions that we will have to consider as we take up the problem of the relationship between

---

28. Others have called attention to Hobbes's optimism. See Ahrensdorf, "The Fear of Death and the Longing for Immortality," 579–87; Kraynak, *History and Modernity in the Thought of Thomas Hobbes*, 28–31, 113, 125; Strauss, *Natural Right and History*, 175–77, 199–200, *The Political Philosophy of Hobbes*, 106–7, 64; Tuck, "The Civil Religion of Thomas Hobbes," 137–38. Contrast Craig, *The Platonian Leviathan*, 490.

Hobbes's political philosophy and his natural philosophy, and as we look at the substance of each.

Still, while these and many other questions remain to be considered, we can already see some features of Hobbes's own approach emerging from his critique of the tradition. In moral or political philosophy, Hobbes will turn away from common opinions in search of a new method that, by abandoning that flawed starting point for a new one, promises to produce a doctrine that is much more solid and scientific than anything previously produced by the moral philosophers. For this reason, Hobbes contends that there are good grounds for his hope that his own doctrine will not suffer the same fate as Plato's useless dream in the *Republic*, but that it will prove possible to "convert this truth of speculation into the utility of practice" (*Lev.* 31.41; see also Latin *Lev.*, 575). As for his natural philosophy, its outlines are at this point even harder to see, but this much may be said: by putting forward a thoroughly materialist account of the universe—of "the whole mass of all things that are"—Hobbes thought that he could help sever the tie that had long bound philosophy to theology, and promote an outlook that would deprive the superstitious belief in incorporeal spirits of its nourishment. Such a change, like bitter medicine given to the sick, would redound to the benefit of both politics and philosophy.

Of course, these formulations, while they may be true as far as they go, are hardly more than broad impressions or rough sketches. Much remains to be fleshed out and filled in. Yet, before we leave Hobbes's critique of the classical tradition and follow him, so to speak, from the darkness of the past toward the enlightenment he promises, a few final considerations are in order regarding his view of the past. The classical tradition provides a point of comparison we should never entirely leave behind. For not only does it always remain a point of comparison for Hobbes himself, but we may wonder—and allow our wondering to linger—about the adequacy of Hobbes's understanding of the tradition he rejects. We have already encountered one reason for doubt: Hobbes does not show any signs of having rigorously followed up on the implications of his suspicion that Aristotle may have written on more than one level, such that some of his most problematic teachings, especially in his natural philosophy, may have been merely exoteric (see pp. 27–28 above). To that consideration—which is important because it raises the possibility that Aristotle's works have hidden depths that contain greater resources for genuine philosophy than Hobbes, in his hostility toward Aristotle, was able to appreciate—let us add a second point that takes us back to the realm of moral philosophy.

In his account of the emergence of moral philosophy as a fountain of anarchy, Hobbes, as we briefly noted, traces the line of moral philosophy back to

Socrates. It was Socrates, according to reports that Hobbes accepts, who was the first to fall in love with "this civil science" and to devote himself to it to the neglect of the other branches of philosophy (see *De Cive*, Pref.). Hobbes thus directs his readers to what has come to be known as the Socratic turn, a turn that Socrates himself took but that, given Socrates' tremendous influence, in a way philosophy as such took, too. Now, whether or not Hobbes is right to suggest that Socrates' turn to moral philosophy led him to neglect the rest of philosophy,[29] his main point concerns Socrates' influence on others: many men, philosophers and gentlemen alike, became captivated by the dignity of this part of philosophy, which surpasses that of all other studies (*De Cive*, Pref.). We have already considered the evils that Hobbes thinks flowed from this development. What is also striking and worthy of consideration, however, is that as much as he bemoans the problems caused by moral philosophy, Hobbes never questions its dignity as a pursuit. That it has been poorly pursued is clear to him, as is the damage that has been caused. But that it is worthy of pursuit he does not doubt. And related to this point is another striking feature of his account: perhaps because he was convinced that Socrates and those who followed him became devoted to moral philosophy because they were captivated by its dignity, Hobbes does not raise the question of whether there was *a philosophic reason* that Socrates and his heirs turned to moral philosophy. Hobbes does not ask—or at any rate, he does not press—the question: Why the Socratic turn?[30]

Hobbes also does not seem to have grasped very well the character of the Socratic investigations. Although he faults Aristotle and others for building their moral philosophy on the flimsy foundation of common opinions, Hobbes does not seem to have had much appreciation, or even much awareness, of another crucial side of classical thought that is more visible in Plato's presentation of Socrates than in Aristotle, even if it retains a place in Aristotle:

29. Among the passages to be considered in this connection (and compared with the preface of *De Cive*) are Plato, *Phaedo* 96a6–102a1, and Xenophon, *Memorabilia* 1.1.11–16, 4.6.1.

30. See Strauss, *Natural Right and History*, 167: "Hobbes was indebted to tradition for a single, but momentous, idea: he accepted on trust the view that political philosophy or political science is possible or necessary." See also *The Political Philosophy of Hobbes*, 136, 152; cf. Schuhmann, "Hobbes and the Political Thought of Plato and Aristotle," 207. Hobbes's failure to examine whether there was a philosophic reason for the Socratic turn to moral philosophy is perhaps connected with his questionable belief that Socrates abandoned the rest of philosophy (see the preceding note). For if Socrates did not abandon the rest of philosophy but merely modified his approach to it, then the question arises as to the connection between the new or revised approach that he took to natural philosophy and his turn to moral philosophy—that is, between the two main aspects of the Socratic turn.

the dialectical analysis of common opinions. Socratic dialectics, understood as the rigorous examination and questioning of ordinary opinions, is missing from Hobbes's picture of classical thought. Its absence may be due to Hobbes's focus on Aristotle, despite his occasional expressions of his higher regard for Plato. But that higher regard seems to be based, in any case, primarily on Plato's emphasis on mathematics, rather than on anything like the point at issue. Hobbes gives no indication that he grasped the importance of this crucial element of Plato's thought, which Plato himself called attention to by putting the Socratic investigations of moral questions—although one would not know it from Hobbes—at the center of his corpus.[31]

If Hobbes did not adequately grasp the impetus and the character of the Socratic turn, he makes it harder for others who follow in his wake to do so as well. For not only does the fact that Hobbes treats the importance of moral philosophy as a matter of course encourage others to do the same, but his turn away from common opinions, as a kind of inversion or reversal of the Socratic turn, has the effect of urging people not to take opinions so seriously. Again, our opinions, according to Hobbes, spring from our diverse and fluctuating passions, and thus our opinions about the virtues in particular "can never be true grounds of any ratiocination." The more one believes that, however, the less likely one is to give much thought to opinions, either those of others or even one's own. And since one form of giving thought is questioning, that means that Hobbes's very disdain for opinions can paradoxically lead—and I would say *has* paradoxically led—many people to cling more unthinkingly to their opinions, including the new opinions that Hobbes helped to instill.

---

31. For Hobbes's favorable view of Plato because of his emphasis on mathematics, see *Lev.* 46.11; Latin *Lev*, 1059; *EW* VII, 346; consider also *A Dialogue*, 124. Regarding Hobbes's neglect of Socratic dialectics, see Strauss, *The Political Philosophy of Hobbes*, 141–53; Burns, "Leo Strauss on the Origins of Hobbes's Natural Science," 124–25.

2

Hobbes's Natural Philosophy

Hobbes's original plan for his work was to produce a comprehensive treatment of the first principles, the "elements," of philosophy that would be divided into three main parts: a first section on body, a second on man, and a third on the commonwealth and the duties of citizens (see *De Cive*, Pref.; *De Corp.*, Ep. Ded., 1.9; *De Hom.*, Ep. Ded.; *Vita* [verse], xc). In a manner and with considerable delays, Hobbes accomplished what he set out to do. When *De Corpore* finally appeared in 1655 and then *De Homine* in 1658, each after many years in the making, Hobbes could claim to have completed the first and second parts of the project he had conceived almost two decades earlier. The third part, unlike the other two, had been produced ahead of schedule. As he tells his readers in a retrospective passage in the preface to *De Cive* (a preface absent from the first edition in 1642, but added to the second in 1647), Hobbes was moved to speed up the completion and publication of that work because he saw the situation in England deteriorating into civil war. Watching as his country began to glow with the conflicts that would soon burst into flames, he put aside for a time the first and second parts of his project and hastened to finish the third. Now, the delay of the first two parts and the early appearance of the third are enough to indicate that, although Hobbes completed his plan, he also departed from it. And then, of course, there is the fact that he did not confine his work, even during the period in question, to the three works that constitute his *Elements of Philosophy*. Not to mention now some of his minor works, where does the mighty *Leviathan*, which appeared in 1651, fit into the three parts of Hobbes's system or program? If the *Leviathan* borrows from all three parts even though it was written before the completion of the first and second (*De Corpore* and *De Homine*), it would seem to be especially closely linked to the third. But it surely expands on *De*

Cive—among other ways, in developing much more extensively a dimension of Hobbes's thought that was already present in *De Cive* but that does not fit neatly into any one of the subject headings of the three parts: Hobbes's treatment of religion and theology.

These considerations begin to indicate the complexity of the question of the unity of Hobbes's thought: How did Hobbes conceive of the relationship between his main works or, better, between the parts of philosophy he treats in them? If his ambition to produce a tripartite treatment of the whole of philosophy, or at least of its "elements," suggests that he thought of his project as a system with a necessary sequence, the fact that the third part could be treated before the others calls into question whether the sequence is truly necessary, or whether it amounts to a system in which each successive part depends on the preceding ones. The doubts that are cast on the systematic character (so understood) of Hobbes's thought by the separability of the third part are strengthened by the reason Hobbes gives to explain why the third part could be treated first. He says that it was possible to separate it from the other two because he saw that, "resting on principles of its own known from experience, it did not need the preceding parts" (*De Cive*, Pref.).[1] This crucial suggestion that political philosophy rests on principles of its own known from experience is echoed elsewhere (see *Lev.*, Intro., 32.1; *De Hom.*, Ep. Ded.; *Elem.* 1.2, 13.4; consider also *De Corp.* 1.9, 6.7; *EW* IV, 275). And with this suggestion we should also put the consideration, raised already in the preceding chapter, that Hobbes makes a much bolder claim to have blazed a new trail in political philosophy than in the other branches of philosophy, especially in natural philosophy, where he pays tribute to Galileo and others. His claim to be the true founder of "civil philosophy," moreover, does not take the form of the claim that he was the first to apply the principles of the new natural science to the study of politics. From here, we can begin to understand how it is possible that Hobbes, who had such a revolutionary impact in political philosophy, never achieved the same level of fame and influence as a natural philosopher.[2]

---

1. My translation here differs in an important way from Silverthorne's in the Tuck and Silverthorne edition of *De Cive*. Silverthorne translates *experientia cognitis* as "known by reason," rather than "known from experience." Consider *Lev.* 32.1 for confirmation that Hobbes means "experience."

2. On Hobbes's relative obscurity as a natural philosopher, see Brandt, *Thomas Hobbes' Mechanical Conception of Nature*, 377–78; Malcolm, *Aspects of Hobbes*, 498–99; Tönnies, *Thomas Hobbes: Leben und Lehre*, 98–99; Shapin and Schaffer, *Leviathan and the Air-Pump*, 7–8. Regarding the independence of Hobbes's political philosophy, see Strauss, *The Political Philosophy of Hobbes*, 3–7, 28–29, 167–70, "On the Basis of Hobbes's Political Philosophy," 177–79; Sorell,

Hobbes's first word, then, on the question of the relationship of his political philosophy to the rest of his thought, and in particular to his natural philosophy, is that his political philosophy stands on its own two feet. Yet, while this is his first word—and, even more than that, a key signpost of which we must never lose sight—it does not tell the whole story. For even if it is true that Hobbes's political philosophy is independent of his natural philosophy in the sense that it is not derivative from it, that does not mean that there are no important connections between the two. Indeed, we have already gotten a glimpse of one such connection. If the Aristotelian-scholastic doctrine of abstract essences was pernicious because it nourished delusions that empowered the "ghostly authorities" who caused epilepsy in the body politic, then a natural philosophic teaching that had the opposite effect—that served as an antidote to that disease—would contribute to the health of the commonwealth. We have already been given reason to think that Hobbes wanted his own natural philosophy, in its unmistakable materialism, to have such an effect and thus to serve as a kind of ground-clearing or sobriety-inducing supplement to his political philosophy. More broadly, Hobbes's natural philosophy presents the view of nature or the universe—of "the whole mass of all things that are"— most conducive to putting men in the disenchanted frame of mind they must be in to be receptive to a political teaching according to which violent death is the worst of all evils and the earthly sovereign the unchallenged authority. But this connection does not exhaust the links between Hobbes's political philosophy and his natural philosophy, and, as much as Hobbes suggests that his political philosophy rests on foundations of its own, there are plenty of indications in his works that there is more to it than that.[3] It would therefore be a mistake, albeit an understandable one often made by scholars and readers of Hobbes, to take the statement quoted from the preface of *De Cive* and its equivalents elsewhere as reason to set aside his natural philosophy and focus exclusively on his political philosophy. Whatever further connections there may be—and that is a question to which we will return, both in this chapter and later—they can be understood only once we can approach Hobbes's political philosophy with a grasp of the main features of his natural

---

Hobbes, 4–13; Weinberger, "Hobbes's Doctrine of Method," 1336–38; Malcolm, *Aspects of Hobbes*, 146–55.

3. For the most striking examples, see *De Corp.* 6.6 and 6.17, where Hobbes suggests that a mechanistic psychology, rooted in a broader mechanistic physics, is an essential precursor to political philosophy. These passages, and other related ones, will be considered at the beginning of Chapter 6.

philosophy. Of course, there is also the simpler consideration that, even if it is far less famous than his political philosophy and rarely studied with much care, Hobbes's natural philosophy is of interest and importance in its own right. Hobbes himself certainly thought so at any rate. In fact, if one judges by the amount of time and effort he devoted to each of his works, *De Corpore* is the work that was of the greatest significance to Hobbes himself.[4]

The aim of this chapter is to examine the main features of Hobbes's natural philosophy as they come to sight not only but above all in *De Corpore*.[5] It is not my intention here to present a step-by-step analysis of the whole of *De Corpore*, a task that would require an entire book devoted exclusively to it. Such an endeavor, despite its attractions, is not essential to my primary purposes of attaining a view of Hobbes's thought that is as comprehensive as possible and preparing the way, in particular, for a more adequate consideration of the relationship between Hobbes's natural philosophy and his political philosophy. My focus in this chapter, therefore, will be not so much on the fine-grain details of *De Corpore* as on the most important aspects, the guiding principles, of Hobbes's natural philosophy, and especially on the theoretical problems with which Hobbes wrestles in this work and elsewhere.

It is possible to give a preliminary sketch of the central questions that will emerge. Hobbes's natural philosophy—this much will surprise no one—is a thoroughgoing effort to understand nature in mechanistic and materialistic terms, that is, as consisting only of matter in its various motions. Brandt's classic work on Hobbes's natural philosophy, *Thomas Hobbes' Mechanical Conception of Nature*, as the title already suggests, has this as its thesis: that Hobbes was the most rigorous and uncompromising, if not the most scientifi-

---

4. See Malcolm, *Leviathan, Vol. 1: Introduction*, 3–5; Brandt, *Thomas Hobbes' Mechanical Conception of Nature*, 171–72, 217; Tuck, "Hobbes and Descartes," 11–27. In the final lines of *Leviathan* (Review and Conclusion, 17), Hobbes expresses his intention to return to his "interrupted speculation of bodies natural." See also *Vita* [verse], xci, where Hobbes speaks of the years he spent working on *De Corpore* "night and day."

5. The other works from which I will draw in this chapter do not include *A Short Tract on First Principles*, because it is uncertain whether Hobbes is its author. It is likely that he is not. Raylor, "Hobbes, Payne, and *A Short Tract on First Principles*," 29–58, argues persuasively, if not decisively, that the *Short Tract* should be attributed to Robert Payne. Leijenhorst, *The Mechanisation of Aristotelianism*, 12–13, objects and defends Tönnies's original attribution of the manuscript to Hobbes. But Leijenhorst's brief argument hardly justifies his contention that "after more than a century of debate, Hobbes's authorship of the *Short Tract* is now beyond doubt" (13). In fact, Hobbes's authorship is so far from "beyond doubt" that Malcolm's recent meticulous study of the evidence (*Aspects of Hobbes*, 80–145) led him to agree with the attribution to Payne.

cally talented, of the early modern proponents of mechanistic materialism.[6] Yet, although that thesis remains intact, not only is it necessary to unpack what mechanistic materialism means in the case of Hobbes, but we also need to examine why Hobbes seems to move, at times, in a more skeptical direction. What problem or problems shook his confidence, such that he was unwilling or unable to leave matters at a simple affirmation of mechanistic materialism as the truth about the character of the world? Strauss put the matter this way, in a striking formulation: "Hobbes had the earnest desire to be a 'metaphysical' materialist. But he was forced to rest satisfied with a 'methodical' materialism."[7] But what exactly led Hobbes to think that his earnest desire to be a metaphysical materialist could not be fulfilled?[8] And insofar as he turned away from metaphysical materialism, to what did he turn in its place? If the answer is indeed "methodical" (i.e., methodological) materialism, what does that mean for Hobbes? And, finally, are there new difficulties that arise from the move from the one kind of materialism to the other, or old ones not solved by it, that can explain why Hobbes wavered, even as he moved, and does not seem to have been wholly satisfied with the only kind of natural science that he regarded as possible?

Hobbes's Mechanistic Materialism

If Hobbes had an earnest desire to be a metaphysical materialist, it is not too hard to understand why. The explanation is only in part that he wanted to sever the problematic connection between philosophy and theology. But that is surely one of the reasons. In the Epistle Dedicatory of *De Corpore*, after discussing the mingling of classical philosophy and Christianity that gave birth to the monster of scholasticism, Hobbes expresses his intention to use "the

6. See especially 6–7, 290–92, 333, 339–40, 345–46, 377–78. See also Burtt, *The Metaphysical Foundations of Modern Physical Science*, 118–27; Willey, *The Seventeenth Century Background*, 102–6.

7. *Natural Right and History*, 174. The terminology that Strauss puts in quotation marks here—"metaphysical" and "methodical" (as applied to Hobbes's materialism)—can be traced to Brandt, although Strauss is disagreeing with Brandt's view that Hobbes was never anything but a "metaphysical" materialist (see Brandt, *Thomas Hobbes' Mechanical Conception of Nature*, 345–46, 355ff.). On this disagreement, see Strauss, *Hobbes's Critique of Religion*, 24, 102n269.

8. This is a question on which Strauss provides some helpful indications, but not a complete answer. Consider *Natural Right and History*, 169–77; see also "On the Basis of Hobbes's Political Philosophy," 178, 181–82, *Hobbes's Critique of Religion*, 94–109. For an illuminating discussion of Strauss's indications, see Burns, "Leo Strauss on the Origins of Hobbes's Natural Science," 115–26.

true and clearly ordered foundations of physics" to "frighten and drive away this metaphysical *Empusa*." He also declares, in the opening chapter of the same work, that the subject of philosophy as it is understood in *De Corpore*— namely, "every body that can be grasped as generated or as having some other property"—excludes theology, because God, whether or not he is a body, is neither generated nor comprehensible (*De Corp.* 1.8). This exclusion of theology is in sharp contrast to the work that Hobbes hoped *De Corpore* would replace, Aristotle's *Metaphysics*, which culminates, at least apparently, in a philosophic theology.[9] And not only does Hobbes's natural philosophy exclude theology, but it works against it in a deeper sense, by presenting a view of the universe that starves the belief in incorporeal beings. Taking away the "superstitious fear of spirits," according to Hobbes, "ought to be the work of the schools," but "they rather nourish such doctrine" (*Lev.* 2.8–9). We can be sure that Hobbes hoped to guide the schools from the old mistake to the new task (see *Lev.* 30.14; *EW* VII, 335–36).

Still, his concern to sever the connection between philosophy and theology and thereby mitigate the dangers caused by that connection is, to repeat, only one of the reasons Hobbes would have had an earnest desire to be a metaphysical materialist. For almost as frequent and every bit as vehement as his warnings about the political dangers of scholasticism are his complaints about the absurdity of its doctrines. In fact, although these latter complaints are surely meant to contribute to his effort to address the political problems, one wonders whether the connection does not also work in the other direction, that is, whether he does not emphasize, and perhaps even exaggerate, the political dangers because he was so hostile to scholasticism on prior theoretical grounds. This much at any rate is clear: Hobbes certainly did have theoretical (and not merely political) objections to the outlook that, whatever its complicated relationship to Aristotle's genuine thought, had turned philosophy into "Aristotelity." To focus for now only on the considerations that would have been foremost in his mind, the doctrines of incorporeal substances and of final causes, in what he regarded as their absurdity, must have been powerful negative forces pushing Hobbes toward a thoroughgoing materialism. For materialism must have come to sight, not only as the best means of combating such doctrines, but also as the sober alternative from which the scholastic doctrines were an all too understandable flight. That flight itself—regarded by Hobbes as a flight into fantasy and thus away from a sober acceptance

---

9. See *Metaphysics* L6–10; cf., however, E1–2, especially 1026a27–32. On Hobbes's exclusion of theology from his natural philosophy, see Leijenhorst, *The Mechanisation of Aristotelianism*, 22–27; Lupoli, "Hobbes and Religion without Theology," 455.

of the truth—may well have helped to cement in his mind the conviction that nature is composed of nothing but bodies and their aimless motions.[10] That a nonteleological, materialistic view was anathema to everything the scholastics stood for, and therefore had long been banished from philosophy, would have seemed to him only further evidence in its favor. And if the flight from it had led philosophy into ever more complicated forms of absurdity, an acceptance of it could easily be seen, not only as a return to sanity, but also as a great simplification that could at last put natural philosophy on a solid foundation. Is this not what Hobbes must have had in mind when he said that Galileo was "the first who opened for us the gate of physics as a whole" by unlocking "the nature of motion" (*De Corp.*, Ep. Ded.)?

Now, as this remark about Galileo indicates, Hobbes's materialism is a mechanistic materialism that has as much to do with motion as it does with matter. But, to see its main features, let us start with Hobbes's central claim about the fundamental ontological status of matter and then turn to his basic principles of motion. Hobbes's central claim about matter, which he equates with body, is that only bodies are real: what is not body is not. In the last chapter, I quoted one of Hobbes's boldest expressions of this claim, which he places, not by accident, immediately after his critique of the Aristotelian doctrine of abstract essences (see p. 24 above). Let me here quote another, which also comes, again not by accident, in the context of a criticism of the scholastic view that the words "body" and "spirit" refer to two different kinds of substances, corporeal and incorporeal. Hobbes states his own, very different position in this way:

> The word *body*, in the most general acceptation, signifieth that which filleth or occupieth some certain room or imagined place, and dependeth not on the imagination, but is a real part of that we call the *universe*. For the *universe* being the aggregate of all bodies, there is no real part thereof that is not also *body*, nor anything properly a *body* that is not also part of (that aggregate of all bodies) the *universe*. (*Lev.* 34.2)

Hobbes goes on from this statement to argue, as he does in many places throughout his works, that the very notion of an "incorporeal substance" is a contradiction in terms: "*substance incorporeal* are words which, when they

---

10. Consider the following remark from the first chapter of *De Corpore*: "I am not unaware how difficult it is to weed out of the minds of men inveterate opinions that have been confirmed by the authority of the most eloquent writers. And the difficulty is greater because true philosophy (that is, accurate philosophy) rejects not only the paint of speeches, but nearly all ornaments of expression, and because the first grounds [*fundamenta prima*] of all science are not only not splendid, but low [*humilia*], arid, and, in appearance, almost deformed" (1.1).

are joined together, destroy one another" (*Lev.* 34.2; see also, e.g., *Lev.* 4.21, 5.5, 34.24; *De Corp.* 3.4; *Elem.* 11.4; *EW* IV, 305–6, 349). Of course, an "incorporeal substance" is a contradiction in terms only if bodies alone can be "substances," or if "substance" and "body" are two names for the same thing. Hobbes's argument in this regard is that the only way to think intelligibly about the beings that exist in themselves, and that underlie or "stand under" (as the Latin *substantia* implies) the changing accidents or qualities that appear to our senses, is to think of them as bodies. Nothing else could serve—at least not in a way that is intelligible to us—as the self-subsistent substratum of accidents, and in any attempt to assign such a status to incorporeal beings, to think of them as real in this sense, one is inevitably compelled to ascribe to them aspects, such as place, extension, and motion, that can intelligibly be ascribed only to bodies. Although one can of course *speak* of incorporeal substances, one cannot truly *think* of them, if thinking means having a coherent conception in one's mind (see *Lev.* 3.12, 4.15–16, 8.27, 34.2, 46.19–21; *De Corp.* 8.1–2, 8.20, 30.15; *Anti-White* 4.3, 7.6; *EW* IV, 308–9, 427).[11]

When Hobbes derides all talk of incorporeal substances as "insignificant speech," then, he means that as more than one of his favorite dismissive insults. He means that the words, taken together, do not reflect in the speaker or call up in the listener a coherent mental conception that they serve to mark or "signify." The consideration of what can and cannot be intelligibly conceived in the mind plays an important role also in Hobbes's further claim about bodies and in his core principles of motion. If Hobbes's first claim about bodies is that they are the true constituents of a universe that is nothing but their aggregate, his second claim is that they do not come into being or perish. Although bodies are of course altered and rearranged in ways that make them appear to us in different forms at different times—so much so that we sometimes call them by different names—bodies, as bodies, are never generated or destroyed, at least not in the sense that a body arises where before there was none or perishes such that no body remains. For if bodies are the only real things, if what is not body is not, such generation or destruction would entail generation of something out of nothing or destruction of something into nothing. But Hobbes argues that, "although it is possible to imagine something arising from nothing, and nothing from something, it cannot be comprehended by the mind in what way that can be done among the natural things" (*De Corp.* 8.20). "And therefore," he goes on, "philosophers, for whom it is not permitted to depart from natural reason, suppose that a body can neither be generated nor destroyed, but only that it can appear to us in differ-

---

11. Compare Tönnies, *Thomas Hobbes: Leben und Lehre*, 124–25.

ent ways at different times." It is possible, then, that what now appears to us as white may later appear as black, or even that "that which is now called man, may later be called not-man," but not that "that which is at one time called body" can ever be called "not-body." Such, at any rate, is the full meaning of Hobbes's conviction that, whereas accidents are generated and not things, the true things are the ungenerated and imperishable bodies (*De Corp.* 8.20, 8.1–3; see also *Anti-White* 5.3–6, 12.1–8, 27.1, 35.1).

The bodies are in motion, of course. In fact, Hobbes thinks that all change can be understood—can be understood *only*—as produced by the motions of bodies impinging on one another. This is the "mechanistic" side of his mechanistic materialism. And just as he defended the central claims of his materialism by an appeal to what is truly conceivable, so too with the central claims of his mechanism. The central claims of Hobbes's mechanism can be laid out, more easily than his claims about bodies, as a set of principles or axioms. Hobbes himself refers to them as such (see *EW* VII, 85). The first axiom is that two bodies cannot simultaneously occupy the same place, nor can one body be in two different places at the same time. Thus, while bodies may displace, pierce, and even mix with one another (see *EW* VII, 136–37), they cannot fully interpenetrate one another such that there would be two bodies in one and the same place. The second axiom is that nothing can move itself in any way: nothing can begin, change, or end its own motion. And the third and final axiom—closely connected with the second, but an extension of it—is that the immediate cause of the motion of any body can be only the motion of another body that is not only external to the first but also contiguous with it. The motion of one body, in other words, can cause or change the motion of another only if the two bodies come into contact with each other, or, as Hobbes puts it in a formulation that unites the second and third axioms, "there can be no cause of motion except in a body contiguous and moved" (*De Corp.* 9.7; *EW* VII, 85–86).[12]

The second of these axioms—the denial that any body can move itself—is the most fundamental to Hobbes's understanding of motion. The first axiom belongs in some sense as much to Hobbes's view of matter as to his principles

---

12. My primary source for this list of three axioms is *EW* VII, 85–86 (a key passage of Hobbes's *Decameron Physiologicum*); but there are many other passages in which Hobbes articulates the same principles, as well as the more basic contention that all change is motion. See, e.g., *De Corp.* 6.5, 8.8, 8.19, 9.6–10, 15.1, 22.7, 26.8; *OL* V, 217–18; *Anti-White* 13.2, 20.8, 27.5, 27.9; *EW* IV, 274, 276. See also Tuck, "Optics and Skeptics," 253–54; Burtt, *The Metaphysical Foundations of Modern Physical Science*, 125–27; Leijenhorst, *The Mechanisation of Aristotelianism*, 188ff.; Jesseph, "Hobbes on the Foundations of Natural Philosophy," 139–41; Tönnies, *Thomas Hobbes: Leben und Lehre*, 140–41.

of motion, and the third axiom, for its part, adds the denial of action at a distance, but, other than that, it rests on and merely works out the implications of the second axiom.[13] What is Hobbes's defense, then, of the second axiom, his case for the impossibility of a body moving itself?

Hobbes argues that if one imagines a body at rest, surrounded either by nothing or by unmoved bodies, it is impossible to conceive of how such a body could begin its own motion. If one supposes for the sake of argument that the body *did* suddenly begin to move by moving itself, then one cannot explain why it moved when it did or where it did. For given that it must already have had within itself all that was necessary to give rise to the motion (otherwise the motion could not have occurred), why did the motion not begin earlier? And why did the body move in this way rather than in that way, given that, with no difference in external impediments or propulsions, it could have moved equally in any direction? The same considerations that make it inconceivable that a body could move itself from rest apply, according to Hobbes, also to the possibilities of bodies altering their own motions or bringing themselves from motion to rest: without the introduction of external causes, we cannot conceive of how such changes could occur (see *De Corp.* 6.5, 8.19, 9.7, 22.17, 26.7–8; *EW* IV, 276; *EW* VII, 85; *Anti-White* 13.2, 20.8, 27.5, 27.9–11).

Now, from Hobbes's denial that bodies can move themselves, extended by the third premise into the claim that there can be no cause of motion except in a body contiguous and moved, there emerges a vision of the universe as a vast conglomeration of bodies constantly displacing each other through the nearly infinite motions that their motions cause in each other. To see the full character of this vision, we need to supplement Hobbes's mechanistic axioms with a consideration of his understanding of causality. Hobbes presents his account of causality most directly and extensively in two crucial chapters of *De Corpore*: Chapter 9, "Of Cause and Effect," and Chapter 10, "Of Power and Act."[14] Perhaps the first thing that ought to be noted about the account in these two chapters is what goes unmentioned in them until the very last para-

---

13. This relationship between the second and the third axioms can be seen in Hobbes's defense of the third. See *EW* VII, 86: "For, *since nothing can move itself,* the movent must be external. And because motion is change of place, the movent must put it from its place, which it cannot do till it touch it" (emphasis added). See also the reliance of Hobbes's argument in *De Corp.* 9.7, that there can be no cause of motion except in a body contiguous and moved, on the argument against self-caused motion in 8.19.

14. On the importance of these two chapters, see Brandt, *Thomas Hobbes' Mechanical Conception of Nature*, 266–92. Brandt even goes so far as to declare: "No doubt Chapters 9–10 are the most crucial ever written by Hobbes" (266). That is an overstatement, but they are important chapters, and I have benefited from Brandt's discussion of them.

graph of the second of them, and is mentioned there only to be denigrated: formal cause and final cause. Hobbes's argument regarding these two of the classic four Aristotelian causes is as brief as it is dismissive: form, understood as the essence of a thing, cannot intelligibly be understood as a cause of the thing whose essence it is, but only as something that plays a role, as a kind of efficient cause, in our knowledge of that thing; and final cause "has no place except in things that have sense and will," and even in those cases it is intelligible as a cause only if it is reduced to an efficient cause (*De Corp.* 10.7).[15] The only causes that are truly causes, according to Hobbes, are efficient and material causes. Hobbes understands them as follows. When, as in all mutation, the motion of one body changes the motion of another such that it generates or destroys some accident of that body, the effect is due, not just to the fact that two bodies, as bodies, collide, but to the accidents or qualities of each of the two bodies and their motions (*De Corp.* 9.1–3; see also *Anti-White* 27.2, 35.2). A fire, for instance, burns a dry leaf because the fire and the leaf are each bodies with certain characteristics and certain motions; without these, the effect (the burning of the leaf) could not occur. An accident on the side of the agent (the fire) that is essential to the effect is a necessary efficient cause, just as an accident on the side of the patient (the leaf) is a necessary material cause. But one cannot leave matters at necessary causes so understood. For necessary causes become sufficient causes only when they all come together. And in the case of any effect, there may be many necessary causes, both on the side of the agent—or of all agents that play various roles in the effect— and on the side of the patient. Thus Hobbes develops his crucial notion of an "entire cause" (*causa integra*) as "*the aggregate of all of the accidents both of the agents, however many there are, and of the patient, which, when they are*

---

15. For a fuller explanation of what Hobbes means by the last point, see *Anti-White* 27.2: "It is common to identify two other kinds of causes, namely, *formal cause* and *final cause*. The latter of these, as far as it is conceivable by man, is entirely the same as efficient cause. For from a delightful object arises the imagination of its enjoyment, from the imagination of its enjoyment arises the imagination of the way to it, and from the imagination of the way arises the motion toward the object of desire—in which series of products, the object, that is, the end, is the agent, and, by this account, the action (*actus*) of the object that is the end is the *efficient cause* of our motion toward *the end*." In the continuation of this paragraph, Hobbes discusses formal cause and considers the way in which form operates, not as a cause of the properties of things, but only as a quasi-cause of our knowledge of them. See also 27.19; *De Corp.* 3.20; *EW* VII, 82. Compare Bacon, *New Organon* 1.48, 1.51; Craig, *The Platonian Leviathan*, 84–105, examines in detail the differences between Hobbes's "Baconian" conception of final cause and the older Aristotelian conception. See also Burtt, *The Metaphysical Foundations of Modern Physical Science*, 125–27; Sorell, *Hobbes*, 53–55; Leijenhorst, "Hobbes's Theory of Causality and Its Aristotelian Background," 436–37.

all supposed, it cannot be understood but that the effect is produced at the same time" (*De Corp.* 9.3). The true efficient cause, then, is an aggregate of accidents, necessary to the effect, in the agent or agents; the true material cause is an aggregate of accidents, necessary to the effect, in the patient (*De Corp.* 9.4). The entire cause, as the combination of these, is "always sufficient for the production of its effect, provided that the effect is in every way possible" (*De Corp.* 9.5, 6.10; see also *EW* IV, 246; *Anti-White* 27.2, 35.2–5).

The significance of Hobbes's notion of an entire cause comes into clearer focus when one considers that, among the agents whose relevant accidents are part of the entire cause, he includes not just those whose action is immediate (that is, those that move the patient by direct contact) but also those whose action is mediated through other bodies in chains that eventually reach the patient (see *De Corp.* 9.2, 6.10; *EW* VII, 86; *OL* V, 217–18). One must also consider, together with this principle of inclusion, that there is no agent, immediate or mediate, that has not itself been the patient of other agents, just as there is no patient that will not be the agent of other patients. To put this last point in the terminology that Hobbes uses when speaking of potential in Chapter 10 of *De Corpore*: no moving body has a "power"—that is, a capacity to produce a specific effect or "act" in another body—that has not itself arisen in that body as the effect or act of the power of some other moving body, which power itself was also an effect or act of yet another, and so on (see 10.1, 10.6, 9.6; *Anti-White* 27.5, 35.8). It is true that, according to Hobbes, we can interrupt "this progress of causation" in our minds by imagining only a part of the chain, such that we can then isolate a beginning and consider something solely as an agent with a power to initiate an act (see *De Corp.* 9.6, 9.2). But in this act of imagination, although we become able to think of a cause only as a cause (and not also as an effect), there is an illusion or at least a distortion, for we are interrupting something that, outside of our minds, can never be interrupted, and we are isolating something that is never truly isolated.

Once one grasps that all causes are themselves caused—because all motions that move bodies are motions of bodies that have themselves been moved—one begins to see the continuous expansion implicit in Hobbes's notion of an entire cause. All of the agents of an effect, to say nothing now of the patient itself, have come to be as they are, and thus to be capable of acting as the agents they are, through chains of causality that themselves involved agents, which had agents, and so on. Thus, since the entire cause of any effect is not limited to the relevant accidents of the agents that immediately cause the effect but includes the relevant accidents of the agents of those agents, what emerges is not just a single, ever-lengthening chain of causes, but many—and endlessly multiplying—such chains interacting with one another. The ultimate conclusion of this line of reflection, especially once one adds the contention, as Hobbes does, that every motion is propagated infinitely through the filled space of a universe without void or vacuum, is the paradoxical thought that the truest cause of any effect is the whole vast aggregate of moving bodies interacting with each other, an aggregate that had no beginning but the flux of which just so happens to have arranged itself in such a way as to provide, at the critical moment, the conditions that make the effect in question possible (see *De Corp.* 9.5, 15.7, 26.5, 30.15; *EW* IV 246–47, 267; *EW* V, 105, 226, 302–5). But it is better to say that the conditions make the effect *necessary*, not just possible. For, according to Hobbes, if something does not occur, then something essential to its occurrence must be missing, and hence it is not truly possible; by the same token, if something does occur, then all of the conditions for its occurrence must be in place, and hence it is necessary, not just possible (*De Corp.* 9.5; see also *Anti-White* 27.5, 35.5–8, 37.11; *EW* V, 380). Hobbes's denial of possibility as a category distinct from necessity is also a denial of chance: our belief that some things happen by chance reflects only our inability to see all of the causes that made them necessary, not any relaxing of the bonds of necessity (*De Corp.* 10.4–5; *Anti-White* 38.1; *EW* V, 189, 450–51). According to Hobbes, "all things come to pass with equal necessity," and, as essential to his vision of the workings of the universe as is the vastness of the causal web that makes the entire cause of any effect untraceable, just as important—or even more so—is Hobbes's conviction that the chains of necessity are never broken (see *De Corp.* 9.10, 9.5, 10.5; *Anti-White* 35.15, 37.14; *EW* IV, 246–47).[16]

It almost goes without saying for Hobbes—even though he was well aware that it hardly does for most other people—that human beings and our actions are as much in the grip of necessity, as enmeshed in the web of moved movers, as are any other bodies and actions. Hobbes's denial that there are incorporeal substances includes the denial that the soul is such a substance and thus that the soul can be separated from the body or act independently of its motions. Life itself, in Hobbes's view, is an accident, or a combination of accidents, generated in a body for a time by an arrangement of its material parts (to say nothing of the conditions that must be in place in external bodies). While the body or the material itself will persist even after its accidents change so profoundly that the body is no longer alive, the notion that an incorporeal essence will detach itself and live on is, for Hobbes, no more conceivable than the separate existence of any other incorporeal substance (see

---

16. On the sovereignty of necessity in Hobbes's conception of the universe, see Brandt, *Thomas Hobbes' Mechanical Conception of Nature*, 266–68, 291; Leijenhorst, *The Mechanisation of Aristotelianism*, 211–14.

Lev. 38.4, 44.15, 46.18–20; *De Corp.* 8.20; Latin *Lev.*, Appendix, 1165–67; *EW* VII, 129; *Anti-White* 5.4–6, 38.10–11). Nor does Hobbes think it necessary—or ultimately intelligible—to have recourse to an unmoved incorporeal mover housed somehow inside the body, whether one calls it the immaterial soul or the pure mind, to explain complex human activities such as deliberation and other forms of reasoning (see *Anti-White* 27.18–20, 30.26–29, 37.8; *De Corp.* 25.7–8, 25.12–13; *Obj.*, no. 2; *Lev.* 3.1–5).[17]

From here, we can begin to see the path to perhaps the most radical and surely the most controversial implication of Hobbes's mechanistic determinism for his view of human life: his denial of free will. Hobbes does not flinch, particularly when provoked by his critics, from arguing from the ubiquity and sovereignty of necessitated causation to the impossibility of the will transcending the concatenations of determined motions and dictating its own course without necessitation by antecedent causes. Although he offers many arguments against free will, especially in his long-running dispute over the matter with Bishop Bramhall, the crux of Hobbes's position is his contention that an act of the will, which he defines as "the last appetite in deliberation," is as thoroughly determined by the necessary causes that make up its entire cause as any other act or motion. Hobbes concedes that the belief that the will is free, just as the belief that some things happen by chance, can easily arise from our inability to see the vast concatenation of causes that determine an action in each instance. But he argues that the belief thus produced is a mirage: "For in the instance of any appetite, the entire cause of the appetite must have preceded the appetite, and hence the appetite itself could not fail to follow; such liberty as is free from necessity, therefore, is not to be found in the will either of men or beasts" (*De Corp.* 25.13, with 9.5). "A free will," according to Hobbes, belongs among those insignificant words "whereby we conceive nothing but the sound" (*Lev.* 5.5; see also *Lev.* 6.53; *EW* IV, 246, 272–78; *EW* V, 105–6, 241, 273, 372–73, 404, 450; *Anti-White* 30.26–29, 37.3–14).[18]

---

17. For fuller discussions of Hobbes's materialistic account of mental activities, see Burtt, *The Metaphysical Foundations of Modern Physical Science*, 119–26; Willey, *The Seventeenth Century Background*, 106–11; Frost, *Lessons from a Materialist Thinker*, Chaps. 1–2; Leijenhorst, "Sense and Nonsense about Sense," 94–98, *The Mechanisation of Aristotelianism*, 89–97; Pettit, *Made with Words*, 11–18.

18. The passages I have cited in parentheses, especially those from *EW* IV and *EW* V (which contain *Of Liberty and Necessity* and *The Questions Concerning Liberty, Necessity, and Chance* respectively), are only parts or moments in a much more extensive critique of free will. But I have listed the passages in which Hobbes's central argument is stated with particular clarity. *EW* IV, 274 (together with 276) is perhaps the most direct statement of the key premise of Hobbes's entire position, namely, his denial that anything can begin or freely dictate its own motion. Many

If human beings and our actions are as much necessitated parts of the web of moved movers as are the other bodies and their motions, what about God? Is he, too, regarded by Hobbes as a body? And are his actions, too, enmeshed in the same web of necessity? These are questions that we will have to consider later, when we turn to Hobbes's treatment of religion and theology. Here, I might appeal to Hobbes's declaration that natural philosophy excludes theology and set the questions aside (see again *De Corp.* 1.8). But that declaration is only Hobbes's first word on the matter, and the questions just raised ultimately cannot be avoided by a thinker who seeks, as Hobbes does, to give an account of the whole (consider *De Corp.* 26.1, 26.5). Let me give, then, a simple, if provisional, answer to the first of them: yes, God is a body, according to Hobbes. Although Hobbes was understandably reluctant to state this position openly in his published writings, it is indeed his position, as he eventually acknowledged (see Latin *Lev.*, 1083–85, Appendix, 1187, 1229–31; *EW* IV, 301–9, 348–49, 426–27; consider also *De Corp.* 26.5).[19] As for the second question, it is a more difficult matter to say whether Hobbes regarded God as bound by necessity in the way the other bodies are. On the one hand, it is hard to see how, as a bodily part of a universe that is the aggregate of all bodies, he could not be. But, on the other hand, Hobbes is aware of the claim that God, as the mysterious creator of the universe for whom nothing is impossible, not only freely brought the universe into being, but can intervene in it in ways that break the bonds of necessity, even to the point of destroying the

---

scholars have discussed Hobbes's critique of free will at greater length than I do here. See, e.g., Frost, *Lessons from a Materialist Thinker*, Chap. 3; Willey, *The Seventeenth Century Background*, 111–15; Leijenhorst, "Hobbes's Theory of Causality and Its Aristotelian Background," 433–34; Sorell, *Hobbes*, 92–95; Foisneau, "Omnipotence, Necessity and Sovereignty," 273–74, 281; Mintz, *The Hunting of Leviathan*, 110–33; Jackson, *Hobbes, Bramhall, and the Politics of Liberty and Necessity*, 294–99.

19. Hobbes is more cautious on this issue in the English *Leviathan*, for instance, than he is in the Latin *Leviathan*, which was published seventeen years later. With the passages cited above, compare *Lev.* 12.7, 34.4–5, 46.15. In a lost letter of 1640 to Mersenne (but forwarded to Descartes), the contents of which can be partially reconstructed from Descartes's response to Mersenne, Hobbes seems already in 1640 to have stated in private correspondence his position that God is corporeal. That helps to confirm that the later shift in his official published position is to be explained as a dropping of his reserve rather than as a genuine change in his thinking. So, too, does the fact that Hobbes concedes in the Appendix to the Latin *Leviathan* that the view that God is a body is already implicit in 4.21 of the English *Leviathan* (see Latin *Lev.*, Appendix, 1229). On the lost letter and Descartes's reply, see Brandt, *Thomas Hobbes' Mechanical Conception of Nature*, 93, 111. Descartes's reply can be found in Hobbes's *Correspondence* (see Letter 29, especially the reference to *anima et deo corporeis* in the fifth line). See also Strauss, *Hobbes's Critique of Religion*, 106–7n285; Curley, "'I Durst not Write so Boldly,'" 582–88.

bodies that natural reason leads one to believe are imperishable. Although we cannot conceive of how matter could be created from nothing or reduced to nothing even "through divine omnipotence," Hobbes acknowledges that, "nevertheless, from the fact that we do not understand how it can be done, it is not rightly inferred that it cannot be done" (*Anti-White* 27.1; see also 7.1, 27.8, 30.34, 33.7, 34.6, 40.1; *De corp.* 26.1). This is quite an admission, and I will return later to the challenge that the possibility that Hobbes cannot exclude poses to the basic premises of his natural philosophy.

Hobbes's Skepticism

Thus far in this chapter, I have tried merely to lay out the basic principles of Hobbes's mechanistic materialism and to bring out the vision of the universe that emerges from them. If we judge by the line of reflection we have followed up to this point, Hobbes's materialism certainly seems to be a thoroughgoing "metaphysical" materialism, that is to say, a conviction regarding the truth of the way things really are. On the other hand, the challenge that emerged at the end of the last section—the challenge posed by the possibility of a creator God who works in mysterious ways, unbounded by necessity—calls into question Hobbes's deterministic principles. And even aside from that challenge, we can see some potential seeds of skepticism, if not of the abandonment of mechanistic materialism, embedded within Hobbes's vision of the whole. For although Hobbes denies the existence of chance in one of its senses (in which it is opposed, as possibility, to necessity), chance in another sense (as the unintended or disordered) would seem to govern hand in hand with necessity in Hobbes's scheme. The vast conglomeration of bodies, determined as it may be in its nearly infinite motions by necessity, does not operate according to any meaningful plan or intelligible order; it merely reflects the ever-changing outcomes of aimless motions. Is knowledge or science possible in such a universe, in which every potential object of thought—and even thought itself—arises from the unfathomably complex workings of accidental causation? Hobbes's answer to this question is not straightforward or simple. But to begin to examine it—to see the ways in which Hobbes both acknowledges and responds to the challenge of skepticism—we need to take a step back and return to a preliminary stage of Hobbes's argument. For in thinking about how Hobbes wrestles with the question of knowledge or science, it is better not to jump immediately to the ultimate implications of his mechanistic materialism, but to begin where his own reflections begin: with sense perception.

Sense perception is the necessary starting-point for any adequate reflections on knowledge, according to Hobbes, because it is only through sense perception that our thinking becomes possible at all. Every conception of which we are capable, he argues, must begin from what we are given through our senses. Although there are of course more complex forms of thought than sense perception, "the rest are derived from that original": "there is nothing in the human intellect that was not previously in the senses" (*Lev.* 1.2; *Anti-White* 30.3; see also *De Corp.* 6.1–2, 25.1, 26.1; *Elem.* 2.1–2).[20] Hobbes's concern to think through sense perception is due to more, however, than his conviction that it is fundamental to all thinking and knowing. The close attention he gives it stems also from his belief that there is a deception in sense perception that leads almost everyone to misunderstand it—a deception that prior thinkers, including "the ancient pretenders to natural knowledge," failed to appreciate and thus allowed to persist (*Lev.* 45.1).

"The great deception of sense," which "also is by sense to be corrected" (*Elem.* 2.10), is the nearly universal belief that sense perception gives us direct access to the things that truly are in the world, such that we perceive them as they truly are. In his repeated efforts to dispel this illusion,[21] Hobbes does not deny that the actions or motions that lead to sense perception begin from the external things that come to be perceived. But he denies that these actions or motions carry with them genuine likenesses of those things or of their qualities as they exist in the things themselves. All that is given by the external objects are, in the case of direct sensations such as taste and touch, direct pressures, or, in the case of indirect sensations such as sight and hearing, motions that ripple through a medium, pressing each successive material part of that medium until they reach our organs of sense perception. From the various organs of sense perception, the motions are then propagated inward until they strike either the heart or the brain,[22] which, by resisting the incoming motions, produces reactive or rebounding motions that give rise to

20. On Hobbes's view of the fundamental role of sense perception, see Brandt, *Thomas Hobbes' Mechanistic Conception of Nature*, 358–59; Leijenhorst, "Sense and Nonsense about Sense," 86; Hood, *The Divine Politics of Thomas Hobbes*, 15–17; Tönnies, *Hobbes: Leben und Lehre*, 118–19, 144–45.

21. Hobbes's account of sense perception can be found in several places in his works, in varying degrees of detail and with some relatively minor differences. The summary that follows in this paragraph is based on the following passages, which I cite here so as to avoid burdening the paragraph with numerous long parenthetical citations: *De Corp.* 6.8–10, 25.1–11; *Elem.* 2.1–9; *Lev.* 1.1–5; *OL* V, 217–21; *Anti-White* 27.19, 30.3–4; *EW* VII, 27–28. Of these passages, *De Corp.* 25.1–11 is the most detailed and should be regarded as the most authoritative. On Hobbes's account of "the great deception of sense," see Garsten, *Saving Persuasion*, 47–49.

22. Hobbes speaks sometimes of the heart, sometimes of the brain, as "the fountain of all sense." For passages in which he attributes this role to the heart, with the brain as a mere way station, see *De Corp.* 6.10, 25.4; *Lev.* 2.4; *Anti-White* 27.19, 30.3. For passages in which he attributes it

the appearances that we experience as the sensible qualities. These appearances or phantasms—be they flashes of light, colors, sounds, waves of heat, or whatever else—seem to be outside of us, according to Hobbes, because the rebounding motions are directed outward. If this last aspect of Hobbes's account is the most speculative and dubious—would a motion that remains internal to a body once it has entered it really produce an appearance of something outside the body merely because of an imperceptible redirection of that motion?—one could perhaps jettison his explanation of exactly how the appearances come to seem external while retaining his central argument. His central argument, to repeat, is that we receive from the external bodies nothing but motions, and hence the sensible qualities reside, not in the external things themselves, but in the reactions within the sentient body. Thus, a sight, for instance, is not fundamentally different from the appearance of light that can arise from rubbing one's eye or being struck in the eye by a ball. In fact, Hobbes appeals to such experiences as evidence that the sensible qualities are not in the external bodies. Such experiences—and others such as echoes, reflections of colors, and seeing double—show, he argues, that the sensible qualities can be separated from the bodies in which they supposedly inhere and thus belie that supposed inherence. It is by examples like these that "the great deception of sense," as Hobbes puts it, "also is by sense to be corrected."

Of the five senses, the one to which Hobbes devotes by far the most attention is sight. The character of Hobbes's account of sense perception as a whole can be seen by considering the example of sight that is of the greatest importance to him: our vision of the light of the sun. In Hobbes's view, there is not really such a thing as "the light of the sun." Rather, according to the explanation he gives in *De Corpore*, the circular motion of the sun—not its dilation and contraction, as he had speculated in earlier works (cf. *Elem.* 2.8; *Anti-White* 9.3; *OL* V, 218; *Tract. Opt.*, 149–50, 153)—casts away the surrounding medium ("the ambient ethereal substance"), thus setting in motion chain reactions that eventually reach our eyes, from which they travel to the heart and there trigger the rebounding motions that give rise to the phantasms we call light (*De Corp.* 27.2). What we see when we look toward the sun, then, is not the sun itself or its light—strictly speaking, it has no light—but only an apparition caused by a reaction to motions that were initiated by the sun's own motions (*De Corp.* 6.10, 25.10, 27.2; *Anti-White* 3.1). In this and other examples of vision, we can see the chasm separating Hobbes's account of sense perception from the account he opposed and sought to replace. The untenable

---

instead to the brain, see *Elem.* 2.7–9 (consider, however: "in the brain, or spirits, or some internal substance in the head"); *OL* V, 220.

alternative, according to Hobbes, is the scholastic account, "grounded upon certain texts of Aristotle," that would explain vision as caused by the emanation of "visible species," which, as genuine disembodied likenesses of external objects, travel from those objects to our eyes (see *Lev.* 1.5). That account attributes to our sense perception a direct and undistorted reception of the world as it truly is. But it does so, Hobbes argues, only by resorting to fantastical explanations that provide yet another display of the "insignificant speech" so prevalent in the universities (see *Lev.* 1.5, 45.2, 46.27; Latin *Lev.*, 1089; *Elem.* 2.4; *De Corp.* 5.4; *EW* VII, 339–40, 469).[23]

There is a question—one not easily answered—as to what exactly Hobbes has in mind when he says that the doctrine he opposes is "grounded upon certain texts of Aristotle." The question is similar to the one we considered earlier regarding Hobbes's view of Aristotle's genuine position on the existence of abstract essences. Did Aristotle himself hold the view in question, according to Hobbes (see pp. 16–17 above)? As in the earlier case, to which the present one is not only similar but also related, the question is difficult to answer because Hobbes, in his disdain for Aristotle, does not seem to have been sufficiently motivated to sift through the details of Aristotle's own treatment of the matter.[24] But this much can be said with confidence: Hobbes did not think that the ancient philosophers—the "ancient pretenders to natural knowledge"—had discovered the nature of sight or any of the other senses (*Lev.* 45.1–2).[25] He must therefore have regarded his understanding of sense perception as a major difference between his own natural philosophy

---

23. For a detailed discussion of Hobbes's disagreement with "the Aristotelians" regarding sense perception, including an account of the diversity and dispute within the "Aristotelian" camp itself, see Leijenhorst, "Sense and Nonsense about Sense," 84–94. See also Pettit, *Made with Words*, 9–10; Flathman, *Thomas Hobbes: Skepticism, Individuality and Chastened Politics*, 16–17. Hobbes himself alludes to the disagreements among his opponents in the Latin *Leviathan* (see 1089). Although Hobbes does not identify any of his scholastic opponents by name when discussing sense perception, Francisco Suárez, one of Hobbes's favorite targets in other contexts, provides a good example of the position Hobbes is attacking. See Suárez, *Opera Omnia*, III, 614–30. See also Thomas Aquinas, *Summa Theologica*, I, Q. 84.1–6, Q. 85.1–2.

24. The key text is Aristotle's *De Anima*. See *De Anima* 424a17–24 for the passage that comes closest to the scholastic position Hobbes criticizes. This passage, however, has to be read in the broader context of Aristotle's very complex treatment of sense perception, which runs from 416b32 to 429a9.

25. See also Latin *Lev.*, 1013: *Quod cum ignorant Philosophi Veteres* . . . (Because the ancient philosophers were ignorant of this [*sc.*, how phantasms are produced in men] . . .). Hobbes speaks elsewhere (*OL* V, 221) of *difficultas maxima in lumine concipiendo tam veterum, quam neotericorum philosophorum ingenia torsit* (the very great difficulties in conceiving of light, which twisted the minds of the ancient philosophers as much as those of the moderns). Compare

and theirs. And that would remain true whatever might be the answer to a further—more discussed, but ultimately less significant—question that can be asked in this connection: whether Hobbes was right to regard his account of sense perception as an original discovery. For that question concerns Hobbes's relationship, not to classical thought, but to the thought of other early moderns, such as Galileo and Descartes.

The question of Hobbes's relationship to Descartes in particular, as it pertains to the issue of sense perception, contains difficulties of its own. Although Hobbes presents his position as if he is breaking new ground, he can be accused—and *was* accused, by Descartes himself—of exaggerating his originality and failing to give credit where it was due. It would go beyond my purposes here, however, to discuss the evidence on each side of this quarrel between Hobbes and Descartes.[26]

Elem. 2.4: "And this opinion [*sc.*, that the qualities perceived are in the perceived objects themselves] hath been so long received, that the contrary must needs appear a great paradox."

26. Brandt and Tuck have done that thoroughly. See Brandt, *Thomas Hobbes' Mechanical Conception of Nature*, 129–42; Tuck, "Hobbes and Descartes," 11–41; see also Tönnies, *Thomas Hobbes: Leben und Lehre*, 99–110; Laird, *Hobbes*, 48–52. The primary documents in the feud between Hobbes and Descartes come from an exchange of letters between the two men, with Mersenne serving as the intermediary, in 1640–41 (see Hobbes, *Correspondence*, Letters 29–30, 32–34, 36). Hobbes declares his own originality also at *OL* V, 221; *EW* VII, 139, 340–42, 471; *EW* IV, 436–37. *EW* VII, 468, is more ambiguous, especially this remark in reference to Descartes' account of light (which follows another claim by Hobbes to originality): "Yet philosophical ground I take to be of such a nature, that any man may build upon it that will, especially if the owner himself will not."

For expressions by Descartes of a view of sense perception very close to Hobbes's in its fundamentals, see *Optics*, Discourses 1, 4; *Principles of Philosophy* 1.66–71, 4.189–98; *The World*, Chap. 1. Although Galileo, for his part, claimed not to know "anything but a trifle" about sight and light, his account of heat in *Il Saggiatore* can be seen as a precursor to the accounts of perception of both Descartes and Hobbes. See Galileo, *Opere* VI, 347ff. Brandt, *Thomas Hobbes' Mechanical Conception of Nature*, 79–84, offers a translation and an account of this passage; see also Burtt, *The Metaphysical Foundations of Modern Physical Science*, 75–76; Tuck, "Hobbes and Descartes," 30; Willey, *The Seventeenth Century Background*, 84–85; Garber, "Natural Philosophy in Seventeenth-Century Context," 107.

Tuck, "Hobbes and Descartes," 30, writes of the "clear sense which modern scholars have now come to possess, that ancient skepticism did not advance to the modern [= Cartesian and Hobbesian] position on perception"; see also *Philosophy and Government, 1572–1651*, 286. This "sense," however, can be challenged by a consideration of passages such as Plato, *Theaetetus* 153d8–154a4 and 156a2–157c3 (with 151e1–152e9). That is not to say, of course, that Plato himself would have endorsed the accounts of Descartes and Hobbes, nor that Descartes and Hobbes took their bearings from such ancient sources, but only that Plato was aware of a position that was strikingly similar, in some of its key aspects, to their "modern position."

More important than the disputed sources of Hobbes's account of sense perception are the problematic implications of that account for his attempt to lay the foundations of a materialistic natural science. Hobbes's account of sense perception is not inconsistent with his materialism or his mechanistic axioms of motion. Far from it: he relies on that materialism and those axioms in his most developed presentation of his account of sense perception (see *De Corp.* 25.2).[27] Yet, while Hobbes's account of sense perception is so far from being inconsistent with his mechanistic materialism that it is even a consequence of it, the account carries with it a problem for our knowledge of a world that consists only of matter in motion. For if his account of sense perception is true, then we do not have direct access to the bodies that are the true things in Hobbes's view; what we experience through our senses are only the appearances or phantasms produced by the various motions of those bodies. But that means that there is a gulf separating the world of our experience, which is a world of mere appearances, and the true but inaccessible world of the moving bodies. Let us consider the problem this gulf poses from the vantage point of each of the two shores it divides.

In our perceptions, we are given what Hobbes variously calls "appearances," "phantasms," "conceptions," "images," "fancies," "ideas." What are these? According to Hobbes's most radical formulations, they are nothing but motions—motions in us as sentient bodies (see, e.g., *De Corp.* 6.10, 25.1–2; *Elem.* 2.7; *Lev.* 1.4, 6.9, 45.1; *Anti-White* 7.1, 30.3). But Hobbes's most radical formulations on this point are not his most precise, for it is more precise to say that the appearances are the *products* or *effects* of motions, effects which are not so much the motions themselves as epiphenomena arising from them (*De Corp.* 25.2–3, 29.2; *Elem.* 2.7–9; *Lev.* 1.4; *Anti-White* 3.2, 30.4).[28] The green of the grass, the bitterness of the lemon, the howl of the wind—these are phantasms caused by, but not simply identical to, the motions that give rise to them in the mind of perceiver. Although Hobbes sometimes speaks of them loosely

27. See Leijenhorst, "Sense and Nonsense about Sense," 89: "sense perception [for Hobbes] is nothing more than an example of the regular mechanical interaction between bodies." See also Gert, "Hobbes on Language, Metaphysics, and Epistemology," 56; Sorell, *Hobbes*, 70; Tönnies, *Hobbes: Leben und Lehre*, 99; Flathman, *Thomas Hobbes: Skepticism, Individuality and Chastened Politics*, 15–16.

28. Although Hobbes does not use the term "epiphenomena," it expresses well what he has in mind, as Gert argues (see "Hobbes on Language, Metaphysics, and Epistemology," 51–52). Consider, e.g., *De Corp.* 25.2: "Let us propose the following as the encompassing definition of sense, drawn from the explication of its causes and from the order of its constant generation: *Sense is a phantasm, enduring for some length of time, produced as a reaction by the endeavor outward of the organ of sense, which is generated by the opposite endeavor inward by the object.*"

as accidents or qualities of the external objects (see, e.g., *De Corp.* 8.20, 9.3; *Anti-White* 27.1, 35.1; *Lev.* 4.15–16; *Obj.*, no. 2; cf. *De Corp.* 8.3), strictly speaking they do not exist in those bodies: the grass is not green, the lemon is not bitter, and the wind never howls. Our perceptions give us, then, merely apparent accidents that are in fact epiphenomena of motions that flow from the external bodies, whose true accidents are not the same as those we perceive (see *Elem.* 2.9–10; *Lev.* 1.4, 5.11; *EW* VII, 28; *Obj.*, no. 1; *De Corp.* 5.6–7, 6.8–10, 25.2–3, 25.10). But what does this mean for the status or being of the phantasms? In what sense do they exist at all? Because they are not bodies or even, strictly speaking, motions, are they "nothing," as Hobbes says at his most extreme and perhaps most consistent (see Latin *Lev.*, 1171; *Lev.* 45.10)? Or is that ultimately an untenable position, given their undeniable reality as at least appearances or mental conceptions?[29] This question, which contains a potential challenge to Hobbes's thoroughgoing materialism, is not a question that Hobbes confronts or pursues.[30] But perhaps it is best to explain his passing over it, not as the avoidance of a challenge, but as one of the consequences of the denigration of the phantasms that is entailed in regarding them as mere phantasms. Does it not become difficult to take seriously, and rigorously to inquire after, that which one sees as mere epiphenomenal appearances produced by a deeper and truer reality? If the world that is given to us is reduced to a realm of mere appearances, it would seem to lose its dignity and importance. And yet there is at least one difficulty here. For the images provided by our senses, phantasmal though they may be, are also the essential starting points of all of our thinking, according to Hobbes.

We will return to this last problem. But first let us look at matters from the other side, so to speak, of the event of sense perception, that is, from the side of the bodies. For there is a difficulty there too—a difficulty at least as weighty. Hobbes, as we have already seen, asserts the fundamental ontological status of the bodies: they are the true things, the only real constituents of a universe that is nothing but their aggregate. His account of sense perception, on one level, only reinforces this central claim: the bodies and their motions are the true world as distinct from the merely apparent world of the phantasms. The bodies are not merely the truth behind the fiction; they are even its source:

29. Brandt, *Thomas Hobbes' Mechanical Conception of Nature*, 355, raises what amounts to the same question. See also Mintz, *The Hunting of Leviathan*, 78.

30. Compare Brandt, *Thomas Hobbes' Mechanical Conception of Nature*, 355–56. A sign of Hobbes's neglect of the question is the frequency with which he wavers, sometimes even within a single passage, between more and less radical formulations of his view of what the phantasms are (see, e.g., *Lev.* 1.4; *De Corp* 25.2, 29.1; *Elem.* 2.7).

"All sense is fancy, though the cause be always in a real body" (*EW* VII, 28; see also *De Corp.* 25.2–3, 25.10; Latin *Lev.*, 1149). But Hobbes's account of perception also poses a problem for the bodies, or at least for our knowledge of them. For if all we know through our senses are the phantasms, if "all of our knowledge of existing things consists in the images produced by the action of the things on our senses" (*Anti-White* 3.2), then how can our minds grasp the bodies themselves? Although we have no direct access to the bodies, we can, Hobbes suggests, use our reason to infer their existence: presumably there must be *something* that gives rise to our perceptions.[31] We can even assume that the bodies must have certain accidents without which they could not produce the effects they do, including giving rise to our various perceptions. But can we know the true character of the bodies and their accidents? There is, of course, a tendency to assume a close correspondence between the accidents of the bodies as things in themselves and the accidents they appear to possess in our phantasms of them. And Hobbes grants that "it is not so easy to distinguish between the things themselves, from which the phantasms proceed, and the many appearances the things produce" (*De Corp.* 6.8; see also 8.3). But it is precisely the illusion that there is a direct or simple correspondence between the true character of the things and the way they appear to us that Hobbes regards as "the great deception of sense."

The problem of the bodies—that is, of *knowing* the bodies—extends even to our conception of body itself: What is meant by calling the bodies "bodies"? Is not "body" a deceptive word, at least in the sense that it gives a misleading impression of clarity concerning a question that is more mysterious than it seems? This further aspect of the problem can be seen in the key chapter of *De Corpore* in which Hobbes struggles to define body, Chapter 8, "Of Body and Accident." Hobbes does, in a manner, define body in this chapter, but it proves to be more difficult than one might expect. Because bodies as bodies are not generated, according to Hobbes, they cannot be understood through

---

31. See *De Corp.* 8.1: *ut non sensibus, sed ratione tantum aliquid ibi esse intelligatur* (it may be understood, not by the senses, but by reason that there is some such thing there); 30.14: *Naturae ergo corporae absque ratiocinatione ab effectu soli sensus idonei testes non sunt* (The senses alone, without reasoning from effects, do not provide sufficient evidence of the nature of bodies); Latin *Lev.*, Appendix, 1171: *quam apparitionem sine aliqua causa & fundamento esse non posse satis intelligimus* (that the appearance cannot be without some cause and foundation, we understand well enough). See also Hobbes's remarks on how "substance" is established ("solely by reasoning") in *Obj.*, no. 9. Compare Gassendi, "Fifth Set of Objections," 189–91; see also Tuck, "Optics and Skeptics," 254, "Hobbes and Descartes," 39–40, *Philosophy and Government, 1572–1651*, 299–301; Leijenhorst, "Hobbes's Theory of Causality and Its Aristotelian Background," 440, *The Mechanisation of Aristotelianism*, 148–50.

their mode of generation (see *De Corp.* 6.13). Nor can they be grasped directly through perception, since the bodies themselves, as opposed to the images produced by them, are not perceived. It seems that, to conceive of bodies, we have to begin by positing the existence of something that exists outside of the images that arise in our perceptions. The warrant for such positing, as we have just seen, lies in the thought that there must be something that causes the images we are given. In a way, then, the bodies can be approached indirectly, through a process of reasoning that, as it were, reverses the process of perception and begins from what is not body.[32] By distinguishing the bodies from the phantasms to which they give rise in our minds, we can arrive at a conception of a body as that which subsists on its own, without any dependence on our thought (*De Corp.* 8.1; see also *Lev.* 34.2; Latin *Lev.*, Appendix, 1185). And a further step is possible through the reflection that, in any such conception, a body must be conceived of as occupying space and thus as extended. In extension, it seems, we can come closest to identifying that which marks a body as a body: it is "on account of its extension" that we call something a body (*De Corp.* 8.1). Hobbes thus defines a body as "that which, without any dependence on our thought, is coincident or coextended with some part of space" (*De Corp.* 8.1; see also 3.3, 8.20, 8.23; *Anti-White* 3.2, 4.3, 27.8). But this definition, which reminds of Descartes's,[33] is not altogether satisfactory even by Hobbes's own lights, because it does not quite do what an adequate definition should do, namely, "by a speech as brief as possible" raise in the mind of the listeners "a perfect and clear idea or conception of the things named" (*De Corp.* 6.13). There are two problems with Hobbes's quasi-Cartesian definition. First, there is a gap between extension understood as the real magnitude of a body, which, like the thing itself, exists apart from our thought of it, and extension understood as our mental conception of the place occupied by the body, which is a mere image in our minds. If the former is "true extension" (*extensio vera*) and the latter "feigned extension" (*extensio ficta*), it would seem to be only "feigned extension" that allows us to place the body in imaginary space and thus to form a conception of it as extended,

---

32. Consider the following exchange between Hobbes's "A" and "B" in the first dialogue of *Decameron Physiologicum* (EW VII, 78–79):

> A: Seeing you say that alteration is wrought by the motion of bodies, pray tell me first what I am to understand by the word body?
> B: It is a hard question, though most men think they can easily answer it, as that it is whatever they can see, feel, or take notice of by their senses. But if you will know indeed what is body, we must first enquire what there is that is not body.

33. Compare Descartes, *Principles of Philosophy* 1.53, 1.63–65, 2.4–11, 2.64.

whereas it is only "true extension" that exists outside of our minds.[34] Second, even in the case of true extension, Hobbes resists a simple equation of body and extension or a reduction of body to extension. Extension is only one accident of any body, and thus a body "is not extension, but a thing extended" (*De Corp.* 8.5; see also 8.2–3. 5.3; *Lev.* 5.10). Similarly, since magnitude is the same as extension, it can be said that a body "has magnitude," but not that it "is magnitude itself" (Latin *Lev.*, Appendix, 1185; see also *De Corp.* 8.15, 15.1; *EW* VII, 227; *Anti-White* 27.1). But what, then, is a body if it is extended but not extension? One might be tempted to say that it is the matter that is extended in real space. But, aside from the difficulty that would remain of bridging the gap between real space and the imaginary space we conceive in our minds, such an answer would only push the question from the word "body" onto the word "matter" without providing any real gain in clarity.[35]

The situation might be different—"matter" might provide a fuller answer—if it were possible to think of all bodies as ultimately constituted by a single *materia prima* or "first matter" of which the particular bodies could be understood as mere forms or mutations. Yet, although Hobbes allows that the notion of *materia prima* can be put to some use, he stresses its limits. The notion is useful for designating "a conception of body without consideration of any form or accident except for magnitude or extension and aptitude for receiving form and accidents"; it can thus serve as a name for "body in general, that is, body considered universally" (*De Corp.* 8.24). But even if *materia prima* is a useful name, it is nevertheless, according to Hobbes, "a mere name" (*De Corp.* 8.24). "*Materia prima* is nothing," it "does not exist," because matter is never in an unformed state in which it is, so to speak, merely awaiting formation into something with characteristics beyond extension or magnitude (*De Corp.* 8.24, 2.14; *Anti-White* 7.3, 27.1; see also Latin *Lev.*, Appendix, 1147). Hobbes's remarks about *materia prima* thus do more to underscore than to overcome the limits of understanding body in terms of extension alone.[36]

---

34. See *De Corp.* 8.5: "*place* is nothing outside the mind, nor *magnitude* anything within it." See also 8.1–2, 8.4, 8.8, 7.2–3, 26.1; *Lev.* 34.2; Latin *Lev.*, 611; *Anti-White* 3.1–2.

35. This account of the difficulties Hobbes encounters in his attempt to define body should be compared with Strauss, *Hobbes's Critique of Religion*, 99–100; Laird, *Hobbes*, 94–97; Tönnies, *Hobbes: Leben und Lehre*, 129–31, 138–39, 297n99. Consider also Herbert, *Thomas Hobbes: The Unity of Scientific and Moral Wisdom*, 44–48; Brandt, *Thomas Hobbes' Mechanical Conception of Nature*, 188–89, 252–53.

36. Even of the "pure ether," Hobbes says only that it can be thought of "as if" (*tanquam*) it were *materia prima* (see *De Corp* 27.1). Regarding Hobbes's position on *materia prima*, see Craig, *The Platonian Leviathan*, 58; Sorell, *Hobbes*, 57; Spragens, *The Politics of Motion*, 90; Leijenhorst, *The Mechanisation of Aristotelianism*, 150–51.

Another possible path, which Hobbes regards as akin to the appeal to *materia prima*, is the attempt of "some philosophers" to conceive of everything as composed of homogenous atoms that differ only in shape (see *Anti-White* 7.2). Yet, although Hobbes himself sometimes speaks of atoms, and even speculates that the space in the universe between the large consistent bodies is filled by minute atoms and fluid ether, he does not regard it as possible to discover the nature of either the atoms or the ether (see *De Corp.* 26.3–5, 27.1; *Anti-White* 7.4; consider also *De Hom.* 10.5; *EW* VII, 78, 133–36, 340–41). Even the very existence of atoms and ether, Hobbes acknowledges, is a matter of speculation or supposition (see *De Corp.* 26.3, 26.5, 29.13, 30.3). And he suggests that attempts to give causal explanations that depend on the specific motions and figures of atoms can easily stray beyond the bounds of reasonable speculation: to place too much confidence in such explanations is "to revolt from philosophy to divination" (*De Corp.* 29.17; see also 27.16; *EW* VII, 146; *Correspondence*, Letter 19).

The further one follows the path of Hobbes's reflections on the bodies, the darker, it seems, the bodies become. It turns out that we can know very little about the bodies, and thus we are confronted with the paradox that the bodies are at once fundamental to Hobbes's entire conception of reality and yet shrouded in such mystery as to make their entire realm a kind of black box. From here, we can understand a remarkable statement of Brandt, the great defender of the view that Hobbes is the most thoroughgoing metaphysical materialist of modern times. In the conclusion to his famous work on Hobbes's conception of nature, Brandt is finally led to concede that, "when Hobbes has been and is still called a materialist, this is in a certain sense misleading. The concept of matter plays an exceedingly small part [in Hobbes's natural philosophy] and has a constant tendency to disappear."[37] Brandt makes this remark in the context of stressing the greater importance Hobbes ultimately places on motion.[38] But since, for Hobbes, motions must always be motions of bodies, there is a problem in trying to cordon off Hobbes's mechanistic account of motions, as Brandt would ultimately like to do, from the problem of matter. For does not the difficulty of knowing the bodies also pose a problem for the clarity with which we can grasp their motions, including those that give rise

37. *Thomas Hobbes' Mechanical Conception of Nature*, 379.

38. Brandt continues on 379: "Hobbes should more correctly be called a motionalist, if we may be permitted to coin such a word. He is the philosopher of motion as Descartes is the philosopher of extension." See also 113. Compare Herbert, *Thomas Hobbes: The Unity of Scientific and Moral Wisdom*, 52–53; Mintz, *The Hunting of Leviathan*, 64–65; Spragens, *The Politics of Motion*, 90–92, 97.

to the appearances we receive through our senses?[39] One might even go so far as to wonder whether Hobbes's fundamental axioms of motion, which he defended on the grounds that they are more conceivable than the alternatives (see pp. 42–44 above), are not called into some doubt by the shadow that the problem of the bodies casts also over the motions of the bodies.

Hobbes does not seem to have gone quite so far. But he did think that the limits of our access to the bodies required a transformation in the approach and character of natural philosophy. That transformation is not, to be sure, a simple succumbing to the skepticism that follows from the conclusion that the true constituents of reality are unknowable and that we have access only to phantasms. Rather, in order to preserve the possibility of philosophy or science in the face of this problem, Hobbes grants the problem and then tries to proceed on the basis of an acceptance of it. We can begin to see something of this new approach by considering the otherwise very puzzling way that Hobbes opens Part II of *De Corpore*, which is entitled *Philosophia Prima* ("The First Grounds of Philosophy").[40] For Hobbes begins there—and thus, in a sense, begins his natural philosophy as such—with a preemptive strike. Since it is a preemptive strike against the implications of the problem we have been considering, or, better, against the thought that those implications are fatal to philosophy, I have waited until now to consider what is, in a certain respect, Hobbes's starting point. That starting point should make more sense than it otherwise would now that we have an awareness of the difficulties to which it is a response.

Hobbes's Thought Experiment

Hobbes begins Part II of *De Corpore* by imagining the annihilation of the entire world except for one man (7.1; compare *Elem.* 1.8; *Anti-White* 3.1).[41] What,

---

39. The reciprocity of grasping bodies and grasping their motions, and thus of the difficulties in doing so, is indicated by this statement of Hobbes from *Anti-White* 7.4: "Thus body or *materia prima* can be altered, and in its parts it can be moved in innumerable ways, and through motions of this sort, it can produce innumerable phantasms in sentient souls, that is, an innumerable variety of images. And since it is impossible to know what motions the individual particles of the whole world have, it follows that it is also impossible for us to know how great is the variety of things, and whether or not there are in the heavens bodies analogous to ours."

40. "The First Grounds of Philosophy" is the Hobbes-approved translation of the Latin title, *Philosophia Prima*, the more common translation of which would be "First Philosophy."

41. The following summary and analysis of *De Corpore* 7.1 may be compared with Tönnies, *Thomas Hobbes: Leben und Lehre*, 121–22; Leijenhorst, *The Mechanisation of Aristotelianism*, 53–55, 105–6.

he asks, would remain for this man such that his thinking would still be possible? Hobbes's answer is that because the phantasms or ideas that arose in his mind before the annihilation of the world would linger as images in his memory, "these are the things to which he could give names, and that he could add and subtract with one another" (*De Corp.* 7.1). Such a man, in other words, would retain the internal contents of his mind or consciousness, even if the bodies that originally produced those phantasms ceased to exist. Thought or "ratiocination" would therefore still be possible under such conditions, so long as memory and imagination allowed the mind to preserve its ideas. The existence—at least the continued existence—of the external world is unnecessary, because the isolated mind could continue its operations by assigning names to the phantasms within the mind itself. Indeed, whether we realize it or not, Hobbes argues, our thinking already works in this way: "if we turn our minds attentively to what we do when we reason, we shall see that, even when the things remain, we compute nothing but our own phantasms" (*De Corp.* 7.1). On one level, then, Hobbes's thought experiment serves merely to clarify a point we have already considered: all thinking originates from the phantasms we receive through sense perception, rather than from direct access to the true constituents of the external world. But the thought experiment is meant to do more than make that point, which could be made without such a strange conceit. The more important purpose of the thought experiment is to make the further point that, not only do we not *have* direct access to the external world, but we do not *need* such access. We do not need a direct grasp of the bodies themselves, because we can proceed, Hobbes suggests, by treating the phantasms or the ideas in our minds *as if* they were the appearances, the "images" (*species*), of external things that exist outside of our minds, even if those things do not exist outside of our minds (*De Corp.* 7.1).

But proceed with what? On the basis of Hobbes's initial presentation of his thought experiment, one might think that he has in mind an approach that would merely articulate the features of the world as it is given to us—the contents, in other words, of the apparent world. By articulating what is given to us without making any claims about the underlying reality that gave rise to the appearances, even as to whether there is any such reality, Hobbes would seem to be on safe ground, and he can go forward with a kind of "phenomenalist" natural philosophy. Yet, although his thought experiment affirms the necessity of a phenomenalist beginning, Hobbes clearly wants to accomplish something more than a mere articulation or description of the appearances as mere appearances. (After all, they are "nothing," or next to nothing.) Thus what follows the dramatic opening of Part II of *De Corpore*, and hence forms the core of the work, is not so much a mere phenomenalist articulation of the given world as it is Hobbes's effort to set forth the key definitions and conceptions that are at the heart of his mechanistic view of nature. What the annihilation thought experiment adds, then, besides the securing of a toe-hold for philosophy in the contents of our consciousness, is a preliminary indication of how Hobbes's definitions are to be taken or what their status is. As another crucial passage will confirm—this one at the end of the development that begins at the outset of Part II—Hobbes's key definitions are meant to lay down a set of first principles for our understanding of nature, but such first principles as "we ourselves make," that is, principles that arise, not from a process of discovery through which nature gradually reveals itself, but from human construction (see *De Corp.* 25.1; see also 15.1, 24.9, 30.15; *De Hom.* 10.4–5; *EW* VII, 183–85).

Now, we will consider further in the next section what is entailed in the kind of construction that Hobbes has in mind and what the relationship is be-tween his constructed definitions and the physics that he also develops in *De Corpore.* For now, let us focus on just one point. The conception of nature that Hobbes presents through his key definitions and his explanations of them is a materialistic as well as a mechanistic conception. There can be no doubt about that. Yet, if we stick strictly to his indications that his definitions do not depend on the actual existence of the bodies because he is merely construct-ing a conception of nature in which the bodies and their motions are *regarded as* the fundamental reality, then it would seem that Hobbes's materialism is merely a methodological materialism. That is to say, Hobbes presents a mate-rialistic conception of nature, and proceeds on its basis, without claiming to know whether nature itself truly conforms to that conception. That question, the ultimate metaphysical question, is left open.[42]

And yet it will be asked—must be asked—whether Hobbes sticks rigor-ously to this understanding of his own enterprise or position. Does he not convey, on nearly every page of *De Corpore*, his settled conviction that, de-spite our lack of access to the true constituents of the world, we can be sure that they are bodies? Even in the thought experiment of the annihilation of the world, does he not display his confidence in the existence of the bodies by treating the annihilation *as a fiction*, and by preserving a role for the bodies as

---

42. On the question of Hobbes's turn toward a methodological materialism, see, in addi-tion to Strauss, *Natural Right and History,* 174 (and context), Strauss "On the Basis of Hobbes's Political Philosophy," 178, 182, and *Hobbes's Critique of Religion,* 99–102; contrast Brandt, *Thomas Hobbes' Mechanical Conception of Nature,* 355–61. For other discussions of the issue, see Leijen-horst, "Hobbes's Theory of Causality and Its Aristotelian Background," 438–40; Kraynak, *History and Modernity in the Thought of Thomas Hobbes,* 129–32; Tuck, "Optics and Skeptics," 252–54.

the original sources of the phantasms that linger as memories even after the bodies themselves have been annihilated?[43]

To the question of whether Hobbes thought that there were serious reasons to doubt the existence of the external world and its fundamentally corporeal character, it does not seem that there is a simple answer. On the one hand, he grants that the existence of the bodies as the true things that abide outside of our consciousness must be merely posited. And his very definition of the bodies as those things, marked by extension, that exist apart from our thought of them is given within the broad section of *De Corpore* that opens with the disclaimer that he will proceed without insisting that the bodies really exist and closes with the declaration that the truth of his definitions is merely a constructed truth (see again 7.1, 24.9, 25.1, 30.15). On the other hand, Hobbes clearly did not think that the answer "bodies" to the question of what lies behind the world of appearances is nothing more than a matter of wholly arbitrary positing or sheer construction. For, as we have seen him reason, not only must *something* lie behind the world of appearances, but "bodies" is the most conceivable answer to the question of what that something is—and "conceivable" in the sense, not of the merely likely, but of that which can be coherently grasped by the mind (see pp. 41–42, 57 above). Although "bodies" is not as fully intelligible an answer as it first appears, surely it remains, in Hobbes's mind, more conceivable than any alternative.

But we must take a further step here, for there is one alternative—in a way, it is *the* alternative—that this last line of reflection is not sufficient to exclude. We can see the relevance of this alternative to the matter at hand by comparing Hobbes's thought experiment regarding the annihilation of the world with the more famous thought experiment of which it cannot but remind one: Descartes's doubt of the existence of the external world in his *Meditations*.[44] Now, Descartes's doubt of the existence of the external world is expressed more radically and rigorously than Hobbes's. One does not find in the *Meditations* the qualification that the absence of the world rests on a fiction or the

43. See Strauss, *Hobbes's Critique of Religion*, 102 (especially n. 268), 105; Laird, *Hobbes*, 132; Sorell, *Hobbes*, 66.

44. See especially Descartes's First Meditation. For a more extensive comparison of the "fundamental reflections" of Hobbes and Descartes, to which my argument in this paragraph is indebted, see Strauss, *Hobbes's Critique of Religion*, 94–109. See also the statement from a 1941 course of Strauss quoted on pages ix–x (n. 4) of the Translators' Preface to *Hobbes's Critique of Religion*. On Strauss's comparison of Hobbes and Descartes, see Burns, "Leo Strauss on the Origins of Hobbes's Natural Science," 115–18.

assumption that, prior to its annihilation, the world must have existed.[45] But this difference may not be as great as it first appears, since Hobbes, in his response to the *Meditations*, grants the legitimacy of Descartes's more radical doubt (see *Obj.*, no. 1; compare *Anti-White* 26.2). More important is that Descartes presents, as one of the grounds for doubt, a troubling alternative to the assumption that moving bodies are the source of the world as it appears to us: perhaps the world we are given through our senses is the work, not of the bodies and their necessary motions, but of an omnipotent God bent on deceiving us.[46] Now, Descartes raises this problem only to solve it through his arguments for the existence of God and God's perfection, the latter of which ensures that neither God nor our clear and distinct conceptions can deceive us.[47] But however Descartes's solution might ultimately have to be understood—whether he regarded it as a genuine solution or as a spurious one meant to indicate a serious problem[48]—Hobbes did not accept it. According to Hobbes, we know too little of God—our powers are too limited and God in his infinity is too unfathomable—to accept such an argument (see *Obj.*, nos. 5, 7, 10, 11, 15; see also *De Corp.* 26.1).[49] Does that mean that Hobbes thinks that we are thrown back on the problem? Admittedly, Hobbes does not explicitly point to the possibility of a mysterious God who might be deceiving us as grounds for his own skepticism. No such *Deus deceptor* appears in his own thought experiment, and even in that experiment, as we have noted, he indicates his confidence in the reality of the external world. Yet the problem pointed to by Descartes must have troubled Hobbes as well. After all, given his acknowledgment that we do not have direct knowledge of the bodies and

45. Laird, *Hobbes*, 132: "[Hobbes's] experiment of feigning annihilation, when compared, say, with Descartes' philosophical doubt, was curiously hesitating, since it presupposed that the memory of real bodies 'before their annihilation' . . . was retained." See also Tuck, *Hobbes*, 41–46.

46. *Meditations* 1.9–12, 3.4. See also *Principles of Philosophy* 1.5, 2.1.

47. See *Meditations* 1.9 together with the whole of the Third Meditation, 4.1–3, and 5.11–15. See also *Principles of Philosophy* 1.13–19, 1.29–30; *Discourse on Method*, Part 4.

48. It is neither possible nor necessary to settle here the question of Descartes's own view of his solution. Among the many passages one would have to consider are *Meditations* 3.22–30, 5.7–12; *Principles of Philosophy* 1.19–27, 3.44–47; *Discourse on Method*, Part IV (25), Part V (28–29); *The World*, Chaps. 6–7. Also worth considering on this question is Krüger, "The Origin of Philosophical Self-Consciousness," 228–37. As Krüger indicates, even if Descartes did not accept his own theological solution, that does not mean that he did not accept his *cogito* argument, which would in fact become all the more important. See also Kennington, *On Modern Origins*, 173–86.

49. Compare Gassendi, "Fifth Set of Objections," 200–201, 205–8; see also Strauss, *Hobbes's Critique of Religion*, 98–99, 108; Tuck, "Hobbes and Descartes," 36–37; Hanson, "Reconsidering Hobbes's Conventionalism," 639–40.

that they must be posited, does he not leave his materialism open to the challenge in question? Since he must be aware that he does, is this not a further reason—perhaps the deepest one—that Hobbes would ultimately have to concede that his materialism is merely methodological?

This last line of reflection may seem to have strayed too far into the realm of speculation. But we have already seen some evidence that Hobbes was aware of the challenge posed to his mechanistic principles by an omnipotent God who can do whatever he wills (see pp. 49–50 above). If an incomprehensible God can create the world and interrupt its operations, then he can create for us appearances that flow, not from the necessitated motions of bodies, but from his freely operating will. "There is no doubt but God can make unnatural apparitions," Hobbes concedes in *Leviathan*, in a remark that, whatever its ultimate intention, at least indicates his awareness of the issue (*Lev.* 2.8.)[50] And we will see further evidence, when we consider Hobbes's physics in the next section, that he was aware of the challenge posed by the possibility of divine intervention in the workings of nature. This possibility, in fact, is one of the most important reasons that Hobbes thought that any possible physics must remain hypothetical.

Hobbes's Twofold Conception of Science

As we turn now to Hobbes's conception of science, we should bear in mind that, for Hobbes, as for all early modern authors, philosophy and science are two words for the same thing. The division within Hobbes's conception, then, is not to be understood as one between philosophy, on the one hand, and science, on the other. Yet there is a division. In fact, the most striking thing about Hobbes's conception is that it is twofold: he divides philosophy on the basis of two different methods that may be used in its pursuit. To understand the distinction between the two methods, each of which Hobbes himself employs, we should begin from his most direct statement of the difference between them. One method, he says, begins from causes or modes of generation and reasons to their possible effects; the other begins from appearances or effects and seeks to discover their causes or at least their possible modes of generation (see *De Corp.* 25.1; see also 1.2, 6.1; *De Hom.* 10.4–5; *Anti-White* 1.1).

If this formulation gives the impression that, in the case of the first method, Hobbes thinks that one can begin from a direct knowledge of natural causes, that impression is misleading. What provides the starting points

---

50. In the Latin *Leviathan* "unnatural apparitions" is replaced by *phantasmata supernaturalia* (supernatural apparitions); see also *EW* VII, 80.

for the first method are rather definitions that "we ourselves make," and what is generated by proceeding from such definitions are not so much accounts of how effects can be produced as demonstrations of what follows if one reasons deductively from postulated definitions (see *De Corp.* 25.1). Since Hobbes's distinction between the two methods of philosophy supplies the central architectural principle of Parts II–IV of *De Corpore*—that is, of the whole of the work after the treatment of logic in Part I—we can place under the heading of the first method both Hobbes's "first philosophy" in Part II and his account of magnitudes and motions, which he also calls his geometry, in Part III. Only in Part IV, his physics, does Hobbes turn to the second method. There, finally calling off his thought experiment regarding the annihilation of the world, he begins from the phenomena of nature, understood once again as produced by existing bodies, and seeks to give causal accounts of how such phenomena are or may be generated (see 25.1; see also 24.9). The fundamental division of science for Hobbes, then, would seem to be between a first philosophy and a geometry that proceed from constructed definitions, on the one hand, and a physics that proceeds from the appearances of nature, on the other. But how exactly are we to conceive of the character and the relationship of these two "halves" of science as Hobbes conceives of it? Are they entirely separate, or do they form a single whole? And if they do form a whole, what can Hobbes's reliance on two different but interconnected approaches tell us about his efforts—perhaps never fully successful—to put the science of nature on a solid footing?[51]

The most obvious difference between the two methods, to start from what is clearer than any connection between them, is the role of construction in the first method. Let us take up each method in turn, and let us begin from this point in trying to get a better grasp of the first method. Now, I have already alluded to Hobbes's turn in a "constructionist" direction when we were considering the path he follows in the wake of the thought experiment with the annihilation of the world, which he announces at the beginning of Part II of *De Corpore* (see pp. 61–63 above). Hobbes's turn to construction is a response, as the structure of *De Corpore* confirms, to the challenge of skepticism.[52] Since the pillars of the structure that he builds in Parts II and III of *De*

51. Hobbes's division of science is discussed also by Brandt, *Thomas Hobbes' Mechanical Conception of Nature*, 191–93; Malcolm, *Aspects of Hobbes*, 146–55; Pettit, *Made with Words*, 18–22; Hanson, "Reconsidering Hobbes's Conventionalism," 637–38, 642. See also Strauss, *Natural Right and History*, 173n9, *Hobbes's Critique of Religion*, 100–101.

52. Compare Hanson, "Reconsidering Hobbes's Conventionalism," 636–46, "Science, Prudence, and Folly in Hobbes's Political Theory," 645–46; Strauss, *Natural Right and History*, 171–74; Kraynak, *History and Modernity in the Thought of Thomas Hobbes*, 119–21.

Corpore are his definitions (see *De Corp.* 6.12–14, 25.1, 30.15), we can think of Hobbes's "constructionism" as guided by the following line of thought. However inaccessible and mysterious the real world of the bodies in motion may be, philosophy can move forward by establishing definitions that are set forth in full awareness of their status as human creations, that is, as first principles that owe their "truth" (see *De Corp.* 25.1) to acts of postulation and agreement. Such definitions and the demonstrations that are possible on their basis are wholly intelligible, unlike nature itself, precisely because they are creations of the human mind (*De Corp.* 3.9, 5.1, 25.1, 30.15; see also *De Cive* 17.28, 18.4; *EW* VII, 184–85, 225–26; *Tract. Opt.*, 147).

The importance of definitions, in Hobbes's conception of science, can be traced all the way back to his account of man's first use of words to register thoughts. The invention of language, Hobbes contends, was a transformative development—it was "the most noble and profitable invention of all other" (*Lev.* 4.1)—because it allowed human beings to rise above the severe limits, both practical and theoretical, previously set by nature. Through a long series of acts of imagination and will, human beings have managed to actualize a tremendous creative potential by building systems of words that vastly expand our capacity for communication, industry, society, and even thought itself (see *De Corp.* 2.1–4; *Lev.* 4.1–3; *Elem.* 5.1–4; *De Hom.* 10.1–3).[53] The scientific formulation of definitions, which explicate and clarify the conceptions conveyed by names, is the continuation of this trajectory by which human beings build an artificial structure over an original wilderness. And cogent deductive demonstrations on the basis of the posited definitions would seem to be the completion of the project, at least on the theoretical plane (see again *De Corp.* 25.1, 30.15; see also 6.12–16).

The model for Hobbes of a successful constructionist science is geometry. The geometers "have administered their province exceptionally well" (*De Cive*, Ep. Ded.), not only in the sense that their work has laid the foundation for almost all civilizing advances in the arts, but also in the sense that they have followed an exemplary method that begins by "settling the significations of words" and proceeds systematically from definitions to demonstrations (*Lev.* 4.12). The allure of geometry for Hobbes, then, is not just the expansion of human power it makes possible, but also the theoretical clarity it exemplifies: the first principles of the science are wholly intelligible because they are

---

53. Hobbes's view of the power of language to improve the human condition is a major theme of Pettit's *Made with Words*; see especially 25–39. See also Gillespie, *The Theological Origins of Modernity*, 236–38; Oakeshott, *Hobbes on Civil Association*, 23–24; Flathman, *Thomas Hobbes: Skepticism, Individuality and Chastened Politics*, 30–38, *Willful Liberalism*, 28–29, 43–44.

human creations, and therefore the demonstrations can proceed without ambiguity or uncertainty (see *De Hom.* 10.4–5; *Lev.* 5.7; *Elem.* 13.3).

Geometry is more than a model for Hobbes. It is also a crucial element of his own endeavor. Part III of *De Corpore*, "Properties of Motions and Magnitudes," is devoted to Hobbes's own geometry, which, by his account, builds on the works of Euclid, Archimedes, Apollonius, and others (*De Corp.* 15.1); ancient geometry is the great exception to Hobbes's disdain for classical philosophy (see *De Cive*, Ep. Ded.; *De Corp.* 1.1; *Lev.* 46.11). Yet, as much as he praises and wishes to continue the work of the ancient geometers, Hobbes's own geometry has an unusual character that reflects his desire to push even geometry in a more constructionist direction. For Hobbes attempts, wherever possible, to bring the motions involved in various acts of construction into the very definitions from which geometry begins its operations. A circle, for instance, is better defined by reference to the circumduction of a body of which one end remains fixed—that is, by reference to the way in which it may be generated—than by reference to an essential property it possesses as a static figure (see *De Corp.* 1.5, 6.13). Hobbes explains this approach, defending it against his critics in mathematics, in this way: "In that part . . . of my book [*De Corpore*] where I treat of geometry, I thought it necessary in my definitions to express those motions by which lines, superficies, solids, and figures were drawn and described . . . supposing I might thereby not only avoid the cavils of the sceptics, but also demonstrate divers propositions which on other principles are indemonstrable" (*EW* VII, 184–85; see also 210–15; *De Corp.* 6.4–6, 15.2; *De Hom.* 10.5; *OL* V, 221).[54]

In his admiration and adaptation of geometry, we can see Hobbes's constructionist tendency taken to a radical extreme. But especially when it comes to applying the model of geometry beyond its sphere, radical constructionism cannot be Hobbes's last word. It is instructive to describe in isolation—as I have just attempted to do—what is indeed one tendency within Hobbes's overall approach to science. To leave it in isolation, however, would give a distorted picture, because there are difficulties that pull Hobbes back from radical constructionism. The first difficulty is that it must remain the case, for Hobbes, that any liberation from nature that human beings can achieve through creative acts of construction is at best only a partial liberation. The universal determinism of the web of moving bodies does not admit of

---

54. On the character of Hobbes's geometry, compare Pettit, *Made with Words*, 19–21; Malcolm, *Aspects of Hobbes*, 153–55; Brandt, *Thomas Hobbes' Mechanical Conception of Nature*, 243–45; Shapin and Schaffer, *Leviathan and the Air-Pump*, 149. See also Strauss, *Natural Right and History*, 172–73.

exceptions for acts of human creativity. Even man's creative acts, then, must ultimately be understood as produced by bodies in motion. Consider, for example, the following passage from Hobbes's objections to Descartes's *Meditations* in which one can see the role of skepticism and construction in Hobbes's thought, but also an ultimate reassertion of his materialism and determinism:

> What shall we say if it proves to be the case that reasoning (*ratiocinatio*) is nothing but the connecting and combining of names or appellations by means of the phrase 'this is' (*hoc est*)? In that case, we gather from our reasoning nothing at all about the nature of things, but only something about the appellations of them—namely, whether or not we are connecting the names of things in keeping with the conventions we established by our declarations regarding their meaning. If this is so, as it may be, reasoning will depend on names, names on imagination, and imagination (as I think) on the motions of bodily organs; and thus thought (*mens*) will be nothing but motion in certain parts of an organic body. (*Obj.*, no. 4)

The final turn in this statement is a turning back, as if Hobbes were compelled to return to a point that he regards as fundamental and undeniable: that all thinking originates in conceptions arising from sense perception and thus has its roots in the motions of bodies. To think of the human mind as freeing itself entirely from its dependence on the world of moving bodies, then, is to contemplate an impossible situation, and one in which the mind would be left with nothing to which it could assign names and begin to think. Even in Hobbes's thought experiment regarding the annihilation of the world, as we saw, the external world was regarded merely as annihilated, not as a pure fiction that has never existed. That qualification, too, testifies to the essential and undeniable role of the moving bodies in Hobbes's conception.

More important for present purposes, however, is another point that also cuts against Hobbes's radical constructionism, but in a different direction. The difficulty concerns definitions, and it can be seen in a simple dilemma: as much as Hobbes describes definitions as arbitrary human creations, he clearly regards some definitions as better than others. Thus, if it might seem that all definitions, as equally arbitrary, should be equally valid, it hardly proves to be the case for Hobbes that one definition is as good as another. Those definitions, for example, that convey a clear and distinct conception of the meaning of the words to be defined are far superior to the muddy and incoherent definitions handed down by the scholastic tradition. After all, is it not a major part of Hobbes's enterprise to revise our understanding of crucial terms by replacing obscure definitions with exact ones "snuffed and purged from ambiguity" (*Lev.* 5.20; see also 4.13, 4.21, 5.5, 5.20; *De Corp.* 3.4, 6.16; *Elem.* 5.7–8,

5.13)? Does that not mean that, before one can build synthetically, or reason deductively from definitions, there must first be an analytical process by which flawed definitions are rejected and sound ones reached? It may well be the case that Hobbes's emphasis on the arbitrary character of definitions has a tendency to obscure that analytical process. But it cannot hide it entirely, for there are reasons and arguments behind Hobbes's definitions—reasons and arguments that must have led him, before they can lead others, to regard his definitions as a superior framework for understanding the world, not just for creating a self-contained realm of artificial constructions (consider *De Corp.* 2.16, 6.17, 6.12, 6.15; *Lev.* 5.17; *Elem.* 6.3–4). Hobbes's definitions, then, are not simply arbitrary, and, although he sometimes insists that they are, we can understand why he cannot stick with full consistency to that view. If one goes too far in that direction, not only does one fail to do justice to the process of thinking that in fact (if not in theory) precedes defining, but one risks turning the world of one's constructs into a kind of imaginary kingdom whose features are announced at its gates but that has no relevance beyond its walls.[55]

Even in Hobbes's geometry one can see the countervailing forces at work, drawing him back from his most extreme constructionism. We have already considered one reason his geometry has the unusual character it does, in which motion is brought wherever possible into the definitions themselves: the more the motions involved in constructing figures can be expressed in the very definitions, the more fully intelligible the system as a human creation (see p. 69 above). But there is another reason for Hobbes's emphasis on motion in geometry that moves in the opposite direction. For the emphasis on motion also brings geometry closer to a world that consists of nothing but moving bodies and the effects they produce. A "kinetic" geometry is a better tool for comprehending a thoroughly kinetic world, and ultimately Hobbes's geometry, which builds on the definitions and axioms of his first philosophy, is meant, not as an imaginary or artificial realm of its own, but as a key part of his natural philosophy as a whole.[56] As he indicates as he is introducing

55. On Hobbes's wavering over the question of whether his definitions are arbitrary, see Sorell, *Hobbes*, 47–49; Hanson, "Reconsidering Hobbes's Conventionalism," 640–46; Pettit, *Made with Words*, 40–41, 49–53; Kraynak, *History and Modernity in the Thought of Thomas Hobbes*, 161–62; Martinich, *Hobbes: A Biography*, 183; Dunlop, "Hobbes's Mathematical Thought," 100–102. Consider also Brandt, *Thomas Hobbes' Mechanical Conception of Nature*, 224–26; Tönnies, *Thomas Hobbes: Leben und Lehre*, 111–12.

56. Consider the following remark Hobbes makes about the leading critics of his geometry, John Wallis and Seth Ward: "For men that pretend no less to natural philosophy than to geometry, to find fault with bringing motion and time into a definition, when there is no effect in nature which is not produced in time by motion, is a shame" (*EW* VII, 242). See also *Lev.* 46.11;

it, his geometry focuses not only on those aspects of geometry that break new ground, but also and especially on those aspects that are "conducive to natural philosophy" (*De Corp.* 15.1). From here we can understand why the geometrical section of *De Corpore*, Part III, begins with definitions of terms that have an obvious bearing on our understanding of the workings of nature. After repeating at its outset the principles of motion developed in his first philosophy of Part II, Hobbes starts his geometry in Part III by defining endeavor, impetus, resistance, pressure, restoration, and force (15.1–2).

Hobbes's geometry, working in conjunction with his first philosophy, is meant to prepare the way for his physics (consider also *De Corp.* 6.5–6, 6.17, 15.3–8, 24.8, 25.1; *De Hom.* 10.5; *EW* VII, 196, 213–20; *OL* V, 221). Thus, the two sides of his natural philosophy, corresponding to the two methods of philosophy, cannot be seen as simply separate. They must be brought together in a single conception, in which each "half" contributes something essential to the other. Their relationship may be conceived of as follows: Hobbes's first philosophy and his geometry provide his physics with a framework of definitions, axioms, and demonstrated propositions; his physics, in turn, restores to his first philosophy and his geometry the necessary contact with nature itself, that is, with the appearances produced by the motions of real bodies, which appearances, epiphenomenal though they may be, constitute the world that science must try to explain.

That the two "halves" of Hobbes's natural philosophy or science are connected in this way can be seen in the passage in which Hobbes most directly describes the difference between them. At the beginning of Part IV of *De Corpore*, as he is making the transition to his physics—so called, by his account, because it aims at knowledge of the causes of "the phenomena of nature"— Hobbes restores the full place and role of the bodies that were abstracted from in the thought experiment regarding the annihilation of the world (25.1). He will now, he says, give causal accounts of how the world as it appears to us may be generated—in other words, he will now follow the second of the two methods of philosophy, which begins from effects and pursues their possible causes (see pp. 66–67 above). These new accounts, Hobbes insists, will be in terms of the motions and magnitudes of bodies regarded as "real and existent," not as abstractions or mere suppositions (with 25.1 see again 7.1 and the last paragraph of 24.9). The new approach, then, may begin from appearances, but it treats the appearances as the products of a genuine reality, and it seeks to search behind the given phenomena for their natural causes. It differs from

Brandt, *Thomas Hobbes' Mechanical Conception of Nature*, 244–46; Malcolm, *Aspects of Hobbes*, 165–66; Dunlop, "Hobbes's Mathematical Thought," 87.

the approach of Parts II and III most notably in that its principles are not constructed: "The principles upon which the following accounts [i.e., those of the physics of Part IV] depend are neither made by us nor set down by us as general definitions, but rather, having been placed in the things themselves by the author of nature, are merely observed by us" (25.1). Yet, although this statement might seem to announce a complete turn away from the constructionism of Parts II and III, an important link remains, connecting Part IV back with what has preceded. For the causal accounts of Part IV will proceed, Hobbes indicates, "not without (*non absque*) the universal propositions demonstrated above" (25.1; consider also 6.6, 6.17; *De Hom.* 10.5; Latin *Lev.*, 125–27; *EW* VII, 196, 225–26). And as Part IV unfolds, Hobbes does in fact rely on the framework of Parts II and III, not only in his account of the causes of sense perception (see 25.2), but also in his cosmology or "sidereal philosophy" (see 26.5–8), and in his explanations of other natural phenomena, such as heat, weather patterns, and gravity (see 27.3, 28.1–6, 30.1–5).[57]

Both the dependence of Hobbes's physics on his first philosophy and geometry and its difference from them shape the character of his physics. On the one hand, the dependence means that, from the beginning, it is predetermined that all of the causal explanations in his physics will be mechanistic explanations. Even in his accounts of phenomena that could well be taken—and were by some of his contemporaries—to defy mechanistic materialism, such as gravity and magnetism,[58] Hobbes sticks to his premises and gives explanations solely in terms of the motions of colliding bodies (see 30.1–5, 30.15; see also 26.7–8; *EW* VII, 147–58; *Anti-White* 10.11). On the other hand, the difference between his physics and the prior framework—that is, the fact that his physics operates, not by constructing definitions and then deducing consequences from them, but by observing the given phenomena and then working back to their natural causes—means that Hobbes's physics must remain hypothetical. For, as Hobbes himself acknowledges, a science that works from the phenomena of nature, of which we ourselves are of course not the causes, can lead to knowledge only of what *may be* their natural causes. Physics, he concedes in many places, can know only *possible* causes (see, e.g., *De Corp.* 25.1, 26.4, 26.11, 27.2–4, 30.15; *De Hom.* 10.5; *EW* VII, 3–4, 10–11, 88, 184).[59]

57. On Hobbes's use in Part IV of the "geometrico-mechanical premises" (Brandt's phrase) from earlier in the work, see Brandt, *Thomas Hobbes' Mechanical Conception of Nature*, 341–42, 370–71 (consider also 241); Sorell, *Hobbes*, 70; Kraynak, *History and Modernity in the Thought of Thomas Hobbes*, 133; Strauss, *Hobbes's Critique of Religion*, 100–101.

58. See Burtt, *The Metaphysical Foundations of Modern Physical Science*, 130–33.

59. This crucial limitation of physics in Hobbes's view is discussed also by Brandt, *Thomas Hobbes' Mechanical Conception of Nature*, 192–97, 341–42, 370–71; Sorell, *Hobbes*, 139; Kraynak,

Why can physics know only possible causes, according to Hobbes? The reasons are worth considering more fully, because Hobbes gives more than one and stresses different aspects of the problem in different places. The most obvious point—or at any rate the most prominent one in his most direct statements on the matter—is that we ourselves are not the causes of the natural phenomena that physics seeks to explain: "the causes of the natural things are not in our power, but in divine will" (*De Hom.* 10.5; see also *De Corp.* 25.1, 30.15; *EW* VII, 184; *Tract. Opt.*, 147). But that is not yet a complete explanation. For why should it be the case that we can know with certainty only what we make? The further reasons flow from the necessity that physics take its bearings from sense perception. Sense perception is the essential starting point of physics, but it is limited: not only do we never directly perceive the moving bodies themselves, as opposed to the appearances they produce in us, but there is the additional difficulty that the causes at work in producing natural phenomena are often extremely small—so small as to be completely imperceptible—and their motions operate over almost unfathomably great distances (see *De Hom.* 10.5; *De Corp.* 6.2, 26.1, 27.1; Latin *Lev.*, 127, *EW* VII, 78, 82). Furthermore, the same effect can in principle be produced by different causes. Thus, even when physics can generate a plausible hypothesis that "saves the appearances" and explains without any impossibilities how a given effect might be generated, we can never be sure that there is not another cause at work instead: "for there is no effect which the power of God cannot produce by many several ways" (*EW* VII, 3; see also 10–11, 88; *Tract. Opt.*, 147; *De Corp.* 30.15, 26.4–5).[60] This last difficulty is compounded by the problem that, by Hobbes's understanding of causality, any account of the cause of a natural phenomenon must inevitably be partial, because it can at most capture a segment of a chain of causes that is itself part of the vast web of interacting causal chains. Hobbes stated that problem in an early letter to Charles Cavendish, in which he had ventured a further hypothesis about the reaction of the medium to save the hypothesis (which he would later abandon) that contractions of the sun are the cause of its light: "yet such is the nature of natural things, as a cause may be again demanded of such [a] hypothesis; and

History and Modernity in the Thought of Thomas Hobbes, 134; Hanson, "Science, Prudence, and Folly in Hobbes's Political Theory," 646–47; Shapin and Schaffer, *Leviathan and the Air-Pump*, 147–51; Tuck, "Hobbes and Descartes," 38–39, "Optics and Skeptics," 252–54; Strauss, *Hobbes's Critique of Religion*, 92, 100; Goldsmith, *Hobbes's Science of Politics*, 41–43; Flathman, *Thomas Hobbes: Skepticism, Individuality and Chastened Politics*, 15–16; Oakeshott, *Hobbes on Civil Association*, 24–25.

60. Compare Malcolm, *Aspects of Hobbes*, 182–84, 187–88; Oakeshott, *Hobbes on Civil Association*, 26–27.

never should one come to an end, without assigning the immediate hand of God" (*Correspondence*, Letter 31 [or *EW* VII, 459–60]; see also *EW* VII 78, 105; *De Corp.* 6.10; consider *Lev.* 12.6).

Hobbes's reference here to "the immediate hand of God," as well as his repeated statements that the causes of the natural phenomena are not in our power but have their ultimate origin in divine will (see again *De Hom.* 10.5; *De Corp.* 25.1; *EW* VII, 3, 88, 105), points to the last and perhaps the most important reason that Hobbes's physics must remain hypothetical. To be sure, one might reasonably ask how seriously such statements should be taken, since the actual explanations that Hobbes gives in his physics, in keeping with the basic premises of his first philosophy, are mechanistic through and through. Are not Hobbes's statements that God is the deepest cause of all natural things best understood merely as signs of the caution of a man who, bold a writer as he was, nevertheless imposed some limits on himself? In some sense, yes—and we will see further reasons for believing so when we turn in the next three chapters to examine his treatment of religion and theology. Still, Hobbes's statements should not be attributed entirely to caution, for they also acknowledge an important possibility, and there is reason to think that, even if he viewed this possibility less with hope than with fear of its implications for science, Hobbes took it seriously. The challenge that an omnipotent God poses to Hobbes's mechanistic materialism has already arisen in the course of our earlier considerations (see pp. 49–50 and 64–66 above). Since it bears on his physics in particular, let us examine some of the evidence that Hobbes was aware of this challenge and concerned about its implications.

As indicated earlier, the primary reason to think that Hobbes *was not* concerned with the problem in question is his explicit exclusion of theology from *De Corpore* (see pp. 40, 49 above; see again *De Corp.* 1.8). But that exclusion, as I also noted, is not his last word. Not only can it be regarded as an aspect of Hobbes's merely methodological materialism, but the exclusion proves not to be complete. The biggest exception to it is the unavoidable question of creation. The question of creation arises at a crucial juncture in Part IV of *De Corpore*, as Hobbes is turning from his account of the workings of sense perception to "the contemplation of those bodies that are the efficient causes or objects of sense" (26.1). Because "the greatest of all bodies or objects of sense" is the world itself, he begins the pivotal Chapter 26 of *De Corpore*, "Of the World and the Stars," by considering the world itself, understood as "one aggregate of many parts" (26.1). There are a few crucial questions, he indicates, that must be asked about the world itself, even if they cannot be definitively answered. Foremost among them is whether the world is eternal or had a beginning, and, if it had a beginning, whether that beginning was, so to speak, a pure beginning or whether the world emerged out of some prior configuration of matter. As Hobbes indicates more clearly in *De Homine*, there would seem to be three possibilities: that the world is eternal in more or less its current form, in which it includes the presence of human life; that it is eternal in one sense but had a beginning in another, if there have always been bodies of some sort but the world as we know it emerged out of a more chaotic mixture of matter; and that it had a pure beginning in the sense that it was created out of nothing by divine fiat (with *De Corp.* 26.1, see *De Hom.* 1.1; see also Latin *Lev.*, 121, Appendix, 1145–49). Hobbes nowhere indicates that he takes the first of these possibilities seriously. But when it comes to the other two—to what would seem to be the fundamental alternatives, in his view—he maintains that the dispute cannot be decided by natural reason alone, because "we who are men," bound by our finitude and forced to begin "from our phantasms," can know only so much of a situation so far removed from our direct awareness (with *De Corp.* 26.1, see *Anti-White* 26.1–2). That is not to say that Hobbes regards each of the two alternatives as equally plausible. For he indicates that creation *ex nihilo* would violate the supposition that nothing can be moved except by that which is already moved, and insofar as that supposition, in his view, is the only intelligible way of conceiving of motion or change, he suggests that creation *ex nihilo* is not something of which we can form a truly coherent conception in our minds. Natural reason, then, is not forced to be simply neutral or to leave the matter entirely open (with *De Corp.* 26.1, see *Anti-White* 5.3, 7.1, 26.7, 27.8–9, 33.7, 35.1). But Hobbes is not led by that thought simply to affirm the truth of the position whose greater plausibility he indicates. Rather, he retreats and declares that the question cannot be settled by reason alone (*De Corp.* 26.1; see also 26.3, 26.7; *Anti-White* 4.3, 26.7, 27.22, 30.34; *EW* IV, 427–28; *EW* V, 176). And that retreat makes sense, because even if a supposition provides the only intelligible way of conceiving of change, one cannot simply assume its truth when one of the two alternatives at issue challenges its validity, and when nothing requires that the origins be such as to be conceivable by the human mind (see again, in particular, *Anti-White* 27.1, as quoted on p. 50 above; consider also 27.14–15).

The possibility cannot be ruled out, therefore, that the world is the work of a mysterious God who created it through an act of will unbound by any prior cause or necessity. If Hobbes merely indicates his awareness of this possibility in *De Corpore*, in other works, especially in his critique of Thomas White's *De Mundo*, where he is responding to a position that affirms creation but also holds that there are knowable limits to what is possible set by the order of created nature, he makes it abundantly clear that he has thought through the implications of the possibility that the fundamental fact of the world is its origin in an omnipotent will (see *De Corp.* 7.2, 26.2, 27.1; *Anti-White* 13.9, 27.15, 27.22, 30.34, 31.1–3, 32.1–2, 33.5–7, 40.1; see also *Lev.* 36.3; *EW* V, 176, 367). The most important implication is that creation would entail the continued possibility of miracles. For if God could create the world from nothing, what is there he could not do? An omnipotent creator, if such there was, presumably "worketh still, and when and where and what he pleaseth" (*EW* VII, 176; see also Latin *Lev.*, 621, Appendix, 1171). Among the many miracles he might perform, a freely acting omnipotent God could create new matter out of nothing (*Anti-White* 13.9), create an entirely new world (*Anti-White* 31.4, 34.6), reduce this one to nothing (*Anti-White* 27.1, 40.1), give spontaneous birth to life (*Anti-White* 5.3; Latin *Lev.*, Appendix, 1169; *EW* VII, 176–77), bring the dead back to life (Latin *Lev.*, Appendix, 1159; *EW* V, 176), or suddenly change the size, shape, or appearance of any body (*De Corp.* 27.1; *Beh.*, 42–43; see also Latin *Lev.*, Appendix, 1153). These, of course, are only a few examples, "for there is nothing in [its] nature able to resist the will of God" (*EW* V, 176).

We will return to Hobbes's position on miracles in Chapter 5 and consider it more fully there. We have not yet seen his whole thought on the matter. Only one point is essential here: if the possibility of creation cannot be ruled out, then the possibility of miracles cannot be ruled out, and if that possibility cannot be ruled out, then the mechanistic explanations of Hobbes's physics must remain hypothetical. For any such explanation—be it of the cause of light, of the motion of the heavenly bodies, or of any other phenomenon—necessarily has an "if" appended to it: *if* the cause of the phenomenon in question operates by mechanistic necessity, not by the miraculous workings of divine will. When Hobbes says, then, that one of the reasons physics can lead to knowledge only of possible causes is that "the causes of natural things are not in our power, but in divine will," he may not be forthrightly expressing his genuine convictions, but neither, I believe, is he merely exercising caution or practicing rhetoric.

✳

There is a further meaning of "possible cause" in Hobbes's physics. It is connected to the last aspect of Hobbes's natural philosophy that we should consider briefly before moving on to other matters. These final considerations may be approached in light of what we have seen in our overview of Hobbes's natural philosophy. To summarize: we have seen Hobbes waver between a thoroughgoing metaphysical materialism, which he believes captures the fundamental truth about nature, and a methodological materialism, to which he is compelled to retreat by his conclusions regarding the limits of our knowledge of nature. So, too, we have seen him move toward a radically constructionist vision of science, according to which we need not know nature since we can know our own constructs, but then try to merge his constructed framework with a physics that reestablishes a necessary connection with nature, even as it is forced to admit that its explanations of natural phenomena can never be more than hypothetical. At the root of Hobbes's wavering, I submit, is the combination of his never-abandoned conviction that the universe is made up of nothing but moving bodies and his troubling awareness that, precisely on the grounds of what mechanistic materialism implies about our access to the world, the bodies themselves are unknowable and the radical alternative to mechanistic determinism cannot be ruled out. Thus, even if Hobbes regarded the new mechanistic science that he and others were developing as a vast improvement over the dreamlike natural philosophy of the classical tradition, he must have remained dissatisfied with the new science insofar as it renounced the hope of decisively settling the most important of all "metaphysical" questions, and thus left it an open matter whether we do in fact live in a universe that consists of nothing but bodies and their determined motions.

From here, we can understand the significance of the further meaning of "possible cause" in Hobbes's physics and the broader point with which it is connected. The primary purpose of Hobbes's use of the term "possible cause" is, of course, simply to acknowledge the uncertain character of the causal accounts given by physics: as plausible as any such account may be, it can tell us only what *may be* the true natural cause or causes at work in a phenomenon under examination. But "possible cause" can also refer to how a given effect—or better, a desired effect—can be generated *by human intervention*. Consider, for instance, the following statements, in which a turn to possible cause in this second sense follows an acknowledgment by Hobbes that physics is limited to possible cause in the first sense:

> The doctrine of natural causes hath not infallible and evident principles. For there is no effect which the power of God cannot produce by many several ways.
>
> But seeing all effects are produced by motion, he that supposing some one or more motions, can derive from them the necessity of that effect whose cause is required, has done all that is to be expected from natural reason. And though he prove not that the thing was thus produced, yet he proves that thus it may be produced when the materials and the power of moving are in our hands: which is as useful as if the causes themselves were known. (*EW* VII, 3–4)

> More cannot be expected from physics than that the motions which it supposes or conceives are imaginable, that the necessity of the phenomenon can be demonstrated from these, and, finally, that nothing false can be derived from them. And yet, in truth, this is no small thing. For if through such hypotheses one can give an account of the reason for the effects, then, even

if they have other causes, nevertheless they may be brought about through these, so that no less do they serve for human use than if they were known and demonstrated. (*Tract. Opt.*, 147; see also *De Corp.* 6.3; *Lev.* 5.17, 11.24, 46.1)

As these passages indicate, the movement toward the second meaning of "possible cause" goes together with a movement toward a more practical or utilitarian conception of the aim of science. Hobbes's bluntest statement of this conception is his famous formulation from the first chapter of *De Corpore*: *Scientia propter potentiam* (Science is for the sake of power) (1.6). *Scientia propter potentiam* does not express the full complexity of Hobbes's position on the end of science: those passages in which he declares that the end of science is to improve the human condition by expanding human power have to be balanced against those in which he praises the pursuit of knowledge for its own sake as the highest human activity (compare, e.g., *De Corp.* 1.6–7; *Lev.* 5.20, 46.1; *De Cive* 17.12, with *De Corp.*, Ep. to the Reader; *De Hom.* 11.9; *EW* VII, 467–68). Still, one can see in Hobbes a tendency that is more clearly visible in some of his contemporaries, especially Bacon but also Descartes— the tendency to reconceive of the ultimate purpose of science as the mastery of nature "for the relief of man's estate."[61]

Is there a connection, in Hobbes's case, between this reconception of the end of science and the character and limits of the new mechanistic science? There is more than one connection, I believe, and each of the several connections can be seen not only in Hobbes's thought but also in the subsequent development of modern science.

First, there is the all but inevitable conclusion to be drawn from the view that nature is a meaningless flux of moving bodies: if this is so, there is no reason to contemplate nature with reverence or gratitude and every reason to exert whatever control we can over the harsh and uncaring world in which we find ourselves. If Hobbes writes, in a rare encomium of philosophy as an end itself, of "what a great pleasure it is for the mind to be carried off in a perpetual and powerful communion with the most beautiful world" (*De Corp.*,

---

61. Bacon, *Advancement of Learning* 1.5.11; see also *New Organon* 1.81, 1.117, 1.124, 1.129; Descartes, *Discourse on Method*, Part 6; preface to the French edition of *Principles of Philosophy*. The turn in Bacon and Descartes to a more utilitarian conception of the end of science is a major theme of Kennington's very helpful *On Modern Origins* (see, in particular, Chaps. 3, 4, and 7). For other discussions of this turn in Hobbes, see Hoekstra, "The End of Philosophy (The Case of Hobbes)"; Craig, *The Platonian Leviathan*, 98–99; Sorell, *Hobbes*, 54; Hood, *The Divine Politics of Thomas Hobbes*, 20; Ahrensdorf, "The Fear of Death and the Longing for Immortality," 586; Mansfield, "Hobbes and the Science of Indirect Government," 105; Strauss, *Natural Right and History*, 175–77, 201 (on these passages in Strauss, see also Burns, "Leo Strauss on the Origins of Hobbes's Natural Science," 126–28), *Spinoza's Critique of Religion*, 90, 210.

Ep. to the Reader), he soon corrects himself: "not only are the first grounds of all science not beautiful, but they appear poor, arid, and almost deformed" (*De Corp.* 1.1). Because Hobbes, even more than Bacon or Descartes, stresses the brutality, penury, and meaninglessness of nature, it is no surprise that he would join in their call to use science to augment man's power over it.

That much follows merely from Hobbes's mechanistic materialism; it does not depend on the more skeptical strand of his thought. But Hobbes's skepticism, too, plays a role in pushing him toward a more utilitarian conception of science. For the more one comes to accept that there are severe limits on what can be known of nature, the more difficult it is for knowledge for its own sake to remain the end of science. In this sense, theory's loss becomes practice's gain, especially since the limits of our knowledge of nature are not such as to prevent us from making great strides in controlling it. Indeed, because man's neediness is a problem that can be at least ameliorated, if not perfectly solved, it is in some sense even a welcome thing that the concern to address that problem is ready to step in, so to speak, to fill the space vacated by the disappointed desire to know.

Scientia propter potentiam, however, is not Hobbes's last word, or at least not the whole of it. For theory, too, has something to gain from the advance of the new science, even if it rests on a merely methodological materialism. After all, the progressive mastery of nature promises to do more than provide men with new powers and relieve our suffering; it promises also to give science itself, if not the certainty it seeks, then at least ever-increasing confidence that the central principles of mechanistic materialism are sound. Hobbes, as we have already begun to see and will continue to see in later chapters, envisioned a great civilizational advancement. The new science has a crucial place in that vision, and in this respect Hobbes's natural philosophy dovetails in its aims with his political philosophy: both are parts of the project by which man can use his ingenuity to exert unprecedented control over his condition. The allure of this vision is theoretical as well as practical, for it promises, with each new advance, to make the doubts about the fundamental assumptions on which the new science rests fade ever further into a dark and musty past that has been left behind by the progress of enlightenment and civilization.

The allure of this vision does not mean, however, that, for Hobbes himself, as he contemplated such a prospect, the doubts could ever fully disappear. Nor does it mean that, for those of us who have come later, and for whom at least the most important doubts have faded still more, the transformation in our consciousness should be seen as an advance in all respects. For the doubts rested on an awareness of the most challenging alternative to the modern scientific outlook, and thus their fading marks the loss of that awareness.

3

Religion and Theology I: "Of Religion"

It would be possible to turn at this point to Hobbes's political philosophy. Now that we have a better sense of the character of his natural philosophy, we could return to the question of the relationship between his natural philosophy and his political philosophy. We will do that—but not yet. Instead, in this chapter and the next two, I want to take what could seem at first a long detour, in order to examine another major aspect of Hobbes's thought: his critique of religion. When one turns from *De Corpore* and takes a sweeping look at Hobbes's corpus as a whole, one sees immediately that Hobbes devoted many pages of some of his most important works, especially *Leviathan*, to questions of religion and theology. Why did he do that? And what are the connections between this realm of his thought and his natural philosophy, on the one hand, and his political philosophy, on the other? Some preliminary reflections on these questions should help to indicate why the apparent detour we are about to take is not a mere detour but a path one must follow if one wants to grasp the full dimensions of Hobbes's thought.

We already have reason to believe that there is an important connection between Hobbes's thinking on theological matters and his natural philosophy. For we have seen that Hobbes's attempt to develop an adequate mechanistic science runs up against the problem posed by the possibility of a creator God who, by freely working miracles, can break the chains of determined causes and thus belie any conception of nature as mechanistically determined through and through. Although the possibility of such a God poses a problem for Hobbes's natural science—a problem he acknowledges in the ways we considered in the last chapter—I alluded at one point to a conception of God, or a kind of God, that would seem more compatible with Hobbes's vision of the whole: perhaps God is a body among the other bodies and thus a part of the universe, of "the whole mass of all things that are," that consists of nothing but bodies (see p. 49 above). Yet, aside from the difficulty that, even if God is a body among the other bodies, the question would remain as to whether he is limited and determined by external causes in the way the other bodies are (see pp. 49–50 above), there is reason to doubt that Hobbes's "acknowledgement" of his view that God is a body should be taken as the frankest expression of his deepest thoughts on the matter. When alluding to this position before, I indicated that it may be a provisional expression of Hobbes's view. To be sure, when he was pressed by his opponents to acknowledge the theological implications of his materialism, Hobbes conceded that he did indeed conceive of God as a body. He even used the occasion of being forced to acknowledge that position to turn the tables on his critics, Bishop Bramhall and John Wallis, by arguing that, because there are no incorporeal spirits, conceiving of God as corporeal is the only way to prevent God from being reduced to nothing (see *EW* IV, 302–13, 348–49, 383–84, 426–27; see also Latin *Lev.* Appendix, 1229–31). Of course, it hardly needs to be said that Hobbes's critics did not take that argument, any more than his materialism in general, to be part of a good faith effort to save God from reduction to nothing. To the contrary, they regarded Hobbes's materialism as the deepest root of his atheism, and they took his argument that God is a body among other bodies as a thin disguise for a position that is thoroughly atheistic.[1] Hobbes himself, moreover, provides at least some warrant for that conclusion. For although he declares in his dispute with Bramhall that God, as a body, must be either the whole universe or a part of it (see *EW* IV, 349), he argues elsewhere that those philosophers who identify God with the whole universe hold a position that, by denying creation, is implicitly atheistic, and he comes at least close to suggesting the same thing about the view that God is a part of the universe (see *Lev.* 31.15 and especially *De Cive* 15.14). Is Hobbes's deepest view, then, best described as atheism?

That is not a conclusion that all scholars of Hobbes would accept, to put it mildly. But neither is it a novel or shocking suggestion. As numerous as are the scholars who regard Hobbes as sincere in his professions of faith, there are just as many who share the suspicions of Bramhall and Wallis, even if the views of these latter-day scholars are not put forward in the same prosecutorial

---

1. See Bramhall, *The Catching of Leviathan*, 525–26, 584; Wallis, *Elenchus Geometriae Hobbianae*, 90, *Hobbius Heauton-timorumenos*, 6. See also Ross, *Leviathan Drawn out with a Hook*, 87; Jackson, *Hobbes, Bramhall and the Politics of Liberty and Necessity*, 235–36; Parkin, *Taming the Leviathan*, 15, 152–53, 192, 262–63 (cf., however, 133–35).

spirit.[2] But what concerns us here is not just the much-disputed question of whether Hobbes is rightly regarded as an atheist. There is a further question at stake, which ties that question back to Hobbes's natural philosophy: If Hobbes's true position *is* atheistic, but he did not think that his atheism could be fully vindicated by his natural philosophy, which cannot decisively settle the question of creation, then did he think that he could vindicate his atheism by means of arguments of a different sort? Is it possible that Hobbes's critique of religion—assuming for now that it is appropriate to speak of such a thing—is not so much an outcome of his natural philosophy as it is a necessary support for it? But what, then, are the arguments in question, that is, those arguments that are best seen not as consequences of but as independent sources of support for his natural philosophy?

If these questions arise when we look back to Hobbes's natural philosophy, another line of reflection emerges if we look ahead—which we must do more tentatively—to his political philosophy. In the main works of his political philosophy, especially *Leviathan*, Hobbes does not follow the approach of *De Corpore*, where he (for the most part) excludes theology from consideration. Far from it. More than half of the very long *Leviathan* is devoted to questions concerning religion and theology. This fact alone should make us doubtful that Hobbes's political philosophy can be understood without a careful examination of his thinking on religious and theological questions. Nevertheless, there does appear to be a certain separation, even in *Leviathan*, between the moral and political, on the one hand, and the religious and theological, on the other. Whereas Parts I and II of *Leviathan* ("Of Man" and "Of Commonwealth") present Hobbes's moral and political doctrines with only occasional references to theological matters, Parts III and IV ("Of a Christian Commonwealth" and "Of the Kingdom of Darkness") take their bearings

2. The dispute over the sincerity of Hobbes's professions of faith is one of the most fundamental and divisive splits in Hobbes scholarship. Although the following list is far from exhaustive (on either side of the question), it includes the leading sources for each of the two starkly opposed views. For examples of works that present Hobbes as a sincere religious believer, see Martinich, *The Two Gods of Leviathan*; Pocock, "Time, History, and Eschatology in the Thought of Thomas Hobbes"; Warrender, *The Political Philosophy of Hobbes*; Hood, *The Divine Politics of Thomas Hobbes*; Glover, "God and Thomas Hobbes"; Taylor, "The Ethical Doctrine of Hobbes"; Lloyd, *Ideals as Interests in Hobbes's Leviathan*. For examples on the other side, see Strauss, "On the Basis of Hobbes's Political Philosophy"; Polin, *Politique et philosophie chez Thomas Hobbes*; Curley, "'I Durst not Write so Boldly'"; Pangle, "A Critique of Hobbes's Critique of Biblical and Natural Religion in *Leviathan*"; Johnston, *The Rhetoric of Leviathan*; Cooke, *Hobbes and Christianity*; Collins, *The Allegiance of Thomas Hobbes*.

from Scripture, and in this second half, *Leviathan* becomes a work of theology. Even in the first half, where religious and theological questions are much sparser but not entirely absent, the two chapters that address such matters most directly, Chapter 12 ("Of Religion") and Chapter 31 ("Of the Kingdom of God by Nature"), stand at the two edges of that section of *Leviathan* (Chapters 13–30) that is most clearly devoted to politics. In a sense, then, Hobbes's political philosophy appears in *Leviathan* as an island in a sea of religious and theological reflections, an island touched only at its shores by the waters that surround it. And this is not only a matter of the structure of the text. More important is that Hobbes's political philosophy does not appear to depend on any theological premises. In fact, if Hobbes's exclusion of theology in *De Corpore* may be regarded as an aspect of the methodological materialism of his natural philosophy, something similar may be said of his political philosophy: by creating the island just described, Hobbes pursues a kind of methodological secularism in his political philosophy. Not only is his political philosophy based on natural reason working from experiences available to all men (see *Lev.* 32.1, 31.1, 31.41; *De Cive* 15.1), but the commonwealth he sketches derives its authority entirely from human sources and is directed entirely to secular ends. This should not be too surprising, since one of Hobbes's chief criticisms of the classical tradition, as we saw in Chapter 1, is that traditional philosophy, by merging with theology, furnished dangerous weapons in the theological-political conflicts that destroyed the peace in England.

Yet Hobbes clearly did not think it sufficient merely to develop a secular political philosophy and to ignore religious and theological questions altogether. The island of his political philosophy, after all, is surrounded in *Leviathan* by the sea of his discussions of religion and theology. What, then, is the role of the sea? We are not yet in a position to answer that question. But a few considerations may provide some orientation. For one thing, had Hobbes left matters simply at the articulation of a secular political philosophy, as many political theorists do in our time, he would have left himself with no response to the charge, which was a serious and even dangerous charge in his time, that he was stripping the political community of its rightful theological orientation. Among the accusations that Bramhall hurled at Hobbes in his attempt to show that Hobbes's principles are "brim full of prodigious impiety" was that "he hath devised us a trim commonwealth, which is founded neither upon religion towards God, nor justice towards man, but merely upon self-interest, and self-preservation."[3] Thus Hobbes's extensive efforts to show that his political philosophy is in accordance with the true teachings of Scripture, when

---

3. *The Catching of Leviathan*, 520–21.

Scripture is properly interpreted, serve a defensive purpose. That defensive or apologetic purpose, moreover, extends beyond the need to provide himself with a shield against his critics and would-be persecutors such as Bramhall. Hobbes also needed to assuage the misgivings of those readers who might be drawn to his political doctrine, especially by its promise of a lasting peace, but held back by their doubts about its permissibility given its conflict with the teachings of Scripture as they had been taught to understand them. By providing a new interpretation of Scripture—one that brings the teachings of Scripture into accord with his own principles—Hobbes tried to remove a major obstacle standing in the way of the widespread public acceptance of his political doctrine. And more than that: by reinterpreting Scripture so as to bring it into harmony with what he regarded as the only sound and scientific political doctrine, Hobbes may have thought that he could turn a long-standing source of conflict into an ally in his quest for peace.[4]

Hobbes did have such aims, I believe. But he also had further and more radical ones, as I will attempt to show. A suspicion that Hobbes was up to something more aggressive arises even from his discussion of the Bible, the more one considers it. For his interpretation of Scripture proves to be so heterodox and even at times outlandish that it becomes difficult to believe, not only that it was guided by a sincere effort to discern the genuine meaning of the biblical text, but also that its deepest purpose was to bring his most demanding readers to accept the harmony between his rational political teaching and the true teaching of Scripture. Might not Hobbes have wanted to bring at least some of his readers to see that his very attempt to harmonize his political teaching with the teaching of the Bible, precisely when that attempt becomes most implausible, points to a deeper critique of the Bible? And is not such a critique in fact necessary for Hobbes's defense of his own position, if he is to provide it not just with the rhetorical trappings necessary for public acceptance, but with an adequate theoretical foundation? Does not a political philosophy whose central premises, established by natural reason, are that violent death is the worst of all evils and that a humanly constructed political order ruled by an unquestioned sovereign is the solution to the human problem have to confront the most powerful text, claimed by many to have been revealed by God himself, that, despite Hobbes's pretensions to the contrary, does not share those premises? A confrontation with the biblical position would seem to be as necessary to Hobbes's political philosophy—as

4. On Hobbes's "defensive" aims, compare Pangle, "A Critique of Hobbes's Critique of Biblical and Natural Religion in *Leviathan*," 28; see also Cooke, *Hobbes and Christianity*, 2–4, 36–38, 81–83, 203–9.

much an essential supplement to it—as it is, for somewhat different reasons, to his natural philosophy.[5]

Now, if Hobbes does have a hidden critique of the Bible—as part of a broader critique of religion in general—the most important task for an interpreter is to uncover the key arguments that make up that critique. As I have already suggested, it is not enough to enter into the dispute over whether Hobbes was a sincere religious believer. It *is* important to try to answer that question with as much certainty as possible. In fact, it is hard to imagine, given the centrality of religious and theological questions to his thought as a whole, that one can make much progress in understanding Hobbes's intentions without an answer to that question.[6] But determining whether Hobbes was a believer, or what exactly he did or did not believe, is ultimately less important than—even if it is not entirely separable from—determining *why* he held the views that he did. Too often, discussions of Hobbes's positions on religious questions do not go far enough in seeking out his *arguments*, as scholars limit themselves to marshaling evidence, historical or textual, of his belief or unbelief. But the attempt to unearth Hobbes's arguments, which will be the primary task of this chapter and the next two, is essential not only for understanding the genuine grounds of his views, but also for reaching a position from which one can pass judgment on the adequacy of his defense of his views. In this regard, however, patience is necessary, because we must first listen to and let ourselves be educated by a man who, even if he was not a believer, approached religion in general and the Bible in particular with a directness and depth rarely found today. Hobbes's arguments about religion can be surprising and even shocking because they are the kind of radical ar-

5. Compare Pangle, "A Critique of Hobbes's Critique of Biblical and Natural Religion in *Leviathan*," 28–29; Strauss, *Hobbes's Critique of Religion*, 26–30.

6. Compare Lessay, "Hobbes's Protestantism," 265: "Recent research on Hobbes's theology and religious thinking has made substantial progress. Writers take up questions in a spirit of tolerance and refrain from striking inquisitorial attitudes. More importantly, they acknowledge that it is impossible to ignore the subject or to treat it with any degree of credibility as peripheral to the political theory or, for that matter, to Hobbes's philosophical system. Most commentators have wisely given up pronouncing on the sincerity of the philosopher's statements." While I agree with Lessay on the importance of confronting "Hobbes's theology and religious thinking," I do not agree with his last statement in this passage: most commentators have not given up pronouncing on the sincerity of Hobbes's statements, nor, in my view, would it be wise of them to do so. Although it may violate the spirit of Hobbes's own principles to say so, one can go too far in seeking peace through the quieting of dispute, especially if peace (among scholars) requires the bracketing of an essential question. Compare, in this connection, Pocock, "Time, History and Eschatology in the Thought of Thomas Hobbes," 162; see also Schotte, *Die Entmachtung Gottes durch den Leviathan*, 1–4.

guments that have disappeared behind the veil of late modern sophistication and the contemporary apathy it has helped to produce. Even if our current religious apathy can be traced in part to Hobbes's own efforts to quiet disputes about religion and push the world in a more secular direction, he himself took questions of religion far more seriously than do either the easygoing believers or the blithe nonbelievers of our time.

A few final words are in order before plunging back into Hobbes's texts. The primary text into which we will now be plunging is *Leviathan*, which is the epicenter of Hobbes's treatment of religious and theological questions. If one compares the various presentations of his political philosophy in the order in which they appeared—*The Elements of Law, De Cive, Leviathan*—it is obvious that religious and theological questions came to play an increasingly prominent role, occupying far more space with each successive work. This holds true up to the English *Leviathan* (published in 1651), after which, in the Latin version published seventeen years later (in 1668), Hobbes removed some key passages and backed off some of his most radical arguments.[7] The more expansive and radical character of the treatment of religion and theology in the English *Leviathan* can be explained in large part, as Hobbes himself indicated, by the transformation of the political and religious situation in England. As troubled as he was by the chaos wrought by the Civil War, Hobbes took advantage in 1651 of the greater freedom of expression during the Interregnum. With the power of the monarchy and the episcopacy temporarily broken, there was for a time no established church in England, and as a result, "every man writ what he pleased" (*EW* IV, 366; see also 355, 407; Latin *Lev.*, Appendix, 1227; *Lev.*, Review and Conclusion, 14).[8] It is no surprise, then, that Hobbes toned down some of his most inflammatory arguments, especially on

---

7. The most important example is *Lev.* 47.19–20, where Hobbes speaks of the untying of the "knots" restricting religious liberty, in a process of liberation that led to a welcome return to "the Independency of the primitive Christians." This passage, which praises even "the putting down of episcopacy," does not appear in the Latin *Leviathan*; it is replaced by a condemnation of the forces behind the English Civil War (see Latin *Lev.*, 1127–31). For other examples, compare *Lev.* 12.30 (on the causes of changes of religion) or 16.16, 41.8–9, 42.3 (on Moses and the Trinity) with their Latin parallels (Latin *Lev.*, 187, 249, 769–73; there is no parallel to 42.3, since the passage was simply removed, but cf. Latin *Lev.*, Appendix, 1233). On the greater reach and radicalism of the treatment of religion in the English *Leviathan*—by comparison not just with the Latin *Leviathan*, but also with Hobbes's other works—see Malcolm, *Leviathan, Vol. 1: Introduction*, 14–15, 35–42, 179–80; Strauss, *Hobbes's Critique of Religion*, 30–33, *The Political Philosophy of Hobbes*, 71–74; Johnston, *The Rhetoric of Leviathan*, 114–15.

8. See Sommerville, *Thomas Hobbes: Political Ideas in Historical Context*, 24, 105–7, 112–13, 136; Malcolm, *Aspects of Hobbes*, 542–43; Jackson, *Hobbes, Bramhall and the Politics of Liberty and Necessity*, 164–65.

ecclesiastical questions, in the post-Restoration Latin *Leviathan*, even if old age and the approach of death—or perhaps just an acceptance that his bluff had been called—made him more forthcoming on a few other points, such as the corporeality of God.[9] Since the partial retreat from the radicalism of the English *Leviathan* is better explained by the return of more restrictive circumstances than by a genuine change of heart on Hobbes's part, the English *Leviathan* should be taken as the most authoritative source for Hobbes's treatment of religion and theology. My primary focus will therefore be on that text, although I will draw from other works when it seems instructive to do so.

I have already indicated something of the place of Hobbes's treatment of religious and theological questions in the structure of *Leviathan*. It is only in Parts III and IV—that is, roughly speaking, in the second half of the four-part text—that such questions manifestly dominate the discussion. This is the section of the work (especially Part III) in which Hobbes presents his interpretation of the Bible, the "interpretation" that proves so heterodox that "confrontation," in my view, is ultimately the better term for it. The second half of *Leviathan* is rarely studied with the same care as the first half; many scholars, to say nothing of general readers, neglect it entirely. This is a tendency that obviously must be resisted by anyone who hopes to understand Hobbes's religious and theological thought. But Hobbes's account of Scripture in the second half of *Leviathan* will be the topic of the fifth chapter, not of this one or the next. For although religious and theological questions play a much less prominent role in the first half of *Leviathan*, they are present and important there, too—and more so than it first appears. I have already mentioned the two chapters in which they are treated most directly: Chapter 12 ("Of Religion") and Chapter 31 ("Of the Kingdom of God by Nature"). In the first of these two chapters, Hobbes presents a psychological account of the "seed" or "seeds" of religion in human nature,[10] and, in the second, he presents what may provisionally be called his "natural theology," that is, his examination of what natural reason teaches us about God. In neither of these chapters is the Bible in the foreground, but in each of them it is in the background. And in any case Hobbes's concern, as we will see, is not just to confront the Bible, but also to give an account of religion as such and to sketch the outlines of a rational theology. The first of these two chapters of *Leviathan*, then, will be the focus of this chapter, and the second will be the focus of the next. But let

9. See Malcolm, *Leviathan, Vol. 1: Introduction*, 180–81.

10. In Chapter 12, Hobbes first speaks of the "seed" of religion in the singular, but then uses the plural, "seeds," as his argument progresses.

us begin by briefly considering two passages from earlier in *Leviathan* that set the stage for the analysis of religion in Chapter 12.

Religion in the Early Chapters of *Leviathan*

Hobbes begins Part I of *Leviathan* in an odd way considering the primary political theme of the book announced by its title: the "great Leviathan" is, of course, Hobbes's name for the commonwealth (see *Lev.*, Introduction). But the surprising beginning of Part I, which seems to turn in a very different direction, allows us to see Hobbes's natural philosophy, political philosophy, and his critique of religion working together. Hobbes begins with a mechanistic account of certain basic human experiences: sense perception, imagination, memory, dreams, and apparitions, in Chapters 1 and 2; more complex forms of thought and reasoning, in Chapters 3, 4, and 5. Although the account of sense perception from which he begins is much briefer than the account given in *De Corpore*, it is fully consistent with it; it may be regarded as a summary of it, even if he was still at work on parts of *De Corpore* at the time. Early in *Leviathan*, then, Hobbes brings an encapsulated version of his mechanistic materialism to bear on the most basic experiences by which man orients himself in the world; he offers the wider audience of *Leviathan* a new outlook on such experiences, one meant to replace the absurd teachings of "the philosophy-schools" (1.5). But what is of greatest interest for our present purposes emerges in Chapter 2, in Hobbes's discussion of dreams and apparitions. For Hobbes inconspicuously weaves into his account of dreams and apparitions an attack on certain interpretations of these experiences—and this attack proves to be the opening salvo of his critique of religion.

Hobbes's discussion of dreams and apparitions follows his discussion of imagination and memory. The discussion of imagination and memory, for its part, necessarily comes after the discussion of sense perception, because imagination and memory, according to Hobbes, are nothing but "decaying sense" (*Lev.* 2.2–3). By Hobbes's account of these experiences, the motions that cause sense perception in its ordinary or immediate forms linger after their original sources, the external bodies, have ceased to bear upon us. Much as waves continue to ripple in water even after the wind has died down, these motions persist within us and are the source—or, in some of Hobbes's formulations, the matter itself—of imagination and memory. Images of past perceptions fade slowly over time as they are crowded out by newer perceptions and by other changes in the body's constitution. Thus imagination is "decaying sense," and it is not truly distinct from memory: "This *decaying sense*, when we would express the thing itself (I mean *fancy* itself), we call *imagination* . . .

but when we would express the decay, and signify that the sense is fading, old, and past, it is called *memory*. So that *imagination* and *memory* are but one thing, which for diverse considerations hath diverse names" (2.3).

If imagination-memories grow weaker over time as they are pushed aside by new experiences, they can suddenly become vivid again when we are asleep and therefore not receiving any new perceptions. Dreams, according to Hobbes, are a species of imagination, rooted, as all imaginations are, in original sense perceptions. But dreams differ from other species of imagination in two respects. First, in the stillness of sleep, the internal agitation of the body—"the distemper of some of the inward parts of the body"—can play a more prominent role than it does when the body is buffeted by external stimuli. More than other acts of imagination, then, dreams are stirred from "within," even if, like all imaginations, they depend on the images originally supplied by sense perception (2.5–6). Second, unlike ordinary memories, dreams can sometimes be hard to distinguish from direct sense perception, for the very stillness of our senses as we sleep, by reducing external stimuli, makes our dreams more vivid (2.5).

Now, Hobbes does not seem to think that it is genuinely difficult to distinguish our waking experiences from our dreams: the discontinuity and frequent absurdity of dreams are sufficient to assure him of the difference (see *Lev.* 2.5). His concern, rather, is to expose a mistake often made by those who take some dreams to be, not exactly the same as ordinary waking experiences, but something different from both such experiences and mere dreams. His key example is what Brutus experienced on the night before the battle of Philippi. According to traditional reports, on the eve of the battle of Philippi, Brutus had a vision of the ghost of Caesar, who warned him of his impending death.[11] Although what Brutus saw is "commonly related by historians as a vision," Hobbes tells a different story about what happened: "considering the circumstances, one may easily judge [the supposed vision] to have been but a short dream" (2.7). What were the circumstances? Brutus was sitting alone in his dark tent, troubled by the horror of his role in the murder of the man to whom he owed his own life; it was cold, which tends to heighten fears; and because he merely nodded off, he could not be sure that he had slept. These are the reasons, according to Hobbes, that Brutus mistakenly thought he had a vision and not a mere dream. And this example, Hobbes suggests, fits a pattern: "this is no very rare accident, for even they that be perfectly awake, if

11. See Plutarch, *Life of Brutus*, 48; *Life of Caesar*, 69; see also Shakespeare, *Julius Caesar* 4.3.274–85. On Hobbes's use of the example of Brutus's "vision," compare Curley, " 'I Durst not Write so Boldly,' " 520.

they be timorous and superstitious, possessed with fearful tales and alone in the dark, are subject to the like fancies, and believe they see spirits and dead men's ghosts walking in churchyards" (2.7; cf. *De Corp.* 25.9).

The significance of the example of Brutus's dream, as illustrative of a broader pattern, becomes clear in what Hobbes says next: "From this igno-rance of how to distinguish dreams, and other strong fancies, from vision and sense, did arise the greatest part of the religion of the gentiles in time past, that worshipped satyrs, fawns, nymphs, and the like; and nowadays the opin-ion that rude people have of fairies, ghosts, and goblins, and of the power of witches" (2.8). Hobbes is very careful in what he says here: the superstitious ignorance in question is the origin only of the religion of the "gentiles," that is, the pagans, "in time past." Yet he manages to indicate that such ignorance has retained its power even in Christian ages; it still operates "nowadays." Is it not likely, then, that it played a role in the rise and spread—and continues to contribute to the persistence—of Christianity as well?

If Hobbes prompts his readers to ask that question without having to go so far as to state it himself, he then takes a further step that allows him simul-taneously to cover his tracks and to extend the subversive line of thought. For he makes this crucial statement:

> Nevertheless, there is no doubt but God can make unnatural apparitions. But that he does it so often as men need to fear such things more than they fear the stay or change of the course of nature, which he also can stay and change, is no point of Christian faith. But evil men, under the pretext that God can do anything, are so bold as to say anything when it serves their turn, though they think it untrue. It is the part of a wise man to believe them no further than right reason makes that which they say appear credible. If this superstitious fear of spirits were taken away, and with it prognostics from dreams, false prophecies, and many other things depending thereon, by which crafty ambi-tious persons abuse the simple people, men would be much more fitted than they are for civil obedience.
>
> And this ought to be the work of the schools; but they rather nourish such doctrine. For (not knowing what imagination or the senses are) what they receive, they teach, some saying that imaginations rise of themselves and have no cause, others that they rise most commonly from the will, and that good thoughts are blown (inspired) into a man by God, and evil thoughts by the Devil, or that good thoughts are poured (infused) into a man by God, and evil ones by the Devil. (2.8–9)

This statement is remarkable in several respects. In the first place, it pro-vides a case study in Hobbes's manner of writing in *Leviathan*. Hobbes is careful here, as before, to keep his analysis within the bounds of Christian orthodoxy: "there is no doubt but God can make unnatural apparitions." But having made that concession—the sincerity of which one may doubt: Did Hobbes really have *no doubt* of God's power to make such apparitions?—he then indicates his intention to counteract, to try to *take away*, the superstitious fear of spirits. He even advances that effort here by encouraging skepticism toward the claims of those who say that they or others have experienced the operation of supernatural spirits: "It is the part of a wise man to believe them no further than right reason makes that which they say appear credible." This exhortation to skepticism, however, is only a minor foray in Hobbes's much larger campaign against the superstitious fear of spirits. Indeed, do we not see here an indication of why Hobbes so eagerly and openly promulgates his mechanistic explanations of phenomena such as dreams, and why he is so concerned to educate his readers about causes? Is this statement not one of Hobbes's most explicit proclamations of the new—much bolder and more aggressive—role that he would have philosophy play in waging war against superstition?

It will be said by some scholars and students of Hobbes that to attack superstition is not necessarily to attack religion as such; it could even be part of an effort to purify religion of that which has contaminated it.[12] But such a response, while plausible and even supported in places by Hobbes himself (consider, e.g., *Lev.* 44.1–3, 44.16, 45.2–4, 45.9–10, 45.38), runs into difficulty if, in order to elaborate the distinction between religion and superstition, appeal is made to Hobbes's own definitions of them: "*Fear* of power invisible, feigned by the mind, or imagined from tales publicly allowed, RELIGION; not allowed, SUPERSTITION" (*Lev.* 6.36). To be sure, Hobbes is careful, even in offering these definitions, not to stray too far from the realm of acceptable opinion. For he immediately adds: "And when the power imagined is truly such as we imagine, TRUE RELIGION." The significance of this pious-seeming addendum, however, must be judged in light of Hobbes's position on the capacity of the human mind to imagine the nature of God. Only five chapters after his definition of "true religion," Hobbes will declare that, although men can be led by apparently sound reasoning to the conclusion that "there is one God eternal," they "cannot have any idea of him in their mind answerable to his nature" (11.25; see also 3.12, 34.4, 45.15; *Elem.* 11.2–3, 11.11; *Obj.*, nos. 5, 7, 9, 10). Can it ever be the case, then, that "the power imagined is truly such as we imagine"?[13]

12. See, e.g., Martinich, *The Two Gods of Leviathan*, 62–66; Pocock, "Time, History and Eschatology in the Thought of Thomas Hobbes," 199–200; Mitchell, "Religion and the Fable of Liberalism," 8.

13. Compare Craig, *The Platonian Leviathan*, 32–33.

In the same context, Hobbes again describes the difference between religion and superstition, and, although the basis of the distinction is not identical to the basis in the earlier statement, it is no more principled or pious than before. Speaking of the "innumerable sorts of gods" that have been created by the human imagination in the grips of fear and ignorance, he declares: "this fear of things invisible is the natural seed of that which everyone in himself calleth religion, and in them that worship or fear that power otherwise than they do, superstition" (11.26). Is this description of the difference between religion and superstition, any more than the earlier one, likely to have been written by a man for whom the distinction was deeply meaningful?[14]

Even early on in *Leviathan*, then, we can see that Hobbes is waging a kind of guerrilla war against "superstition," and we have reason at least to suspect that his enemy is more formidable and dwells, so to speak, closer to home than it first appears. If the first skirmish in Hobbes's struggle is the passage in Chapter 2 on dreams and apparitions, Hobbes waits until Chapter 12 to launch his major offensive. In that chapter, "Of Religion," he will expand and deepen his psychological account of the origin of religion that only begins in Chapter 2. The psychological account of the "seed" of religion that he gives in Chapter 12, moreover, will prove to be only one feature of one of the

---

14. For two very different discussions of Hobbes's statements on the distinction between religion and superstition, compare Curley, "'I Durst not Write so Boldly,'" 523–27, with Martinich, *The Two Gods of Leviathan*, 50–59. Curley's account is much closer to my own. Martinich's account, in my view, illustrates some of the difficulties faced by scholars who regard Hobbes as a sincere Christian when they are confronted by Hobbes's most radical statements. Because Martinich cannot adequately explain away the seemingly irreligious character of Hobbes's statements, which make the distinction between religion and superstition dependent first on the dictates of the political authorities and then on the subjective convictions of the one drawing the distinction, he is forced to revise what Hobbes wrote (see 56–57: "The correct Hobbesian definitions are these . . .") and to argue that what he regards as Hobbes's needlessly confused and confusing way of expressing himself was due to his failure to grasp the nature of definitions and his "logical confusion" (52–59, especially 56 and 59). If Hobbes had written as Martinich would have him write—by, among other things, deleting a key portion of the inflammatory statement in *Lev.* 6.36—"Hobbes would have saved himself much grief" (52). But he did not do that—not even in the Latin *Leviathan*, where Hobbes easily could have revised or deleted the "confused" statements that had provoked his critics. (There are some minor changes in the Latin version of 6.36, but they do not resolve the problems that trouble Martinich.)

Hobbes's account of the distinction between religion and superstition is one of several matters on which Hobbes's contemporary critics can be better guides to his thought, in their very accusations of him, than his present-day defenders, who often dull the edges of his knives in their efforts to exonerate him. See, e.g., Bramhall, *The Catching of Leviathan*, 521–22; Ross, *Leviathan Drawn out with a Hook*, 9–10; Hyde, *A Brief View and Survey*, 21; see also Latin *Lev.*, Appendix, 1233; Mintz, *The Hunting of Leviathan*, 40–41.

most radical chapters of *Leviathan*. Before we turn to Chapter 12, however, we should take up another passage from the earlier chapters. For there is an oddly placed passage in Chapter 8 that also speaks to the question of the psychological basis of religious experience, and in this passage, too, Hobbes's argument is more polemical and far-reaching than it first appears.

The passage in question is oddly placed because Hobbes's ostensible concern in Chapter 8 is merely to consider various intellectual qualities, good and bad, that men possess either by nature or by cultivation. The chapter bears the innocuous title "Of the Virtues Commonly Called Intellectual, and Their Contrary Defects." One would hardly expect anything particularly controversial under such a heading. Yet, although the chapter begins blandly enough, with discussions of qualities such as discretion and dullness, Hobbes's real target in the chapter comes into view as he turns to consider the relationship between "wit" and the passions. For it turns out that the passions, especially the most intense ones, not only are essential for spurring the mind beyond dullness—since a man without strong desires "cannot possibly have either a great fancy or much judgment" (8.15)—but are a dangerous source of the intellectual vice that becomes the focus of Chapter 8: madness. Hobbes proves to be far more interested in Chapter 8 in the depths of madness than in the heights of intellectual achievement.

Madness, as Hobbes explains it, arises from an excess of passion in either direction—that is, it arises when men get either too high or too low, when they are consumed by vainglory, on the one hand, or devastated by dejection, on the other (see 8.18). That these tendencies have some relevance to the question of religion is first indicated by Hobbes's suggestion that one of the madness-fueled delusions that can arise with an "excessive opinion of a man's own self" is the belief that one is distinguished by "divine inspiration" (8.19); so, too, can dejection lead to the "haunting of solitudes and graves" and other "superstitious behavior" (8.20). Of these two manifestations of madness, Hobbes is more concerned with the former: the question becomes, above all, what leads men to believe they are divinely inspired. Hobbes's answer, to repeat, is that claims to divine inspiration arise from a species of madness rooted in excessive passions. Excessive passions, like too much wine, can deprive men of their sober judgment and untether their most extravagant thoughts from the usual restraints. And there is no more extravagant thought, in Hobbes's view, than the belief that one is divinely inspired.[15]

---

15. See 8.21: "If there were nothing else that bewrayed their madness, yet that very arrogating such inspiration to themselves is argument enough." Compare Latin *Lev.*, 581: "He who claims

In describing the madness that manifests itself in claims to divine inspiration as rooted in excessive passions, Hobbes knows that he is taking a position in a long-running dispute: "The opinions of the world, both in ancient and in later ages, concerning the cause of madness, have been two" (8.24). The divide between the two sides in this dispute is clear enough: whereas some have attributed madness to passions alone, thereby giving a wholly psychological explanation of its sources, others have derived madness "from demons or spirits, either good or bad, which they thought might enter a man, possess him, and move his organs in such strange and uncouth manner as madmen use to do" (8.24). It is also clear on which side of the divide Hobbes himself stands, since he has just given his own psychological explanation of madness. But equally important is where he places others. Hobbes makes it obvious that he thinks that the "spiritualist" view of madness dominated the ancient world. He gives examples from Greek antiquity that indicate its ubiquity there (see 8.25). And then he remarks: "And as the Romans in this held the same opinion with the Greeks, so also did the Jews; for they called madmen prophets or (according as they thought the spirits good or bad) demoniacs, and some of them called both prophets and demoniacs madmen, and some called the same man both demoniac and madman" (8.25; see also 45.4).

There would seem to be nothing too surprising about the suggestion that the Jews, like all other ancient peoples, believed in possession by spirits. But Hobbes suggests that this *is* surprising and in need of an explanation. If "for the gentiles it is no wonder" that they believed in demons and possession by spirits, "for the Jews to have such opinion is somewhat strange" (8.25). It is "somewhat strange," Hobbes contends, because such a view is foreign to the Bible itself. Now, it is indeed surprising—even very hard to imagine— that the early Jewish view was not also the view of the biblical prophets. Yet that is precisely what Hobbes argues here. He argues that neither Abraham nor Moses claimed to have prophesied through possession by a spirit, and he contends that there is nothing in the Mosaic Law—indeed in the entire Old Testament—that supports the notion of such possession (8.25). The key question for understanding Hobbes's intention here, however, is whether he is serious in making this argument. For not only is it hard to imagine that the Bible would so starkly diverge in its teaching from the views of the ancient Jews, who shaped and in turn were shaped by it,[16] but the very passages

that some new doctrine has been inspired into him supernaturally by God will be understood, by the wise, to be raving, out of admiration of his own mind." See also *Elem.* 10.9–10; *Beh.*, 187–88.

16. Relevant in this connection is Hobbes's view (to be discussed in Chapter 5) that the Old Testament was written much later than was traditionally thought. He argues that Moses was not

Hobbes gives as examples to show the antispiritualism of the Bible would seem, by any straightforward reading, to show precisely the opposite. Hobbes points, in his first example, to Numbers 11:25, where God is said to have come down in a cloud to take from Moses his—that is, *God's*—spirit and give it to the seventy elders. Is it really plausible, as Hobbes contends (or pretends), that by "the Spirit of God in man" in this passage, the Bible means nothing more than "a man's spirit, inclined to godliness"? Or, to take Hobbes's other example, when God speaks in Exodus 28:3 of those whom he has "filled with the spirit of wisdom to make garments for Aaron," can the Bible really have meant, not "a spirit put into them that can make garments," but merely "the wisdom of their own spirits in that kind of work"? More generally, it is hard to believe that Hobbes seriously believed that there are no claims to possession by spirits in the Old Testament.[17] By making that argument, however, he puts himself in a position to pose the question obviously raised by it—"How then could the Jews fall into this opinion of possession?"—to which he can respond with this naturalistic, all-too-human explanation:

> I can imagine no reason but that which is common to all men, namely, the want of curiosity to search natural causes, and their placing felicity in the acquisition of the gross pleasures of the senses and the things that most immediately conduce thereto. For they that see any strange and unusual ability or defect in a man's mind, unless they see withal from what cause it may probably proceed, can hardly think it natural; and if not natural, they must needs think it supernatural; and then what can it be but that either God or the Devil is in him? (8.25)

Hobbes's "interpretation" of the Old Testament and his account of the source of the Jews' belief in possession set up his approach to the New Testament. For he uses his explanation of the supposedly nonbiblical but nevertheless very intense spiritualism of the Jews to explain why the scribes and others regarded Jesus as possessed by the Devil and lesser demons (8.25).[18] He also extends his explicit argument regarding the Old Testament to the New Testament,

---

the author of the Pentateuch, and that the primary author of the Old Testament as a whole was Ezra, who composed it after the return of the Jews from the Babylonian captivity.

17. For an even clearer counterexample than those to which Hobbes points in Chapter 8 of *Leviathan*, see 1 Samuel 18:10 (mentioned in *Lev.* 36.8). Consider also the following passages, among the many to which Hobbes points in Chapter 34, where his strategy is similar to the one in Chapter 8: Exodus 31:3–6, 35:31 (see *Lev.* 34.6); Judges 3:10, 13:25, 14:6, 1 Samuel 19:23 (*Lev.* 34.7); Job 27:3, Ezekiel 2:2 (*Lev.* 34.10); Exodus 33:11–14 (*Lev.* 34.22); Joel 2:28 (*Lev.* 34.25). See also the different characterization Hobbes gives of the Bible's position on possession in his dispute with Bramhall (*EW* IV, 327); cf. *Elem.* 11.5.

18. Hobbes refers here to Mark 3:21–22 and John 10:20. See also *Lev.* 45.4, where Hobbes points to John 7:20 and 8:52.

at least in this sense: whatever may have been the case with the scribes and many other Jews, Jesus himself, Hobbes contends, did not believe in possession by spirits (8.26). But Hobbes's effort to assimilate the teaching of Scripture to his own antispiritualist position is even more transparently flimsy as it applies to the New Testament than as it applies to the Old. In fact, he himself all but explicitly acknowledges as much by indicating that he has no good answer to the question that he allows himself to pose: "But why then does our Saviour proceed in the curing of [madmen] as if they were possessed, and not as if they were mad?" (8.26; compare *Lev.* 45.5, 45.8). Hobbes does not stop with this question. He goes on to remind his readers that Jesus spoke to diseases as if they were people, that he rebuked the winds and chastised a fever, and that he warned of an unclean spirit that might depart from a man, wander about, and then return accompanied by seven still more wicked spirits (8.26).[19] To be sure, Hobbes keeps up the pretense of attempting to explain away all of these examples either as merely metaphorical expressions or as accommodations by Jesus, in his speech, to his superstition-soaked audience. But it is more reasonable to conclude—and to suppose that Hobbes wanted at least some of his readers to conclude—that Jesus himself shared the outlook that was so prevalent in his time, and that he was, if anything, more rather than less steeped than most in the spiritualism of his age. The true purpose of Hobbes's argument, I submit, is to indicate the climate of opinion that prevailed in the world in which Jesus lived, and thereby to indicate the roots and character of Jesus' own thoroughly spiritualist teaching. That is not to say that Hobbes would object if some of his readers were persuaded by his attempt to give a despiritualized "interpretation" of Scripture; but such readers would not grasp his deepest intention.[20]

19. Hobbes is drawing here from these passages: Matthew 8:26, Luke 4:39, and Matthew 12:43–45. Again, Chapter 34 provides many similar examples. Among them are Romans 8:9 (see *Lev.* 34.13); Luke 4:1, Matthew 4:1–2 (*Lev.* 34.14; see also 45.6); Matthew 25:41 (*Lev.* 34.23); John 20:22 (*Lev.* 34.25); consider also, on the general issue of prophecy and possession, 2 Peter 1:21 (*Lev.* 34.25).

20. On Hobbes's intentions in Chapter 8, compare Curley, "'I Durst not Write so Boldly,'" 538–41; Johnston, *The Rhetoric of Leviathan*, 104–6; Pangle, "A Critique of Hobbes's Critique of Biblical and Natural Religion in *Leviathan*," 38–40. Pangle points out that one of the passages Hobbes cites is the very passage in which Jesus declares that blasphemy against the Holy Ghost shall never be forgiven (see Mark 3:21–29). Since Hobbes's argument regarding spiritual possession, especially as it applies to Jesus and the Holy Spirit, comes at least very close to such blasphemy, Pangle comments: "Hobbes, I daresay, was a singularly rash spirit" (38–39). Those who take a very different view of Hobbes's intention on religious questions face a problem when it comes to the question of the Holy Spirit. Consider, e.g., Pocock, "Time, History and Eschatology in the Thought of Thomas Hobbes," 188: "[Hobbes's] drastic handling of the term 'spirit' render[s] it more than usually difficult for him to give a satisfactory account of the Third Person of the Trinity."

There was one genuine exception, according to Hobbes, to the rampant spiritualism among the Jews of Jesus' time, even if it was not Jesus himself. The Sadducees were the only Jews of the time who did not believe that "whosoever behaved himself in extraordinary manner" was possessed by spirits (8.25). In fact, the Sadducees, Hobbes says, "erred so far on the other hand as not to believe there were at all any spirits (which is very near to direct atheism) and thereby perhaps the more provoked others[21] to term such men demoniacs rather than madmen" (8.25). Hobbes's declaration here that the view of the Sadducees is "very near to direct atheism" is striking, because that view also seems very near to Hobbes's own position.[22] But we can understand why Hobbes distances himself from the Sadducees by considering his suggestion that the Sadducees may have ("perhaps") provoked a backlash that drove their rivals to cling all the more fiercely to their opposed view. Hobbes's statement on the Sadducees even contains, whether intentionally or not, a kind of warning and challenge to Hobbes himself and to those he can recruit to his side: Is it possible to attack the belief in supernatural spirits in such a way that one does not end up intensifying the very opinions one is trying to undermine?[23]

"Of Religion"

Let us turn now to Chapter 12, "Of Religion." If the passages we have considered so far provide initial glimpses of Hobbes's account of the sources of religious experience and belief—both the general fear of "power invisible" by which

---

21. Latin *Lev.*: "the Pharisees."

22. Compare *Lev.* 34.2–4; Latin *Lev*, Appendix, 1185–87. See also *Lev.* 34.18 and Latin *Lev.*, Appendix, 1235, where Hobbes speaks favorably of the Sadducees' denial that angels are genuine substances. In the Appendix to the Latin *Leviathan*, Hobbes also praises the Sadducees *inter Philosophos* (among the philosophers) because they, unlike "the followers [*sectatores*] of Plato and Aristotle," did not believe that there are any created spirits, and thus they did not recognize "any existence of the soul, other than that called life" (1167); compare Acts 23:8. For Hobbes's Sadducee-like view of the soul, see *Lev.* 44.14–15, 44.23–25; *Elem.* 11.5. On the similarity between Hobbes and the Sadducees, see Strauss, "On the Basis of Hobbes's Political Philosophy," 183; Pangle, "A Critique of Hobbes's Critique of Biblical and Natural Religion in *Leviathan*," 38.

23. That it is sometimes possible to win a battle in the struggle against spiritualism Hobbes indicates in Chapter 8 by reporting the following story, perhaps as a parable of sorts: "[T]here reigned a fit of madness in [a] Grecian city, which seized only the young maidens and caused many of them to hang themselves. This was by most then thought an act of the Devil. But one that suspected that contempt of life in them might proceed from some passion of the mind, and supposing they did not contemn also their honor, gave counsel to the magistrates to strip such as hanged themselves and let them hang out naked. This, the story says, cured that madness" (8.25). Hobbes's source for this story is probably Plutarch (see *Moralia*, "The Virtues of Women," XI).

Hobbes defines religion (see again 6.36) and the more intense experiences that can drive some men to believe they are inspired prophets—Chapter 12 is Hobbes's most extensive and decisive statement on the psychological origins of religion. Hobbes does not conceal his primary intention in Chapter 12: he seeks to give an account of the human sources—that is, the sources in human nature and the human condition—of the rise and persistence of religion. As he puts it in the opening sentence of the chapter, "Seeing there are no signs nor fruit of religion but in man only, there is no cause to doubt but that the seed of religion is also only in man, and consisteth in some peculiar quality, or at least in some eminent degree thereof, not to be found in other living creatures" (12.1).[24]

By the time he opens Chapter 12, Hobbes has already given us an inkling that he thinks the "quality" in question is a certain kind of fear that blends with a certain kind of ignorance to give rise to religion. In the last few paragraphs of Chapter 11, Hobbes argues—in keeping with what he already began to indicate in Chapter 2—that men who are ignorant of natural causes and worried about what the future has in store for them are prone to conjuring up, through the fertile and diverse workings of the human imagination, all kinds of "powers invisible" or "innumerable sorts of gods" (11.26, 11.23). It is important to note, however, that this is only one of two human tendencies or possibilities that Hobbes describes near the end of Chapter 11. Other men, those driven by curiosity more than by fear, are led by their "love of the knowledge of causes" to inquire into the causes of things, and that inquiry keeps them from "feigning," as "they that make little or no inquiry into the natural causes of things" tend to do, that all kinds of invisible powers are operative in the world (see 11.25–26). Although Hobbes suggests, then, that those who are driven by their desire to know natural causes will eventually be led by their search to conclude—or, at any rate, will become "thereby inclined to believe"—that "there is one God eternal," this God, of whose nature they acknowledge they know nothing, is not to be confused with the "invisible powers" that are conjured up by the imaginations of those who remain ignorant of natural causes (compare 11.25 with 11.26; 6.35 with 6.36). In short, Hobbes draws an important distinction between two kinds of men whose different concerns lead them down two different paths—one path leading, it seems, to the mysterious God at the beginning of any chain of causes, the other to the many gods spawned by the fear-gripped fantasies of the human imagination.

These two paths reappear in Chapter 12. But the primary task of Chapter 12 is to provide a more precise specification of the fear and ignorance that

---

24. On the importance of this sentence in setting the tone and agenda for Chapter 12, see Lilla, *The Stillborn God*, 77–78.

drive men down the only one of these paths that culminates in what Hobbes terms "religion." Now, the kind of fear that Hobbes has in mind is not simple terror; it is a distinctively human form of anxiety. Anxiety, according to Hobbes, is an inescapable feature of the human condition. Human beings are much more acutely aware than are other living creatures that events in our lives have causes, and, unlike the beasts, who have "little or no foresight of the time to come," we dwell in the future as much as in the present (12.2–4). Only human beings can be "famished even by future hunger" (*De Hom.* 10.3). Constantly worried about the turns of fortune that await us, always wishing to procure the goods we desire and ward off the evils we fear, human beings cannot but be "in perpetual solicitude of the time to come" (*Lev.* 12.5). Yet, while anxiety grips all men, it is especially intense, Hobbes suggests, in those who are "over-provident" and consumed by worry about the future. Just as Prometheus, the foresighted man, awaited the eagle who would devour his liver each day, "so that man which looks too far before him, in the care of future time, hath his heart all the day long gnawed on by fear of death, poverty, or other calamity, and has no repose, nor pause of his anxiety, but in sleep" (12.5). It is such men who are most prone to conjuring up—whether by their own imaginations or by the trust they put in the reports of others—mental images of "powers invisible," especially when their anxiety is combined with an ignorance of causes. In short, anxiety as perpetual worry about the future, intensified and made more conducive to credulity by an ignorance of causes, prepares the mind to attribute turns of fortune to the operation of "some power or agent invisible." "In which sense, perhaps," Hobbes concludes, "it was that some of the old poets said that the gods were at first created by human fear" (12.6; compare *Hist. Eccles.*, lines 1389–95).

This is Hobbes's opening account in Chapter 12 of the seed of religion. He will return to it in order to expand on the kind of ignorance that combines with anxiety to allow for the growth of religion. Before he does so, however, he pivots and digresses from his main line of argument. Hobbes's digression here can be seen, in the first place, as a retreat from, not to say a compensation for, his provocative suggestion that the gods were created by human fear.[25] This suggestion, he now claims, is "very true," but only when it is applied to *the gods*, that is, to "the many gods of the gentiles" (12.6). Thus, as we saw him do in earlier passages, Hobbes again pulls back from explicitly extending the most radical implications of his argument beyond their applicability to the pagan religions of the past. In the present passage, he contrasts

---

25. Among those the provocative suggestion provoked was Bramhall. See *The Catching of Leviathan*, 521.

the anxiety-produced gods of the gentiles with God, that is, the "one God, eternal, infinite, and omnipotent" (12.6). But who or what is this God whom Hobbes here distinguishes from the gods of the gentiles? Is it the God of the Bible? It would seem more clearly to be the same God whom Hobbes introduced near the end of Chapter 11, in his statement regarding the view eventually reached by those curious seekers whose inquiries are motivated by "love of the knowledge of causes" (see again 11.25; cf. *Elem.* 11.2). As in that passage, the God of whom Hobbes now speaks is the product of—or, better, the conclusion drawn from—a search after causes, driven not by anxiety and ignorance but by "the desire men have to know the causes of natural bodies and their several virtues and operations" (12.6). Hobbes explains the path to this God in this way:

> For he that from any effect he seeth come to pass should reason to the next and immediate cause thereof and from thence to the cause of that cause, and plunge himself profoundly in the pursuit of causes, shall at last come to this, that there must be (as even the heathen philosophers confessed) one first mover, that is, a first and an eternal cause of all things, which is that which men mean by the name of God; and all this without thought of their fortune, the solicitude whereof both inclines to fear and hinders them from the search of the causes of other things, and thereby gives occasion of feigning of as many gods as there be men that feign them. (12.6)

The search for causes would seem to lead, according to what Hobbes says here, to belief in and even knowledge of God, the one God at the beginning of all things. But the question remains: Who or what is the God of whom Hobbes speaks here?

The movement of Hobbes's argument, with his statement on God coming immediately after his debunking remarks about the pagan gods as the products of anxiety, gives the impression that Hobbes thinks that a profound investigation into causes will lead to a monotheistic view that vindicates the biblical God. Yet, although he allows and even cultivates that impression, Hobbes does not quite draw the conclusion it leads one to expect. As he goes on to argue, those who "by their own meditation" reach the conclusion that there is "one infinite, omnipotent, and eternal God" "choose rather to confess that he is incomprehensible, and above their understanding, than to define his nature by *spirit incorporeal*" (12.7). Hobbes insists—emphatically—that we cannot know anything of the nature of the God who lies at the beginning of any chain of causes. In particular, we should not draw the conclusion that he is an incorporeal spirit, a conclusion that would be both presumptuous and unintelligible (12.7). Thus, if those who search into causes sometimes give

God the title of "*spirit incorporeal*," they do so "not *dogmatically*, with intention to make the Divine Nature understood, but *piously*, to honour him with attributes of significations as remote as they can from the grossness of bodies visible" (12.7; see also *Elem.* 11.4). More important, Hobbes indicates that the God in question—God as the "first mover"—was acknowledged even by "the heathen philosophers."[26] This is quite remarkable, since Hobbes elsewhere describes the views of at least some of these philosophers as atheistic (see again 31.14–16; *De Cive* 15.14; consider also Latin *Lev.*, Appendix, 1147). But when one thinks it out, why could not the "God" whom Hobbes describes here be some kind of nondivine matter? Would that possibility not be more consistent with the materialism of Hobbes's own natural philosophy? Admittedly, Hobbes uses the name "God" here, and he attributes to God, not only existence, but eternity, infinity, and omnipotence, the latter two of which are very hard to conceive of as attributes of matter. But is there any good reason to attribute infinity and omnipotence to God, according to Hobbes, other than the desire to honor him with exalted, if ultimately unintelligible, terms (consider 3.12; *Elem.* 11.2–4; *EW* IV, 296–97)?

The difficulties posed by this passage can be approached in another way: How emphatic is Hobbes's affirmation that the first mover at the beginning of any chain of causes is a being that merits the name "God"? In describing the conclusion reached by an investigation of causes, Hobbes states it as the proposition that "there must be (as even the heathen philosophers confessed) one first mover, that is, a first and eternal cause of all things, *which is that which men mean by the name of God*" (emphasis added; see also 11.25; *Elem.* 11.2; *Obj.*, no. 5). Let us leave aside for present purposes—we will return to them later—the questions of whether it is in fact reasonable to conclude that there must be only one first mover and whether natural reason truly supports the view that there was a first movement. It suffices here to note that Hobbes has identified little more than a certain point of overlap between an apparent philosophic conclusion and the view of most believers in the God of the Bible: the belief that there is a first and eternal source of all things, who (or which?) is incomprehensible to finite human beings. But do those who accept the biblical account stick with full consistency to their view that God is incomprehensible? Or do they, rather, ascribe to him important attributes—such as justice, goodness, and a providential concern for human beings—that are difficult to reconcile with the incomprehensibility of God (see *Elem.* 11.2–3; *De Hom.* 14.1)? How close, then, in truth, is Hobbes's

---

26. The Latin *Lev.* replaces "the heathen philosophers" with "the sounder of the ancient philosophers" (*veterum Philosophorum sanioribus*).

doctrine of God as the incomprehensible x at the beginning of any chain of causes to the biblical view, if it belongs to the latter both to affirm and to deny God's incomprehensibility?[27]

The resolution of the questions raised by Hobbes's doctrine of God as the incomprehensible x would carry us well beyond the scope of this brief passage in Chapter 12. We will return to this doctrine and to the questions raised by it when we take up Hobbes's natural theology in Chapter 31 of *Leviathan*, "Of the Kingdom of God by Nature." For now, however, it is better to return to the main line of argument in Chapter 12.

Now, to repeat, it was *by way of contrast* with the gods produced by the anxiety-gripped imaginations of men who are ignorant of causes that Hobbes digressed to discuss God as the incomprehensible first cause.[28] When he returns from the digression to his analysis of the gods of men's anxiety-gripped imaginations, Hobbes expands his account of the kind of ignorance that joins with anxiety to form "the natural seed of religion." The ignorance in question is an "ignorance of causes," but not in the inescapable sense that it is impossible for human beings to identify all of the causes that make up the entire cause of any given phenomenon. A more problematic ignorance displays itself in the tendency of men to regard apparitions and other figments of the imagination as "real and external substances," that is, as ghosts capable of producing effects in the world (12.7). Further, "men that know not what it is that we call *causing* (that is, almost all men)" are prone to attributing causality to things that have no such power, as the Athenians believed that the mere name of a certain general could ensure their success in battle, or as some believe that words alone have the power to "turn a stone into bread, bread into a man, or anything into anything" (12.8). The ignorance and credulity of most men also display themselves in the worship of and devotion to "powers invisible," as well as in the frequent interpretation of random events as meaningful signs by which such powers reveal the future (12.9–10). In sum, when anxiety

27. Compare Glover, "God and Thomas Hobbes," 291. Glover remarks on "the lacuna between the impersonal cause of all things and the personal sovereign who by virtue of his power is 'King, and Lord, and Father.'" Yet, because he believes that Hobbes was an orthodox if somewhat unconventional Christian, Glover is led to claim that Hobbes must have been unaware of this lacuna. See also Milner, "Hobbes on Religion," 413–15; Hepburn, "Hobbes on the Knowledge of God," 92.

28. Craig, *The Platonian Leviathan*, 36–37, 44–45, emphasizes this point about the structure of Hobbes's discussion; see also Tuck, "The Civil Religion of Thomas Hobbes," 130; Lupoli, "Hobbes and Religion without Theology," 459–61; Flathman, *Willful Liberalism*, 22–23; Oakeshott, *Hobbes on Civil Association*, 105. Contrast Hood, *The Divine Politics of Thomas Hobbes*, 68–69.

blends with these all-too-human forms of ignorance and credulity, the human soul is ready for the growth of religion. As Hobbes puts it:

> [I]n these four things, opinion of ghosts, ignorance of second causes, devotion towards what men fear, and taking of things casual for prognostics, consisteth the natural seed of religion, which, by reason of the different fancies, judgments, and passions of several men, hath grown up into ceremonies so different that those which are used by one man are for the most part ridiculous to another. (12.11)[29]

Hobbes's identification here of the four elements that constitute the seed of religion, coupled with his remark about the diverse growths that the seed produces, reminds of his earlier definition of religion, which collapsed any important distinction between religion and superstition. The present statement, in tone as well as content, is hardly more respectful of religion.[30] To be sure, some scholars insist that Hobbes's analysis of the seed of religion in this section is limited to pagan religion.[31] But Hobbes himself draws no such line here, and his inclusion of the example of the belief that mere words can turn bread into a man suggests that his target is not restricted in the way these scholars contend.

That is not to deny that Hobbes draws an important distinction in Chapter 12 between pagan religion and biblical religion. In fact, on the heels of the argument just sketched—perhaps the most inflammatory of all his arguments in Chapter 12—Hobbes provides himself with some cover by turning from the question of the *constitution* of the seeds of religion to the question of their *cultivation*. Here, at least, he distinguishes between pagan religion and biblical religion—and thus, it would seem, saves biblical religion from reduction to just another form of superstition rooted in anxiety and ignorance. But what he says about the cultivation of the seeds of religion is complicated, and its bearing needs careful consideration. Here is the key paragraph in full:

29. In the version of this paragraph in the Latin *Leviathan*, Hobbes concludes by speaking, not of those ceremonies "which are used by one man," but of those "which are sanctioned by law in one commonwealth" (*quae Lege in una Civitate comprobantur*). He also adds "and purposes" (*& Consilia*) after "passions" earlier in the same sentence.

30. This is one of the passages to which Bramhall pointed to show that Hobbes's principles are "brim full of prodigious impiety": "What is now become of that dictate or 'precept of reason,' concerning 'prayers, thanksgivings, oblations, sacrifices,' if uncertain 'opinions, ignorance, fear,' mistakes, the 'conscience' of our 'own weakness,' and 'the admiration of natural events,' be the only 'seeds of religion'?" (*The Catching of Leviathan*, 521). See also Curley, "'I Durst not Write so Boldly,'" 529; Willey, *The Seventeenth Century Background*, 117; Craig, *The Platonian Leviathan*, 37–40.

31. See, e.g., Hood, *The Divine Politics of Thomas Hobbes*, 68–69; Martinich, *The Two Gods of Leviathan*, 62–64.

For these seeds have received culture from two sorts of men. One sort have been they that have nourished and ordered them according to their own invention. The other have done it by God's commandment and direction. But both sorts have done it with a purpose to make those men that relied on them the more apt to obedience, laws, peace, charity, and civil society. So that the religion of the former sort is a part of human politics, and teacheth part of the duty which earthly kings require of their subjects. And the religion of the latter sort is divine politics, and containeth precepts to those that have yielded themselves subjects in the kingdom of God. Of the former sort were all the founders of commonwealths and lawgivers of the gentiles; of the latter sort were *Abraham, Moses,* and our *Blessed Saviour,* by whom have been derived unto us the laws of the kingdom of God. (12.12)

It is undeniable that Hobbes suggests here that biblical religion differs from pagan religion: they should not be understood merely as two manifestations of the exact same process of growth. Although it is true that Hobbes continues to suggest, even here, that they share at least some common ground— for he does not retract, but even reiterates, his suggestion that the seeds of religion are the same in the two cases—that commonality would seem to be less important in this context than the difference indicated by his distinction between "human politics" and "divine politics." But what exactly is meant by that distinction? And in favor of which of the two sorts of religion does it cut?

Of course, the overwhelming impression conveyed by this famous statement[32] is that Hobbes means to elevate biblical religion, cultivated by "God's commandment and direction," above the superstitious religions of the gentiles, which grew from merely human sources. And that impression is heightened by what follows this first statement on the distinction between "human politics" and "divine politics." For Hobbes turns immediately to a long and amusing diatribe on the absurd carnival of deification that was pagan religion. "There is almost nothing that has a name," he proclaims, "that has not been esteemed amongst the gentiles, in one place or another, a god or devil, or by their poets feigned to be inanimated, inhabited, or possessed by some spirit or other" (12.13; cf. *De Hom.* 14.11). To make sure this point does not go unnoticed or unsupported, Hobbes gives examples and then more examples, in a cascade of ridicule. An excerpt should suffice to convey the tenor of the passage:

The unformed matter of the world was a god, by the name of *Chaos.*

The heaven, the ocean, the planets, the fire, the earth, the winds, were so many gods.

---

32. It is famous in part because it supplied the title for F. C. Hood's well-known book, *The Divine Politics of Thomas Hobbes.* See Hood, 70–71.

> Men, women, a bird, a crocodile, a calf, a dog, a snake, an onion, a leek, deified. Besides that, [the gentiles] filled almost all places with spirits called *demons*: the plains, with *Pan* and *Panises*, or satyrs; the woods, with fawns and nymphs; the sea, with tritons and other nymphs . . . They have also ascribed divinity and built temples to mere accidents and qualities, such as time, night, day, peace, concord, love, contention, virtue, honour, health, rust, fever, and the like—which, when they prayed for or against, they prayed to, as if there were ghosts of those names hanging over their heads, and letting fall or withholding that good or evil for or against which they prayed. They invoked also their own wit, by the name of *Muses*; their own ignorance, by the name of *Fortune*; their own lust, by the name of *Cupid*; their own rage, by the name *Furies*; their own privy members, by the name of *Priapus*; and attributed their pollutions to *Incubi* and *Succubae*—insomuch as there was nothing which a poet could introduce as a person in his poem which they did not make either a *god* or a *devil*. (12.14–16)

Hobbes's description here of the polymorphous deification that saturated the pagan world is only the beginning of his diatribe. He follows it with an account of the even crazier beliefs of the gentiles concerning prognostication and divination—an account capped off by a sentence of over thirty lines that displays the full range of Hobbes's marvelous powers of mockery (see 12.17–19).

But to what purpose does Hobbes let his rhetorical capacities romp so freely? The most obvious aim of his long description of the absurdities of pagan religion is to continue to compensate for his earlier suggestion that religion as such is rooted in anxiety and ignorance. Hobbes creates the impression that the polytheistic excesses of the gentiles deserve a form of mockery to which he would never submit monotheistic religion. Yet, at the same time, by directing his fire at pagan religion and thereby freeing himself of any restraint, Hobbes is able to teach a lesson about the fathomless depths of human credulity. How could the gentiles come to believe all of the bizarre things they came to believe? Hobbes ends his account with a blunt explanation and conclusion: "So easy are men to be drawn to believe anything from such men as have gotten credit with them and can with gentleness and dexterity take hold of their fear and ignorance" (12.19; cf. *De Hom.* 14.11–12; *Hist. Eccles.*, 106–7, 1389–90). It is hard to believe that Hobbes would not have expected at least some of his readers to apply that lesson universally, that is, as extending beyond the bounds of pagan religion, and hence into the realm of "divine politics" as well. After all, Hobbes has already indicated that the ignorance of causes that was a seed of the many bizarre pagan convictions and practices has grown into certain Christian beliefs and rituals as well, including the

Eucharist (see again 12.8; consider also 30.6, 44.1–3, 45.4–6, 45.23–25, 45.29–30, 45.38; *Elem.* 11.6).[33]

But a further question must be asked about Hobbes's attitude toward pagan religion: Despite its nuttiness, was there not, in Hobbes's view, something politically sensible and sound about pagan religion? This question emerges as Hobbes turns from listing the crazy beliefs of the gentiles to consider the aims of the cultivators of those beliefs, which were not so crazy. In fact, seen from the perspective of the political aims of its cultivators, pagan religion appears in Hobbes's presentation as the product of an entirely reasonable concern to secure law and order within the various commonwealths.[34] Elaborating his claim that pagan religion was a part of "human politics," Hobbes indicates that the most important "authors" of religion among the gentiles were political men—"the first founders and legislators of commonwealths"—who sought to reduce civil unrest and encourage adherence to their laws. Their goal was "only to keep the people in obedience and peace" (12.20; see also 42.67, 45.2; *Elem.* 25.2). As Hobbes tells the story, moreover, their efforts were generally successful (see 12.20–21). Indeed, this form of "human politics" was so successful in pacifying the public that, once established, it allowed for a considerable degree of toleration. Among the ancient Romans, Hobbes notes, "men were not forbidden to deny that which in the poets is written of the pains and pleasures after this life, which divers of great authority and gravity have in their harangues openly derided" (12.20). Hobbes describes the advantages of the skillful use of religion among the Romans:

> And therefore the Romans, that had conquered the greatest part of the then known world, made no scruple of tolerating any religion whatsoever in the city of Rome itself, unless it had something in it that could not consist with their civil government; nor do we read that any religion was there forbidden, but that of the Jews, who (being the peculiar kingdom of God) thought it unlawful to acknowledge subjection to any mortal king or state whatsoever. And thus you see how the religion of the gentiles was a part of their policy. (12.21)

Even more striking than Hobbes's praise of the moderation and toleration made possible by the political use of pagan religion is his indication that the religion of the Jews was the one religion that the Romans found it difficult

---

33. Contrast Martinich, *The Two Gods of Leviathan*, 62–64; Hood, *The Divine Politics of Thomas Hobbes*, 68–69.

34. Collins, *The Allegiance of Thomas Hobbes*, 43–45, makes a similar suggestion about Hobbes's estimation of the political utility of the religion of the gentiles. See also Kraynak, *History and Modernity in the Thought of Thomas Hobbes*, 22. Compare Rousseau, *Social Contract* 4.8.

to tolerate. Hobbes mentions this fact immediately before returning to the distinction between "human politics" and "divine politics" (12.22). Coming as it does at the end of a passage in which he is praising pagan religion for its political utility, this allusion to the political problem posed for the Romans by the religion of the Jews invites us to wonder whether there is not something more problematic, at least from a civic perspective, about "divine politics." For it was not mere prejudice, by Hobbes's account, that made the Romans intolerant of the religion of the Jews. After all, the Romans were ready to tolerate any religion "unless it had something in it that could not consist with their civil government." But the Jews "thought it unlawful to acknowledge subjection to any mortal king or state whatsoever." Why did the Jews hold that belief? Because they regarded themselves as subjects of "the peculiar kingdom of God," that is, because they believed that they were the recipients of a supernatural revelation that gave them laws as God's own subjects meant to live in God's own kingdom (compare 12.21 with 12.22; see also *De Cive* 16.9). Now, Hobbes, of course, explicitly attests to his own belief in the truth of that conviction. That is one meaning—the most obvious one—of his distinction between "human politics" and "divine politics." But the deeper purpose of that distinction, especially as he returns to it after having indicated that the religion of the Jews posed a special problem for the Roman authorities, may be to suggest that "divine politics," by making "laws civil" subordinate to religion and thereby inverting the relationship characteristic of "human politics," is in fact a more problematic form of politics (consider 12.22; compare 16.11–12). If Hobbes does intend to convey such a suggestion, it would not be limited to the religion of the Jews, for he mentions not only Abraham and Moses but also "our *Blessed Saviour*" as among the cultivators of religion as a form of "divine politics." And, of course, the notion of the kingdom of God may carry a very different meaning in Christianity, but it is certainly no less important than it is in Judaism. Not surprisingly, the Roman authorities also found it difficult to tolerate some of those who professed their allegiance to the kingdom of God as it was proclaimed by Christ (compare 12.21–22 with 42.12–16, 43.13, 44.2; see also *De Cive* 17.3, 17.25, 18.1, 18.7; *Beh.*, 5–8, 16, 63–64).[35]

Admittedly, if Hobbes is suggesting that the "divine politics" of biblical religion is a particularly problematic form of politics, he is doing so elliptically. But that can be explained by his desire not to exacerbate the problem by

---

35. Compare Collins, *The Allegiance of Thomas Hobbes*, 43–47, on Hobbes's view of the political superiority of pagan religion and the special problem posed by biblical religion. See also Lilla, *The Stillborn God*, 84–86; Cooke, *Hobbes and Christianity*, 87–89; Schwartz, "Hobbes and the Two Kingdoms of God," 13–16, 20n50. See again Rousseau, *Social Contract* 4.8.

acknowledging its true grounds too openly. He will go further later in *Leviathan* by offering an interpretation of the Bible that would solve or at least mitigate the problem by denying that there is any conflict between adherence to the dictates of Scripture and obedience to civil authority. We can see only the first flickers of this interpretation in the early chapters of *Leviathan*, since, as Hobbes tells us in the second of his two statements on "divine politics" in Chapter 12, "to speak more largely of the kingdom of God, both by nature and covenant, I have in the following discourse assigned to another place" (12.22). But even in Chapter 12, we can discern something of the aims that will shape his later discussions of the kingdom of God, especially in Part III of *Leviathan*. On the one hand, Hobbes will reinterpret Scripture so as to bring its teaching into harmony with his own teaching on the supremacy of civil authority. That is, he will reshape "divine politics" on the model of a civil religion under the sovereign's control, so as to make biblical religion as compatible as possible with "human politics." On the other hand, he will indicate, on a deeper if more oblique level, the nature of the problem that he is trying to address, and he will suggest that its deepest roots lie in the Bible itself, which does not in fact consistently or even primarily teach the supremacy of civil authority. The oblique manner in which Hobbes must pursue this second prong of his complex strategy is dictated by the fact that it is in some tension with the first. That makes it harder to see what is ultimately his deeper line of argument: his critique of biblical religion as containing, from each of its two inceptions, the roots of a profound and dangerous religious challenge to political authority.

This interpretation, of course, would hardly be accepted by all scholars of Hobbes. Yet, although further elaboration of it will have to wait until we turn to the second half of *Leviathan*, it receives some additional support from the remarkable final step that Hobbes takes in Chapter 12. Immediately after the second of his two statements on the "divine politics" of the kingdom of God, *Hobbes turns to consider how religions are destroyed.* As if he were merely an analyst turning to consider the inverse of a process under examination, he writes the following:

> From the propagation of religion, it is not hard to understand the causes of the resolution of the same into its first seeds or principles—which are only an opinion of a deity, and powers invisible and supernatural—that can never be so abolished out of human nature, but that new religions may again be made to spring out of them by the culture of such men as for such purpose are in reputation. (12.23)

Hobbes does not leave matters at this general statement on the "resolution" of religion back into its first seeds; he goes on to describe the causes of the decline and ultimate collapse of religions. Because all "formed religion" is founded on the faith people place in the extraordinary claims of a human founder, and then on deference to the authorities who perpetuate what the founder established, religions can fall, Hobbes says, when doubt spreads about the wisdom, sincerity, or love of those who "have government of religion" (12.24). He then lays out the ways in which the reputations of religious authorities are undermined. When such men come to be seen as "enjoining a belief in contradictories," they lose their reputation for wisdom; when they fail to live by the principles they preach, they lose their reputation for sincerity; and when they are discovered to be pursuing private ends, they lose their reputation for love (12.25–27). More important than these first three "causes of the weakening of men's faith" is the last one Hobbes mentions: because miracles are the crucial testimony of "divine calling," faith tends to fade when such testimony is not forthcoming or no longer accepted. "For," Hobbes explains, "as in natural things men of judgment require natural signs and arguments, so in supernatural things they require signs supernatural (which are miracles) before they consent inwardly and from their hearts" (12.28).

In laying out the causes of the weakening of men's faith, Hobbes does not limit his analysis to pagan religion, although he does suggest that the rise of Christianity was due in large part to the contempt that the pagan priests had brought upon themselves (12.31; see also *De Hom.* 14.13; *Hist. Eccles.*, 1355–70). He points out that examples of the weakening of religion can be found in the Bible itself (12.29–30).[36] Still, even if he includes biblical religion in his analysis, the main example he would seem to have in mind is one that would have been familiar and unobjectionable to most of his English readers: the revolt against the Catholic Church in England and "many other parts of Christendom" (12.31). The Reformation is Hobbes's chief example of a change in religion, because, as he argues, the contradictions and absurdities enjoined by the Catholic Church, as well as the abuse of power by its authorities, conform perfectly to his model of the causes of the weakening of men's faith (12.31–32; see also *De Hom.* 14.13; *Hist. Eccles.*, 2174–2216). It is tempting to conclude, therefore, that the sole intention of Hobbes's brief discussion of the causes of changes in religion is to give a thumbnail sketch of the problems that led to the Reformation.[37] But such an interpretation cannot explain why Hobbes

---

36. Hobbes points to Exodus 32, Judges 2, and 1 Samuel 8. The last of these is one of Hobbes's favorite chapters of the Bible, for reasons that will be discussed in Chapter 5.

37. See, e.g., Hood, *The Divine Politics of Thomas Hobbes*, 71; Martinich, *The Two Gods of Leviathan*, 65–66; Lessay, "Hobbes's Protestantism," 267–68 (but cf. 289). Contrast Johnston, *The Rhetoric of Leviathan*, 203–4.

concludes his discussion of the changes of religion by extending his argument beyond the Church of Rome. After railing against the various forms of power-seeking by religious authorities, he ends Chapter 12 with the acerbic remark that "all the changes of religion in the world" may be attributed to "one and the same cause," namely, "unpleasing priests, and those not only amongst Catholics, but even in that Church that hath presumed most of reformation" (12.32). Why does Hobbes conclude his argument by extending its reach beyond the Reformation? Why does he suggest that his analysis of the causes of the decline of religion applies even to the Church of England?[38]

The conclusion of Chapter 12 provides an important clue, I believe, to one of Hobbes's most far-reaching aims in *Leviathan* and beyond. Especially when one considers that it comes at the end of a chapter in which Hobbes has argued that religion grows out of anxiety and ignorance, and in which he has pointed to the politically problematic character of biblical religion, the conclusion of Chapter 12 indicates that Hobbes was ultimately seeking nothing less than to initiate yet another "change in religion." Going beyond those who "hath presumed most of reformation," Hobbes was seeking—to use his own formulation—a "resolution" of religion "into its first seeds or principles," which consist only of "an opinion of a deity, and powers invisible and supernatural."[39] In light of his manifest efforts to undermine the belief in powers invisible and supernatural, and what we will see in the next chapter

---

38. Curley suggests, *contra* Clarendon, that by "that Church that hath presumed most of reformation," Hobbes is referring to the Presbyterians, not the Church of England (see note 20 to Chapter 12 of the Curley edition of *Leviathan*; see also Martinich, *The Two Gods of Leviathan*, 65; cf. Hyde [= Clarendon], *A Brief View and Survey*, 25). It is true that it seems odd, *prima facie*, to take Hobbes's formulation as referring to the Anglicans, since they were hardly the most radical reformers. There is thus some basis for Curley's claim that it is "more natural" to suppose that Hobbes is referring to the Presbyterians. But Hobbes's criticism of "unpleasing priests" (which fits the Anglican priests better than it does the Presbyterian presbyters) supports Clarendon's reading, as does a much later passage, in Chapter 47, in which Hobbes speaks favorably of the Presbyterian attack on episcopacy (see 47.19–20; consider also 42.71, 47.34). In the manuscript version of *Leviathan* presented to Charles II, Hobbes replaced the formulation here in Chapter 12 with a more anodyne statement, and in the post-Restoration Latin edition, he deleted it (together with the passage from Chapter 47) entirely. These facts, too, suggest that the original reference is to the Church of England, for there would be no need to alter or remove a reference to the Presbyterians. It is also noteworthy that Hobbes is more cautious in a parallel passage in *De Homine* (14.13). Compare Lessay, "Hobbes's Protestantism," 289; Collins, *The Allegiance of Thomas Hobbes*, 122–23, 275; Malcolm, *Leviathan, Vol. 1: Introduction*, 36–37, 46–47.

39. Compare the remarkable passage at 47.19–20, which begins with a classic Hobbesian line: "But as the inventions of men are woven, so also are they ravelled out; the way is the same, but the order is inverted." This passage will be discussed in Chapter 7.

is his less conspicuous critique of the "opinion of a deity," we may even wonder whether Hobbes was seeking to go further than his explicit formulation
suggests. In that very formulation itself, moreover, he declares only that the
"first seeds or principles" of religion "can never be *so* abolished out of human
nature, but that new religions *may* again be made to spring out of them."[40]
That statement is less emphatic in its assertion of religion's hold on the human heart than it first appears. And might not Hobbes have wanted to see
just how invincible religion really is by attacking it at its very roots or "seeds"?

40. Consider also the qualification in parentheses in the Latin version, "if suitable cultivators emerge" (*si Cultores accesserint idonei*), which replaces the English version's "by the culture
of such men as for such purpose are in reputation." On the ambiguity of the statement as a
whole, see Strauss, "On the Basis of Hobbes's Political Philosophy," 186; Johnston, *The Rhetoric
of Leviathan*, 118; Willey, *The Seventeenth Century Background*, 118; contrast Cooke, *Hobbes and
Christianity*, 209–10, 229–31; Sherlock, "The Theology of *Leviathan*," 46–47.

4

Religion and Theology II:
Hobbes's Natural Theology

Hobbes's interest in the dissolution of full-grown religion at the end of Chapter 12 of *Leviathan* is all the more striking when one considers that Chapter 12 is immediately followed by a series of crucial chapters, beginning with the famous Chapter 13 on the state of nature, in which Hobbes presents the central principles of his political philosophy. That Hobbes presents the core of his political philosophy immediately after his analysis of religion suggests that there is a connection between the two, at least in a negative sense. Could it be the case that Hobbes's political philosophy, which begins, not from any theological premises, but from an account of our natural condition as a brutal state of perpetual danger mitigated only by the "providence" of men taking the necessary steps to protect themselves, has an important role to play in Hobbes's attempt to undermine religion? If Hobbes can lay the theoretical foundations of a secular state supported by a rational morality, can he direct his readers toward a new kind of political order that will endure and even thrive without the support of religion? These are far-reaching questions that will have to wait until we turn in later chapters to a direct consideration of Hobbes's political philosophy.

For now, however, we can observe that at least the suggestion that Hobbes's political philosophy does not depend on any theological premises is confirmed at the beginning of the other chapter in the first half of *Leviathan* that is devoted to religious and theological matters: Chapter 31, "Of the Kingdom of God by Nature." This chapter, which stands at the other end of Hobbes's presentation of his political philosophy, is the last chapter of Part II of *Leviathan* and thus serves as a bridge between the first half of the book and the more explicitly theological second half. It begins with these questions: What are the laws of God? And do they conflict with the moral and political principles presented in the first half of *Leviathan*? To raise these as questions still to be considered implies that it was possible for Hobbes to bracket them as he was laying out his moral and political principles (see 31.1; see also 32.1–2; *De Cive* 15.1; Latin *Lev.*, 1125–27). This is an aspect of what I meant earlier when I compared Hobbes's political philosophy to an island surrounded by religious and theological reflections that touch it only at its shores (see p. 84 above).

But can Hobbes's political philosophy remain untouched once theological questions are given their full due? This is the concern with which Hobbes opens Chapter 31. Having completed his presentation of his political philosophy, he declares that he must now turn to consider the laws of God, lest his readers be led either by excessive obedience to civil authority to offend God or by excessive fear of that danger to transgress the laws of the commonwealth. "To avoid both these rocks," Hobbes says, "it is necessary to know what are the laws divine" (31.1). Now, Hobbes suggests that the "laws divine" are known in three different ways: by natural reason, by revelation, and by prophecy. Because it is only through natural reason and prophecy, however, that universal laws are given, "there may be attributed to God a twofold kingdom, *natural* and *prophetic*" (31.3–4). The purpose of Chapter 31, Hobbes suggests, is to investigate the natural kingdom of God; his prophetic kingdom will be taken up in Part III. The opening of Chapter 31 thus leads us to expect that the main purpose of the chapter will be to consider the laws of God insofar as they are knowable to natural reason. Yet, as the chapter progresses, Hobbes proves to be less interested in considering any laws of God than in examining what natural reason teaches, first, about God's kingdom or sovereignty and, second, about God's attributes. In his discussion of each of these problems, moreover, Hobbes is more concerned to raise difficult questions than to provide edifying answers: it is a question whether God, according to Hobbes, even has a kingdom in the strict sense of the word by nature, and what, if anything, natural reason can teach us about God's attributes. Chapter 31, then, is worth examining in detail, because it proves, no less than Chapter 12, to be part of Hobbes's critique of religion. Hobbes presents here what may be called his "natural theology." But his is a natural theology of an unusual—not only nontraditional, but even antitraditional—sort. To see the true argument of Chapter 31, however, it is necessary to follow the movement of the chapter step by step. For Hobbes is at some pains not to make his path too clear or direct.

"Of the Kingdom of God by Nature"

Hobbes's path in Chapter 31 begins to twist and turn almost from the start, with the first question he takes up: the question of God's kingdom or sovereignty. Scripture teaches, of course, that God reigns as a king over all men. Hobbes acknowledges as much by quoting at the outset two passages from the Psalms proclaiming that "God is king" (31.2).[1] Yet, although the position of Scripture is clear enough, the task of Chapter 31 is to examine what natural reason teaches. And if natural reason cannot begin from Scripture, neither can it begin from universal agreement about God's sovereignty, because no such universal agreement exists. Hobbes goes out of his way, early in Chapter 31, to point to the existence of atheists and those who accept God's existence but deny his providence (31.2; cf. *De Cive* 15.2, 16.1). That Hobbes mentions atheists and those who deny God's providence helps one, in turn, to see the most important omission in his initial argument regarding "the right of nature whereby God reigneth over men" (31.5). Although this argument depends on the premise of God's omnipotence—a premise that at least some would deny—Hobbes does not offer any argument to establish that premise. Rather, he simply accepts it and then uses it to think through the implications of God's omnipotence for his right to rule. He argues as follows. If God is omnipotent, then he is like a man in the state of nature, who has a right to all things, including a right to assert his rule over others, but he must also be without the weakness and vulnerability that lead men to relinquish their rights out of a concern for their safety. From God's irresistible power, then, follows his continual right to treat all men at his discretion (31.5; compare *EW* IV, 236).

Why does Hobbes offer this strange argument? To be sure, it establishes in a certain manner God's right to rule over men, if one accepts the premise of God's omnipotence. But it also raises some troubling questions. Why would an omnipotent being rule, or exercise his "sovereignty," which is really only his irresistible power, by giving laws and entering into covenants?[2] Why would he be concerned to guide and protect the weaker beings under his control, especially if he has no needs of his own? Or perhaps the better way of casting these questions is to ask whether natural reason gives us any good reason to think that there is a being who, while omnipotent and thus free to act entirely at his own discretion, exercises benevolent providential rule over human beings. Without posing that question directly, Hobbes confirms its legitimacy and makes it more pointed by also raising the problem of the

---

1. The passages in question are Psalms 97:1 and Psalms 99:1. It is worth nothing that the first of these passage stresses God's goodness ("The Lord reigns; let the earth rejoice") whereas the second stresses his power ("The Lord reigns; let the people tremble").

2. Compare Curley, "The Covenant with God in Hobbes's *Leviathan*," 207–9, "Hobbes and the Cause of Religious Toleration," 316. See also *De Cive* 16.4.

prosperity of the wicked and the suffering of the righteous, a problem that, he notes, "hath shaken the faith, not only of the vulgar, but of philosophers, and which is more, of the saints, concerning divine providence" (31.6). It will not suffice to solve this problem, he further indicates, by arguing that all men are sinners, because some men are born with afflictions, such as blindness, and the suffering caused by disease and death also afflicts "other living creatures that cannot sin" (31.6).[3]

Already at this early point of Chapter 31, we can begin to see that Hobbes's intention is more to critique or debunk traditional natural theology than it is to support it by giving his own version of it.[4] But we need to follow Hobbes's path further. After speaking of the right of God's sovereignty, Hobbes quickly brushes aside, as already covered by his discussion of the laws of nature in earlier chapters of *Leviathan*, the question of the divine laws insofar as they concern the natural duties men owe to one another. He turns instead to the question of "what precepts are dictated to men by their natural reason only, without other word of God, touching the honour and worship of the Divine Majesty" (31.7). Once he turns to the question of honor and worship, Hobbes's discussion necessarily expands to consider God's goodness in addition to his power. For honor and worship, as Hobbes emphasizes, imply thoughts of both. Honor and worship are ways of soliciting the favor of a being in whom we see both the capacity to benefit us and the inclination to do so, at least if he is swayed by our praises and other signs of submission (31.8). Such, at any rate, is the nature of honor and worship as they are displayed among men, and in his discussion of the various forms of honor and worship that men display toward God, Hobbes reasons from "those rules of honor that reason dictateth to be done by the weak to more potent men, in hope of benefit, for fear of damage, or in thankfulness for good already received from them" (31.13; cf. *De Hom.* 14.8, 14.10).

---

3. Hobbes points to the problem of the prosperity of the wicked and the suffering of the righteous in many other places as well. See, e.g., *De Cive* 15.4; *EW* IV, 248–51; *EW* V, 17, 103–4, 115–16, 145; consider also Latin *Lev.*, 1093, 1127–29; *Anti-White* 31.4, 38.2. In his quarrel with Bramhall over liberty and necessity, Hobbes makes a further argument: if God is omnipotent, then he is the cause of sin (see *EW* V, 6–15, 104–6, 117, 142, 212–18, 297–99, 450; see also *EW* IV, 257, 278, 390, 399; *Lev.* 46.31; Latin *Lev.* 1091–93; *Anti-White* 35.16, 38.2). On this further argument, see Strauss, "On the Basis of Hobbes's Political Philosophy," 183; Foisneau, "Omnipotence, Necessity and Sovereignty," 276–78; Milner, "Hobbes on Religion," 422n17; Mintz, *The Hunting of Leviathan*, 122.

4. Compare Pangle, "A Critique of Hobbes's Critique of Biblical and Natural Religion in *Leviathan*," 46–48.

Or does Hobbes not so much reason by his own lights from such rules as try to reproduce by his argument the tendency of those who honor and worship God to do so in the forms and with the expectations they know from their interactions with other men? Hobbes's argument certainly makes that tendency apparent. But it also leads one to wonder whether it is a tendency that reason truly endorses. If, as Hobbes reminds us, "God has no ends" (31.13)—if God does not stand to profit, as a powerful man would, by the signs of submission shown by his inferiors, or enjoy the feelings of triumph that come from witnessing such signs (cf. *De Cive* 15.13)—why would God wish to be honored or worshiped? Just as Hobbes's preceding argument about God's sovereignty pointed to the unanswered question of why an omnipotent God would exercise his right to providential rule, so too his discussion of honor and worship leaves us with a question. Hobbes states the problem more bluntly in the Latin version of the passage: "As for an end on account of which God omnipotent would wish to be worshiped, I see none, other than that it may benefit us" (Latin *Lev.*, 565; cf. *Anti-White* 32.2).

This problem, however, does not keep Hobbes from turning to the question of God's attributes, "that we may know what worship of God is taught us by the light of nature" (31.14). The premise of Hobbes's discussion of honor and worship thus far in Chapter 31 has been that God, whether or not he desires honor and worship, certainly deserves them. This, at any rate, has been the premise insofar as Hobbes's discussion is to be understood as an argument about the submission dictated by natural reason, and not as a mere description of the ways in which human beings are led, whether reasonably or not, to honor and worship God. Yet, if his earlier argument about God's sovereignty did not establish the key premise of God's omnipotence, Hobbes has also yet to demonstrate that God is of such a character as to merit honor and worship. And, just as he did earlier, Hobbes points to the existence of those who would deny the premise in question. He does so by way of laying out the basic attributes that God must possess for reason to dictate that he be honored. First, God, of course, must exist—"for no man can have the will to honour that which he thinks not to have any being" (31.14)—and, second, God must care for human beings. But there are those, Hobbes reminds us, who deny God's existence and others who deny his providential concern for human beings. It is striking who these men are. They are not the open atheists and deniers of divine providence to whom Hobbes referred earlier. Rather, they are "those philosophers" who hold one or more of three positions: that the world (or the soul of the world) is God; that the world was not created, but is eternal; and that God is inactive (31.15–17). In laying out these three positions, Hobbes indicates that the first two amount to a denial of God's existence. "For by God is understood the cause of the world," and thus to say the world is God or that the world is eternal "is to say there is no cause of it, that is, no God" (31.15–16; see also *De Cive* 15.14).

What is Hobbes's response to these positions? He argues that they are incompatible with the will to honor God (31.14–17). That is surely true. But it is hardly much of an argument for demonstrating that they are false. Does it not put the cart before the horse to argue that we ought to attribute existence, for instance, to God because otherwise we would not be led to honor him?[5] Or does Hobbes mean, once again, to point to a prevalent human tendency that is questionable when seen in the cold light of reason, the tendency, namely, to attribute to God those qualities he must have in order for a prior concern to honor him to make sense? And does not that prior concern have its source, not in a grasp of God's true nature, but rather in the wish that there be a being who, like a supremely powerful man, can and will come to our aid if we show our due submission?

If Hobbes leads us to these questions about the human roots of the common, anthropomorphized conception of God, he quickly pivots from them to direct us to another, related difficulty. For his argument about God's attributes becomes primarily a doctrine of negative attributes, that is, an account of those attributes that should not be ascribed to God and those that should be but only as negations of conceivable positive attributes.[6] The transition comes with the turn to the question of whether God is finite. Although there are those who maintain that God is finite, Hobbes argues that they, too, just like those who deny God's existence or his providence, dishonor God, since they attribute to him "less than we can" (31.18; see also 45.12). The concern to honor God as much as possible, then, would seem to lead necessarily to a denial of God's finitude. Once one says that God is infinite, however, one must then acknowledge that we cannot conceive of him, "for whatsoever we conceive is finite" (31.20). But that, in turn, means that all intelligible attributes of God are, in effect, erased by his infinity. Not only does it no longer make sense to attribute to God figure, parts, totality, place, motion, rest, and other such qualities of finite bodies; even to ascribe to him passions such as anger and mercy, a will anything like our own, or perception and understanding is to dishonor him, because these qualities, as we know them, depend on the limitations and interactions of finite natural beings (31.18–27; see also 3.12; *De Cive* 15.12; *Elem.* 11.3; *Obj.*, no. 10).

5. Compare Milner, "Hobbes on Religion," 413.
6. Compare Maimonides, *The Guide of the Perplexed* 1.57–58.

How should we understand the character and purpose of this line of argument? And why does Hobbes press it as vigorously as he does? On the one hand, Hobbes's argument is consistent, as he himself indicates, with the traditional biblical conception of God, according to which God is unfathomable or incomprehensible (31.28; see also 46.12; *Obj.*, no. 10). Hobbes's argument begins from what would seem to be a consideration of irreproachable piety: if God is to be honored as highly as possible, we should not ascribe to him attributes that imply limits or deficiencies. On the other hand, Hobbes then shows that if one follows this path to its end, one must abandon along the way all of God's positive attributes, or, at any rate, one must reinterpret them, not as comprehensible significations of God's true nature, but either as exalted but indeterminate superlatives ("highest," "greatest," and so on) or as indefinite words of praise that indicate merely our own desire to honor God with the grandest terms our feeble powers can muster (31.28). As God's positive attributes are cast aside with the movement to his incomprehensible infinity, our conception of God is reduced, it would seem, to a mere "I AM," the ultimate meaning of which is mysterious. The name "God" may still imply that he is our "Father, King, and Lord," but the nature of the relationship to us implied by those terms has faded into a mist that our limited vision cannot penetrate (31.28; compare *De Cive* 15.14).[7]

In this argument about God's attributes, Hobbes uses one element of the traditional view of God to call into question all the others. He shows, in other words, that if one pulls on the thread of men's conception of God that is the acknowledgment of his incomprehensible infinity, the rest of the cloak comes unraveled and one is left with nothing but a mystery. In this way, Hobbes's argument operates as an *ad hominem* critique of the traditional conception of God, showing that one aspect of it undermines or invalidates all the others. But this is not yet the end of his argument, nor even its most important part. For it is not only by accepting the premises of the tradition, or by thinking through what follows from the assertion of incomprehensible infinity arising from the concern to honor God, that one is led to the conclusion that God's nature is unknowable. Hobbes's *ad hominem* argument gives way to a simpler

---

7. For a similar argument by an associate of Hobbes, see Gassendi, "Fifth Set of Objections," 200–201: "God is infinitely beyond anything we can grasp, and when our mind addresses itself to contemplate him, it is not only in darkness but is reduced to nothing. Hence we have no basis for claiming that we have any authentic idea which represents God; and it is more than enough if, on the analogy of our human attributes, we can derive and construct an idea of some sort for our own use—an idea which does not transcend our human grasp and which contains no reality except what we perceive in other things or as a result of encountering other things." See also 205–7. Compare Hepburn, "Hobbes on the Knowledge of God," 99–100.

but ultimately more far-reaching argument, which takes as its starting point not so much the traditional view of God or the concern to honor God as an awareness of the natural limits of our knowledge.

The crucial passage in this regard comes as Hobbes is discussing the dictates of natural reason for the worship of God. In an apparent digression from a list of eight such dictates, as he is discussing the careful consideration with which men should speak of God, Hobbes makes this statement:

> And [hence followeth from the dictate to speak considerately of God] that disputing God's nature is contrary to his honour. For it is supposed that in this natural kingdom of God, there is no other way to know anything but by natural reason, that is, from the principles of natural science, which are so far from teaching us anything of God's nature as they cannot teach us our own nature, nor the nature of the smallest creature living. And therefore, when men, out of the principles of natural reason, dispute of the attributes of God, they but dishonour him. For in the attributes which we give to God, we are not to consider the signification of philosophical truth, but the signification of pious intention, to do him the greatest honour we are able. (31.33; cf. *De Cive* 15.15; *Hist. Eccles.*, 1087–90)

In its beginning and its end, this statement appears to be simply a repetition of the argument we have been considering. Hobbes seems once again to be reasoning outward from the presupposed concern to honor God. But he also speaks now of the limits of the knowledge "natural reason" can attain "from the principles of natural science." This consideration supplies, at the core of the statement, a different basis for the argument, and one that changes its character. Indeed, in the light provided by this new consideration, we can see more clearly that the movement of the earlier argument was guided, not by the direct pursuit of the "philosophical truth" about God insofar as it is knowable to natural reason, but by the attempt to spell out the implications of the "pious intention" to do God "the greatest honour we are able." We can thus see more clearly the *ad hominem* character of the earlier argument, which was only somewhat dimly visible before.[8] But that, in turn, leads us to a new set of questions: What if one does not share—as we already have good reason to suspect that Hobbes himself does not genuinely share—the concern that drove the earlier argument? Must one not return to and restart the examination of the nature of God? Or have we just encountered a further reason— and, from Hobbes's own point of view, a more decisive one—why that examination cannot be carried out?

8. For further confirmation, see *Lev.* 46.12, 46.22–23; *Obj.*, no. 11; *De Corp.* 1.8; *EW* V, 6.

The answer to this last question, I believe, is yes. But it is not enough to leave matters at a simple "yes," because at least two important questions remain. First, is it the case, in Hobbes's genuine view, that natural reason leaves us unable to say *anything* about the nature of God, such that *any claim* about his nature is just as plausible, because just as speculative and groundless, as any other? Is our situation like that of men shooting arrows in the dark, for whom there is no reason to shoot in one direction rather than another? And, second, how can this passage about the impossibility of natural knowledge of God be squared with Hobbes's doctrine, which we saw in Chapters 11 and 12 of *Leviathan*, about God as the first cause? For even if the new argument is largely in agreement with that earlier argument, insofar as both stress the incomprehensibility of God, it is not in complete agreement with it, since that earlier argument held that we can know of God at least that he is the first cause. Must we not, then, return to and reconsider Hobbes's thoughts on the question of the origins?

God as the First Cause?

To pursue these questions we must go beyond Chapter 31 and pull together some points we have already seen in other places. Let us return, first, to Hobbes's position that God is corporeal. For even if that position is not a full or frank expression of his final view, at least this much may be said: this is the only conception of God that would be compatible with Hobbes's materialism, and it is the only conception of God that, given his view of the absurdity of the notion of incorporeal substances, Hobbes would recognize as coherent and intelligible. Hobbes argues for the view that God is a body on precisely these grounds. As I noted earlier, when he was attacked by his critics, who pointed to his materialism as decisive evidence—indeed, as the very root—of his atheism,[9] Hobbes argued in response that *they* were the ones

---

9. For Bramhall's accusation, see *The Catching of Leviathan*, 536: "Though we be not able to comprehend perfectly what God is, yet we are able perfectly to comprehend what God is not: that is, He is not imperfect, and therefore He is not finite, and consequently He is not corporeal. This were a trim way to 'honour' God indeed, to honour Him with a lie. If this that [Hobbes] says here be true—'that every part of the universe is a body, and whatsoever is not a body is nothing'—then, by this doctrine, if God be not 'a body,' God is 'nothing': not an incorporeal spirit, but one of the 'idols of the brain,' a mere 'nothing,' though they [i.e., the Hobbesians] think they dance under a net, and have the blind of God's incomprehensibility between them and discovery." See also 525: "My next charge is, that [Hobbes] destroys the very being of God, and leaves nothing in His place but an empty name. For by taking away all incorporeal substances

who, by holding God to be an incorporeal spirit, reduced God to nothingness (see p. 82 above; see again *EW* IV, 302–13, 348–49, 383–84, 426–27; Latin *Lev.*, 1229–31). Now, Hobbes does not—cannot—deny that God is a spirit. Such a claim, by openly adopting the position of the Sadducees, would come too close to "direct atheism" (see again 8.25). But what, then, is God, according to Hobbes? "God is indeed a perfect, pure, simple, infinite substance" (*EW* IV, 302); "he is a most pure and most simple corporeal spirit" (*EW* IV, 306); he is a "thin, fluid, transparent, invisible body" (*EW* IV, 309); he is "an infinitely fine spirit" (*EW* IV, 310; see also 313, 384, 426–27; Latin *Lev.*, 1231). Because God is such a spirit, that is, a spirit that is also a body, "and because God has a be-ing," "it follows," as Hobbes insisted to Bramhall, "that he is either the whole universe or part of it" (*EW* IV, 349).

Hobbes nowhere gives any sign of accepting the view that God is the whole universe. After all, that is one of the positions that he indicates amount to a denial of God's existence (see again 31.15; *De Cive* 15.14). But if that position implicitly denies God's existence by denying that there is a cause of the uni-verse, what about the more plausible alternative that God is a bodily part of a universe that consists of nothing but bodies? There are several questions one could raise about this, Hobbes's, so to speak, official position.[10] Is the view that God is a body, and therefore a determinate magnitude in a place and with parts, truly compatible with his infinity (consider *EW* IV, 295–97, 300–301, 308–9; *Lev.* 3.12, 31.20–22; *De Cive* 15.14; *De Corp.* 8.1–5; *Anti-White* 2.2)?[11] And if no two bodies can occupy the same place, and none can act upon another except by being itself set in motion by another external body, can any body, even a divine one, truly be omnipotent (consider *EW* IV, 296, 309–10; *De Corp.* 8.8, 8.19, 9.6–7; *EW* VII, 85–86; *Anti-White* 27.5, 27.9)? Rather than pursue these difficult questions concerning the infinity and omnipotence of a corporeal God, let us focus on the question of creation. For the position that God is a corporeal part of the world is uncomfortably close to the view that God is the soul of the world, another of the philosophic positions to which Hobbes has pointed in Chapter 31 as implicitly denying God's existence by

---

he taketh away God Himself . . . This—that there is no incorporeal spirit—is that main root of atheism, from which so many lesser branches are daily sprouting up." Bramhall was not alone in making this accusation, as Mintz, *The Hunting of Leviathan*, 45, 58–59, 63–79, 83–84, 109, 153, shows at length.

10. Compare Milner, "Hobbes on Religion," 406, 421n15.

11. Gillespie, *The Theological Origins of Modernity*, 249, acknowledges this problem: "To say that God is some small and subtle matter interspersed in everything, as Hobbes at times does, seems to deny the divine infinity that Hobbes repeatedly insists upon."

denying that the world has a cause (see 31.15).[12] If that implication is less clear for the position that God is only a part of the world than it is for the view that he is the entire world, the matter would seem to hinge on creation, that is, on whether natural reason truly teaches, in Hobbes's view, that the world or universe was created by that part of it which is God. Indeed, Hobbes himself points to this as the decisive question for natural theology as such. Natural reason, he says, can find no argument "besides the creation of the world" that suffices "to prove a Deity" (*EW* IV, 427; cf. *Obj.*, no. 5). But what is Hobbes's genuine position on creation? Is there not a difficulty insofar as we have encountered *two positions* that are at odds with one another?

The two positions in question are, on the one hand, the view that we were led to attribute to Hobbes by our consideration of his natural philosophy, especially as presented in *De Corpore*—a view that regards creation as less plausible than the alternative—and, on the other hand, the view presented in Chapters 11 and 12 of *Leviathan* (and elsewhere) that holds that there must be a first mover at the beginning of any chain of causes (compare p. 76 above with p. 101). Now, if the first of these positions casts more doubt on creation than the second, one might try to close the gap between them by asking whether a first mover is necessarily the same as a creator. Could not the first mover, as we wondered earlier, be some kind of nondivine material principle (see p. 102 above)? Still, Hobbes does call the first mover "God," and he speaks of him as the first cause of all things. The better approach, then, is not to try to reconcile the two positions but to ask which more accurately reflects Hobbes's own deepest view of the matter. For even if Hobbes uses the name "God" only because one thing men mean by God is the first cause of all things (see again *Lev.* 11.25, 12.6), the two positions would still seem to differ over whether there must be a first mover or a first movement. And there is reason to think that one of the positions, rather than the other, should be taken as Hobbes's more considered word on the matter.[13]

We should recall here that in the crucial passage on the origin of the world in *De Corpore* (26.1), Hobbes took up the question of whether the world had a beginning or is eternal. He approached that question there *as an open*

---

12. The similarity appears even greater if one considers the parallel passage of *De Cive* (15.14), where Hobbes, after mentioning the view that God is the soul of the world, adds in parentheses *id est partem* (that is, a part).

13. On the difference and tension between the two positions, compare Curley, " 'I Durst not Write so Boldly,' " 574–77. See also Brandt, *Thomas Hobbes' Mechanical Conception of Nature*, 365; Sorell, *Hobbes*, 57–58; Craig, *The Platonian Leviathan*, 41–44; Milner, "Hobbes on Religion," 405–6; Sommerville, *Thomas Hobbes: Political Ideas in Historical Context*, 138; Hepburn, "Hobbes on the Knowledge of God," 92–95.

question. And one result of the more probing approach in *De Corpore* was that the key premise of his doctrine of God as the first mover, namely, the supposition that there cannot be an endless regress of causes with no first cause, was called into question. Hobbes argued that although it is true that no one can pursue cause after cause without eventually giving up the chase, he who abandons it, out of weariness if nothing else, will do so "without knowing whether it is possible for him to proceed to an end or not" (*De Corp.* 26.1; see also 26.3, 26.7). Hobbes was also concerned in that passage of *De Corpore* to think through the implications of a supposition that he presented as sounder than the supposition that there cannot be an endless regress of causes. This is the supposition that nothing can move itself or be moved except by that which is already moved. From this supposition, it would seem to follow, as at any rate the most plausible view, that any eternal mover, be it one or many, must have been moved, and moved by something other than itself, by something which, in turn, must have been moved by something else (see again *De Corp.* 26.1 and p. 76 above). In the same context, and in part as a result of this line of reflection, Hobbes declared that he "cannot commend" those "that boast of having demonstrated, by reasons drawn from natural things, that the world had a beginning" (*De Corp.* 26.1). He confirms elsewhere that he did not think that the creation of the world could be established by natural reason (see *EW* IV, 427–28; *EW* VII, 445; *De Hom.* 1.1; *Anti–White* 26.2–6, 27.1, 29.2, 33.7).[14]

If there is no argument from natural reason "besides the creation of the world" that suffices "to prove a Deity," but natural reason, far from establishing the creation of the world, actually casts doubt on it, what does that mean for Hobbes's natural theology as a whole? It means that his doctrine of God as the first cause cannot be an essential part of it. Or rather, insofar as that doctrine can be regarded as an essential part of his natural theology, his own critique of that doctrine reveals that Hobbes was in fact a thoroughgoing critic of natural theology, understood as the attempt, not only to grasp God's nature, but also to demonstrate his existence by reason alone (see again *Anti–White* 26.1–2, 28.3; *Obj.*, nos. 10, 11). But does that mean that Hobbes affirms the truth of those philosophic positions that, by denying that the world had a beginning or a cause, deny creation and thus the existence of God as the creator? Not quite. For we must remember that, even in the key passage of *De Corpore* to which we have just returned, Hobbes indicated that such views are more plausible than the alternative, and more intelligible insofar as they are consistent with the supposition that nothing can be moved except by

---

14. Compare Curley, " 'I Durst not Write so Boldly,' " 576–78, "Hobbes and the Cause of Religious Toleration," 315; Strauss, "On the Basis of Hobbes's Political Philosophy," 184.

that which is already moved, but he did not claim that he could demonstrate their truth. To the contrary, he indicated that each of the two fundamental alternatives remains an open possibility, at least in the sense that neither can be ruled out (see pp. 76–77 above). And that is just one example, if the most important one, of a broader consideration that reappears in Hobbes's critique of natural theology: the very great limits of the knowledge attainable by natural reason. It is striking that Hobbes reaffirms these limits in Chapter 31 of *Leviathan*, in the statement that echoes the skepticism of his natural philosophy. For the limits of the knowledge attainable by natural reason have consequences in both directions. On the one hand, they disclose the boastfulness and groundlessness of all claims that reason can discover the truth about God's nature or prove his existence. On the other hand, they leave reason unable to rule out the existence of a creator God whose powers we cannot fathom. By pointing at its most decisive stage to these limits, then, Hobbes's critique of natural theology does more to reaffirm than to overcome the inconclusiveness of his natural philosophy.

Hobbes's natural theology, which has now come to sight more as a negation than as an affirmation of natural theology, is placed, as noted earlier, at the very end of Part II of *Leviathan*. It therefore concludes the first half of the work as a whole. But that means that it also sets the stage for Hobbes's turn to Scripture in the second half of the work, especially in Part III. This transition can be understood in light of the limits of natural theology in Hobbes's view. But in what sense? The most straightforward way of understanding the connection would be to suppose that the limits of natural theology provide one with an inducement to turn from an exclusive reliance on reason and to defer to Scripture.[15] Hobbes often seems to take precisely this step. He does so—at least apparently—even in the key section of *De Corpore* that we have just considered again, where he follows his indication that the question of creation cannot be settled by reason alone by concluding that one should accept the answer given in "the Sacred Scriptures" (26.1; compare *Anti-White* 33.7). But however that suggestion, which is an anomaly in *De Corpore*, should be understood, the far more important example of a turn from reason to Scripture is the one to which we have now come: the transition from the first half of *Leviathan* to the second. It is impossible to deny that a crucial transition

---

15. See Mitchell, "Religion and the Fable of Liberalism," 9; Glover, "God and Thomas Hobbes," 288, 291. Consider also Pocock, "Time, History and Eschatology in the Thought of Thomas Hobbes," 192–94 with 160–63.

occurs at this point in the book (see especially *Leviathan* 32.1–3, 31.4; compare Latin *Lev.*, 575; *Elem.* 11.7–8; *De Cive* 16.1). Yet, like so many things on the surface of his texts, Hobbes's turn from reason to Scripture in *Leviathan* is in need of interpretation. And the most straightforward interpretation is cast into doubt by the fact that Hobbes, as we will see in the next chapter, begins Part III of *Leviathan* by making some radical arguments regarding the basis of the authority of Scripture. Hobbes proves to be at least as concerned in Part III to reveal the problems with establishing the authority of Scripture as he is to resolve them. Nonetheless, that does not mean that there is no serious meaning to his indication that the limits of natural theology dictate a turn to Scripture. For that indication can be taken as confirmation that Hobbes's natural theology, that is, his critique of natural theology, is a mere part of a broader critique of religion—and necessarily so, since it cannot stand alone.

Hobbes's natural theology cannot stand alone because it does not decisively settle the most important question to which it points. Even if we take Hobbes's natural theology together with the other major line of argument regarding religion that we have seen in the first half of *Leviathan*—Hobbes's account of the psychological sources of religion—we still have not seen a decisive critique of religion. If Hobbes's natural theology does not enable him to deny the possible existence of a creator God, the earlier account of the seeds of religion has the limitation that belongs to any such psychological account: an argument of that sort can never do more than offer a plausible natural explanation of experiences and convictions whose supernatural sources cannot be ruled out. And that is to say nothing of a question that we will take up later, once we have considered Hobbes's complete critique of religion: whether it is in fact plausible to explain religion in terms of anxiety and ignorance alone, and to dismiss claims of divine inspiration as a form of madness. As for whether Hobbes himself regarded his critique of religion, in any of its parts or in all of them together, as decisive, that, too, is a question that should be left open for now. It is to his credit that Hobbes all but explicitly acknowledges the limits of his critique of natural theology, and it is hard to believe that he could have regarded a psychological explanation of religion as a decisive refutation of the position he opposed. But we still need to consider his confrontation with Scripture in the second half of *Leviathan* before trying to take stock of the results of his critique of religion.

5

Religion and Theology III:
Hobbes's Confrontation with the Bible

It is sometimes argued by scholars who regard Hobbes as a pious Christian that the sheer number of pages of *Leviathan* devoted to religious and theological matters, especially to the interpretation of the Bible, is sufficient testimony to the sincerity of Hobbes's professions of faith. Why would "a notoriously arrogant thinker, vehement in his dislike of 'insignificant' speech," have "written and afterwards defended sixteen chapters of what he held to be nonsense, and exposed them to the scrutiny of a public which did not consider this kind of thing nonsense at all"?[1] In an influential essay devoted mostly to the neglected second half of *Leviathan*, J. G. A. Pocock posed this question as a challenge to all who doubt Hobbes's "sincerity of conviction." He was echoing Willis Glover, who found his own argument about Hobbes's sincerity so compelling that he was moved to declare at its completion that "the legend of Hobbes the atheist is doomed except as a historical curiosity." Glover put the challenge in this way: "In view of the fact that Hobbes devoted more than a third of his political writings to discussion of religion and wrote several polemical books to combat the charge of atheism and show himself, not only a theist, but a sound Anglican Christian, it is incumbent on any who think he did not mean what he said to provide some principle of interpretation that will show what he did mean or at least to explain why he should write insincerely at such length."[2]

---

1. Pocock, "Time, History and Eschatology in the Thought of Thomas Hobbes," 162; see also 167–68.

2. Glover, "God and Thomas Hobbes," 294, 279. See also Gillespie, *The Theological Origins of Modernity*, 247; Warner, "Hobbes's Interpretation of the Doctrine of the Trinity," 299–313; Sutherland, "God and Religion in *Leviathan*," 373–80; Lloyd, *Ideals as Interests in Hobbes's Leviathan*, 17–18.

This much must be granted to Pocock and Glover: Hobbes did indeed devote quite a few pages, especially in the second half of *Leviathan*, to religious
and theological matters, and he does offer an extensive interpretation of the
Bible there. It should also be granted, given the heterodoxy of much of his interpretation of the Bible and the angry reactions it predictably provoked, that
Hobbes's intentions cannot plausibly be reduced merely to the desire to avoid
persecution.[3] But there are reasons beyond a desire to avoid persecution that
a man with a complicated political project, to say nothing of a simple concern
to defend the truth of his own principles, might write extensively about the
Bible. The alternative to regarding everything Hobbes wrote as sincere is not
to conclude that he wrote pages upon pages of intentional "nonsense." It is
imaginable that a writer of Hobbes's ingenuity might advance important aims
and even make serious arguments without necessarily expressing himself in
the most straightforward manner.

But what, then, are Hobbes's aims in those parts of *Leviathan* in which he
most directly confronts and interprets the Bible—that is, above all in Part III,
but also in Part IV? Despite Glover's injunction, it is best not to postulate
"some principle of interpretation" at the outset, but to allow the answer to un-
fold gradually. For the answer is likely to be complicated, and Pocock is right
to insist that, in approaching these parts of *Leviathan* in particular, one ought
to begin "not by making prior assumptions about Hobbes's beliefs when he
wrote them, but by paying attention to what he actually wrote."[4] Yet, precisely
if we follow that advice more strictly than Pocock himself does, our doubts
that Hobbes's intentions are as simple and pious as Pocock and Glover suppose
will be aroused from the very beginning—by the way Hobbes opens Part III
of *Leviathan*. Let us take a close look at how Hobbes sets the stage for this
part of the work.

Hobbes begins Chapter 32 of *Leviathan*, the opening chapter of Part III,
"Of a Christian Commonwealth," by indicating not only that he intends to
turn at this key juncture from the question of the nature and rights of sovereign power as such to the nature and rights of a Christian commonwealth,
but also that this transition requires that he place his argument on a new
foundation. Because the nature and rights of a Christian commonwealth is a
matter "whereof there dependeth much upon supernatural revelations of the
will of God," he says, "the ground of my discourse must be, not only the natu-

3. Glover, "God and Thomas Hobbes," 280; see also Lloyd, *Ideals as Interests in Hobbes's
Leviathan*, 17–18; McClure, "Hell and Anxiety in Hobbes's *Leviathan*," 18–19.

4. Pocock, "Time, History and Eschatology in the Thought of Thomas Hobbes," 162.

ral word of God, but also the prophetical" (32.1). Hobbes declares, in other words, that he will now take his bearings by Scripture. And yet his very next word is "nevertheless":

> Nevertheless, we are not to renounce our senses and experience, nor (that which is the undoubted word of God) our natural reason. For they are the talents which he [i.e., God] hath put into our hands to negotiate till the coming again of our blessed Savior, and therefore not to be folded up in the napkin of an implicit faith, but employed in the purchase of justice, peace, and true religion. For though there be many things in God's word above reason—that is to say, which cannot by natural reason be either demonstrated or confuted—yet there is nothing contrary to it; but when it seemeth so, the fault is either in our unskillful interpretation or erroneous ratiocination. (32.2)

Several things are striking in this crucial statement that prepares the way for the interpretation of the Bible that will follow in Part III. First is Hobbes's remark, offered merely as an aside, that natural reason is "the undoubted word of God." (What, then, is the questionable or "doubted" word of God? Must it not be Scripture itself?) Second is Hobbes's rather free and imaginative use of Jesus' parable of the talents to try to establish a foothold in Scripture for the use of natural reason in its interpretation.[5] But most important is the principle that Hobbes expresses at the end, a principle that will shape his entire approach to the interpretation of Scripture: by claiming that there is nothing in Scripture contrary to reason, Hobbes grants himself license to undertake a more "skillful" interpretation of Scripture whenever it "seemeth" that Scripture and reason diverge.

Hobbes's path here at the outset of Part III continues to weave. He follows the statement just quoted with a declaration that appears at first sight to move in a different direction, and thus leaves one at least momentarily puzzled about the character and extent of the use he intends to make, and to urge others to make, of natural reason:

> Therefore, when anything therein written [i.e., in Scripture] is too hard for our examination, we are bidden to captivate our understanding to the words, and not to labour in sifting out a philosophical truth by logic, of such mysteries as are not comprehensible, nor fall under any rule of natural science. For it is with the mysteries of our religion as with wholesome pills for the sick, which, swallowed whole, have the virtue to cure, but chewed, are for the most part cast up again without effect. (32.3)

---

5. Compare Matthew 25:14–30; Luke 19:12–27. The version in Luke explains the meaning of the "napkin of an implicit faith" to which Hobbes refers.

The first impression conveyed by this statement is that there is a limit—a rather strict limit—that Hobbes intends to respect when it comes to any potential conflict between what is written in Scripture and what can be comprehended by natural reason: "we are bidden to captivate our understanding to the words." But *by whom* are we bidden, and in what sense? It is not so clear that we are bidden by Hobbes himself, at least not in the most obvious sense. Doubts arise not only from the irreverent metaphor that Hobbes chooses to describe how one might "swallow whole" the "pills for the sick" that are "the mysteries of our religion." (As Basil Willey nicely puts it, "A man in love with mystery would not, one feels, have used the image which Hobbes employs in this connection.")[6] A more decisive reason not to take Hobbes's statement in the most straightforward way emerges as he goes on to explain what it means to "captivate our understanding": "But by the captivity of our understanding is not meant a submission of the intellectual faculty to the opinion of any other man, but of the will to obedience, where obedience is due" (32.4). As long as one's internal questioning does not lead to acts of disobedience, Hobbes proves to have no objection to "chewing the pills." In fact, according to what he says next, we could not truly submit our "intellectual faculty" even if we tried: "For sense, memory, understanding, reason, and opinion are not in our power to change, but always and necessarily such as the things we see, hear, and consider suggest to us, and therefore are not effects of our will, but our will of them" (32.4). We are not simply free, Hobbes suggests, to believe or not to believe, to accept or not to accept various "opinions," by acts of our own undetermined will (with 32.4 see 26.41, 40.2; *De Cive* 4.24; *EW* IV, 339; *Obj.*, no. 13). Thus it would seem to make a big difference what exactly we "see, hear, and consider," and if Hobbes should go on to raise troubling questions about some of "the pills," he must expect that at least some of his readers will be unable to avoid some "chewing"—perhaps even enough that the pills will be "cast up again without effect." Should this happen, such readers ought not to be blamed for what might otherwise be regarded as sinful doubts, because Hobbes provides them with a preemptive defense: it is not within one's power to change that which dictates the will rather than being dictated by it.

That Hobbes does indeed intend to provoke quite a bit of questioning or "chewing" is confirmed by the course of his argument in the remainder of this opening chapter. For Hobbes turns to the matter of God's speech to men, and, as if the remarks we have just considered were not provocative enough, he lays out a set of challenging questions and considerations concerning proph-

---

6. *The Seventeenth Century Background*, 121. See also Hobbes's use of the same image in *De Cive* 18.5. Compare *Hist. Eccles.*, lines 617–28, 1091–94.

ecy. He introduces what may be called the problem of prophecy. In introducing this problem, Hobbes does not deny that God sometimes speaks to men, both immediately and through the mediation of other men who act as prophets. But he presents two difficulties for consideration by those to whom God has not spoken directly when they are confronted by the claims of others who say that he has. First is the difficulty of understanding the means or mode of God's communication with men. Can those to whom God has not spoken directly understand *how* he has communicated with those with whom he purportedly has? While God's communication may be understood "well enough" (Latin *Lev.*: *fortè*, perhaps) by a man to whom God has spoken, "how the same should be understood by another is hard, if not impossible, to know" (32.5). And then there is the further difficulty—the deeper one—of whether the experience of the self-proclaimed prophet is a genuine experience that has been correctly interpreted by him. For while a man may claim that God has spoken to him in a dream or vision, Hobbes reminds his readers of his earlier analysis of dreams and visions: especially when a man is in the grips of intense passions and deluded opinions—full of "self-conceit, and foolish arrogance, and false opinion of a man's own godliness, or other virtue, by which he thinks he hath merited the favour of extraordinary revelation"—he may well mistake a mere dream for a vision or believe that he had a vision when in fact he merely failed to realize that he had fallen asleep (32.6; see pp. 90–91, 94–95 above). And not only may a man easily delude himself in this way, but he may lie, as Hobbes also reminds his readers (32.6). Are there not examples even in the Bible itself of false and deceptive prophets?[7] "How, then," Hobbes asks, "can he to whom God hath never revealed his will immediately (saving by the way of natural reason) know when he is to obey or not to obey his word, delivered by him that says he is a prophet?" (32.7).

By raising the problem of prophecy, Hobbes calls into question, from the very the beginning of Part III of *Leviathan*, the basis on which Scripture is or is not to be accepted as the genuine word of God. For what is Scripture itself but the report of God's word as it has been passed down in a line that goes back to men who claimed to be prophets? Now, Hobbes does suggest that an answer to the challenge he poses regarding prophecy can be given "out of Scripture." Scripture indicates that there are "two marks" by which, "together, not asunder," a true prophet may be known: the performance of miracles and

---

7. Hobbes points here to the story of Micaiah and the four hundred false prophets in 1 Kings 22 and to the deception of one prophet by another in 1 Kings 13, as well as to Moses' warning about false prophets in Deuteronomy 13:1–5 and Jesus' warning about false Christs at Matthew 24:24.

"the not teaching any other religion than that which is already established"
(32.7). We will have to take up later the question of whether this test of true
prophecy is sufficient in Hobbes's view, or whether his appeal to it is not part
of his fuller articulation of the problem of prophecy. For Hobbes will return
to consider at much greater length the problem of prophecy and the closely
connected problem of miracles. We should not try to dig, however, straight to
what will prove to be the deepest stratum of Hobbes's confrontation with the
Bible. It is better to begin by taking a broader look at his interpretation of the
Bible to see what headway we can make on the question of his guiding intentions. Since we are entering a realm of Hobbes's thought that is too often neglected or treated in a cursory way—despite its undeniable prominence in his
greatest work—we must be patient in exploring its different aspects and pondering their various connections to Hobbes's project as a whole.

Hobbes's Interpretation of the Bible

Few scholars of Hobbes, even among those who regard him as a sincere
Christian, would deny that his interpretation of the Bible is highly idiosyn-
cratic and unorthodox.[8] How could one reasonably deny that when Hobbes
acknowledges it himself? In the Appendix to the Latin *Leviathan*, as he is reflecting on his earlier efforts to use the freedom prevailing when he wrote the
English *Leviathan* to defend the rights of the sovereign as vigorously as possible, Hobbes acknowledges that he got himself into hot water for an interpre-

---

8. Even Glover, for instance, who regards Hobbes as a sincere Anglican, writes of Hobbes's
unconventional "minority positions" (see "God and Thomas Hobbes," 280, 294). Hood, who
holds the same view of Hobbes's fundamental convictions as Glover does, grants that many of
Hobbes's specific doctrines are "odd" and even declares his overall view of Christian politics
"unacceptable" (see *The Divine Politics of Thomas Hobbes*, 3, 24). Similar is Lloyd's acknowledgment that "the religious view Hobbes develops in the second half of *Leviathan* is extremely unorthodox and inflammatory" (*Ideals as Interests in Hobbes's Leviathan*, 17; see also 112). Although
Lessay, for his part, refuses to pronounce on Hobbes's sincerity, he calls attention to the radicalism of several of Hobbes's doctrines, especially his view of the Trinity, and declares that "[t]he
author of *Leviathan* was indeed difficult to situate in the constellation of Protestant creeds"
("Hobbes's Protestantism," 286; see also 283–85; "Hobbes's Covenant Theology and Its Political
Implications," 260–64). The closest to an exception is Martinich, who argues with the fewest
qualifications for Hobbes's orthodoxy. But even Martinich speaks of Hobbes's "reinterpretation"
of the Bible over against "the standard interpretations that either conflict with modern science
or are used to destabilize existing governments" (*The Two Gods of Leviathan*, 216). On the question of the orthodoxy, or lack thereof, of Hobbes's interpretation of the Bible, see also Malcolm,
Leviathan, Vol. 1: Introduction, 179–80; Gillespie, *The Theological Origins of Modernity*, 246–53;
Collins, *The Allegiance of Thomas Hobbes*, 31–32.

tation of Scripture that "fell into unusual doctrines, which have been accused of heresy and atheism by a great many theologians" (1227; see also 1125). This result can hardly have taken Hobbes by surprise, since he predicted it in the Epistle Dedicatory of the English *Leviathan*: "That which perhaps may most offend are certain texts of Holy Scripture, alleged by me to other purpose than ordinarily they use to be by others." But when Hobbes acknowledges the "unusual" character of much of his interpretation of the Bible, what exactly does he have in mind?

It may be helpful, especially since the second half of *Leviathan* is less familiar to many people than the first, to give an overview of some of the most striking and radical features of Hobbes's interpretation of the Bible or what may be called his "revealed theology."[9] According to Hobbes, the Bible does not teach that there are incorporeal spirits, despite the fact that God himself is often described as if he were one (34.1–5).[10] There are angels in the Bible, but they are either mere supernatural apparitions that arise in men's brains or corporeal substances (34.16–24). There are no devils, corporeal or incorporeal (38.12, 45.4–7), and the soul, which is mortal by its nature, cannot exist apart from the body (38.4, 44.14, 44.23). By the "kingdom of God," Scripture does not refer to a heavenly realm to which the souls of the redeemed will ascend after death or to the universal spiritual community of the Church (35.1–2, 38.3–4). Rather, the kingdom of God refers either to God's rule by consent over the Israelites, which ended when God was deposed through the election of Saul (35.2–9), or to the future kingdom that will be established upon Christ's second coming (35.11–13). Jesus, whom God used as a representative in the same way he used Moses (41.7–9, 42.3), did not establish a kingdom, spiritual or otherwise, while he was on earth (35.11–13, 41.3–6, 42.128). There is, then, no present kingdom of God, although there will be one in the

9. For this term, see Strauss, "On the Basis of Hobbes's Political Philosophy," 185; Oakeshott, "Introduction," lxii.

10. In this instance and in the rest that follow in this paragraph, I give only one, or in some cases two or three, references to passages in which Hobbes makes the claim in question. The passages I cite are usually not the only ones that could be cited, but I did not want to burden the paragraph with many long lists of passages. I have therefore limited myself to the clearest or most decisive passages. All of my references are to the English *Leviathan*, although there are plenty of corroborating passages in other works. It is true that Hobbes excised a few of his most inflammatory statements from the Latin *Leviathan*—for example, his suggestion that Jesus represented God in the same way Moses did (see 41.9, 42.3)—but such retractions were more likely the result of caution, or a reconsideration of whether he should express himself so openly, than a genuine change in his views. See pp. 87–88 above on the relationship between the English and the Latin texts on religious questions.

future—*on earth*. What is promised for the elect upon Christ's second coming is a new life on earth, in which they will live forever in spiritual bodies and thus will not eat, drink, or procreate (38.1–5, 38.17–24, 44.27–29). The reprobates, who will enjoy such bodily pleasures in their second lives, will suffer the penalty of a second death, from which they will never again be resurrected (38.14, 44.27–29), but they will not burn in hell for eternity, because, although the fire of hell—which is not a literal fire—may be eternal, no one is tormented for eternity (38.6–14, 44.26–29). All that is necessary to avoid even the punishment of a second death and annihilation, that is, all that is necessary for salvation, is belief in Jesus' claim that he is the Christ, in the sense of the king promised by the Old Testament prophecies, and obedience to the laws (43.3–5, 43.11–19). Obedience to the laws, however, means obedience to the laws established by *the civil sovereign*, for any apparent law in Scripture is binding as law only if it is made so by a civil sovereign who, as sovereign, is the authoritative interpreter of Scripture: there is no such thing in Scripture as divine law, as opposed to mere advice, without this validation by the civil sovereign (26.40–41, 42.36–47, 42.96, 43.5, 43.22). Therefore, one should obey the commands of the sovereign in all instances, even in the extreme case in which the sovereign commands one to deny Christ. One may obey even that command, because only the original disciples of Jesus were obligated to martyr themselves in Jesus' name (42.11–14, 43.23); for all others, there is no obligation to martyrdom, just as there is no basis in Scripture for any human being to claim spiritual authority over and against temporal authority (39.4–5, 42.124–28). In keeping with the primacy of temporal authority, there is no "Church" in the sense of a separate spiritual community whose leaders exercise a rightful authority that is not derived from the civil power: the commonwealth and the Church, in a well regulated Christian state, are one and the same thing, and the civil sovereign is the chief pastor (39.4–5, 42.79–80).

It is not too hard to see why Hobbes provoked the ire of so many theologians with this interpretation of the teachings of the Bible. Even if some of his doctrines overlap in certain ways with positions taken by various strands of radical Protestantism in the seventeenth century, Hobbes's revealed theology, by the unprecedented extremes to which it pushed specific claims, as well as by the shocking character of the whole, brought him under intense criticism as beyond the pale of acceptable opinion. That he was willing to pay that price only underscores the question—which would arise in any case—of what led him to such a strange interpretation of the Bible. To be sure, in presenting his interpretation, Hobbes claims that he is simply bowing to the true meaning of the biblical text and articulating its genuine teachings over against the misinterpretations of Scripture that have arisen through a long theological tradition (see, e.g., 32.9, 34.1, 43.24, 44.3–4). It would be a mistake to dismiss out of hand his claim to be recovering what the Bible, faithfully and carefully read, really teaches. Yet it is hard to ignore the fact—and to avoid pondering its implications—that the Bible's teachings as Hobbes interprets them harmonize remarkably well with his own philosophic and political principles. His interpretation, in fact, seems to be very nearly exactly the "interpretation" one might develop if one's primary concern were to remove any possible tension between the teachings of the Bible and Hobbes's own doctrines. And this remarkable coincidence has led many scholars to suggest that that was precisely Hobbes's guiding concern. It has often been suggested that the best way of making sense of Hobbes's revealed theology is to look to its political intentions: Hobbes was seeking to bring the teachings of the Bible into accordance with doctrines that, by this point of *Leviathan*, he had already established on the basis of natural reason.[11]

Of course, the harmony between his interpretation of the Bible and his own political teaching, while it is certainly suggestive, is not in and of itself decisive proof regarding Hobbes's intentions. Without insisting, then, that the coincidence in question proves that Hobbes was guided by concerns other than a good faith effort to bring out the genuine meaning of the biblical text, and without conceding, in the other direction, that the common political explanation is the last and deepest word on Hobbes's intentions, let us consider the character of the coincidence. How does Hobbes's interpretation of the Bible bring it into accordance with his own principles?

To answer this question, it makes sense to start from the basic political problems that Hobbes thought were caused by the traditional interpretations of the text. It is a telling fact in its own right that Hobbes repeatedly points to these problems in the course of his analysis of the Bible, sometimes even as a way of introducing or concluding his own examination of specific biblical doctrines—for example, when he takes up the meaning of eternal life and eternal torments in Chapter 38 of *Leviathan* (see 38.1, 38.5), the meaning of a Church in Chapter 39 (see 39.5), or the question of what is necessary for salvation in Chapter 43 (see 43.1–2, 43.22–23). In these passages, and other

11. Different versions of this suggestion can be found, for instance, in Johnston, *The Rhetoric of Leviathan*, 164–77, 181–83; Curley, "Hobbes and the Cause of Religious Toleration," 313–14; Cooke, *Hobbes and Christianity*, 203–38; Collins, *The Allegiance of Thomas Hobbes*, 31–32; Beiner, "Machiavelli, Hobbes, and Rousseau on Civil Religion," 624–31; Lessay, "Hobbes's Protestantism," 286–91, "Hobbes's Covenant Theology and Its Political Implications," 262–65; Sherlock, "The Theology of *Leviathan*," 47–58; Farneti, "Hobbes on Salvation," 298–302; Milner, "Hobbes on Religion," 408–10; Malcolm, *Aspects of Hobbes*, 40; Parkin, *Taming the Leviathan*, 92–93. See even Pocock, "Time, History and Eschatology in the Thought of Thomas Hobbes," 187–92, 201.

similar ones (see, e.g., 29.15, 36.20, 42.25, 42.67, 44.2–8; cf. *De Cive* 6.11, 17.27, 18.1, 18.14; *Elem.* 25.1), Hobbes identifies two chief problems that the misinterpretation of Scripture can pose to peace and civic stability. The first is the propagation of doctrines so complex and demanding that they inevitably give rise to disputes among those who try to understand and adhere to them. The second problem—and the more serious one, judging by the greater emphasis it receives—is that the traditional interpretations teach men to believe that they have more to hope and fear for from their obedience or disobedience to spiritual authorities than they do from their obedience or disobedience to temporal authorities. If men's allegiance is divided, if they believe that they ought to serve two masters and that one of these masters can determine the eternal fate of their souls, the commonwealth has contracted a disease that will eventually destroy it (see especially *Lev.* 29.15; *De Cive* 6.11).

Hobbes cannot deny that men ought to serve God and follow God's word (see, e.g., *Lev.* 37.1, 43.1). But he can take steps to minimize—in the best case, to eliminate—the possibility of conflict between spiritual authority and temporal authority. Consider, for example, his teaching on the requirements for salvation. By reducing the requirements for salvation to two simple demands that everyone can readily understand—belief that Jesus is the Christ and obedience to the laws—Hobbes draws his readers away from a long-contested battleground of doctrinal dispute and makes it unnecessary for them to turn to spiritual authorities whose guidance might conflict with the laws established by the civil sovereign. The requirements for salvation, Hobbes claims, are easy to fulfill (*Lev.* 43.14; see also *De Cive* 18.8). One need not trouble oneself with abstruse matters of doctrine or accept numerous articles of faith. A single article is sufficient, and, as Hobbes reminds his readers, "more than sufficient is not necessary" (43.15; see also *Beh.*, 55).[12] In his teaching about the kingdom of God, Hobbes removes another potential challenge to the supremacy of civil authority. According to his interpretation of the Bible's teaching on the kingdom of God, we live between the two epochs in which the kingdom of God may rightly be regarded as a literal kingdom; we live in the gap, so to speak, between the once active but now defunct kingdom in which God himself ruled over the Israelites and the yet to be established kingdom over which Jesus will rule upon his return. In the interim, that is, in our present situation, there is no kingdom of God to which claimants of spiritual authority can point as the source of an authority that flows from

---

12. On the political advantages of Hobbes's minimalist doctrine of salvation, see Farneti, "Hobbes on Salvation," 298–302; Lessay, "Hobbes's Protestantism," 290–91; Curley, "Religion and Morality in Hobbes," 109–10; Vaughan, *Behemoth Teaches Leviathan*, 67–71.

a higher source and thus supersedes the authority of the civil sovereign. In sum, because there is no present kingdom of God, there can be no legitimate challenge to the supreme authority that Hobbes claims for the civil sovereign in his own political philosophy. Only the civil sovereign represents a literal kingdom, and only his declarations have the binding force of genuine law.[13]

Still, the would-be spiritual authorities might claim in response that, even if the present Church is not the kingdom of God or its direct representative, the kingdom of God retains its meaning as the heaven to which the souls of the redeemed will be transported after death, and they hold the keys to that realm. From here, we can grasp the advantages of Hobbes's highly unusual eschatology. What is to be gained, from Hobbes's perspective, by convincing people that the Bible teaches that after the general resurrection the redeemed will continue to live on earth, and that the damned will merely die a second death rather than burning in hell for all eternity? The attractions of the latter claim are perhaps more obvious: by denying the reality of eternal torments, Hobbes takes the most terrifying threat away from those theologians and clergymen who have used it to exert their power over believers (see *Lev.* 38.5–6, 44.14–16, 44.26–30).[14] But there is also an advantage in bringing heaven, as it were, down to earth. For that doctrine, too, works against the belief that there is a higher realm or another dimension of reality that transcends the one in which the civil sovereign holds sway. Hobbes's strange eschatology not only is consistent with his radically Erastian politics; it reaffirms—and gives purported biblical approval to—his materialism. These two points ultimately work together, for there is a connection, as we saw earlier, between the metaphysical—or, better, the denial of the metaphysical—and the political: if there is no realm beyond the world of matter in motion, if there is no "spiritual" dimension of reality beyond the bodies moving in time, then there is no font of a separate and higher form of authority (compare p. 37 above).[15]

---

13. Regarding Hobbes's treatment of the kingdom of God in the Bible, and its compatibility with his own political teaching, see Lessay, "Hobbes's Protestantism," 286–88, "Hobbes's Covenant Theology and Its Political Implications," 262–65; Sherlock, "The Theology of *Leviathan*," 47–51; Milner, "Hobbes on Religion," 407–10; Schwartz, "Hobbes and the Two Kingdoms of God," 9–10, 23–24; Beiner, "Machiavelli, Hobbes, and Rousseau on Civil Religion," 624–31.

14. See Sherlock, "The Theology of *Leviathan*," 54–57; Johnston, *The Rhetoric of Leviathan*, 147, 181–82; Tuck, "The Civil Religion of Thomas Hobbes," 130–32.

15. Although Pocock reaches very different conclusions than I do regarding Hobbes's sincerity and ultimate convictions, I have found helpful his treatment of the connection between the metaphysical positions expressed in Hobbes's eschatology and Hobbes's ecclesiastical-political argument "directed against new presbyter as well as old priest, and against new saint as well as old scholastic—against anyone, that is, who may claim that the process of salvation authorizes

Hobbes goes quite far in reinterpreting the Bible such that it supports rather than contradicts his materialism: it is not only in his claim that salvation will entail eternal bodily life on earth, but also in his interpretation of the biblical teachings on spirits, angels, and the soul, that he insists that the Bible rejects the very notion of incorporeal substances. The Bible—the Hobbesian Bible, at any rate—stands with Hobbes in all aspects, even the metaphysical aspects, of his multifront struggle against the claimants of "ghostly" authority.

Hobbes's Critique of the Bible

But does the Bible really stand with Hobbes? Did he really think that it does, or even want all of his readers to think that it does? There is a problem with leaving matters at the common suggestion that Hobbes interprets the Bible so that its teachings conform to his own doctrines established on the basis of natural reason. The most important difficulty with that suggestion is not that it implies that Hobbes was willing to play fast and loose with the Bible to interpret it according to purposes that are more political than pious. That difficulty recedes as Part III of *Leviathan* progresses and it becomes harder and harder to ignore the signs of Hobbes's intentional manipulation of the biblical text for political ends. The serious difficulty lies in a different direction, and it emerges as one ponders the question of whether Hobbes really had to interpret the Bible in *such* a radical and inflammatory way to accomplish his political purposes.[16] This difficulty comes into clearer view, moreover, the more one considers the "evidence" that Hobbes marshals ostensibly to show that the Bible teaches what he says it does. For the more closely one examines Hobbes's "evidence" for his novel interpretations of various biblical doctrines, the flimsier that evidence seems, and the less plausible it becomes, not only

---

his civil actions or power in the present" (see "Time, History, and Eschatology in the Thought of Thomas Hobbes," 174–87; the quoted statement comes at the end of the passage). It is puzzling, however, that Pocock argues that "neither the use of apocalyptic in *Leviathan*, nor its mortalism and materialism, suffice to place Hobbes outside the mainstream of Protestant thinking" (180), even though he himself is led to call Hobbes's interpretation of Christ's messianism "almost brutally political" (173–74), and to speak of Hobbes's denial of "the reality of 'spirit' in the ordinary accepted sense of the term" as "ruthless" (182), "drastic" (188), and hard to square with "a satisfactory account of the Third Person of the Trinity" (188).

    16. See, e.g., Milner, "Hobbes on Religion," 416: "[Hobbes] would scarcely bother to pick so many theological quarrels if his deepest intention were to fashion a marriage of convenience between sovereignty and religion." Johnston, *The Rhetoric of Leviathan*, 136–37, 183–84, makes the same point. See also Parkin, *Taming the Leviathan*, 93; Lloyd, *Ideals as Interests in Hobbes's Leviathan*, 17–18.

that Hobbes thought he was bringing out the genuine meaning of the biblical text, but also that his deepest intention was to offer a new "Hobbesian" reinterpretation of the Bible for political reasons.[17] It is in the details that Hobbes proves to be playing a kind of double game with the Bible or pursuing a strategy that works on two levels at once. The Hobbesian reinterpretation of the Bible is only the surface level; beneath it is a deeper critique of the Bible.

Now, the suggestion that Hobbes pursues a two-pronged strategy of this sort could seem implausible for the obvious reason that there is a tension between the two aims it ascribes to Hobbes: the deeper critique requires that Hobbes indicate that the Bible does not genuinely support his own rational doctrines, and thus it would seem to undermine his efforts toward the more evident goal.[18] Yet, although there is some tension between Hobbes's two aims—although they do, to some extent, work at cross purposes—that tension is not so great as to make it impossible for him to pursue both at once. In fact, the two prongs of Hobbes's strategy can even work together. For under the guise—which is not merely a guise, but also not the whole story—of pursuing his more obvious aim, Hobbes puts himself in a position to cite chapter and verse from the Bible without having to acknowledge what he is really trying, on a deeper level, to indicate about the passages he cites. And it is in the very moments when his surface arguments are least plausible—that is, when he points to passages in the Bible that hardly support, on any straightforward reading of them, the views he claims they support—that Hobbes directs his most attentive readers to his deeper arguments. By letting the seams of his weaving show, in other words, he reminds some of his readers that a cloak has been woven, and, even as he leaves it in place to do its work, he indicates what lies underneath. If the cloak that Hobbes weaves is the contention that the teachings of the Bible are in complete accord with the principles arrived at by natural reason, what lies underneath, the deeper critique, is the indication of the many ways in which that contention is far from true.

Let me give several examples of this two-pronged strategy at work. I will focus on examples that reveal not merely the strategy itself but important aspects of the critique it serves.

The first example takes us back to an issue that arose earlier, when we considered Hobbes's treatment of madness and spiritual possession in Chapter 8

---

17. Compare Pangle, "A Critique of Hobbes's Critique of Biblical and Natural Religion in *Leviathan*," 28–29.

18. Glover, "God and Thomas Hobbes," 279–80, makes a version of this objection. But he regards it as more decisive than I think it is, for reasons that I will indicate in the rest of the present paragraph.

of *Leviathan* (see pp. 94–98 above). In Chapter 34, Hobbes takes up a similar but broader set of questions. Here he begins his account of the meanings of crucial words in the Bible with the terms "spirit," "angel," and "inspiration," and he uses his discussion of these terms to launch an attack to which the earlier skirmish in Chapter 8 proves to have been merely a prelude. In Chapter 34, Hobbes reaffirms his denial of spiritual possession, that is, of "inspiration" strictly understood, but he now goes much further: he denies the very existence of incorporeal spirits and contends that this denial reflects the true teaching of the Bible. He argues, in short, that the Bible is in complete agreement with a thoroughgoing materialism, an outlook that he now spells out more fully and radically than in any earlier part of the book. In fact, Hobbes comes close in Chapter 34 to arguing openly for the position of the Sadducees, that is, for that very denial of all spirits that he described in Chapter 8 as "very near direct atheism." Yet he argues, at the same time, that he is merely articulating the genuine teaching of the Bible.

How can he do this? The procedure of Hobbes's argument is complicated, but the complications themselves are revealing. Hobbes begins by announcing his intention to turn in Chapter 34 to the meanings of certain key words as they are used in Scripture. He will begin, he says, with the words "body" and "spirit," "which in the language of the Schools are termed *substances, corporeal* and *incorporeal*" (34.1). Although he leads one to expect that the chapter will be devoted entirely to the articulation of the meaning of these and related terms ("angel" and "inspiration") in Scripture, Hobbes immediately pivots and prefaces his turn to Scripture with a remarkable statement that takes its bearings, not from Scripture, but from natural reason, and that speaks, not to the meaning of both body and spirit, but to the question of body alone. For body, as he argues here, is all that there is in the universe. Hobbes inserts at this point—that is, *before turning to Scripture*—one of the two boldest statements of his materialistic vision of the universe in all of *Leviathan* (34.2; the other is 46.15).[19] According to this statement, the universe is corporeal through and through: "For the universe, being the aggregate of all bodies, there is no real part thereof that is not also *body*, nor anything properly a *body* that is not also part of (that aggregate of all *bodies*) the *universe*." From this position it would seem to follow—and this would seem to be the point of its inclusion here—that there are no such things as spirits, at least if by spirits one understands incorporeal substances. And Hobbes reminds his readers that "substance"

---

19. Compare Johnston, *The Rhetoric of Leviathan*, 145: "This opening argument belies Hobbes's claim that his interpretation is based upon Scriptural usage alone. The basis of his definitions is a strict, materialist metaphysics." See also Strauss, *Hobbes's Critique of Religion*, 63.

and "incorporeal" are "words which, when they are joined together, destroy one another" (34.2).

After presenting what he regards as the rational view of the matter, Hobbes then turns, *still not yet to Scripture*, but to the common view, which he indicates diverges from the scientific position that he has just sketched: "But in the sense of common people, not all the universe is called body, but only such parts thereof as they can discern by the sense of feeling to resist their force, or by the sense of their eyes to hinder them from a farther prospect" (34.3; see also 46.16). The common view, unlike the more thoroughly materialistic view that Hobbes presented first, leaves a place for the existence of incorporeal spirits understood as genuine substances and not mere fancies born of turbulence in the brain. When confronted with "those idols of the brain which represent bodies to us where they are not"—those "idols" that Hobbes himself dismisses as "nothing" ("nothing at all, I say, there where they seem to be")—the common view is not so debunking: "men that are otherwise employed than to search into their causes know not, of themselves, what to call them." Because they are ignorant of the nature and causes of such idols, ordinary men "may therefore easily be persuaded by those whose knowledge they much reverence, some to call them *bodies*, and think them made of air and compacted by a power supernatural (because the sight judges them corporeal), and some to call them *spirits* (because the sense of touch discerneth nothing, in the place where they appear, to resist their fingers)" (34.3; see also *Elem.* 11.4–6).

It is only in the wake of these remarks that Hobbes turns at last to Scripture and begins his argument that Scripture itself does not support the notion of spirits understood as incorporeal substances. Why did he delay that turn by setting the stage as he did? On the one hand, Hobbes's procedure in Chapter 34, which begins from the rational or scientific view before arguing for the conformity of Scripture to that view, provides an indication of how his strategy works on its more obvious level: he will interpret Scripture so as to make it conform to a view already reached on rational grounds. On the other hand, by going out of his way also to indicate the divide between the scientific and the common view of the matter—a step that is unnecessary for the more obvious purpose—Hobbes plants a question that opens up a deeper line of reflection. For if the scientific view is held only by those few who rigorously employ themselves in "the search into causes," if a thoroughgoing materialism, in other words, requires a process of inquiry that leads to a break with the common view, which of the two views is Scripture more likely to reflect? It may well be true, as Hobbes argues, that one cannot find in Scripture the term "incorporeal substance," a term that itself depends on a scientific development, albeit one of a very different sort from that which leads to Hobbesian materialism (see 34.24, 46.15–19; *Elem.* 11.5; Latin *Lev.*, 621, 1021, 1083–85; Appendix, 1175–87, 1229–31). But can one not find the notion of such substances in the way the Bible speaks of "spirits"?

Hobbes cannot deny, of course, that the Bible, in keeping with the common view, speaks often of spirits. The most he can do is to argue that nowhere in the Bible does the word "spirit" carry the meaning of a real substance without a body. But how convincing is that argument? Let us consider a few of the passages to which Hobbes points. In the second verse of the Bible, for instance, it is said, "the Spirit of God moved upon the face of the waters" (Gen. 1:2). Hobbes responds: "Here if by the *Spirit of God* be meant God himself, then is *motion* attributed to God, and consequently *place*, which are intelligible only of bodies, and not of substances incorporeal; and so the place is above our understanding, that can conceive nothing moved that changes not place or that has not dimension" (34.5). Does Hobbes not suggest here that the Bible presents God himself as an incorporeal spirit who nevertheless acts in ways that only a body could? Is this inconsistency or incoherence not why "the place is above our understanding"? Or consider the example of 1 Samuel 11:6, where it is said, "The Spirit of God came upon Saul, and his anger was kindled greatly." Hobbes replies that by "the Spirit of God," "it is not probable was meant a Ghost, but an extraordinary *zeal* to punish the cruelty of the Ammonites" (34.7). But is Hobbes's reading really more "probable" than the usual and more straightforward interpretation of the passage, according to which "the Spirit of God" means much more than Saul's own zeal? A more important example is Luke 4:1, where Jesus himself is said to be "full of the Holy Ghost" (see 34.15). Is that, too, to be taken, as Hobbes contends, for a mere "*zeal* to do the work for which he was sent by God the Father," and not as referring to a real ghost? It may be true, as Hobbes suggests, that there is a difficulty in understanding the Holy Ghost in this instance as a ghost: "to interpret it of a ghost is to say that God himself (for so our Saviour was) was filled with God, which is very improper and unsignificant" (34.14). Yet, not only does the Bible speak of it as a ghost, but Jesus himself draws a distinction between himself (and thus by implication his own zeal) and the Holy Ghost in his famous warning at Matthew 12:32: "Whosoever speaketh a word against the Son of man, it shall be forgiven him; but whosoever speaketh against the Holy Ghost, it shall not be forgiven him, neither in this world, nor in the world to come" (see *Lev.* 44.32; cf. Mark 3:28–29).[20] If all but denying the existence of

---

20. Consider also *Lev.* 36.13, where Hobbes refers to Colossians 2:9 and acknowledges that, at least according to what Paul says there, the Holy Spirit ("the Godhead") "dwelleth bodily" in Christ. In the same passage, Hobbes argues that to claim that God spoke to Moses "by the Holy

something, reducing it to a mere metaphor for a psychological state, amounts to "speaking against" it, then Bramhall was right to warn Hobbes that he had run dangerously afoul of Jesus' warning.[21] But Hobbes is compelled to deny the existence of the Holy Ghost as an incorporeal substance if he is going to argue that ghosts are nothing but "the imaginary inhabitants of man's brain" and—however implausibly—that the Bible does not teach otherwise.[22]

Hobbes cannot go quite as far with angels as he does with ghosts. Angels would seem to be the clearest instances of spirits that are presented in the Bible, not as mere metaphors, but as real beings. Although the bounds of even remote plausibility thus keep Hobbes from mounting the same argument about angels as he did about ghosts, he nevertheless argues that the angels in the Old Testament are not to be understood as real substances or "things permanent" but merely as images that arise supernaturally in the imaginations of men. Hobbes grants and even stresses that there are many angels in the Old Testament: "to mention all the places of the Old Testament where the name of angel is found would be too long" (34.23). He also indicates that the common or vulgar view among both the Jews and the gentiles in the ancient world was that angels are real beings independent of men's imaginations (see 34.15, 34.18). Nevertheless, he argues that nothing in the Old Testament requires or even supports that belief: the Sadducees were right to deny that angels are real beings, and, even if the Sadducees were the only ones who held that view, they have the Bible on their side (see 34.18; see again 8.25; compare Latin *Lev.*, Appendix, 1167, 1235). Yet this argument is despite such passages—to which Hobbes also calls his readers' attention—as Genesis 19, where two angels, who seem every bit real beings, arrive in Sodom to stay with Lot and test the

---

Spirit," understood merely as "the graces and gifts of the Holy Spirit," is objectionable because it is "to attribute nothing to him supernatural." See also 36.15.

21. See *The Catching of Leviathan*, 529–31.

22. That Bramhall's indignation at Hobbes's treatment of the Holy Ghost was not without warrant is further indicated by the irreverent "interpretation" Hobbes will go on to give of Jesus' warning that blasphemy against the Holy Ghost will never be forgiven: Jesus, according to Hobbes, was merely making a prediction or offering a prophecy about "the severity of the pastors after him against those which should deny their authority, which was from the Holy Ghost." "[It is] as if [Jesus] should say, you that deny my power, nay, you that shall crucify me, shall be pardoned by me, as often as you turn unto me by repentance; but if you deny the power of them that teach you hereafter by virtue of the Holy Ghost, they shall be inexorable, and shall not forgive you, but persecute you in this world, and leave you without absolution (though you turn to me, unless you turn also to them), to the punishments (as much as lies in them) of the world to come. And so the words may be taken as a prophecy or prediction concerning the times, as they have long been in the Christian Church" (*Lev.* 44.32).

city, and the Book of Daniel, where the angels Gabriel and Michael are even given proper names (see 34.20, 34.23).[23]

If Hobbes indicates by pointing to such examples that his denial that angels are ever presented as real substances in the Old Testament is highly dubious, he does not even attempt to repeat that denial in the case of the New Testament. He indicates that he would if he could. He remarks that, on the basis of his reading of the Old Testament and his own reflections on "the nature of dreams and visions that happen to men by the ordinary way of nature," he found himself "inclined to this opinion, that angels were nothing but supernatural apparitions of the fancy, raised by the special and extraordinary operation of God" (34.24). The difficulty, however, is that there is simply too much evidence in the New Testament on the other side: "But *the many places of the New Testament, and our Saviour's own words* . . . have extorted from my feeble reason an acknowledgment and belief that there be also angels substantial and permanent" (34.24, emphasis added). The New Testament, even more than the Old, abounds with angels, good and evil, who travel from heaven to earth, and can even be sent to hell (see 34.23). Hobbes thus retreats to the position that, although the angels of the New Testament are substantial and permanent, they are not incorporeal. That much, he argues, "cannot by Scripture be evinced" (34.24). Yet, whatever one may think of that questionable claim,[24] the damage of Hobbes's deeper argument has already been done. For the key point conveyed by Hobbes's treatment of angels is that a spiritualism that was already on full display in the Old Testament is even more rampant and extreme in the New Testament.

If this conclusion, in one sense, merely reflects the unsurprising fact that the Bible shares the common or vulgar view of spirits—and not the scientific view, which would deny them altogether[25]—the conclusion is important be-

---

23. See also, among the other passages to which Hobbes points, Genesis 16:7–12, 22:11–18 (*Lev.* 34.21); Exodus 14:19–20, 33:2–14 (*Lev.* 34.22). Compare Ross, *Leviathan Drawn out with a Hook*, 38–39.

24. Consider Luke 24:39 (*Lev.* 45.5), 20:34–36 (*Lev.* 44.29); Matthew 22:30 (*Lev.* 34.23); Ephesians 6:12 (*Lev.* 44.1); 2 Peter 2:9–12. Compare *De Corpore* 1.8, where Hobbes drops the fiction that angels are corporeal substances and grants that they are held to be "neither bodies nor properties of bodies." If he disagreed with that view—at least in the direction of regarding angels as genuine corporeal substances—he could not use the view, as he does in *De Corpore* 1.8, as grounds for excluding angels from philosophic investigation.

25. See again *De Corp.* 1.8. As mentioned in the preceding note, Hobbes here treats angels as incorporeal substances, but for that reason he excludes them, and all other such things, from philosophic investigation. (The full meaning of the passage can best be seen by taking it together with *Lev.* 34.2 and 46.15.)

cause it indicates that the Bible is far from affirming Hobbes's own rational materialism. And more than that: Hobbes indicates that the Bible is one of the primary sources of resistance or opposition to a rational materialism. For not only does the Bible reflect the common view of spirits, which is not consistently materialistic, but it emerged from an ancient world in which that view was even more dominated by an irrational spiritualism than in Hobbes's own time. By giving the endorsement of purported revelation to such an outlook, moreover, the Bible makes it harder for later ages to move beyond it and toward the scientific view. On one level, Hobbes's argument—rather obviously—is an effort to promote that movement by enlisting a radically reinterpreted Bible in its cause. But, on the deeper level, by showing just how radical the "reinterpretation" must be, it provides an indication of why the task is so difficult and where the most serious obstacles lie.

Before turning to the most important and complicated example of Hobbes's two-pronged strategy at work, let us consider another fairly simple one: his doctrine of hell. Hobbes's doctrine of hell is a critical part of his unusual eschatology, according to which all rewards and punishments after the general resurrection will be meted out on earth. Hobbes's central claim about hell is that it is not a place of eternal punishments, and not even a separate place at all. Hobbes denies that the reprobates will live eternally, and so he denies that they can suffer eternally (see *Lev.* 38.14, 44.14–15, 44.27–29). "Hell fire" and other ways of describing the suffering of the wicked in the New Testament (e.g., "weeping and gnashing of teeth") are merely metaphorical expressions for the grief the wicked will feel at the sight of others enjoying the eternal happiness they have forsaken through their disbelief and disobedience (38.11–14). In addition to their "grief and discontent of mind," the reprobates will suffer bodily pains in their second lives, in which they will be in the same state Adam and his posterity were in after the Fall; but they will be released from all of their pains, psychological and physical, by their second deaths. The phrase "second death," according to Hobbes, refers not to a state of continual existence and suffering, but to the final annihilation of the reprobates (38.14, 44.14–15, 44.27–29; cf. Rev. 20:10–14, 21:8). The second lives of the reprobates, then, do not differ all that much from the first lives of all men, if one were to assume that our lives are followed by nothing other than annihilation.[26]

26. See Bramhall's indignant remark: "It is to be presumed that in those their second lives, knowing certainly from T. H. that there is no hope of redemption for them from corporal death upon their well-doing, nor fear of any torments after death for their ill-doing, they will pass their times here as pleasantly as they can. This is all the damnation which T. H. fancieth" (*The*

Hobbes's doctrine of hell can be understood, as I suggested earlier, as part of his effort to weaken the threats that the self-proclaimed spiritual authorities can use to frighten people into obedience to their authority (see p. 137 above). But how seriously should it be taken as an interpretation of the biblical text? Consider the following remarkable passage, in which Hobbes begins by granting that there are some passages in the New Testament—many, in fact—that cut against his claim about the mortality of the souls of the wicked and his account of hell:

> But there be other places of the New Testament where an immortality seemeth to be directly attributed to the wicked. For it is evident that they shall rise to judgment. And it is said besides, in many places, that they shall go into *everlasting fire, everlasting torments, everlasting punishments, and that the worm of conscience never dieth*; and all this is comprehended in the word *everlasting death*, which is ordinarily interpreted *everlasting life in torments*. And yet I can find nowhere that any man shall live in torments everlastingly. Also, it seemeth hard[27] to say that God, who is the father of mercies, that doth in heaven and earth all that he will, that hath the hearts of men in his disposing, that worketh in men both to do and to will, and without whose free gift a man hath neither inclination to good nor repentance of evil, should punish men's transgressions without any end of time, and with all extremity of torture that men can imagine and more. We are therefore to consider what the meaning is of *everlasting fire* and other the like phrases of Scripture. (44.26)

Hobbes accomplishes several things at once with this statement and others like it (compare, e.g., *Lev.* 38.1, 38.14). First and most simply, he calls attention to the fact that the Bible *does speak* in "many places" of eternal punishments.[28] Second, he indicates that there is nevertheless a hatch through which one can escape from what would seem to be the obvious meaning of such passages: it is never said in so many words that any individual man will be punished eternally, and so it is possible to claim that the torments themselves are eternal but not the suffering of individual sinners.[29] Hobbes makes extensive use of this interpretive escape hatch (see 38.14, 44.27–29; Latin *Lev.*, Appendix,

---

Catching of Leviathan, 538–39). See also the objections of Ross, *Leviathan Drawn out with a Hook*, 67–68, 72–74, and Hyde, *A Brief View and Survey*, 221, 224–27. For a more detailed account of Hobbes's doctrine of hell, see McClure, "Hell and Anxiety in Hobbes's *Leviathan*," 4–7.

27. Latin *Lev.*: "too hard" (*nimis durum*).

28. Among the places Hobbes has in mind are passages such as these: Matthew 8:12 (*Lev.* 38.14), 10:28 (*Lev.* 44.15), 25:41 (*Lev.* 34.23; see also *EW* IV, 352); Mark 9:44, 9:46, 9:48 (*Lev.* 38.14); Revelation 21:8 (*Lev.* 38.8).

29. Consider, however, Isaiah 66:24; Mark 9:43–48; Revelation 20:10. See Sherlock, "The Theology of *Leviathan*," 56, on Hobbes's "curious piece of scriptural exegesis."

1161–63). Third and most important, however, in his explanation of why one would wish to take the biblical passages on eternal torments in a way other than what would seem to be their straightforward meaning, he points to a difficulty with the biblical teaching as it appears on the surface of the text, and therefore as it is "ordinarily interpreted." The difficulty is not just that the (apparent) biblical teaching on hell is very harsh. The real sting of Hobbes's statement lies in his indication of what that teaching implies about the biblical God. For God, as he is presented in the Bible, has power enough to keep men from sinning, and yet he punishes some men's transgressions with unending torments. Is not a God who punishes human beings so severely for actions he could easily prevent—nay, for actions of which he, who "hath the hearts of all men in his disposing," is even the truest cause—more like a cruel tyrant than "the father of mercies" he is said to be?

What is Hobbes's response to this problem? "We are therefore," he says, "to consider what the meaning is of *everlasting fire* and other the like phrases of Scripture."[30] This is an instance of Hobbes letting the seams of the garment show even as he is weaving it. For he allows us to see that his "interpretation" is guided not by an unbiased reading of the Bible—which, again, speaks repeatedly of eternal torments—but by the desire to find a pretext in the text to read away the massive surface message so as to mitigate its severity. By revealing what he is doing, and by indicating how creatively he must mine and twist the biblical text to make its message humane and reasonable, Hobbes leaves some of his readers to chew on the pill that is the difficulty of comprehending the justice of an omnipotent God who punishes men eternally for sins that he allows or even compels them to commit.[31]

---

30. Latin *Lev.*: "Let us therefore consider what else can be meant by eternal fire" (*Videamus ergo, per ignem aeternum quid aliud significari possit*).

31. The passage just considered should be compared with other passages in which Hobbes suggests that God's omnipotence means that he is the cause of sin. These passages, most of which are from Hobbes's dispute with Bramhall over free will, are listed in note 3 to Chapter 4 above. See, in particular, Hobbes, *EW* V, 100, where Bramhall, with his sharp eye for the heretical implications of Hobbes's positions, accuses Hobbes of imputing a cruel tyranny to God for punishing men despite "the infiniteness of his power and the absoluteness of his dominion" (see also Bramhall, *The Catching of Leviathan*, 523, 581). Hobbes's reply to the charge that he imputes cruelty to God is hardly one that fully exonerates either himself or the biblical God: "And what cruelty can be greater than that which may be inferred from this opinion of the Bishop; that God doth torment eternally, and with the extremest degree of torment, all those men which have sinned, that is to say, all mankind from the creation to the end of the world which have not believed in Jesus Christ, whereof very few, in respect of the multitude of others, have so much as heard his name; and this, when faith in Christ is the gift of God himself, and the hearts of all men in his hands to frame them to the belief of whatsoever he will have them believe? He hath

Let us turn now to the most complicated but also the most revealing case in which Hobbes's "interpretation" of the Bible works on two levels at once. This is his account of the two meanings of the kingdom of God in the Bible. In his discussions of the kingdom of God—first as it appears in the Old Testament, and then as its meaning changes in the New Testament—Hobbes tells the story of what may be called "biblical politics."

The basic story, as Hobbes tells it, is straightforward and initially appears unproblematic, even if it requires an unorthodox reading of the Bible. It is an account that has already been touched on. Hobbes argues that by "the kingdom of God," the Bible means a literal kingdom on earth: such a kingdom once existed in the form of God's rule over the Israelites, which was rejected by the election of Saul, and it will exist again when Jesus establishes a new earthly kingdom upon his second coming. The most important implication of this account, as noted earlier, is that, by denying that there is a present kingdom of God, it removes a dangerous weapon from the arsenal of the would-be representatives of that kingdom who challenge the supremacy of the civil sovereigns in present commonwealths. There is thus a great political advantage, from Hobbes's point of view, in affirming that we live in the interim between the two kingdoms of God (see pp. 136–37 above). And Hobbes goes further in interpreting the politics of the Bible so as to make its teaching supportive of his own politics. He argues that even when there *was* a kingdom of God, the Old Testament properly read shows that it was based, as all sound commonwealths are, on a contract established by consent, and that authority was always united in the hands of the civil sovereigns (see, e.g., *Lev.* 35.2–5, 26.41; *De Cive* 16.3–10). Thus the politics of the Old Testament conform to the Hobbesian model. And so too, in a different way, do the politics of the New Testament. Upon his second coming, Jesus will establish an earthly commonwealth, which, like God's original rule over the Israelites, will conform to sound principles. During his first mission on earth, Jesus posed no threat to the supremacy of the civil authorities. Not only did Jesus, according to Hobbes, come not to command but only to teach, but his central political teaching was the salutary message that men should respect the authority of their established sovereigns: "Render unto Caesar" (see, e.g., *Lev.* 41.5, 42.6–10, 42.43, 20.16; *De Cive* 17.6–11). In these ways, then, both the Old Testament and the New Testament, as Hobbes interprets them, show the fundamental

---

no reason therefore, for his part, to tax any opinion, for ascribing to God either cruelty or injustice" (*EW* V, 214). See also *EW* V, 212–13; *De Cive* 4.9; *EW* IV, 354; *Elem.* 18.11. On the vehemence of Bramhall's hostility to Hobbes's suggestion that God is the cause of sin, see Jackson, *Hobbes, Bramhall and the Politics of Liberty and Necessity*, 115–16.

soundness and rationality of the politics of the Bible. But what does one find if one digs more deeply into the details of the story as Hobbes tells it?

The difficulty of reading the Bible such that the political story conforms to Hobbesian principles arises almost from the very beginning—with Abraham. Hobbes must, of course, begin his account of the kingdom of God in the Old Testament with Abraham, because it was Abraham with whom God first established his covenant with his chosen people. In Hobbes's telling of the story, God's covenant with Abraham was a contract, a contract "between God and Abraham, by which Abraham obligeth himself and his posterity, in a peculiar manner, to be subject to God's positive law . . . as by an oath of allegiance" (*Lev.* 35.4; see also 40.1–2). Now, by telling the story such that it is no longer a tale of God announcing to Abraham his intention to establish a covenant, but becomes one of two parties mutually consenting to a contract (compare *Lev.* 35.1, 40.1–2 with *Gen.* 12:1–3, 17:1–19), Hobbes recasts the biblical account so that it conforms more closely to his own principles. In doing so, however, he also points to a question: How could those who followed Abraham—the members of his household and his "seed"—have been bound by the agreement reached between God and Abraham? The importance of this question is underscored by the fact (to which Hobbes calls his readers' attention) that the covenant between God and Abraham was formed through a series of dreams or visions in which God revealed himself to Abraham alone (*Lev.* 26.41, 40.1; see also *De Cive* 16.4). Hobbes argues that such experiences can obligate only the person who has them, not others, to whom they are merely reported (see *Lev.* 32.5, 36.19, 26.40–41). How, then, could Abraham pledge not just his own obedience but that of others, too? The answer—Hobbes's answer, at any rate—is that the members of Abraham's household were bound, not by their subjection to God himself or by direct participation in the contract, but by their prior obligation to Abraham as "their father, and lord, and civil sovereign" (40.2; see also 26.41; *De Cive* 16.6–7). But this answer raises a further difficulty, for, although Abraham was the head of a large household, he was not really a civil sovereign, and at the time of the covenant he was not yet even a father through Sarah. Of course, God solved the latter problem through the miraculous birth of Isaac. But that makes it all the more puzzling why he did not solve—at least not with any haste—the other problem. If God's intention was to create a great nation that would be a beacon and a blessing to the other nations of the world, why did he not make Abraham a civil sovereign ruling over a full-fledged nation living under God's law? Why did he choose to work through a man whom he himself had made a wanderer in foreign lands (see *Gen.* 12:1), and to whom he had no intention of giving full sovereignty over an independent nation? Indeed, why did God choose a path that he himself knew, at the time of the original covenant, would include four hundred years of bondage for his chosen people before the final realization of the promise of full nationhood (see Gen. 15:13)?

One possible response to these questions is that God wanted his chosen people to appreciate the depth of their need for him and to be steeled for the difficult task of rising to become a kingdom of priests and a holy nation (see Exod. 19:3–6). By this frequently offered explanation, the early struggles of the Israelites, even the long experience of slavery in Egypt, provided a necessary preparation for the formation of a unique nation ruled by God and dedicated to his service. Hobbes does not altogether disagree with this view. Whatever may have been the case with God's intentions in his view, Hobbes agrees that the Israelites emerged from Egypt transformed by the experience of bondage. As he puts it in *De Cive*, the people who found themselves in the desert near Mount Sinai were "not only very free, but also extremely hostile to subjection to human beings because of their memory of their recent servitude in Egypt" (*De Cive* 16.8; see also 16.9, 17.7; *Lev.* 40.6). In Hobbes's account, however, this appears less as an essential stage in God's plan than as one of the two massive challenges facing Moses as he set out to secure his rule. The other was that Moses had no claim by inheritance to govern the Israelites as a successor in the line of Abraham, and for this reason, among others, there was opposition to his ascension (*Lev.* 40.6–7; see also *De Cive* 16.9, 16.13; *Elem.* 26.2). Hobbes presents Moses' rise to power as a renewal of the covenant, but in the sense of a new beginning, a new and more decisive founding of something that could for the first time properly be called a kingdom (*Lev.* 33.20, 35.13, 40.5, 40.7, 42.37; see also *De Cive* 16.9). And Hobbes's Moses, like Machiavelli's, responded to the challenges with which he was confronted with *virtù*, at least in the Machiavellian sense of the term.[32] Hobbes calls attention to the severity with which Moses dealt with his rivals (see *Lev.* 40.7; *De Cive* 16.13, 17.10; *Elem.* 26.2),[33] and he underscores Moses' insistence that he alone had a special direct line of communication with God (*Lev.* 40.6–7, 42.37; *De Cive* 16.13). Hobbes acknowledges that Abraham believed—whether rightly or wrongly, nevertheless sincerely—that the voice he heard was God's and that he had experienced genuine revelations (see *De Cive* 16.4). In the case of Moses, that

32. Compare Machiavelli, *The Prince*, Chap. 6, *Discourses on Livy* II.8.2, III.30.1.

33. Hobbes points to examples such as Moses' reaction to the making and worship of the golden calf (Exod. 32), the outcome of Aaron and Miriam's objections to Moses' marriage to an Ethiopian (Num. 12), and the fate of the rebellion led by Korah, Dathan, and Abiram (Num. 16). Aubrey, *Aubrey's Brief Lives*, 159 remarks of Hobbes: "I have heard him inveigh much against the cruelty of Moses for putting so many thousands to the sword for bowing to the golden calf." See also, *Lev.*, Review and Conclusion, 10–11.

is harder to say (consider *Lev.* 40.7–8; *De Cive* 16.13). But this much is clear: because he was dealing with a people who were so hostile to human rule, and because his claim to authority was so tenuous and contested, Moses secured his power in the only way he could, by claiming that he was no more, but also no less, than God's spokesman (see *Lev.* 40.7; *De Cive* 16.13; *Elem.* 26.2–3, 26.7). That claim—not in itself, but because it was believed by the Israelites (consider *Lev.* 40.6, 42.37; *De Cive* 11.1, 16.9)—allowed him to establish his sovereignty in matters both civil and religious (*Lev.* 40.7; *De Cive* 16.13). But it also put a permanent stamp on the order that Moses established.

After Moses' death, sovereignty over the kingdom passed to the high priests, first to Aaron's son Eleazar. Although Moses had managed to maintain his own supremacy over Aaron himself, the first high priest, Moses' claim that he was merely doing God's bidding contributed to the Israelites' belief that the new order was to be a sacerdotal kingdom. Thus, even as Joshua was given charge of the army, his claim to authority was at least officially subordinated to Eleazar's (see *Lev.* 40.9, 35.5–7; *De Cive* 16.14).[34] After Joshua's death, moreover, the situation, at least regarding the locus of sovereignty *de jure*, became less ambiguous: the high priest, according to Hobbes, held the sovereignty for the entire period from Joshua's death to the election of Saul (*Lev.* 40.9–10; *De Cive* 16.15). But Hobbes indicates that the rule of the high priests was hardly rule worthy of the name. The problems pointed to in *Leviathan* are spelled out more fully in *De Cive* (compare *Lev.* 40.9–10, 49.12 with *De Cive* 16.15). There, Hobbes says that, although supreme civil power belonged *by right* to the high priest, "that power *in fact* was in the prophets, who were raised up by God in extraordinary ways" (*De Cive* 16.15, emphasis added). The Israelites, by Hobbes's account, submitted to the prophets not only because they were "a nation ardent for prophets"—that is, because they had a "high esteem for prophecy," which had already shown itself in their willingness

---

34. In *Leviathan* 40.9, Hobbes quotes from Numbers 27:21, where God says of Joshua, "He shall stand before Eleazar the priest, who shall ask counsel for him before the Lord; at his word shall they go out, and at his word they shall come in, both he and all the children of Israel with him." In the Latin *Leviathan*, Hobbes quotes the fuller passage (Num. 27:18–21) of which this statement of God is a part (see Latin *Lev.*, 749). Hobbes's interpretation of this passage from Numbers is not beyond challenge. Spinoza, *Theological-Political Treatise* 17.10, for instance, argues that Numbers 27:21 indicates that authority was divided between Eleazar and Joshua, and that the post-Mosaic order was a kind of mixed regime in which no one had supreme authority (see also 17.11–15). See also Calvin, *Institutes* 4.20.8; Thomas Aquinas, *Summa Theologica*, I-II, Q. 105.1; Hyde, *A Brief View and Survey*, 340–41; Pangle, "The Hebrew Bible's Challenge to Political Philosophy," 79. The novelty of Hobbes's interpretation of Numbers 27 is noted by Sommerville, *Thomas Hobbes: Political Ideas in Historical Context*, 118.

to follow Moses only because they believed he spoke for God—but also because they needed protection and arbitration. In the sacerdotal kingdom that emerged after the deaths of Moses and Joshua, the high priests were unable to preserve law and order; theirs was a kingdom "without strength, even if it was not without right" (*De Cive* 16.15). Hobbes describes this post-Mosaic period in which the high priests were nominally in charge but frequently pushed aside by prophets and judges as a period of anarchy: during this period, "*there was no sovereign power* in Israel"—at least if one judges power by its "act and exercise" (*Lev.* 40.10; see also 40.12; *De Cive* 11.4). Although the absence of a clear sovereign exercising firm authority made this period very different from Moses' own reign, the chaos that emerged after Moses' death, rooted as it was in the belief in God's demand for a sacerdotal kingdom and the zeal with which the Israelites turned to prophets, can be traced to Moses' founding influence. Hobbes might excuse Moses because he dealt in the only way he could with the difficulty of ruling a people "extremely hostile" to human rule; but Moses nevertheless planted the tree of theocracy that bore such bitter fruit.[35]

Only with a grasp of his view of the deepest sources of the "civil troubles, divisions, and calamities" (*Lev.* 40.12) that beset God's kingdom after Moses can we appreciate Hobbes's quiet but discernible sympathy with one of the most controversial actions in the Bible: the demand of the elders of Israel, in Chapter 8 of 1 Samuel, for a king "like all the nations." Judging by the frequency with which Hobbes cites it and the key role it plays in his narrative of the politics of the Bible, 1 Samuel 8 seems to have been Hobbes's favorite chapter of the Bible.[36] He treats the moment described in that chapter, the

---

35. In my view, it is not widely enough recognized, even by scholars who regard Hobbes as a critic of traditional biblical religion, that Hobbes wanted to reveal the problems of the kingdom of God as it functioned in the period between Moses and Saul. See, for example, the analysis of Johnston, who, although a perceptive reader of Parts III and IV of *Leviathan*, focuses too exclusively on Hobbes's surface argument that sovereignty over civil and religious affairs was never divided during this period (*The Rhetoric of Leviathan*, 168–69, 193–94). Closer to my own analysis is Schwartz, "Hobbes and the Two Kingdoms of God," 11–18. Schwartz provides the fullest discussion of Hobbes's account of the problems during this period; but see also the brief remarks of Strauss, "On the Basis of Hobbes's Political Philosophy," 188; Beiner, "Machiavelli, Hobbes, and Rousseau on Civil Religion," 625–28; Garsten, "Religion and Representation in Hobbes" 531–32; Pangle, "A Critique of Hobbes's Critique of Biblical and Natural Religion in *Leviathan*," 40. For an account similar to Hobbes's, compare Spinoza, *Theological-Political Treatise* 17.26–30.

36. Hobbes cites or alludes to I Samuel 8, by my count, fourteen times in *Leviathan* alone: 12.30, 20.16, 29.13, 33.20, 35.8–10, 36.13, 38.4, 40.11, 40.13, 42.31, 42.62, 42.88, 42.118, 44.4. Hobbes also mentions the election of Saul, the eventual outcome of the Israelites' demand, at 35.11, 35.13, 40.9, 41.4, 42.135, 44.17.

demand for a king, not just as a first step toward a new and more sensible form of government, but as a rejection of theocracy as such, that is, a casting off of God's rule that brought an end to the kingdom of God through the revocation of the Israelites' consent (see *Lev.* 36.13, 40.11, 42.88, 44.4). It is true that Hobbes sometimes portrays the demand of the Israelites as an act of rebellion (see, e.g., 12.30, 29.13, 35.10, 33.20, 40.11, 42.88); but in other passages—and sometimes even in the same ones—he underscores God's consent to their demand and portrays the demand itself as wholly understandable (see, e.g., 12.30, 40.11, 40.13, 20.16; *De Cive* 16.16).[37] Especially when it is considered in the context of Hobbes's account of the flawed and contested rule of the high priests, prophets, and judges—only the last manifestation of which was the corruption of the sons of Samuel—the Israelites' demand for a king appears as a reasonable attempt to find a desperately needed solution to a terrible problem.

The solution, however, was incomplete. In fact, it was not much of a solution at all. For the turn to the rule of the kings, beginning with the election of Saul, did not really reflect a deep and abiding change of heart among the Israelites. Although they accepted the rule of the kings and the subordination of the priests it entailed (see *Lev.* 40.11, 36.13; *De Cive* 16.16), the Israelites imposed limits on the kings. They would not allow them "to change the religion which they thought was recommended to them by Moses," and, as a result, "they always kept in store a pretext, either of justice or religion, to discharge themselves of their obedience, whensoever they had hope to prevail" (*Lev.* 40.13; see also *De Cive* 16.16). When they wanted to challenge the authority of their kings, moreover, the Israelites turned where they had always turned: "generally, through the whole history of the kings, as well of Judah as of Israel, there were prophets that always controlled the kings, for transgressing the religion, and sometimes also for errors of state" (*Lev.* 40.13).[38] Thus, Hobbes

37. Compare Pocock, "Time, History and Eschatology in the Thought of Thomas Hobbes," 171: "Innumerable were the emphases which could be selected in interpreting this event [sc., the election of Saul], and Hobbes's treatment can be seen as it were suspended between two of them: emphasis that it constituted a 'rejection' and 'deposition' of God from his direct kingship over Israel, and insistence that this nevertheless occurred with his permission and consent, so that the authority of the kings was not merely natural, but had his express and positive sanction." See also Milner, "Hobbes on Religion," 408; Lessay, "Hobbes's Covenant Theology and Its Political Implications," 249; Beiner, "Machiavelli, Hobbes, and Rousseau on Civil Religion," 626.

38. "Controlled" in this statement carries the sense, as Malcolm notes, of "challenged" or "found fault with." (Compare the Latin version: *criminati sunt*.) The dynamic of prophets "controlling" the kings set in quickly, as Hobbes indicates in 40.13 by pointing to the example of Samuel's rebuke of Saul and his anointment of David after Saul "observed not his counsel in destroying Agag as God had commanded" (see 1 Sam. 15–16). Hobbes also gives the examples of Jehu's rebuke of Jehoshaphat (2 Chron. 19:2) and Isaiah's of Hezekiah (2 Kings 20:14–19). See

concludes, "though the power both of state and religion were in the kings, yet none of them were uncontrolled in the use of it but such as were gracious for their own natural abilities or felicities" (*Lev.* 40.13). Of course, the Israelites were not lucky enough always to have such "gracious" kings, and thus authority, especially over religious matters, was frequently contested and resided in different hands at different times (*Lev.* 40.13, 42.40; *De Cive* 16.16). From here we can understand why the period that began with the kingship of Saul and the promise of a new beginning ended with the ruin of the nation and another period of captivity, during which "the Jews had no commonwealth at all" (*Lev.* 40.14, 40.12, 42.40; *De Cive* 16.16–17).[39]

Throughout his account of the main stages of the political history of the Old Testament, Hobbes preserves the façade that his main purpose is to demonstrate that sovereignty *by right* was always united in the hands of a single sovereign, even as he indicates the more important point that *in actual practice* that was far from the case. The still deeper point is that the problems that emerged in practice—the divisions, chaos, and weakness—were rooted in the Israelites' abiding addiction to prophecy and their commitment to theocracy. Regarding the period after the Captivity, Hobbes's account is brief. When the Jews returned from Babylon, they were, once again, in no mood to submit to ordinary human rule: "though they renewed their covenant with God, yet there was no promise made of obedience, neither to Esdras nor to any other" (*Lev.* 40.14; see also *De Cive* 16.17). And when they later came under Greek domination, "their religion became much corrupted," and they were in such dire straits that "nothing can be gathered from their confusion, both in state and religion, concerning the supremacy in either" (*Lev.* 40.14; see also *De Cive* 16.17). The most important development of the Captivity and the postexilic period—more important even than the partial restoration of the rule of priests (*De Cive* 16.17) and the infiltration of pagan demonology into the religion of the Jews (*Lev.* 40.14, 42.88)—was the intensification of the hope for a Messiah who would at last save the Jews from their troubles (*Lev.* 40.14; *De Cive* 17.1).

The title of Chapter 41 of *Leviathan* is "Of the Office of our Blessed Saviour." By placing his discussion of Jesus' "office" immediately after his account of

---

also *Beh.*, 49, where Hobbes speaks of the prophets "that vehemently from time to time preached against the idolatrous Kings of Israel and Judah"; compare Spinoza, *Theological-Political Treatise* 17.20, 17.29. On Samuel's rebuke of Saul, see Hobbes, *EW* IV, 331; see also François du Verdus' letter to Hobbes of 1 January 1657 (*Correspondence*, Letter 108).

39. See also Latin *Lev.*, 755, especially the added *quae Israelitarum Gentem tandem everterunt* (which in the end destroyed the nation of the Israelites).

the political history of the Old Testament, Hobbes urges his readers to consider Jesus' venture in light of that history, and to bear in mind the problems that remained unsolved at the time of his first coming. There may also be a certain irony, not to say a blasphemous joke, in the title of this chapter, since Hobbes goes on to indicate that Jesus' first coming hardly brought an immediate solution to those problems. From a certain perspective—which would seem to be Hobbes's own perspective—the transition described in Chapter 41 looks less like a resolution of a terrible difficulty than it does a leap from the frying pan into the fire. But to see what Hobbes wants to indicate about Jesus' "office" and about the character and effects of his attempt to fulfill it, we need to consider the details of Hobbes's account. The surface message is by now familiar: Jesus came not to command or legislate but only to teach; he posed no threat to the established authorities, since he consistently urged his followers to obey them in all things; and because his kingdom will be established only upon his second coming, he established nothing that can rightly pose a challenge to civil or temporal authority. But what do the details indicate?

The original meaning of "Messiah," as Hobbes repeatedly emphasizes, was a *king*—a king who would restore the kingdom of God in the sense of God's rule over his chosen nation. The Old Testament prophecies vary in their description of the figure who would arise, but the dominant picture—and hence the prevalent expectation among the Jews—was of a man of strength who would restore, perfect, and expand the weakened and trouble-ridden nation of the Jews (see *De Cive* 17.1–2; *Lev.* 35.10, 35.13, 38.16–23, 41.5, 41.7, 42.88; *Elem.* 25.6–7).[40] Jesus, Hobbes suggests, thought of himself as the Messiah in this original sense. In his own eyes, Jesus, as Hobbes puts it, "was the Messiah, that is, the Christ, that is, the anointed priest and the sovereign prophet of God; that is to say, he was to have all the power that was in Moses the prophet, in the high priests that succeeded Moses, and in the kings that succeeded the priests" (*Lev.* 41.3; see also 16.12, 33.20, 43.11–13; *De Cive* 17.3, 18.5–6; *Elem.* 25.7). Of course, Hobbes is well aware that such a statement about Jesus' claim to be the Messiah can be taken as referring only to the power that Jesus will possess upon his second coming. Hobbes's primary rhetorical intentions dictate that he himself interpret Jesus' claim in that way, or at least that he urge such an interpretation on his readers (see *Lev.* 41.3; *De Cive* 17.5). By suggesting that interpretation, however, Hobbes also puts himself in a position to pose the question: "If then Christ, whilst he was on earth, had no kingdom

40. Among the many passages to which Hobbes points are Isaiah 11:1–5, 11:11–16; Daniel 7:13–14; and Zechariah 9:9.

in this world, to what end was his first coming?" (*Lev.* 41.4). To that question, Hobbes gives this reply:

> [The end] was to restore unto God, by a new covenant, the kingdom which, being his by the old covenant, had been cast off by the rebellion of the Israelites in the election of Saul. Which to do, he was to preach unto them that he was the *Messiah*, that is, the king promised to them by the prophets; and to offer himself in sacrifice for the sins of them that should by faith submit themselves thereto; and in case the nation generally should refuse him, to call to his obedience such as should believe in him amongst the Gentiles. So that there are two parts of our Saviour's office during his abode upon the earth: one to proclaim himself the Christ; and another, by teaching, and by working miracles, to persuade and prepare men to live so as to be worthy of the immortality believers were to enjoy at such time as he should come in majesty to take possession of his Father's kingdom. (*Lev.* 41.4)

Hobbes suggests here that the first—in the sense of the primary or original—purpose of Jesus' first coming was to restore the kingdom of God that had been "cast off" by the election of Saul. It was this political problem, more than the original sin of Adam (compare *Lev.* 35.11 with 43.11 and *EW* IV, 354), that, by Hobbes's account, Jesus sought to rectify by preaching to his fellow Jews that "he was the *Messiah*, that is, the king promised to them by the prophets" (with *Lev.* 41.4, see also *De Cive* 18.3; *Elem.* 25.7).[41]

If Jesus did seek to become a king even in his first coming, that attempt of course failed. But Hobbes suggests that Jesus was prepared for that eventuality: "in case the nation generally should refuse him," he would then "call to his obedience such as should believe in him among the Gentiles." Now, whether or not Jesus had all along such a twofold intention—a primary plan and, so to speak, a backup plan—is not the key question for understanding Hobbes's suggestion. The better way of thinking about Hobbes's account is as a commentary on the origins of Christianity.[42] For Hobbes suggests that Christianity rose from the ruins of a failed political movement, the original goal of which was to establish Jesus, the self-proclaimed Messiah in the original Jewish sense, as king over a nation whose greatness was in desperate need of restoration. That this political goal is what Jesus intended is shown, Hobbes suggests, by Jesus' imitation of Moses in the way he conducted himself and arranged his followers (see *Lev.* 41.7–8; *De Cive* 17.3; *Elem.* 26.4, 26.10).

---

41. On the "almost brutally political" character of Hobbes's "messianism," see Pocock, "Time, History and Eschatology in the Thought of Thomas Hobbes," 172–74.

42. Compare Strauss, "On the Basis of Hobbes's Political Philosophy," 188–89.

It is also how his disciples originally understood his mission: "they under-stood the Messiah to be no more than a temporal king, till after our Saviour's resurrection" (*Elem.* 25.7; see also *Lev.* 32.7, 43.12–13; *De Cive* 18.6–7). More important, Jesus' claim to be the Messiah in the original Jewish sense ex-plains, Hobbes indicates, why Jesus *did* at times claim an authority to issue commands, and why he *did* insist that his dictates were of a higher author-ity than the merely human dictates of the established authorities. What did Jesus intend, for instance, when he commanded his apostles to preach that "the kingdom of heaven is at hand," promised to punish those cities that re-jected his message, and told his apostles to "fear not those who kill the body, but cannot kill the soul" but rather to "fear him who can destroy both soul and body in Gehenna"?[43] Or what did Jesus imply when he told two of his disciples, as he was approaching Jerusalem, to go into a nearby village, un-tie an ass and a colt, and bring them to him, with the justification that "the Lord hath need of them"?[44] Hobbes is understandably reluctant to point too frequently to passages of the New Testament in which Jesus asserts a kingly authority, since doing so undermines his argument that Jesus came only to teach. But he must do so at least occasionally if he wants some of his readers to see the truth of the matter and to appreciate his deeper argument. Hobbes's deeper argument, to repeat, is that Jesus *did not* come only to teach and to prepare men for his second coming. Jesus had much more immediate ambi-tions, which posed a genuine threat to the established authorities, Jewish and Roman, and Christianity itself is best understood as an attempt to salvage a failed revolution by radically reinterpreting its character and aims. If some of the materials for that reinterpretation were provided by Jesus himself, who not only proclaimed himself the Messiah, but also, in executing the other part of his "office," worked miracles and taught men "to live so as to be worthy of the immortality believers were to enjoy," the full reinterpretation occurred after his death—as it had to, since a large part of that reinterpretation was a response to the challenge of making sense of Jesus' claim to be the Messiah after his life had culminated, not in his triumphant rule, but in his death at the hands of the civil authorities (consider *Lev.* 43.12; *De Cive* 17.14, 18.6–7).

If this is indeed Hobbes's account of the origins of Christianity—an ac-count that he wants, for competing reasons, to conceal and to reveal—what conclusions can be drawn from it? In keeping with his desire not to tell the full story too openly, Hobbes argues vigorously and frequently that insofar

---

43. Matthew 10:7–28, cited in *Lev.* 42.16, 42.84, 43.2, 43.13, 44.15; *De Cive* 17.25, 18.1; *Elem.* 25.7.
44. Matthew 21:2–3, cited in *Lev.* 20.16, 25.10; *De Cive* 11.6.

as Christianity came to pose a threat to civil authority by becoming a source of claims to spiritual authority, that development was a departure from the original message of Jesus himself (see, e.g., *Lev.* 41.5, 42.31, 44.1–3, 47.1–4, 47.33–34). But that argument, as he quietly indicates, is not entirely true. The truth of the matter is that Jesus himself and then, in a somewhat different way, the early Christians were involved in a movement within the Roman Empire that was of dubious legality and a threat to peace and stability (see *Lev.* 33.20, 35.11, 42.2–4, 42.12–19, 42.32, 42.57, 43.12–13; Lat. *Lev.*, Appendix, 1239; *De Cive* 17.24, 18.6–7; *Elem.* 25.4). It is also true, as Hobbes much more loudly proclaims, that the later Church, once it had risen to power in the Roman Empire and then retained its influence after the Empire's collapse, raised an especially problematic claim to spiritual authority that became the main source of the "darkness" that caused Christendom to be riven for so long by foreign and civil wars (*Lev.* 44.2–9, 47.1–4, 47.17–18, 47.21; see also *Beh.*, 4–12). But even this claim can be traced back to Jesus himself. For Jesus provided a model that was not in fact one of consistent deference to temporal authority, and he furnished the materials for the later dualism of powers by inspiring belief in miracles, appealing to spirits, and proclaiming a kingdom that is at once not of this world and yet extremely important in it. That Jesus' claim to be a divinely sent king was later transformed into the Church's assertion of spiritual authority, then, is not rightly seen simply as an abuse of his teaching.[45]

Hobbes's indication of the deepest roots of the political problems caused by biblical religion, both in its original Jewish form and then in its transformed Christian form, is a key part of his critique of the authentic teachings of the Bible, as opposed to his reinterpretation of them to bring them into accordance with reason. Again, the greater the need for the reinterpretation in each instance, the more severe the implicit critique. But the critique that emerges from his account of the politics of the Bible goes beyond politics in the narrow sense. This is the best place to sketch the outlines of Hobbes's critique of biblical morality, especially in its Christian form, for the character of that morality is due, Hobbes's account suggests, not only to the already strict demands

---

45. Kraynak, *History and Modernity in the Thought of Thomas Hobbes*, 45–46, argues that, unlike other modern philosophers who analyze the political effects of Christianity, such as Machiavelli, Rousseau, and Nietzsche, Hobbes "shows that the problem of Christian politics has little or nothing to do with the doctrines that are peculiar to Christianity . . . The distinctiveness of Hobbes's historical analysis, in other words, lies in deemphasizing the distinctiveness of Christian politics or, more generally, in treating opinions and doctrines as mere instruments of domination regardless of their content." Both my immediately preceding and my immediately following analysis should indicate why I disagree with this view.

put in place by Moses' theocratic legislation, but also to the circumstances in which Christianity arose.[46]

Christianity arose, by Hobbes's account, first as a movement coming from outside—that is, a movement *challenging*—an already established order, and then as an attempt, once the original movement had failed, to turn defeat into triumph by reinterpreting Jesus' message in an even more radical manner. By considering these circumstances, it is possible to understand the emergence of a moral teaching that proclaims that man's overriding concern should not be prudent action within the confines of ordinary political life, but preparation for an ultimate divine reckoning. Once again, Hobbes's serious argument—this time about the character of Christian morality—must be coaxed out from under his surface argument. His surface argument is that Christian morality, or the divine law of Scripture, is in full accord with the rational morality that he presents in his own doctrine of the laws of nature (see *De Cive* 4.1–24; *Elem.* 18.1–12; *Lev.* 14.5, 15.35, 43.5). To accept that argument as Hobbes's last word, however, one has to accept such incredible propositions as that Hobbes's revised version of the Golden Rule, "Do *not* that to another, which thou wouldst *not* have done to thyself," is essentially the same as the far more demanding original; that peace on earth and not salvation in heaven is the true end of Christian morality; and that "to be delighted in the imagination only of being possessed of another man's goods, servants, or wife, without any intention to take them from him by force or fraud, is no breach of the law, that sayth, *Thou shalt not covet*" (see *De Cive* 4.3, 4.12, 4.16, 4.23; *Elem.* 18.3, 18.6, 18.9; *Lev.* 15.35–36, 15.40–41; *Lev.* 27.1). By thinking about the differences that Hobbes points to by his conflation of the Christian teaching with his own—that is, by the implausibility of that conflation—we can begin to appreciate what Hobbes wants to indicate about Christian morality.[47]

Hobbes underscores, in the first place, the far greater demands that Christian morality places on its adherents than a rational morality would. Christianity teaches, for instance, that even the inward anger of a man against his brother, if it is without cause, is a sin tantamount to homicide and punishable by hellfire (see *Lev.* 44.37 and *De Cive* 4.10 with Matt. 5:22). By teaching that passions that lead men merely to imagine the enjoyment of certain pleasures

---

46. Compare Goethe, *Maximen und Reflexionen*, 376: "Die christliche Religion ist eine intentionierte politische Revolution, die, verfehlt, nachher moralisch geworden ist" (The Christian religion is an intended political revolution which, having failed, later became moral). I am indebted to Hannes Kerber for pointing me to this remark of Goethe.

47. The paragraph that follows should be compared with Pangle, "A Critique of Hobbes's Critique of Biblical and Natural Religion in *Leviathan*," 29–31; Curley, "Religion and Morality in Hobbes," 13–14; Strauss, "On the Basis of Hobbes's Political Philosophy," 187–88.

are sinful, Christian morality fights against human nature to such an extent as "to make sin of being a man"; as it is understood by its true proponents, it is "too severe" (*Lev.* 27.1; see again 44.37; compare 13.10; see also *Hist. Eccles.*, lines 1097–1110). Furthermore, by placing so much emphasis on the purity of men's intentions—by "accepting the will for the deed" (*Lev.* 43.4, 43.20; see also *Elem.* 18.10, 25.10; *De Cive* 4.21)—Christianity makes men ever fearful of a God who can look into their hearts, and desperate to satisfy his demands even as their natures render them unable to do so (see *Lev.* 46.37, 42.107; *De Cive* 4.21). It is true that Christianity teaches that men can make up for their moral failings, in their actions and even in their intentions, through their faith in Christ (see *Lev.* 25.10, 43.19–21; *De Cive* 17.9, 18.3, 18.10; *Elem.* 18.10). But that solution addresses one problem only by creating further ones. For not only is it a question whether it is reasonable to accept faith over works "as well in good as in evil men" (see *Lev.* 43.20–21), but Christianity demands that men have unquestioning faith in a proposition that, because it is not evidently true, reason necessarily leads those in whom it is active to doubt (see *Lev.* 32.4–5, 42.9; *De Cive* 17.28; *EW IV*, 339; *Elem.* 11.8–10; *Obj.*, no. 13). According to the very premises of Christianity itself, moreover, faith depends on divine grace, and thus it cannot be summoned by acts of one's own will (*Lev.* 26.41, 40.2, 43.9; *De Cive* 4.24, 17.13; *Elem.* 11.9). These dilemmas of faith understandably, if not reasonably, drive men to a fierce insistence on orthodoxy, both in themselves and in others (see *Lev.* 44.32, 46.37; *EW IV*, 340; *A Dialogue*, 126; consider also *De Hom.* 13.3; *Elem.*, 18.11; *Hist. Eccles.*, lines 1021–30). And because this insistence must fight against forces woven into the nature of men, including reason itself, one can understand why the God of the Old Testament, who was already extremely harsh, becomes even more threatening and punitive in the New Testament. One can also understand, from here, why men who live in zealous devotion to that God are not well suited to be sensible citizens of Hobbes's rational commonwealth, in which the demands of peace take precedence over the demands of piety.

Prophecy and Miracles

It hardly needs to be said that the critique I have just sketched is not the kind of critique that would be undertaken by a man who approached the Bible with reverence for it as the authentic word of God. If Hobbes's radical reinterpretation of the Bible to make it support his own teachings gives one reason to doubt that he regarded the Bible as divine revelation, that is all the more true of the critique of the Bible that runs beneath that surface. But does even the critique we have just considered lead us to the most important reasons why Hobbes did not accept the Bible as genuine revelation? Does it show the deepest grounds on which he thought the fundamental claim of the Bible could be rejected? It is true that the more one comes to the conclusion that the biblical teachings are at odds with the teachings of natural reason, the more likely one is to doubt the revealed character of the Bible. It is hard, in such a case, to avoid asking why an omnipotent and benevolent God would reveal a text full of irrational teachings and lead his followers down such rocky paths. But that problem carries only so much weight. For there remains the response that God's ways are mysterious and that what appears to natural reason as irrational or foolish may serve a hidden purpose, perhaps even the purpose of putting the faithful through a difficult trial before leading them to salvation. Given Hobbes's own teaching on how little can be known of God and his ways, it is unlikely that he thought that he could reject such a response with complete confidence.[48] At any rate, we have not yet considered the most radical level of Hobbes's confrontation with the Bible. Hobbes provides other reasons—perhaps weightier ones, but certainly reasons that go more to the root of the matter—for his refusal to accept the Bible as genuine revelation. These reasons come out, above all, in his chapters on prophecy and miracles when they are read with due attention to Hobbes's complex manner of writing.

These chapters, Chapters 35 and 36 of *Leviathan*, are best approached by way of a brief consideration of Hobbes's broader treatment of the question of the authority of Scripture. As Hobbes himself indicates, the question of the authority of Scripture can be posed in different ways, such that it asks about different things. The question may concern how it can be *known* that Scripture is the word of God, or it may ask why it is *believed* to be so (see *Lev.* 33.21, 43.7). If the question is put in yet a third way—Hobbes's preferred way—as what gives Scripture the binding status of law, Hobbes's answer is clear: only the established civil sovereign can make the precepts of Scripture legally binding (see *Lev.* 26.41, 42.36–48, 33.21–24, 43.5; *EW* IV, 369). In denying that the dictates of Scripture have the obligatory force of laws prior to their validation by the civil sovereign, Hobbes takes a heterodox position that would seem already to rest on his doubts about the revealed status of Scripture. This is especially so since Hobbes defends his position by arguing that it is precisely because it cannot be known whether purported revelation

---

48. Consider *Lev.* 45.8, where Hobbes raises a number of "curious" questions about Jesus' conduct in presenting his teaching and leading men to salvation—such as why he left some truths obscure and why he gave faith only to some and not to all—but then acknowledges that "nevertheless, there may be alleged probable and pious reasons."

is genuine revelation that men are not obligated to follow its dictates unless they are commanded to do so by the sovereign (*Lev.* 26.40–41, 33.21–24). Hobbes asks his readers to consider the situation—which is clearly his own situation and which he assumes is the situation of each of his readers—of someone who has not received direct revelation. Such a person cannot know, he argues, whether another person who claims to have received a revelation has interpreted his experience correctly and is reporting it honestly. For this reason, the person without direct revelation cannot be obligated by the claims of the purported prophet, for one can be obligated only when one has knowledge of the legitimacy of the authority to which one is asked to submit (*Lev.* 26.40–41 and 33.31–24; see also *Lev.* 32.6, 42.37, 43.1, 43.6; *EW* IV, 363–65; *EW* V, 179; *Beh.,* 46).

What follows from this situation, according to Hobbes? It follows that the civil sovereign, whose legitimate authority *is* known, can command us to adhere to his dictates—and not only to his own direct dictates, but even to the dictates of Scripture, which he can turn into binding laws. Yet there is a limit even here. Although the sovereign can command our obedience, he cannot command our belief: "to obey is one thing, to believe is another," and belief, as opposed to obedience, is not subject to the sovereign's control (*EW* IV, 339–40; see also *Lev.* 26.41, 32.4–5, 42.9, 42.43; *De Cive* 4.24). In Hobbes's view, then, *no one* can obligate men who have not received direct revelation to believe claims that others have—not purported prophets, because we cannot be assured of the truth of their claims, and not civil sovereigns, because they cannot command the uncommandable. Yet, even if we are not obligated to believe, *should* we believe, according to Hobbes? In the same context in which he makes the striking remark that "to obey is one thing, to believe is another," Hobbes declares, even more arrestingly, "Where there is no reason for our belief, there is no reason we should believe" (*EW* IV, 339). To gauge the bearing of this latter remark properly, it must be stressed that Hobbes acknowledges that men who accept Scripture as genuine revelation *do* have reasons for what they believe—at least reasons of a sort. Hobbes argues, in many places, that most men who believe do so "by hearing," that is, because they have repeatedly been told certain things by other human beings—first by their parents, but then also by the leaders of the Church—and they put their trust in these human beings. Belief or faith, as Hobbes repeatedly points out, is not just in what human beings say, but also in the virtue and reliability of those who say it (*Lev.* 7.5–7, 29.8, 43.8; *De Cive* 18.4; *Elem.* 6.7, 11.9–10). But if this trust is the reason that most men believe, is it, in Hobbes's view, a *good* reason?

Hobbes's argument that those who have not received revelation cannot know but can only believe that the claims of others are true has led some to describe his position as "fideistic."[49] And his argument that believers put their trust in human authorities, especially the Church,[50] is in some ways close to the traditional Catholic view. But coming from Hobbes, these arguments have a different tone and intention than they do when they come from other sources. When Hobbes takes a "fideistic" position, it is to emphasize what is not known and therefore cannot impose a genuine obligation. And when he emphasizes that faith involves belief not just in claims or propositions but also in the human beings who make or transmit them, it is to cast doubt on the reliability of these all too human sources. What, for instance, could be his motive for reminding his readers that, "If Livy says the gods made once a cow speak, and we believe it not, we distrust not God therein, but Livy" (*Lev.* 7.7), if not to invite his readers to apply the same spirit of skepticism to more important sources? Hobbes's opposition to the traditional Catholic view—which, of course, is not fideistic, and thus against which "fideism" can be used as a weapon—comes out most clearly in a passage in which he directly challenges both the traditional Catholic and the newer Protestant arguments as to how it can be known that the Bible is the authentic word of God. Against the Catholics, who "ground their knowledge upon the infallibility of the Church," Hobbes argues that the infallibility of the Church, based as it is on certain key passages in Scripture itself, cannot be known without first knowing the infallibility of Scripture. This dilemma renders the Catholic argument circular (see *Lev.* 43.7). As for the contention on "the other side," which appeals, not to tradition, but to "the testimony of the private spirit," Hobbes dismisses it with this question: "How shall a man know his own private spirit to be other than a belief, grounded upon the authority and arguments of his teachers, or upon a presumption of his own gifts?" (*Lev.* 43.7; see also 33.24, 43.9).[51] Because there is no solid reason to regard either the Church or individual men as infallible, "it is manifest," Hobbes concludes, "that Christian men do not know, but only

49. See, e.g., Pocock, "Time, History and Eschatology in the Thought of Thomas Hobbes," 192–94, 199–201; Glover, "God and Thomas Hobbes," 288–92; Martinich, *The Two Gods of Leviathan,* 208–19; Oakeshott, "Introduction," xx; Hepburn, "Hobbes on the Knowledge of God," 103–7. Compare Tuck, *Hobbes,* 80–83, *Philosophy and Government, 1572–1651,* 329; Leijenhorst, *The Mechanisation of Aristotelianism,* 28–29.

50. See *Lev.* 7.7: "when we believe that the Scriptures are the word of God, having no immediate revelation from God himself, our belief, faith, and trust is in the Church, whose word we take, and acquiesce therein."

51. On Hobbes's rejection of the Catholic and the Protestant modes of establishing the authority of the Bible, compare Sommerville, *Thomas Hobbes: Political Ideas in Historical Context,* 108–10; Milner, "Hobbes on Religion," 411–12; Strauss, *Hobbes's Critique of Religion,* 74–76, "On the Basis of Hobbes's Political Philosophy," 185.

believe the Scripture to be the word of God" (*Lev.* 43.8; see also 26.40; *Elem.* 11.8). If this is fideism, it is fideism with a sharp Hobbesian edge.

Still, much would seem to depend on whether there are good reasons, even if they fall short of supplying knowledge, for accepting Scripture as the word of God. Hobbes's rejection of both the Catholic appeal to the infallibility of the Church and the Protestant appeal to the inner testimony of the Holy Spirit does not so much settle the matter as push him toward an investigation that goes back to the prior links in the chain transmitting Scripture from its original sources. Part of this investigation is carried out in Hobbes's famous historical-critical analysis of the Bible in Chapter 33 of *Leviathan*, where he examines the authorship, antiquity, and history of the books of the Bible. This chapter is best known for Hobbes's argument that the Pentateuch cannot have been written by Moses because it speaks, for instance, of the location of Moses' own grave as unknown "to this day" and describes other matters too from the perspective of someone looking back from a much later age (*Lev.* 33.4). That argument belongs to a broader effort to show, on the basis of evidence internal to the Bible itself, that almost all of the books of the Old Testament were written much later than was traditionally supposed, and that the work as a whole was not set forth in its final form until after the return of the Jews from Babylon. Ezra, not Moses or the other prophets, is the man most plausibly regarded as the primary author of the Old Testament (see especially *Lev.* 33.19; see also 42.39–41; *De Cive* 16.12). Hobbes also insinuates in Chapter 33—at least for those attuned to his irony—that although the books of the New Testament were written shortly after the events they describe, there is reason to suspect that they were tampered with at the Council of Laodicea, when the canon of the New Testament was first established. After noting that at the time of this council, in 364 AD, the "great doctors of the Church" had become so ambitious that they regarded Christian emperors as sheep to be herded by themselves as "absolute governors," and that they viewed even frauds as pious if they made the people "more obedient to Christian doctrine," Hobbes then declares: "Yet I am persuaded they did not therefore falsify the Scriptures—though the copies of the books of the New Testament were in the hands only of the ecclesiastics—because if they had an intention so to do, they would surely have made them more favorable to their power over Christian princes and civil sovereignty than they are" (*Lev.* 33.20).[52]

---

52. The irony of this conclusion extends also to the broader statement that follows it: "I see not therefore any reason to doubt but that the Old and New Testament, as we have them now, are the true registers of those things which were done and said by the prophets and apostles" (*Lev.* 33.20). As Curley, "'I Durst not Write so Boldly,'" 568, points out, this statement carries a

Hobbes's historical-critical analysis of the Bible is indicative of his general disposition toward the Bible as a book of human origins, bearing the marks of a complicated and messy history. Nevertheless, the arguments of Chapter 33, as telling and important as they are, are not as fundamental as what follows them in the later chapters on prophecy and miracles.[53] For one thing, it is clear in the case of the historical-critical arguments of Chapter 33 that they can do no more than cast doubt on the revealed character of the Bible. It is possible to respond to them with an objection similar to the one that can be raised against Hobbes's political and moral critique of the Bible (see p. 161 above). Could not an omnipotent and mysterious God have given Moses, for instance, prophetic insight into the future, such that he could foresee things like the later uncertainty about the location of his grave?[54] Or, even if God did not inspire Moses to write the Pentateuch, could he not have inspired Ezra and guided his hand as he did his work?[55] More important, perhaps, than these questions is one that cuts in the other direction, but also shows the limits of Hobbes's historical-critical arguments: Even if Moses *were* the author of the Pentateuch, would Hobbes have regarded that as sufficient reason to accept it as genuine revelation?[56] The answer to this last question can

---

very different message when it is read in context than when it is quoted on its own, as it sometimes is, as support for the view that Hobbes was a sincere Christian. Curley and Malcolm disagree about whether it is possible to know that Hobbes is being ironic in the conclusions he draws about the Council of Laodicea (compare Curley, "'I Durst not Write so Boldly,'" 567–69, and "Hobbes and the Cause of Religious Toleration," 318–320, with Malcolm, *Aspects of Hobbes*, 428). Although it is perhaps impossible ever to be absolutely certain about irony, I agree with Curley that Hobbes's irony in this instance is fairly obvious. Consider also the implication of Hobbes's remark in *Lev.* 34.24 on those texts of the New Testament (which he indicates does not include all of them) "wherein is no suspicion of corruption of the Scripture."

53. For fuller treatments of the arguments of Chapter 33 than I have given here, see Malcolm, *Aspects of Hobbes*, 381–431; Curley, "'I Durst not Write so Boldly,'" 556–71; Cooke, *Hobbes and Christianity*, 155–82; see also Strauss, *Spinoza's Critique of Religion*, 102–4, *Hobbes's Critique of Religion*, 74–75.

54. Consider Exodus 4:10–12.

55. Consider the passages from the apocryphal 2 Esdras (which Hobbes suggests should be "credited") that Hobbes quotes in *Lev.* 33.19, especially Ezra's plea to God: "But if I have found grace before thee, send down the holy spirit into me, and I shall write down all that hath been done in the world, since the beginning, which were written in thy law, that men may find thy path, and that they which will live in the later days may live."

56. See Strauss, *Hobbes's Critique of Religion*, 75–76: "[Hobbes's] unbelief is not the consequence but the presupposition of the historical critique: the proof of the inauthentic character of the biblical writings is only a still further, subsequent confirmation that they were not revealed. One fully appreciates how little depends on the historical critique for Hobbes if one supposes for a moment that Hobbes could have been convinced by the *authenticity* of the biblical writings: he

be gathered from Hobbes's treatment of prophecy, which takes us to a deeper
level of his argument.

Hobbes's primary treatment of prophecy comes in Chapter 36 of *Leviathan*,
"Of the Word of God, and of Prophets." The treatment of prophecy in Chapter 36, however, is prepared by remarks that we have already briefly considered
when we looked at Chapter 32, the chapter that opened Part III of *Leviathan*
and thus began Hobbes's direct confrontation with the Bible. In that earlier
chapter, Hobbes introduced what I called "the problem of prophecy" (see
p. 131 above). He raised two main difficulties: the difficulty of understanding
the manner of God's communication with prophets, and the difficulty of distinguishing between genuine prophetic experiences and the delusions and
deceptions that arise from men's dreams, visions, and reports. Hobbes did not
go so far as to deny the possibility of supernatural communication between
God and man. But he did remind his readers of his own debunking analysis of
dreams and visions, and he pointedly urged them to remember that intense
passions and false opinions can lead men to misinterpret their experiences.
He also bluntly declared that, if men "may err," so also they "may lie" (see
again 32.6). He pointed out, too, that the problem of prophecy appears in the
Bible itself, in which there are many stories of false prophets and important
warnings not to be deceived by them (see again 32.7).

    When Hobbes returns to the question of prophecy in Chapter 36, he re-
turns to the same set of difficulties. As in the earlier chapter, he does not deny
in Chapter 36 that God can communicate with prophets. Yet, by affirming
that among the many significations of the word "prophet" in Scripture the
most frequent is "him to whom God speaketh immediately," he prepares the
way to take up again the question of how such communication occurs: "And
hereupon a question may be asked, in what manner God speaketh to such
a prophet. Can it (may some say) be properly said that God hath voice and
language, when it cannot be properly said he hath a tongue, or other organs,
as a man?" (36.9). This difficulty would seem to loom largest in the case of
those prophets whom Hobbes sets apart as the "supreme prophets of perpetual calling" in the Old Testament: Moses, the high priests, and "those kings
which submitted themselves to God's government" (see 36.11, 36.13). Of this
group, the exemplar—the supreme of the supreme—is Moses. Moses is the
most important Old Testament prophet because it is clearest in his case that

---

would not thereby have been in the least convinced of their *revealed character*." See also Strauss,
Spinoza's Critique of Religion, 140–44; compare Malcolm, *Aspects of Hobbes*, 428–29; Johnston,
The Rhetoric of Leviathan, 179–80.

the Bible suggests that God communicated with a man directly—indeed, "in such manner as a man speaketh to his friend" (*Lev.* 36.11). Hobbes points to passages such as Numbers 12:6–8, where God declares that he will speak to Moses "mouth to mouth," and Exodus 33:11, where it is said that "the Lord spake to Moses face to face" (*Lev.* 36.11). If the Bible clearly suggests that God's communication with Moses was extraordinary in its directness, that makes it all the more difficult to comprehend. It seems impossible to deny, on the one hand, that God's communication with Moses was unlike that with other, more ordinary prophets: "To say that when Moses went up to God in Mount Sinai, it was a dream or vision, such as other prophets had, is contrary to that distinction which God made between Moses and other prophets [Numb. 12:6–8]" (36.13). Yet it also seems impossible to claim, on the other hand, that Moses had a direct perception of God himself: "To say God spake or appeared as he is in his own nature is to deny his infiniteness, invisibility, incomprehensibility" (36.13). Hobbes also rules out that God spoke to Moses by inspiration in the sense of a direct infusion of the Holy Spirit, and that he spoke by the Holy Spirit understood in the sense of the merely natural gifts with which he graced Moses: the former is unacceptable because it would make Moses equal with Christ, "in whom only the Godhead [as St. Paul speaketh, Col. 2:9] dwelleth bodily," the latter because it would "attribute nothing to him supernatural" (36.13).[57] Since Moses is the exemplar of the supreme prophets of perpetual calling, Hobbes can then point to the broader implications of the dilemma he is sketching: "And as these ways cannot be applied to God in his speaking to Moses at Mount Sinai, so also they cannot be applied to him in his speaking to the high priests from the mercy-seat." "Therefore," Hobbes concludes, "in what manner God spake to those sovereign prophets of the Old Testament, whose office it was to enquire of him, is not intelligible" (36.14).

Now, in the presentation manuscript of *Leviathan* given to Charles II, Hobbes added at this point, after "not intelligible," the phrase "otherwise than by a voice." This addition would seem to indicate the only way in which Hobbes thinks the mystery of God's communication with Moses and the other supreme prophets can be solved, insofar as it is solvable at all.[58] He suggests

---

57. Notice what Hobbes acknowledges here about the genuine biblical teaching about Jesus' inspiration by the Holy Spirit—if only to deny such inspiration to Moses. Hobbes also acknowledges here that to treat the action of the Holy Spirit merely as an expression that "signifieth the graces or gifts of the Holy Spirit" is to reduce it to something "natural and ordinary." Compare p. 97 and pp. 142–43 above.

58. Consider also Hobbes's reformulation of the broader statement (of which this sentence is a part) in the Latin *Leviathan*: "In what way, then, God spoke to the prophets of perpetual calling when they consulted him, I do not find it written, except that he spoke to the high priests in the

a solution, not only by this addition, but also by his contention that those passages in which God's communication with Moses is explicitly said to be by the mediation of an angel may serve as a template for the other, more mysterious instances in which the mode of communication is left obscure. In keeping with his earlier account of the meaning of angels in the Old Testament, Hobbes suggests that any passage that says that God spoke to Moses by the mediation of an angel may be taken to mean that Moses merely had a vision, "though a more clear vision than was given to the other prophets," and he further suggests that all of God's communication with Moses should be understood along such lines (36.11; cf. Review and Conclusion, 12).[59] In this way, even as he calls attention to the special status that Scripture accords Moses and the other supreme prophets of perpetual calling, Hobbes weaves them back into a general account of prophecy as occurring by means of dreams, visions, and voices.[60] The warrant for this assimilation of the supreme prophets to the other prophets would seem to be that it is the only intelligible way of making sense of their experiences. But does this step truly solve the problem of understanding God's communication with man? There remains the difficulty of understanding how exactly God works through "angels" (which are not real beings, according to Hobbes's interpretation of the Old Testament) to influence men's minds when they have dreams, see visions, or hear voices. And more important, by suggesting that *all* prophecy, even that of Moses and the other supreme prophets, occurred by such means, Hobbes brings even the most important cases of prophecy in the Old Testament within the

---

Holy of Holies [*Sancto Sanctorum*] by a voice from between the cherubim. But that voice, just as all other signs of the divine presence, can be called an angel, in the same way as dreams and other supernatural signs" (669). See also *Lev.*, Review and Conclusion, 12. Compare Malcolm, *Leviathan, Vol. 1: Introduction*, 206–7.

59. As examples of passages in which it "appears expressly" that God communicated with Moses by the mediation of an angel or angels, Hobbes points to Acts 7:35, Acts 7:53, and Galatians 3:19. The fact that these passages are from the New Testament does not keep Hobbes from interpreting them in light of the meaning he suggests angels carry in the Old Testament. He also points to the following passages of the Old Testament as "conformable" with his interpretation of the passages from Acts and Galatians: Deuteronomy 13:1, Joel 2:28, and 1 Kings 3:15.

60. See the conclusion of 36.11: "So that generally the prophets extraordinary in the Old Testament took notice of the word of God no otherwise than from their dreams or visions, that is to say, from the imaginations which they had in their sleep or in an ecstasy—which imaginations in every true prophet were supernatural, but in false prophets were either natural or feigned." See also 36.10, 36.19; *EW* IV, 334. Compare Lessay, "Hobbes's Covenant Theology and Its Political Implications," 259.

purview of his own analysis of dreams and visions. He does not fail to deliver the message he thus sets up:

> Seeing, then, all prophecy supposeth [a] vision or dream (which two, when they be natural, are the same), or some especial gift of God so rarely observed in mankind as to be admired where observed, and seeing as well such gifts as the most extraordinary dreams and visions may proceed from God, not only by his supernatural and immediate, but also by his natural operation, and by mediation of second causes, there is need of reason and judgment to discern between natural and supernatural gifts, and between natural and supernatural visions or dreams. And consequently, men had need to be very circumspect, and wary, in obeying the voice of [a] man that, pretending himself to be a prophet, requires us to obey God in that way which he in God's name telleth us to be the way to happiness. For he that pretends to teach men the way of so great felicity pretends to govern them—that is to say, to rule and reign over them—which is a thing that all men naturally desire, and is therefore worthy to be suspected of ambition and imposture, and consequently, ought to be examined and tried by every man before he yield them obedience, unless he have yielded it them already, in the institution of a commonwealth, as when the prophet is the civil sovereign, or by the civil sovereign authorized. (36.19)

This passage cannot but remind one of Hobbes's earlier admonitions not to give credence too readily to purported prophets who claim that God has spoken to them in dreams, visions, or voices (see again *Lev.* 2.7–8, 32.6; see also 7.5–7, 26.40–41). The primary difference between this statement and the earlier ones is that Hobbes places somewhat less emphasis here on the possibility that purported prophets may be deluded and somewhat more on the possibility of intentional deception. If he reminded us earlier that men "may err" or "may lie," he here stresses the latter danger.[61] By stating the reasons for suspecting such deception, moreover, he makes the admonition to wariness more explicit and pointed.

Hobbes's admonition to be wary of purported prophets is also an argument for the necessity of a rational examination of purported prophecy: "there is need of reason and judgment to discern between natural and supernatural gifts, and between natural and supernatural dreams." But how should such an examination proceed? The Bible itself provides an answer, Hobbes suggests. Given what might otherwise come across as the impious skepticism of his admonition to be wary of false prophets, it is very helpful to Hobbes— very convenient, one is tempted to say—that the Bible, too, confronts the

---

61. See Hoekstra, "Disarming the Prophets," 126.

problem of false prophets. Hobbes can thus recast his argument for the need
for a rational examination of purported prophecy as an appeal to apply to all
prophecy "those rules which God hath given us, to discern the true from the
false" (*Lev.* 36.20). Yet, although Hobbes is certainly on solid ground in pointing to the problem of false prophets in the Bible, there is a difficulty here: Is
Scripture itself not purported prophecy? How, then, can its criteria be used
to test prophecy before its own status as true prophecy—that is, as genuine
revelation—has been established by some other means? After all, to use a
test derived from Scripture itself in order to establish that Scripture is rightly
regarded as the source of the decisive criteria for judging prophecy would be
to argue in a circle.[62]

This difficulty—which Hobbes makes visible by his procedure—is not the
only one that besets the test of prophecy that Hobbes claims to derive from
Scripture. The scriptural test, as Hobbes stated it in Chapter 32, was that there
are "two marks" by which a true prophet may be known, or two criteria that
must be met: the performance of miracles and "the not teaching any other
religion than that which is already established" (see again 32.7). In Chapter 36,
Hobbes returns to this test, but with some modifications. The test in the case
of the Old Testament, he now says, was that prophets could be true prophets
only if they taught "conformable doctrine to that which Moses the sovereign
prophet had taught them" and displayed "the miraculous power of foretelling
what God would bring to pass"; in the New Testament, "there was but one only
mark," namely, "the preaching of this doctrine, *That Jesus is the Christ*, that
is, the king of the Jews, promised in the Old Testament" (*Lev.* 36.20).[63] There
are a number of questions one could raise about the biblical test as Hobbes
presents it. Is or is not the performance of miracles, for instance, essential according to the New Testament version of the test (compare 36.20 with 32.7;
cf. *Elem.* 11.7; *De Hom.* 14.12; *EW* IV, 330)? But the most serious difficulty with
the test, in any of its forms, is the following. By making one essential mark
of true prophecy conformity with a prior religion or doctrine—whether it be

62. See Curley, " 'I Durst not Write so Boldly,' " 535; Strauss, *Hobbes's Critique of Religion*, 76;
Lupoli, "Hobbes and Religion without Theology," 468–69. Consider *De Cive* 16.11: "The whole
and sole word of God is what God is proclaimed to have said by a true prophet. Now, the writings of the prophets, which include what God says, as much as what the prophet himself says,
are called the word of God because they contain the word of God. Yet, because the whole and
sole word of God is what is presented as such by a true prophet, it is not possible to know what
is the word of God before one knows who is a true prophet; nor can one believe the word of God
before one believes the prophet." See also *Elem.* 11.8.

63. The key passages from which Hobbes derives these criteria are Deuteronomy 13:1–5 and
1 John 4:1–3.

that religion "which is already established," or the doctrine of Moses, or the doctrine that Jesus is the Messiah—the test begs the question in the case of the decisive prophets who originated the lines by which the others are to be judged. This difficulty is akin to that of establishing the validity of Scripture itself as the source of the criteria. But now the question must be asked about Moses and Jesus themselves: How should the claims of these most important of all purported prophets be tested? Moses could perhaps be judged by his conformity with the religion that Abraham put in place; but that would merely push the crucial question back to Abraham.[64] And Jesus, for his part, might be judged by the consistency of his teaching with the "doctrine" of the Old Testament; but that would mean that his case too would ultimately lead back to Moses and Abraham. At some point, the line must begin. The religion or doctrine by which all later prophets are to be judged must be established. But rather than judging Moses and Jesus as links in a chain that begins with Abraham, it is more reasonable to acknowledge that each of them broke with an established order and inaugurated something new. Each of these rebellious and path-breaking prophets, although continuous in certain ways with a prior religion or doctrine, was also and more fundamentally an innovator or a founder (consider *Lev.* 12.12, 37.13, 40.5–7, 41.4, 42.37; *De Cive* 18.9; *EW* V, 338–39; *Hist. Eccles.*, lines 39–42). But does that not mean that the test as Hobbes lays it out cannot be applied in their cases, or that, insofar as it can be applied, in the form that requires "the not teaching any other religion than that which is already established," Moses and Jesus would fail it?[65]

---

64. Consider *De Cive* 16.11: "Moses was believed by the people of Israel on account of two things, *miracles* and *faith*. For, however great and evident were the miracles he performed, they would not have believed him—at least they ought not to have—had he called them out of Egypt to a worship other than that of the God of Abraham, Isaac, and Jacob, their fathers." In *De Cive*, Hobbes states the Old Testament version of the test of true prophecy somewhat differently from the way he states it in *Leviathan*, placing more weight on Abraham: "There are two things— namely, *supernatural prediction of the future*, which is an enormous miracle, and *faith in the God of Abraham, their liberator from Egypt*—which God proposed to all the Jews as marks of a true prophet" (16.11). Consider also *De Cive* 16.1, 16.4; *Lev.* 40.1–3.

65. This difficulty is underscored in Chapter 36 when Hobbes concludes by arguing that "the sovereign prophet," whose "doctrine" should be used to judge prophets, is the established civil sovereign. See the last two (very long) sentences of Chapter 36, which are even more pointed in the Latin *Leviathan* (679–81); compare *EW* V, 270. In response to the passage at the end of Chapter 36, the ever-perceptive Bramhall objects: "and Christ, who had the approbation of no sovereign prince, upon his [*sc.*, Hobbes's] grounds, was to be reputed a false prophet everywhere" (*The Catching of Leviathan*, 528; Hobbes's question-begging response is at *EW* IV, 329). See the similar objection that Hyde, *A Brief View and Survey*, 196–97, raises regarding the implication of Hobbes's argument for Moses (see also 205–7). On the main difficulty sketched in the paragraph

But what about the miracles that Moses and Jesus performed? Hobbes's appeal to the biblical test enables him to argue that, according to the Bible's own criteria, miracles are not enough by themselves to verify that a purported prophet is a true prophet. After all, even false prophets in the Bible can sometimes perform miracles (*Lev.* 32.7, 36.19; see also *De Cive* 18.9; *Elem.* 11.7). Thus the difficulty would seem to be insuperable in the case of the decisive founding prophets, whose credibility cannot be demonstrated by the necessary combination of miracles and conformity with a prior doctrine or established religion. Still, Hobbes's efforts to sketch this problem, or to lead his readers to see it, does not settle the matter. For does not the Bible, as it were, anticipate the objection and respond to it by suggesting that, in the cases of Moses and Jesus, their miracles were so remarkable, so extraordinary, that they *do* provide sufficient evidence of their divine calling?[66] At any rate, Hobbes's treatment of the problem of prophecy points to the need for a more direct confrontation with the question of miracles. For if miracles are possible, then genuine prophecy is possible, even if its operation is difficult to understand and its authenticity difficult to verify. Hobbes has not even tried to deny this possibility. In fact, he has clearly left it open (see *Lev.* 2.8, 32.6, 36.19). He has also yet to confront the crucial claim that goes beyond the contention that miracles in general are possible: the claim that the specific miracles of the most important prophets *actually occurred*. It is fitting, then, that Hobbes's chapter on prophecy is followed by Chapter 37, "Of Miracles, and their Use." Here we come to the most decisive stage in Hobbes's confrontation with the Bible.[67]

The question of miracles arose earlier, in our examination of Hobbes's natural philosophy. There we reached the conclusion that Hobbes was aware that his natural philosophy was not such as to allow him to exclude the possibility of miracles. If it could be known that the world was not created out of nothing by a freely acting divine will and that the chains of necessitated mechanistic causation can never be broken, then it could be known that miracles are impossible. But the eternity of the world and the inviolable reign of necessity are precisely what Hobbes thought he could not establish with certainty

---

above, compare Curley, "'I Durst not Write so Boldly,'" 536–37; Cooke, *Hobbes and Christianity*, 142–43, 149–50; Lessay, "Hobbes's Protestantism," 293.

66. See *Lev.* 37.6. Consider the remark Hobbes makes near the end of *Anti-White* 30.2, when proceeding by "a preferable and more Christian method": "[The Apostles] believed the same doctrines that Christ himself taught; but Christ, whatever he taught, he very much confirmed with miracles that provided demonstrations." See also *EW* IV, 329; *De Hom.* 14.12; *Hist. Eccles.*, lines 39–42, 679–93, 779–83.

67. Compare Strauss, *Hobbes's Critique of Religion*, 85.

(see pp. 49–50, 65–66, 76 above). Another conceivable way of trying to rule out the possibility of miracles would be to attempt to demonstrate that miracles are incompatible with the nature of God as a perfect being. But that path, too, is closed for Hobbes, who would argue that any such attempt would inevitably founder on the rocks of the incomprehensibility of God and the limits of our knowledge. Hobbes's natural theology, as we saw, does not seek to discover or articulate the true nature of God; it moves in the other direction, conveying a lesson about the implications of God's incomprehensibility and, more simply and deeply, about the limits of human knowledge (see pp. 119–20, 124–25 above). Thus far, then, it would seem that Hobbes has not ruled out the possibility of miracles. And he may never do so. But what does he say about miracles in Chapter 37, his most direct and extensive statement on the matter?

In Chapter 37, Hobbes focuses on miracles in their purpose of vindicating the missions of prophets. "A MIRACLE," as he defines it here, "*is a work of God (besides his operation by the way of nature, ordained in the creation) done for the making manifest to his elect the mission of an extraordinary minister for their salvation*" (37.7; see also 37.1, 37.6, 12.28). Hobbes's discussion of miracles is thus closely connected to his preceding account of prophecy: if that account pointed ahead to the need for a more extensive consideration of miracles, as one of the criteria for establishing true prophecy, the present discussion looks back throughout to the question of prophecy. Moreover, in Chapter 37 Hobbes takes an approach to miracles—or, at any rate, to what men regard as miracles—that is similar to his approach to prophecy in Chapter 36, where he laid out a test of true prophecy in terms of criteria that must be met. Miracles, as he argues at the outset of Chapter 37, are "admirable works of God," and for that reason "they are also called *wonders*" (37.1); but that means that to understand miracles, "we must first understand what works they are which men wonder at and call admirable" (37.2). According to Hobbes, there are two requirements, because "there be but two things which make men wonder at any event": the first is that the event must be strange, in the sense of rare or unusual; the second is that it must be inexplicable in terms of natural causes, such that "we cannot imagine it to have been done by natural means, but only by the immediate hand of God" (37.2).

Hobbes's presentation of these criteria has the effect of directing attention as much to the audience, the "spectators," of miracles as to the events themselves. And that enables him to develop the further suggestion that miracles at least in some cases are relative to the condition of those who observe them: "Furthermore, seeing admiration and wonder is consequent to the knowledge and experience wherewith men are endowed, some more, some less, it followeth that the same thing may be a miracle to one and not to another"

(37.5).[68] Now, in suggesting that miracles are relative in this way, Hobbes must not be understood as suggesting that the different experiences, or the different interpretations of experiences, of different men are to be regarded as equally reliable or beyond appeal. He makes that clear with his next remark: "And thence it is that ignorant and superstitious men make great wonders of those works which other men, knowing to proceed from nature (which is not the immediate, but the ordinary work of God), admire not at all" (37.5). Experience shaped by knowledge of nature is decisively superior, Hobbes suggests, to experience, or interpretation of experience, shaped by ignorance and superstition, even if the former is less likely to produce "admiration." Hobbes underscores this point by giving two examples in which ignorant men are deceived because of their ignorance. The first is eclipses, which "have been taken for supernatural works by the common people," even though others "could from their natural causes have foretold the very hour they should arrive." The second is a case of intentional deception in which one man secretly gains knowledge of the prior actions of "an ignorant, unwary man," and then tells him what he did earlier in his life. To the ignorant man, Hobbes says, "it seems a miraculous thing," but "amongst wise and cautelous men, such miracles as those cannot easily be done" (37.5).

At this point in his argument—having put forward a suggestion that cannot but encourage skepticism toward claims of miracles—Hobbes turns from a general account of miracles to a consideration of some of the biblical miracles. In returning to the Bible, he goes straight to the most important cases: the miracles performed by Moses and Jesus. He argues, first, that the essential purpose of Moses' miracles in Egypt was to convince the Israelites that he had indeed been sent by God to deliver them from bondage (37.6). Moses, in this respect, provides the model of how miracles are to be understood in their relationship to prophecy: "In like manner [to Moses' miracles in Egypt], if we consider all of the miracles done by the hand of Moses and all the rest of the prophets till the Captivity, and those of our Saviour and his apostles afterwards, we shall find their end was always to beget or confirm belief that they came not of their own motion, but were sent by God" (37.6). Now, one might expect at this point that Hobbes would issue a reminder of the other criterion of true prophecy—conformity with the established religion or with a prior doctrine—and insist upon an application of the test of prophecy from

---

68. Compare Latin *Lev.*: *Admiratio dependet plerumque a scientia & experienta hominum, ita ut alii videatur, quod vidit Miraculum, alii non videatur* (Admiration depends in large part on the knowledge and experience of men, such that it may seem to one man that what he sees is a miracle, while it does not seem so to another).

Chapter 36. He does not do that here. But that can be taken as a sign that he has moved to a more fundamental level of his argument. His attention is now squarely focused on the decisive founding prophets and their miracles. What replaces an appeal to the earlier test of prophecy is a new suggestion: that the purpose of the key biblical miracles was "to beget belief, not universally in all men, elect and reprobate, but in the elect only, that is to say, in such as God had determined should become his subjects" (37.6).

This new suggestion would seem to be Hobbes's way of giving a pious response to a problem that, because he has a response at the ready, he is able to call to his readers' attention. The problem is that the biblical prophets, even Moses and Jesus, did not convince everyone they encountered of their divine missions. This problem is perhaps not so perplexing in the case of Moses, since the recalcitrance of Pharaoh, for instance, can be explained by God's decision to harden his heart (37.6). But what is one to make of the fact that Jesus seems to have been unable to perform miracles in his own country? Hobbes touches on this delicate matter by pointing to Matthew 13:58, where it is said that Jesus did not perform many miracles in his own country because of the unbelief of his countrymen, and to Mark 6:5, where it is said that Jesus could not perform miracles in Nazareth.[69] In addressing the latter passage, Hobbes says that it would be blasphemous to say that Jesus lacked the power to perform miracles anywhere he wished. But he also objects to those who would read away the difficulty by saying that when Mark wrote that Jesus "could not" perform miracles in his own country, he meant merely that he "would not." To suggest that the phrase "he could not" may stand in for "he would not," Hobbes says, is "without example in the Greek tongue" (*Lev.* 37.6). What, then, is Hobbes's response to this problem, an inadequate resolution of which, he notes, can "lay a stumbling block before weak Christians, as if Christ could do no miracles but amongst the credulous" (37.6)? His response is to suggest that Jesus could perform miracles only before those whom God had elected for salvation, and not before "those whom his father had rejected." But this resolution has the difficulty of making one wonder why God would have rejected Jesus' own countrymen,[70] and thus it encourages

---

69. In his quotation of Mark 6:5 in *Leviathan* 37.6, Hobbes leaves out the second part of the verse, which qualifies the first. The full verse reads: "And he [*sc.*, Jesus] could there do no mighty work, save that he laid his hands upon a few sick folk, and healed *them*." In the Latin *Leviathan*, Hobbes quotes the full verse, and also adds the beginning of 6:6: "And he marveled because of their unbelief" (see 687).

70. See Curley, " 'I Durst not Write so Boldly,' " 549. Curley points to Clarendon's (= Hyde's) objection to Hobbes's "new doctrine": "besides the barbarity of it, [it] is irrational to think that all the People of *Nazareth*, where our Saviour had vouchsafed to live, and converse above thirty

one to keep pressing the question of whether there was not something else about Jesus' countrymen that made them less receptive to taking his works as miracles. If Hobbes cannot go so far as to claim in his own name that "Christ could do no miracles but amongst the credulous," does he not manage to convey that suggestion indirectly, by pointing to the limits of Jesus' power to work wonders before a group of people who would have been less credulous for the simple reason that they had known Jesus from his childhood?

Hobbes does not dwell on this delicate matter concerning the apparent limits of Jesus' ability to perform miracles before an audience that knew his background. He leaves it quickly and returns to the case of Moses—but only to bring out another difficulty that emerges from the biblical accounts of miracles. Hobbes referred earlier to Moses' miracles, before he turned to consider the dilemma of Jesus in Nazareth (see 37.6). When he returns to Moses, he calls attention to the Egyptian sorcerers who were able to match at least some of the feats of Moses. They, too, apparently, could turn rods into serpents, change water into blood, and bring frogs upon the land (37.10).[71] Should their feats, too, be regarded as genuine miracles? Hobbes had suggested so in an earlier passage (32.7); but now he says no (37.10–11; cf. 44.11). And the fact that he is considering the case of the Egyptian sorcerers allows him to spell out a debunking argument. There is a difficulty in trying to understand the feats of the Egyptian sorcerers and other instances of apparent magic in the Bible, because the Bible itself does not clearly explain the nature of such feats: "there is no place in Scripture that telleth us what an enchantment is" (37.10). Hobbes, however, is willing to fill that void. He argues that an "enchantment" is not, "as many think it," the direct effect of spells or magical words, but rather "imposture and delusion, wrought by ordinary means" (37.10). Enchantments are "so far from supernatural as the imposters need not the study so much as of natural causes, but the ordinary ignorance, stupidity, and superstition of mankind, to do them" (37.10). Nothing is enchanted in such cases, Hobbes declares, "but the spectator" (37.11). And he stresses how easy it is to "enchant"— that is, to deceive—most spectators: "For such is the ignorance and aptitude to error generally of all men, but especially of them that have not much knowledge of natural causes, and of the nature and interests of men, as by innumerable and easy tricks to be abused" (37.12).

To repeat, Hobbes is able to deliver this blunt argument about human cre-

---

years of his life, should be reprobated by God to everlasting damnation" (*A Brief View and Survey*, 217).

71. Hobbes quotes from Exodus 7:11, 7:22, and 8:7.

dulity and the "aptitude of mankind to give too hasty belief to pretended miracles" (37.13) because he raised the problem of the Egyptian sorcerers. But is his real concern to cast doubt on the magical powers of the Egyptian sorcerers? When he was directly addressing Moses' own feats, Hobbes of course made no suggestion that they were due to deception or that Moses exploited the ignorance of his spectators. Yet, since Moses' spectators were the same as those of the Egyptian sorcerers in the case of at least some of his feats, does not Hobbes urge his readers to put the pieces of his argument together and ponder its implications for Moses' purported miracles? If one were among the spectators, but in the cautious and skeptical frame of mind that Hobbes advocates, would one be likely to think the two cases so different? Hobbes gives the appearance of fending off this question, or at least its blasphemous answer, by returning at last to the test of prophecy from Chapter 36 and reminding his readers that it is necessary to consider the doctrine as well as the feat "before we give credit to a pretended miracle or prophet" (37.13). By referring back to the test of prophecy, Hobbes covers his tracks by distancing Moses from the Egyptian sorcerers in a way that suggests that Moses' feats pass muster as genuine miracles whereas their mere enchantments do not (see also 37.11). But he also manages, at the same time, to remind his readers of what—or who—is really at issue. And since the problem we saw earlier in the application of the test of prophecy to Moses himself remains, he encourages at least some of his readers to dwell on the deeper difficulty he is indicating here. That difficulty, to put it simply, is that Moses' purported miracles were performed before a highly credulous audience who, owing to their ignorance of natural causes and human motivations, would have been especially prone to deception. Hobbes's explicit position, as we have seen, is that the key biblical miracles were intended to persuade only the elect. But he leaves one suspecting that, in the case of both Moses' and Jesus' miracles, "the elect" is a name he borrows for a group he would prefer to call, if he could, "the credulous."[72]

There is a historical dimension to Hobbes's argument that is ultimately its most important aspect. When Hobbes gives examples of the ways in which men are easily deceived, one of his examples is that of eclipses, an example making its second appearance in Chapter 37 (37.12; see 37.5 and p. 174 above). In this second instance, Hobbes argues that it would have been much easier in earlier times, "before it was known that there was a science of the course

---

72. Compare Strauss, *Hobbes's Critique of Religion*, 93: "In this sense it is true [according to Hobbes] that miracles are directed only to the 'elect': the 'elect' are precisely those same poor in spirit who are without any scientific culture."

of the stars," to deceive men by predicting an eclipse. This example brings out a thought that runs throughout Hobbes's treatment of miracles, as one of its main threads: because the propensity to interpret strange events as miraculous depends, not just on their strangeness, but also on the inability of the spectators to imagine their natural causes, a rise in the knowledge of natural causes should produce a corresponding decline in the propensity of men to interpret unusual occurrences as miracles (see again especially 37.4–5, 37.12).[73] Indeed, near the end of Chapter 37, Hobbes makes a striking statement in which he suggests that that propensity has already all but vanished:

> For in these times, I do not know one man that ever saw any such wondrous work, done by the charm, or at the word or prayer of a man, that a man endowed but with a mediocrity of reason would think supernatural. And the question is no more [i.e., no longer] whether what we see done be a miracle— whether the miracle we hear or read of were a real work, and not the act of a tongue or pen—but, in plain terms, whether the report be true or a lie. (37.13)[74]

This statement is perhaps best taken not as an accurate description of a historical stage that Hobbes thought had already been reached— in that respect, it is surely an exaggeration—but as an indication of a trajectory and its anticipated end. Yet, even if it is taken in that way, two things stand out in what Hobbes says here. First, Hobbes suggests that a stage can be reached, even if it has not yet been reached, when the spirit of skepticism has so replaced the older credulity that no sensible man would be fooled any longer by purported miracles. With the advance of a general enlightenment, he indicates, the interpretation of "wondrous works" as miracles would fade away. And second, he suggests that such a change would affect, not just the interpretation of present experiences, but also the attitude of men toward reports of miracles from the past, those reports "we hear or read." Since such reports surely include those in the Bible itself, Hobbes suggests that a time could come in which the general run of men, led by a vanguard of men like Hobbes

73. Consider also the following passages in which Hobbes points to the connection between "miracles" and a remediable simplicity and ignorance: *Lev.* 44.3, 45.9, 46.41; *De Hom.* 14.13; *EW* IV, 231; *Hist. Eccles.*, lines 129–43. Compare Johnston, *The Rhetoric of Leviathan*, 162–63; Strauss, *Hobbes's Critique of Religion*, 93–94.

74. Hobbes expresses himself slightly differently and somewhat more clearly in the Latin *Leviathan*: "For today, I do not know even one man who has seen done, whether through an incantation or by the voice or oration of a man, a work so wonderful that it could appear supernatural to a moderately cautious man. Thus the question today is not whether a miracle that we have seen or read about or heard rumors of really occurred, but whether the miracles of which we read, or that we accept by rumors, are not merely the works of tongue or pen" (697).

himself, would be willing to look upon the Bible and its purported miracles with a sober skepticism, and thus to regard them as relics of a primitive age.

*

Through his discussion of miracles—which is better called his critique of miracles—Hobbes is able to point those who are willing to follow the indications of his arguments to the grounds on which he thinks a sensibly skeptical man should doubt the reality of the miracles reported in the Bible. But his critique does not amount to a refutation of the very possibility of miracles. Nor is it plausible that Hobbes himself thought that it did. For the historical argument with which Hobbes's critique culminates manifestly falls short of a demonstration of the impossibility of miracles. Indeed, the very fact that Hobbes must resort to the argument that miracles are relics of a primitive age that will be left behind as science and enlightenment advance is testimony to his awareness that he cannot rule out the possibility of miracles. If he thought that he could give a truly demonstrative argument that miracles are impossible, would we not find such an argument presented, or at least intimated, in Chapter 37? Moreover, Hobbes, as I noted earlier, explicitly affirms in many places in his works, including *Leviathan*, that miracles are possible (see again, e.g., *Lev.* 2.8, 12.12, 32.6; see also 37.6). I suggested earlier that even if such affirmations are rhetorical concessions that conceal Hobbes's doubts as to the actuality of miracles and even his belief in their impossibility, they are also more than rhetorical concessions insofar as they reflect his awareness that he cannot confirm his doubts or convert his belief into knowledge (compare p. 77 above). Our examination of Hobbes's critique of miracles in Chapter 37 does not change—rather, it confirms—the conclusion to which we were led by our examinations of Hobbes's natural philosophy and his natural theology: Hobbes did not think that he could demonstrate the impossibility of miracles. In the end, Hobbes could accomplish, and knew that he could accomplish, only the more limited aim of showing that there is no compelling reason for those who have not had direct experience of revelation or witnessed miracles themselves to put their trust in the reports of others. Since such reports, in the most important cases, come down to us as messages in a bottle from the primitive past, not only can we not know that they are true, but we have every reason to doubt them and to regard them as the products of the ignorance rampant at their origins.

But has Hobbes shown even that much? In trying to take stock of Hobbes's critique of miracles and of his broader critique of religion, it is necessary to distinguish, as far as possible, between those limits of his arguments of which he was aware and those limits of which he may have been unaware. In the former category, I believe, is the limit just considered, namely, that Hobbes cannot demonstrate the impossibility of miracles, but can only argue that the most important purported miracles are relics from the primitive past. But there are other difficulties in Hobbes's critique of religion that may belong in the latter category. As an example of broader significance than it may first appear, consider Hobbes's dismissive rejection of the Protestant argument that the authenticity of the Bible as genuine revelation, and thus the reality of the miracles reported in it, can be known through the inner testimony of the Holy Spirit. Hobbes, as we saw, rejects that claim on the grounds that a man may easily take "his own private spirit" to be the testimony of the Holy Spirit when in fact nothing supernatural is at work; such a man's "spirit" may be nothing more than a belief grounded upon his trust in the authority of other men or upon a false presumption of his own gifts (see again 43.7; see also 29.8; *Elem.* 11.9; *EW* IV, 333–34; pp. 163–64 above). Is that response an adequate refutation of those who would claim that true faith is not what Hobbes says it is—that is, an unreasonable trust in what one has heard from dubious authorities and an unreliable tradition—but rather a revelatory experience in its own right that gives the faithful a special form of knowledge? A defender of this view of faith might respond to Hobbes's exhortations to skepticism by arguing that Hobbes encourages in his readers, and displays in his own case, an attitude that makes it harder to hear the voice of a God who speaks in faith, but who speaks with clarity only to those who are willing to lay down the sword of skeptical reason and humbly submit themselves to his higher authority. In this connection, it is important that the very fact to which Hobbes points regarding the biblical miracles—namely, that they were performed before primitive and credulous spectators—permits of an alternative interpretation. For it may be precisely such "primitive" men—men who lived long before the emergence of the skeptical spirit of modern science—who were least estranged from God and thus chosen to be the conduits of his revelation. And it can be argued, at least, that those who live in later ages need not merely *believe* that this is the case, because they can *know* it through a present experience that is not, to be sure, the same as the experience of those who witnessed the original miracles, but is nevertheless a miraculous gift of God's grace.[75] If Hobbes can exploit for his

75. See Calvin, *Institutes* 1.7.4–5, 1.8.13 (with 1.8.5–10); Ross, *Leviathan Drawn out with a Hook*, 28–29. See also Sommerville, *Thomas Hobbes: Political Ideas in Historical Context*, 109–10, 142; Milner, "Hobbes on Religion," 411–12; Pocock, "Time, History and Eschatology in the Thought of Thomas Hobbes," 194; cf. Strauss, *Spinoza's Critique of Religion*, 124–25, 145, 192–93, 213–14.

own skeptical purposes the Protestant doctrine that miracles have ceased (see *Lev.* 32.9 with 37.13), that does not entitle him to dismiss the claims of those who say that experiences can still be had, by those whose hearts are open to them, that confirm that the biblical miracles were real and that God remains active in the lives of men.

Hobbes's dismissive rejection of the claim that the inner testimony of the Holy Spirit confirms the truth of Scripture is only one difficulty that raises the broader question of whether Hobbes adequately confronts the challenge posed to skeptical reason by claims that religious experiences provide an illumination unavailable to reason alone. Of course, Hobbes could—and, I think, would—deny that he himself has had any such experiences. And he would claim that he can explain what is at work in the case of others without recourse to anything supernatural and thus in such a way as to debunk their claims to have received genuine illumination. In the course of our examination of Hobbes's critique of religion, we have encountered Hobbes's mechanistic explanation of dreams and visions, his argument that purported prophets are either deluded to the point of madness or perpetrating intentional deceptions, and his account of religion as rooted in a combination of anxiety and ignorance that makes men prone to imagining invisible powers at work in all sorts of ways they are not. These arguments are Hobbes's response to claims of "religious experience." Because he makes them, it would be unfair to say that he simply ignores such claims. Yet, precisely because the main intention of his arguments is to debunk what others take to be authentic experiences of God's communication with man, it is necessary to question the adequacy of his arguments. Hobbes seems—so far, at least, as one can judge from his writings—never to have made a serious attempt to understand religious experiences, or, better, the view of those who claim to have had them, *from the inside*, that is, by taking seriously the self-understanding of men such as the original biblical prophets, the theologians who provide the most compelling interpretations of their messages, or even the ordinary faithful who find in their faith an experience of quasi-revelatory illumination. Is it possible that Hobbes, appalled as he was by the destruction and ignorance fostered by religion, had become so contemptuous toward his opponents that he was unwilling to confront their position on its own terms? On this question, one consideration is especially important: Hobbes does not seem to have looked very deeply into the *moral dimension* of the claims and outlook of serious religious believers. To be sure, he sketches out, by means of scattered indications, a critique of biblical morality as irrational. To direct one's readers to such a critique, however, is not the same as taking seriously the moral outlook of one's opponents as they themselves understand it. As evidence of Hobbes's dismissiveness and even shallowness on this score, his opponents could point to his argument that the seeds of religion are nothing more than anxiety and ignorance. If his opponents were to argue, as some of them did,[76] that such an account is too crude to be convincing, would they not be right? Is it really plausible that at the basis of religious experiences, which include experiences of the conscience, moral obligation, and even love—each of which are often interpreted as intimations of the divine—lies nothing but anxiety and ignorance? Does Hobbes's psychological reductionism do full justice to, or even offer a genuinely plausible explanation of, the ways in which religious believers conceive of their relationship to a God who makes unconditional demands and calls them to an exalted task?

Hobbes might respond to this line of criticism with something akin to his historical argument regarding miracles. He might argue that the reductionism of his account of religion is bound to seem unconvincing to those who remain in the grips of a traditional outlook that makes excessive demands and inspires irrational hopes, but that outlook can give way over time to a new one that is, even or precisely if more disillusioned, more sober and rational. The spread of a more sober and rational outlook, he might argue, will vindicate over time a position that appears to be an unwarranted distortion of men's experience only so long as the "Kingdom of Darkness" retains its power (consider *Lev.* 30.6, 30.14, 44.2–3; *De Cive*, Pref., 1.2; *Elem.* 1.1). This much, at any rate, is certain: Hobbes was making every effort compatible with his safety to promote a new outlook, and he was doing so, not only by trying to convince men to accept the basic premises of his mechanistic materialism and by raising doubts about the Bible, but also by setting forth a new moral and political doctrine. Hobbes's political philosophy, too, plays an important role—in some respects, the most important role—in his project of civilizational transformation. And his political philosophy, too, may bear, if in a less obvious way, on the question of religious experiences. For Hobbes might reply to the charge that he overlooks the crucial moral dimension of religious experiences by saying that, rather than ignoring that dimension, he was seeking, not indeed to appreciate it or to see it from the inside, but to *change it*. If men could be brought to hold more sober and rational moral opinions— opinions that made their view of morality at once less demanding and less inspiring of naïve hopes—might that not lead over time to a transformation of their experience, such that the tendency of men to interpret certain experiences as "religious" would fade away? And if that happened, would it not

---

76. See, e.g., Bramhall, *The Catching of Leviathan*, 521–22; Ross, *Leviathan Drawn out with a Hook*, 9–10.

provide a kind of demonstration that Hobbes was right all along in his denial that such experiences are genuine sources of an illumination unavailable to reason alone? Of course, one could ask again in such a case, as in the case of miracles, whether what Hobbes would regard as progressive enlightenment could not be interpreted instead as estrangement from God. But those who would offer that response would be fewer, and the power of their position would seem ever weaker, as most men came to be persuaded of the truth of Hobbes's moral and political teaching and enjoyed the fruits of its success. Whether Hobbes had such a vision in his mind's eye is a question we should keep in mind as we turn, at long last, to Hobbes's political philosophy.

6

Hobbes's Political Philosophy I:
Man and Morality

Let us begin our examination of Hobbes's political philosophy by returning to a question that we began to consider much earlier, at the beginning of Chapter 2: the question of the relationship between Hobbes's political philosophy and his natural philosophy. In our earlier consideration of this question, we pursued it far enough to begin to see how complicated it is. To recall the basic puzzle: by announcing (and never renouncing) his ambition to produce a tripartite system that moves from body to man to citizen, Hobbes suggests that he conceived of his political philosophy as dependent on and even derivative from his natural philosophy. Yet, by declaring that the third part of his project—his political philosophy proper—could be severed from the other two parts and presented first (in *De Cive*), he suggests that his political philosophy is independent, in its foundation and principles, from his natural philosophy (see p. 36 above and the passages cited there). Now, as I indicated earlier, the apparent contradiction in Hobbes's direct remarks about his tripartite project is only the beginning of the difficulty of making sense of the relationship between his political philosophy and his natural philosophy. We need now to plunge more deeply into the problem—a problem with which Hobbes scholars have long struggled and over which they have come to widely divergent conclusions. The struggle and the disagreement are understandable, because Hobbes himself does not offer a clear resolution of the problem. One is forced to sift through conflicting evidence, and some measure of speculation is unavoidable.

The evidence that Hobbes *did* regard his political philosophy as derivative from his natural philosophy is not limited to those remarks in which he speaks of his ambition to create a tripartite system encompassing the "elements" of philosophy. Hobbes also makes other statements that indicate more explicitly that he conceived of the parts or branches of philosophy as having a necessary order, in which the later parts are dependent on the earlier ones. The most striking such statement is in Chapter 6 of *De Corpore*, where Hobbes speaks most directly of the procedure to be followed as one moves from one part of philosophy to the next. In this chapter, "Of Method," Hobbes suggests that physics, as the culmination of natural philosophy, must follow a prior study of "first philosophy" and a form of geometry that is directed above all to the understanding of motion. But more important for present purposes is what he says about what comes after physics: "After physics, one comes to moral philosophy (*moralia*), in which part of philosophy one considers the motions of the mind, namely, *appetite, aversion, love, benevolence, hope, fear, anger, emulation, envy*, etc., what causes they have, and of what they are causes. The reason why these are to be considered after physics is that they have their causes in sense and imagination, which are subjects of physical contemplation" (*De Corp.* 6.6). This statement and others that would seem to corroborate it (see above all *De Corp.* 6.17, but also Latin *Lev.*, 125–29) have led some to the conclusion that Hobbes believed that there is a necessary sequence to the parts of philosophy, with the implication that his political philosophy must be understood as a mere application or extension of his natural philosophy to the understanding of human life in its moral and political dimensions. In support of this view would seem to be this key fact: in *The Elements of Law* and *Leviathan*, Hobbes prefaces his presentation of his political philosophy proper with a mechanistic account of human psychology. Is not Hobbes's mechanistic psychology the middle term, so to speak, linking his physics with his political philosophy in such a way that the latter is merely the working out of the human consequences of the former? Is not Hobbes's distinction as a political philosopher that he was the first to apply the new science of mechanistic materialism to human life in general and to moral and political life in particular?[1]

1. See, for example, Alan Ryan, *The Philosophy of the Social Sciences*, 102–3: "Hobbes believed as firmly as one could that all behaviour, whether of animate or inanimate matter, was ultimately to be explained in terms of particulate motion: the laws governing the motions of discrete particles were the ultimate laws of nature, and in this sense psychology must be rooted in physiology and physiology in physics, while the social sciences, especially the technology of statecraft, must be rooted in psychology" (see also the reference on p. 15 to "the fanciful world of Hobbes's 'Leviathan,' where social science would be a sub-department of physics"). Although Ryan offers the most extreme expression of the view that Hobbes's political philosophy is derivative from his natural philosophy, similar claims, if somewhat more qualified and complicated ones, can be found in Peters, *Hobbes*, 69–74, 86–88 (cf. 134–38); Spragens, *The Politics of Motion*, 101–4, 129–218; Macpherson, *The Political Theory of Possessive Individualism*, 9–17, 29–34, 78–79

This view, which at first seems so compelling, runs into difficulties when one considers the full range of Hobbes's methodological statements and compares them with his actual procedure in his political philosophy. The first and most obvious difficulty is that the view just sketched makes it impossible to account for the anomaly of *De Cive*, where Hobbes begins from a brief consideration of human nature but not from a mechanistic psychology. This aspect of *De Cive*, moreover, should remind us of the crucial statement we considered earlier in which Hobbes says that the reason he was able to write *De Cive* (the third part of his tripartite project) before completing *De Corpore* and *De Homine* (the first two parts) is that it did not need the preceding parts because the work "rests on principles of its own known from experience" (*De Cive*, Pref.; see p. 36 above). One might be tempted to confine the significance of that statement to *De Cive* and to explain the anomaly of *De Cive* as due to Hobbes's desire, for reasons having to do with the political crisis in England, to rush that work to completion. After all, Hobbes himself gives that explanation in the same passage. But the statement cannot be so easily dismissed or downplayed, because there are similar statements in Hobbes's other works. Perhaps the most important—certainly the most famous—is in the introduction to *Leviathan*. There, Hobbes indicates that, before turning to the theme of the commonwealth itself in Part II of *Leviathan*, he will begin in Part I from "the *matter* thereof, and the *artificer*, both of which is *man*." He then goes on to explain his procedure in investigating man, indicating that his examination of human nature aims, above all, at the discovery of the fundamental passions common to all men. He *does not* claim that the key to the discovery or understanding of the passions is the rigorous application of his mechanistic materialism. Rather, he suggests that the method to be used by "him that searcheth hearts" is a combination of close observation of

---

(see also 68–70); Goldsmith, *Hobbes's Science of Politics*, 13–14; Lubienski, *Die Grundlagen des ethisch-politischen Systems von Hobbes*, 14–17; Gillespie, *The Theological Origins of Modernity*, 222–39; Laird, *Hobbes*, 89–90. Consider also Brandt, *Thomas Hobbes' Mechanical Conception of Nature*, 244, 346, 370–71; Watkins, *Hobbes's System of Ideas*, xiii–xv, 1–13, *et passim*; Burtt, *The Metaphysical Foundations of Modern Physical Science*, 124–27; Mintz, *The Hunting of Leviathan*, 23–38; Cassirer, *The Philosophy of the Enlightenment*, 19, 254–56. Malcolm, for his part, suggests in the introduction to his edition of *Leviathan* that Hobbes's political theory was "derived from, or at least built on, his mechanistic account of human nature" (*Leviathan, Vol. 1: Introduction*, 13). But not only does the demurral "or at least built on" indicate a reservation, but Malcolm takes a somewhat different and more complex position in Chapter 5 of *Aspects of Hobbes* (see especially 155: "Hobbes's formal science of rights and obligations assumes the existence of a human nature which can be described by a mechanistic science of causes; but it is not itself a product of that science").

men's actions and a form of introspection in which one reads in oneself "not this or that particular man, but mankind." Hobbes then calls on his readers to consider, as they move through his text, whether they find in themselves the same reading of human nature that he has arrived at by such a method, *"for this kind of doctrine admitteth no other demonstration"* (emphasis added). This crucial statement should be taken together with others, both in *Leviathan* and in his other works of political philosophy, where Hobbes suggests that the best way to know human nature is to reflect on experience (see, e.g., *Lev.* 32.1; *Elem.* 1.2; *De Hom.*, Ep. Ded.). Even in *De Corpore*, in the very same chapter that supplies the strongest evidence for the view that his political philosophy is derivative from his natural philosophy, Hobbes acknowledges that it is not essential to study natural philosophy first. Although one can proceed by a "synthetic" method from geometry and physics to civil philosophy, one can also forgo that method and turn directly to civil philosophy: "for the causes of the motions of the mind are known, not only by ratiocination, but also by the experience of anyone who observes those motions within himself," and, therefore, "even those who have not learned the prior part of philosophy, namely, geometry and physics, can nevertheless arrive at the principles of civil philosophy by the analytical method" (*De Corp.* 6.7). It would seem to be this "analytical" method, not the "synthetic" one, that Hobbes himself primarily relied on in his political philosophy.

There are reasons of substance, in addition to those of method, not to regard Hobbes's political philosophy as derivative from his natural philosophy. For if one tries to understand Hobbes's political philosophy as merely derivative from his natural philosophy, it becomes difficult to preserve some of the crucial features that give it its distinctive character. What comes to sight if one applies the principles of Hobbes's natural philosophy directly and rigorously to human life and looks at human life only through that lens? The picture that emerges is this: every human action, just like every other event in the world, is necessitated by chains of mechanistic causation; we live in a world of appearances produced by the motions of unknowable bodies; but at neither level—that is, at neither the level of the appearances, nor that of the underlying bodies—is there anything real except matter in motion and the epiphenomena produced by colliding bodies; in particular, there is nothing to which one could attach any moral significance. Now, it is undeniable that there are many passages in which Hobbes presents precisely such a picture of human life as wholly determined by chains of mechanistic causation. And on some level Hobbes surely accepted the view just sketched as the truth about human life (consider pp. 47–48 above). But is it possible on such a basis—on the basis of what may be called a completely necessitated "naturalism"—to understand the full dimensions of Hobbes's political philosophy? After all, Hobbes's political philosophy has at its core a claim about natural *right*—a claim that would seem, at any rate, to rest on a moral distinction between the fear of violent death, as a morally legitimate motive, and the desire for glory, as a morally illegitimate motive. More broadly, Hobbes's political philosophy is obviously meant to do much more than merely describe the mechanistic causes of moral and political life; it also prescribes a new moral outlook and a new kind of politics. Hobbes's political philosophy is, as we would say today, normative.[2] But can these features of it be understood if it is approached merely as a consequence of his natural philosophy? Although Hobbes's overall view was certainly naturalistic, "consistent naturalism," as Strauss puts it, "would have been the ruin of his political philosophy," because consistent naturalism would obscure, not to say destroy, the moral and normative character of Hobbes's political philosophy.[3]

Are there, then, *no connections* between Hobbes's political philosophy and his natural philosophy? That would be going too far in the other direction from the view that Hobbes's political philosophy is derivative from his natural philosophy. For even if that view is wrong and Hobbes's political philosophy rests on its own foundations, that does not mean that these two parts of philosophy belong, for Hobbes, simply to separate worlds. They *are* connected—and in more than one way.

The first connection appears from the already raised question of Hobbes's method. It is true—and, with respect to the primary question considered thus far, decisive—that Hobbes proceeds in his political philosophy from experience and introspection. But how are his statements about the need to begin from experience and introspection to be put together with the claim, which he also makes, to have discovered a new method of political philosophy to replace the older orientation by common opinions (see p. 32 above)? The new method is often called the "resolutive-compositive" method, which Hobbes applied to political philosophy in apparent imitation of Galileo, its pioneer in natural philosophy.[4] By this method, the understanding of a complex whole is pursued through a process that first breaks down the object of study by an anal-

---

2. See Sorell, *Hobbes*, 16–17, 21, 24; Peters, *Hobbes*, 158–62.

3. *The Political Philosophy of Hobbes*, 169 (cf. viii–xi, 28–29, 168); see also "On the Basis of Hobbes's Political Philosophy," 178–79, 192; "Some Notes on the Political Science of Hobbes," 127. Compare Sorell, *Hobbes*, 17.

4. For discussions of the "resolutive-compositive" method and Hobbes's application of it to political philosophy, see Cassirer, *The Philosophy of the Enlightenment*, 255–56; Watkins, *Hobbes's System of Ideas*, 32–35, 43–50, "Philosophy and Politics in Hobbes," 133; Strauss, *The Political Philosophy of Hobbes*, 2, 6, 151–52; Lloyd, *Ideals as Interests in Hobbes's Leviathan*, 235–41; Gauthier, *The Logic of Leviathan*, 2–5; Peters, *Hobbes*, 64–65, 158–60.

ysis that reduces it into its first principles or elements, and then reconstructs it on the basis of the discovered elements. Hobbes's most direct account of his adaptation of this method to political philosophy is in the preface of *De Cive*:

> As for my method, I came to the conclusion that the order of an oration, although clear, would not suffice by itself. I decided instead to begin from the matter of a commonwealth, then turn to the generation and form of it, and proceed from there to the first origin of justice. For a thing is best known from its constituents. Just as in the case of an automatic clock or any other machine of some complexity, it is impossible to know the work of each part and wheel unless it is taken apart and the matter, shape, and motion of each of them is inspected separately, so too in the case of the right of the commonwealth and the duties of citizens, the task is, not indeed to take the commonwealth apart, but rather to consider it as if it were taken apart, that is, to understand correctly what the character of human nature is, and in what respects it is suitable and in what unsuitable for uniting in a commonwealth, and in what way men who want to join together ought to be combined.

The crucial premise that Hobbes's method in political philosophy shares with the Galilean approach in natural philosophy is captured by the simplest line in this passage: "a thing is best known from its constituents." The guiding thought of the resolutive-compositive method is that the constituents of any given object of study can be discovered by a mental process of analysis that precedes a subsequent (re)synthesis.

The constituents that Hobbes has in mind in the case of the commonwealth are not so much the citizens *per se* as the most important aspects of human nature, and these aspects, in Hobbes's view, are the fundamental human passions. Hobbes's political philosophy begins, then, with an examination of human nature that seeks to discover the passions that are the building blocks—or the obstacles, in the case of some passions—for the construction of a solid commonwealth. This conception of his procedure is not at odds with Hobbes's other claim that he begins from experience and introspection. For the question must be asked: How does one take apart the "clock"? To what evidence does one look to see its parts? And that question can be answered only by understanding Hobbes's resolutive-compositive method, not as opposed to his turn to experience and introspection, but as cooperating with it, or even as a somewhat more technical expression of the same guiding thought.[5] Now, this could seem to mean—in a way, it does mean—that in

---

5. Immediately after the passage in which he compares his method to the taking apart of a clock, Hobbes speaks of the "principles" discovered by his method as "known to all men by experience" (*De Cive*, Pref.). See also *De Cive*, Ep. Ded.; *De Corp.* 6.7.

using a method adapted from natural philosophy, Hobbes is, as it were, filling the shell of that borrowed method with content derived from an independent consideration of experience. For, as we have already noted, it is not so much Hobbes's mechanistic psychology as his examination of experience and introspection that lead the way in his attempt to analyze human nature into its key components. Thus we can understand why Hobbes's most explicit account of his resolutive-compositive method can come at the outset of a work—*De Cive*—in which his mechanistic psychology is almost entirely absent.

We must tread carefully here, however. For the fact remains that, at least in *The Elements of Law* and *Leviathan*, Hobbes *does* present a mechanistic psychology, which he blends with his reflections on experience and the results of his introspection. And the difficulty one encounters is this: although it may be true that the content or substance (as opposed to the method) of Hobbes's political philosophy comes from reflections that, strictly speaking, are not derivative from any prior scientific account, it is impossible to deny that Hobbes's mechanistic psychology seems to have left an imprint on his interpretation of what he finds by reflecting on experience and by looking into himself. A particularly striking example can be found in the pivotal chapter on the passions in *Leviathan*, Chapter 6. In this chapter, Hobbes makes a series of important claims about the human good and the character of our striving for it. First and foremost, he denies that there is any simple or absolute good to which all men are directed by nature (*Lev.* 6.7; see also *Elem.* 7.3). But he does not leave matters there. He also claims that any attraction men have to the noble or the beautiful (the *pulchrum* in Latin) is nothing more than a version of desiring the good: the noble is distinguished by the promise of something good, not by the transcendence of all considerations of benefit and harm (*Lev.* 6.8; see also *Elem.* 7.3). He then goes on to argue that our desire for the good, in all of its forms, can be reduced to the pursuit of pleasure or power or some combination of those two ends (*Lev.* 6.9–12, 6.39–43; see also *Elem.* 7.2–4, 7.7–9, 8.3–4). In keeping with the tendency of this line of argument, Hobbes includes in his list of (mere) passions in Chapter 6 qualities such as courage, magnanimity, and liberality, which were traditionally regarded as virtues (*Lev.* 6.17, 6.26–28; see also *Elem.* 9.4, 9.20); and he denies the possibility of happiness understood as a state of perfect contentment or "perpetual tranquility of mind" (*Lev.* 6.58; see also *Elem.* 7.6). We will consider these claims more fully later in this chapter. For present purposes, we may limit our attention to the following dilemma. On the one hand, the claims just sketched are not derived in Chapter 6 from Hobbes's mechanistic psychology. If one searches for an argument that may be regarded as a strict and rigorous derivation, one comes up empty-handed.[6] Moreover, it is possible to imagine someone accepting the claims in question while rejecting Hobbes's mechanistic psychology; the two are not so inseparable that such a position is inconceivable. Yet, on the other hand, Hobbes's mechanistic psychology is very much on display in Chapter 6. The title of the chapter is "Of the Interior Beginnings of Voluntary Motions, Commonly Called the PASSIONS, and the Speeches by which they are Expressed," and Hobbes begins the chapter with an account of the small, initially imperceptible motions "within the body of man" that he regards as sources of appetite and aversion (*Lev.* 6.1–2; see also *Elem.* 7.1–2). Is it not likely that this conception—the view that at the roots of all change, including human desires and aversions, lies nothing but the motions of bodies—colored the way Hobbes saw the passions? At least this much may be said with confidence: Hobbes's claims about the human good and the character of our pursuit of it—the judgments he makes about human experience—have a deep kinship with his mechanistic psychology. The kinship lies in a shared reductionism and in the conviction that life in a world of ceaseless motions is incompatible with any notions of transcendence, teleology, or repose.

It is impossible to know for sure just how deeply Hobbes's mechanistic psychology, or his mechanistic view of nature more broadly, shaped his interpretation of human experience, including his evaluation of the results of his introspection. But the kinship just indicated should remind us of another way in which there is at least some connection between Hobbes's natural philosophy and his political philosophy. In our earlier consideration of the relationship between these two parts of Hobbes's thought, I suggested that Hobbes's natural philosophy plays a ground-clearing role, in the sense that it fosters a kind of sobriety that is necessary if Hobbes's readers are to be receptive to his political philosophy (see p. 37 above). Let me spell out that suggestion a bit more fully here. One could ask why Hobbes includes his natural philosophy in his works of political philosophy at all. Hobbes's natural philosophy *does* appear there, and especially in *Leviathan* it makes more than a cameo appearance. But why? One reason—and this is the explanation that Hobbes himself gives in the passage in which he directly addresses the question—is that he thought it necessary to combat certain Aristotelian-scholastic doctrines,

---

6. Berkowitz, "*Leviathan*, Then and Now," and Macpherson, *The Political Theory of Possessive Individualism*, 32–33, suggest otherwise, but neither of them identifies an argument that qualifies as a strict and rigorous derivation of the claims in question from Hobbes's mechanistic psychology.

especially the doctrine of abstract essences, that had equipped the "ghostly authorities" with philosophic weapons and thereby helped to undermine secular authority and the stability of the commonwealth (see *Lev.* 46.15–18; see also 2.8–9; Latin *Lev.*, 1125–31). Hobbes regarded it as necessary to fight fire with fire or, perhaps better, to douse fire with cold water. Thus he presents a vision of nature that, unlike the teachings of traditional metaphysics, which had the opposite effect, could be expected to bring men to their senses and prepare them to embrace a political teaching that depends on the thought that violent death is the worst of all evils (see p. 37 above). But this suggestion can be stated more broadly. It helps in this regard to reflect on the likely psychological and cultural effects of spreading the view that reality consists of nothing but matter in motion—that is, on the human significance and impact of mechanistic materialism. Is not the predictable impact of that doctrine to move men away from a superstitious form of fear, which grips men by nature and leads them to imagine invisible powers, to a new, more rational kind of fear before a vast and unresponsive universe? Does not the doctrine also have the effect of humiliating a dangerous form of pride or vanity, by teaching men that we are not the special darlings of nature, and that nature threatens us as much as it does any other beings? Is it not plausible—indeed, more than plausible—that Hobbes thought that the new kind of fear, together with the humiliation of men's pride, would put those who accepted the new view of nature in a better frame of mind to do the work necessary, including accepting the restrictions necessary, to build the only kind of commonwealth that can provide the security we desperately need in our dangerous world?[7]

These reflections suggest that Hobbes thought that his natural philosophy, by articulating the view of nature most conducive to the success of his political project, could serve as a kind of handmaid of his political philosophy. Hobbes did think that, I believe. But one can also turn the question around and ask whether Hobbes's political philosophy contributes in any way to his natural philosophy. To understand how that might be the case, we need to bear in mind what came to sight in our earlier examination of Hobbes's natural philosophy. Hobbes's natural philosophy presents, to be sure, a thoroughly mechanistic and materialistic view of nature. But we should not forget the

---

7. See Strauss, "On the Basis of Hobbes's Political Philosophy," 181; Johnston, *The Rhetoric of Leviathan*, 120–21. At the very beginning of *Leviathan*, Hobbes brings together a mechanistic account of life and a portrait of the Leviathan, the commonwealth, as an artificial man who will provide for the protection and defense of natural men (see Intro.). Regarding the human significance of mechanistic materialism, consider *Anti-White* 37.8; see also Burtt, *The Metaphysical Foundations of Modern Physical Science*, 4–11, 126–27, 236.

strand of skepticism that also emerged in response to certain problems and led Hobbes to waver between a bold metaphysical materialism and a more modest methodological materialism. Most important is the problem that Hobbes's natural philosophy cannot rule out the possibility of a mysterious God who created the universe and can miraculously intervene in its workings (see pp. 64–66 and 76–77 above). Near the beginning of Chapter 3, I suggested that Hobbes's critique of religion, which we have examined in the last three chapters, should be regarded as a supplement to his natural philosophy in the sense that it is meant to address that problem (see p. 83 above). Yet, even if that is true, we can now see the limits of that suggestion. For Hobbes's critique of religion does not resolve the critical issue either: it has proven to be no more decisive than his natural philosophy in ruling out the possibility of God's miraculous intervention in the world (see pp. 125–26 and 179–80 above).

Hobbes must have remained dissatisfied, then, with his direct efforts to settle the deepest theological question, which is at the same time the deepest question of natural philosophy. And that conclusion should make us open to the possibility that Hobbes thought that his political philosophy could contribute, not just practically but also theoretically, to his battle against his most fundamental foe. This thought is not altogether new at this point. We have already observed Hobbes's interest in the "resolution"—that is, the dissolution or destruction—of religion. And the striking fact that his expression of that interest immediately precedes his chapter on the state of nature, the core of his political philosophy, led us to wonder whether Hobbes's political philosophy has an important role to play in his attempt to undermine religion (see p. 113 above). So, too, in our consideration both of his natural philosophy and of his critique of religion, we were ultimately led to suggest that Hobbes's political philosophy is an essential part of the project of civilizational advancement by which he could provide a certain kind of indirect response to the challenge posed by claims of miracles and religious experiences (see pp. 80 and 182–83 above). Finally, we have already noted that Hobbes's political philosophy does not rest on a theological foundation or depend on any theological premises. To the contrary, not only does it rest on principles discovered by reason alone, but it aims to establish the primacy of secular political ends and to promote a rational morality that does not need religious support (see pp. 84 and 113–14 above). Can the zeal with which Hobbes pursued this moral-political project be explained, at least in part, by the hope that its success would help to vindicate his view that claims of miracles and religious experiences belong to a backward age that men can become ever more confident has been rightly left behind? We may never be able to answer that question with certainty, for it is difficult—perhaps impossible—to see into Hobbes's mind and to gauge whether or in what way he was guided by such a vision. But it is possible to show that Hobbes hoped that his political philosophy would undermine and replace a traditional view of human life and morality that, in its high demands and summons to transcendence, had long worked with other forces to keep men "in the dark" (see *Lev.* 44.2).

Hobbes's Account of Human Nature and Human Striving

In Chapter 1, we examined Hobbes's critique of the classical tradition of political philosophy, especially of Aristotle, the most influential but also the most problematic source of that tradition in Hobbes's view. It is not necessary to review here every aspect of Hobbes's critique. But to begin to see what is distinctive about Hobbes's own political philosophy, in both approach and content, it will help to remind ourselves of two key points: Hobbes criticized Aristotle and his heirs for taking their bearings by common opinions, and he attacked their foundational conviction that man is naturally drawn into society—that man is, in Aristotle's famous formulation, "a political animal." There is a connection between these two points, not only because the belief in man's natural sociality is an example of an opinion that earlier philosophers accepted too uncritically, but also for a broader reason: both points reflect Hobbes's conviction that the classical tradition was naïve. Aristotle and his heirs accepted too readily men's exalted speech about themselves, and the insufficient skepticism of nearly all earlier philosophers led them to embrace lofty but false conceptions of what moves men and leads them into communities. Precisely because of its naïve deference to common opinions, the classical tradition, in Hobbes's view, lacked an adequate starting point, unwittingly inflamed the diverse passions that underlie opinions, and thus failed to provide a firm foundation for a truly secure order (see pp. 18–20 above).

If we start from this line of criticism and search for Hobbes's alternative approach, our attention is likely to be drawn immediately to his doctrine of the state of nature. Is it not in his state of nature teaching, more than anywhere else, that Hobbes displays his new approach of applying the "resolutive-compositive" method to the commonwealth? Is it not through the thought experiment of that teaching that Hobbes takes apart the "clock" of the commonwealth, views it as dissolved into its constituent elements, and then discovers a superior composition of those elements? The answer to that question is surely yes, and in some sense it is obvious that Hobbes's state of nature teaching is the centerpiece of his new political philosophy. Yet it would be a mistake to jump straight to Hobbes's state of nature, because in each of his presentations of his political philosophy, his state of nature teaching is preceded by an account of human nature.

This is true even in *De Cive*, where Hobbes does not begin from a mechanistic psychology but rather turns in short order to the state of nature. The title of the first chapter of *De Cive* is "On the State of Man outside of Civil Society." Even in this opening chapter, however, Hobbes does not begin by turning directly to the state of nature. Instead, he begins with a striking line of argument that displays, in another way, the difference between his approach and the traditional one. He opens with an immediate attack on the view that man is a political animal naturally directed toward society. Leaving no doubt as to whom he regards as its original proponent—since he quotes Aristotle's famous phrase that man is a ζῷον πολιτικόν (political animal)—Hobbes argues that this view has supplied the foundation on which most earlier writers on politics have built their doctrines (*De Cive* 1.2). He then bluntly declares that the view rests on a superficial understanding of human nature that is belied by careful observation of the actions of men. We can see something here of what Hobbes means when he says that he argues from experience. Against those who would claim that there is a natural fellowship among men, Hobbes contends that men seek the company only of those who are useful to them, either by adding to their prestige or by benefiting them in more concrete ways. Hobbes does not deny that bonds of a sort develop between men. But he argues that human relationships are rooted more in fear and in the desire for glory or benefit than in love or natural goodwill. "Honor and advantage" are what we are primarily after, even in our friendships; friends themselves are "secondary" (*De Cive* 1.2).

To see "the purpose for which men congregate," Hobbes says, we need only look at "what they do when they congregate" (*De Cive* 1.2). What sort of observations does Hobbes make about the congregations of men? He points out that when men meet to do business with one another, they are manifestly seeking profit, not fellowship. If the purpose of their gathering is political, they are guided more by fear or factional interests than by love or goodwill. Even in gatherings that are merely for the sake of entertainment, each man, according to Hobbes, finds his greatest delight in those incidents and jokes that display his superiority at the expense of others. In these social gatherings, men tend to ridicule those who are not present, or even those who depart; it is therefore a wise policy, Hobbes quips, always to be the last to leave. Similarly, men are always eager to talk about themselves. If one produces a story about himself, the rest will typically respond in kind. Even in philosophic gatherings, everyone wishes to be regarded as a master, and resentments quickly arise when those wishes are not fulfilled. On the basis of observations like these, Hobbes draws a far-reaching conclusion: "it is clear from experience to everyone who considers human affairs with even a modicum of attention that every voluntary congregation arises either from mutual need or from the pursuit of glory; when men congregate, what they are eager to get is either some benefit or that εὐδοκιμεῖν, that is, esteem and honor among their fellows" (*De Cive* 1.2).

Two things stand out in this passage from the opening pages of *De Cive*. The first is the sheer bluntness, not to say the almost gleeful cynicism, with which Hobbes asserts that the primary concern of each and every human being is for his own good. Hobbes is amazingly direct, here and elsewhere, in his assertion that the fundamental motive of all human action is the desire to benefit oneself (see also, e.g., *De Cive* 1.13, 3.21; *Elem.* 16.6; *De Hom.* 11.6; *Lev.* 14.8, 15.16; *EW* IV, 273; *EW* V, 357; *Anti-White* 32.1, 39.5). Hobbes's claim in this regard is reasonably called an "assertion," not because he does not support it with empirical observations, but because one could well question whether observations of the sort he offers suffice to demonstrate its truth. Are Hobbes's highly selective observations adequate to settle so complex a question as the character of men's deepest motives in their dealings with one another? One could also ask why Hobbes so eagerly and unabashedly puts forward an assertion that most human beings would regard as an unsettling or even repugnant claim about our inescapable selfishness.[8] Rather than dwell on these difficulties at this point, let us turn to the other striking feature of the passage: if Hobbes asserts, on the one hand, a basic uniformity of all human actions as driven by the desire to benefit oneself, he also suggests, on the other hand, a crucial bifurcation between those actions that arise from need and those that are for the sake of glory or reputation. In the passage under consideration, this bifurcation emerges from mere observation on Hobbes's part. One wonders, however, how Hobbes conceived of its roots in human nature and the human condition. For we can see even from the opening pages of *De Cive* that Hobbes regarded the pursuit of glory as no less natural but far more problematic than the concern to meet one's basic needs. As he goes on to say in the passage we have been considering, the desire for glory may be

---

8. This is another claim in the bundle of rank-smelling "weeds" that Bramhall gathers out of Hobbes's works (see *The Catching of Leviathan*, 544–45). Bramhall objects to Hobbes's claim that "of all voluntary acts, the object is to every man his own good" by declaring that "Moses, St. Paul, and the Decii were not of this mind" (545). See also the similar objection of Hyde, *A Brief View and Survey*, 28. On the broader "repudiation of [Hobbes's] egoistic psychology" in Restoration England, see Mintz, *The Hunting of Leviathan*, 142–46.

a natural passion, but "no large or lasting society can be based on the passion for glory," because glory, unlike safety, is not something that can be widely shared (De Cive 1.2). Does that mean that those who are driven by the passion for glory are more culpable for their aggressive actions—more deserving of blame, in Hobbes's eyes—than are those who act for the sake of self-preservation (see De Cive 1.4)? But how can that be if the former, no less than the latter, are driven by a passion woven into the very fabric of human nature itself (see De Cive, Pref.)?

It would be a mistake to try to answer these questions too quickly. The division of human motives that is visible from the outset in De Cive emerges more gradually in Hobbes's other presentations of his political philosophy. And an examination of key sections of those other presentations, especially of Leviathan, can help us with the prior question of how Hobbes conceived of the roots of the difference in motives. In Leviathan, Hobbes attempts to reconstruct human experience and the character of human striving from the ground up. In his account there, observations of the sort one finds at the beginning of De Cive play a role, but they do not come on stage quite so quickly; they emerge only after an analysis of the passions in particular. The account of the passions in Leviathan shares with the opening passage of De Cive a debunking intention; but it differs from it insofar as it provides a more comprehensive account, built up step by step, of human striving—an account that is woven together with a broad consideration of the human condition and of the kind of happiness that is possible for human beings.

I have already sketched some of the most notable features of Chapter 6 of Leviathan, the crucial chapter on the passions. But let us now consider it in greater detail. The full title of Chapter 6, as already noted, is not "Of the Passions," but "Of the Interior Beginnings of Voluntary Motions, Commonly Called the PASSIONS, and the Speeches by which they are Expressed." From the last part of this title ("and the Speeches by which they are Expressed"), one could easily get the impression that Hobbes intends to give more weight here than he did in De Cive to common opinions. That proves not to be the case. In fact, in his account of the passions in Leviathan, Hobbes explicitly warns his readers not to be misled by the frequently deceptive ways in which men speak of their passions (see 6.56). Rather than taking his bearings by the opinions men express in speech, Hobbes begins from a mechanistic account of the origins of the passions in minute motions—motions either toward certain objects (in the case of appetites) or away from them (in the case of aversions). As noted earlier, Hobbes's mechanistic materialism is very much on display at the beginning of Chapter 6, and, even if it fades into the background as the chapter proceeds, Hobbes's analysis remains consistent with it throughout.

The passions begin, according to Hobbes, as motions triggered by the interaction of external stimuli and the internal constitutions of men's bodies
(see *Lev.* 6.1–2). Since both the external stimuli affecting men and the internal
constitutions of men's bodies are in "continual mutation," Hobbes is led to
stress in the first place the great diversity and fluctuation of men's appetites
and aversions (6.6). From this diversity alone it does not necessarily follow
that there is no natural hierarchy of the ends men pursue, nor that there is no
single end they *should* pursue. Yet those are precisely the claims Hobbes goes
on to make, in his famous statement about the absence of an absolute good
and the relativity of all notions of good and evil:

> But whatsoever is the object of any man's appetite or desire, that is it which
> he for his part calleth *good*; and the object of his hate and aversion, *evil*; and
> of his contempt, *vile* and *inconsiderable*. For these words of good, evil, and
> contemptible are ever used with relation to the person that useth them—
> there being nothing simply and absolutely so, nor any common rule of good
> and evil to be taken from the nature of the objects themselves. (6.7; see also
> *Elem.* 7.3; *De Hom.* 11.4, 13.8; *Anti-White* 30.24)

Hobbes emphasizes here the ineluctable variety within men's striving to attain what is regarded (by various men at various moments) as good and to
avoid what is regarded (by various men at various moments) as evil. And yet,
if there is an obvious pluralistic and relativistic thrust to his analysis, Hobbes
also moves in the other direction, toward affirming a basic commonality of all
human striving. For, as diverse as the objects of our striving are according to
Hobbes, there is also a sense in which he thinks all men are seeking the same
thing. All men are seeking what is good for themselves—even when they are
attracted by the noble or the beautiful (see 6.8; see also *De Hom.* 11.5, 11.13)—
and the good that draws men to it would seem to consist in various forms of
pleasure. "*Pleasure*," Hobbes writes, "is the appearance, or sense, of good, and
molestation or *displeasure*, the appearance, or sense, of evil. And consequently
all appetite, desire, and love is accompanied with some delight, more or less,
and all hatred and aversion, with more or less displeasure and offence" (6.11).
Hobbes contends that pleasure and pain, delight and distress, are mere appearances caused by underlying motions (6.9–10; see also *Elem.* 7.1–2); but it
would seem to be our lived experiences of these appearances that, in his view,
dictate our passion-driven actions.

Now, if one stopped at this point in Chapter 6, it would seem that Hobbes's
account of human striving is thoroughly hedonistic. It is certainly the case that
Hobbes does not pass any moral judgments against the seeking of pleasure or
draw any distinctions between higher and lower pleasures. To the contrary,

even as he distinguishes between "pleasures of sense" and "pleasures of the mind," he objects to those who would use the word "sensual" to condemn the former as baser than the latter; such a usage has "no place till there be laws" (6.12). In keeping with the moral neutrality, or amorality, of his analysis is an aspect of Chapter 6 already mentioned: Hobbes treats as mere passions what were traditionally regarded as moral virtues. Courage, for instance, he defines merely as the hope of avoiding hurt by resistance (see 6.17). Similarly, in the cases of magnanimity and liberality (6.26–28), Hobbes does not enter into the kind of nuanced analysis of the motives of the morally virtuous that one finds, for example, in Aristotle's *Ethics*. Rather, he defines each passion tersely, usually in a line or two, and he does not describe any passion as especially admirable or contemptible. Still, even if Hobbes assiduously refrains from the language of moral praise and blame, one cannot leave matters at saying that his account of the passions is simply hedonistic. For, as the account unfolds, another human concern, besides the desire for pleasure, enters the picture. This further concern can be seen, for instance, in Hobbes's definition of glorying as a joy or "exultation of the mind" arising from "imagination of a man's own power and ability" (6.39), or in his definition of dejection as "grief from opinion of want of power" (6.40). In his definitions of glorying and dejection—and so, too, in his descriptions of the sudden eruptions of these passions in bouts of laughter and weeping—Hobbes points to the importance to men, not just of pleasure, but also of power. If men laugh when the revelation of a defect in another causes them to rejoice in their own relative power, they weep when turns of fortune "suddenly take away some vehement hope, or some prop of their power" (6.42–43; see also *Elem.* 9.13–14). Laughter and weeping, of course, are only two manifestations of a concern that displays itself more broadly in human life. As Hobbes will go on to say in a later chapter: "The passions that most of all cause the differences of wit are, principally, the more or less desire of power, of riches, of knowledge, and of honor—all of which may be reduced to the first, that is, desire of power, for riches, knowledge, and honor are but several sorts of power" (*Lev.* 8.15).

Power is ultimately as important in Hobbes's account of human striving as pleasure is. But if pleasure is the delight that appears as the result of underlying motions, what is the root of the human concern for power in Hobbes's view? There would seem to be more than one root, and thus the question does not admit of a simple answer. One way of answering it is to say that the concern for power is a consequence of the relative and fluctuating character of the good: if the good is relative and fluctuating, then it makes sense that each man, necessarily unsure what his future desires will be, should want "the present means to obtain some future apparent good"—which is how Hobbes defines power (see *Lev.* 10.1). We do not know precisely *what* goods we will want in the future, but as needy, desirous beings, we know that we will want *some* goods, and so it makes sense to prepare ourselves in the present by accumulating the power that is the wherewithal to get the goods we want when we come to want them.[9]

Although a rational calculus of this sort is part of Hobbes's explanation of the human concern for power, it is not the whole of it. To see the rest of it, let us consider why the desire for power, in Hobbes's account, is a uniquely human phenomenon: the beasts share with us the desire for pleasure, but not the desire for power (consider *Lev.* 3.5, 10.1, 12.4; *Elem.* 8.2–3; *Anti-White* 38.8). Now, upon first encounter, this observation may seem surprising coming from Hobbes, because so much of his thinking has the tendency to minimize the difference between men and the beasts. Hobbes insists, for instance, that human beings no more have free will than do the beasts, and he argues that our deliberation works in essentially the same way as theirs (see, e.g., *Lev.* 3.9, 6.51–53, 27.1; *De Cive*, Pref.; *De Corp.* 25.13; *EW* IV, 244; Latin *Lev.*, Appendix, 1168; *Anti-White* 30.10–13, 37.8). But Hobbes does single out one way in which the human mind operates differently from the minds of the beasts. According to Hobbes, even the beasts, when they want something, can seek the causes or the means to produce "an effect imagined." Only human beings, however, "when imagining anything whatsoever," can "seek all the possible effects that can by it be produced." That is, only human beings are able, when pondering a given thing, to imagine "what we can do with it when we have it" (3.5). Hobbes identifies this kind of causal thinking as the most important difference between men and the beasts prior to the emergence of language (with *Lev.* 3.5, see also 2.1, 5.6, 6.35; *Elem.* 9.18; *De Hom.* 10.3, 12.12).[10] And this difference between men and the beasts, which enables us to see ourselves as causes of effects whereby we can increase our power, is closely tied to another feature of our humanity that also contributes to the human concern for power: because human beings are far more aware of the future than are the beasts, we are gripped in a way they are not by anxiety about what will befall us (*Lev.* 3.5, 11.1–2, 11.24, 12.4–5; *Elem.* 8.3; *Anti-White* 38.7–8). We have already seen the importance Hobbes places on anxiety about the future in his account of the seeds of religion in human nature (see p. 100 above). It is important to his

---

9. See Pangle and Burns, *The Key Texts of Political Philosophy*, 255–56.

10. On the importance of Hobbes's emphasis on this difference between men and the beasts, see Strauss, "On the Basis of Hobbes's Political Philosophy," 176n2; see also Manent, *The City of Man*, 114; Brandt, *Thomas Hobbes' Mechanical Conception of Nature*, 352–54; Mansfield, "Hobbes and the Science of Indirect Government," 105.

account of power as well. Our intense anxiety about the future, when coupled with the awareness that we can increase our power through inventive
causal thinking, awakens and emboldens us with the realization that we are
not simply thrown by nature into an inescapable condition: we can improve
our situation by augmenting our power. Yet it is not only through inventive
causal thinking that we can increase our power. The final piece of the puzzle
is that human beings are also far more aware than are the beasts that power is
relative, that is, that each man's power is meaningful primarily in comparison
with that of others, whose help he needs and whose threats he must be able to
ward off (see *Lev.* 10.3–16; *Elem.* 8.4; *Anti-White* 38.7–8; *De Hom.* 11.6). If, as
human beings, we live much of our mental life in the future, we also live in a
social world of comparisons, competition, and interdependency—a nexus of
relative power relationships.

These, then, are the roots of the human concern for power: the relative and
fluctuating character of the good, the human capacity for a distinctive kind
of causal thinking, our anxiety about the future, and our awareness that each
man's power is relative to that of others. The last of these plays the most important role in Hobbes's description of the ways in which the pursuit of power
structures almost all relationships among men. Because men know that power
is relative, every man is constantly seeking to build himself up by finding
ways to convince others that he possesses the wherewithal to help or harm
them—that he is, so to speak, a force to be reckoned with (see *Lev.* 10.2–15).
And because the truth of the matter—that is, whether he is in fact a force to
be reckoned with—depends so heavily on the power that stems from the *belief*
of others that he is powerful, every man, ever uncertain of his own power, is
constantly seeking the signs of its recognition in the deference and respect of
others. The broad term that Hobbes uses to capture the many forms of such
deference and respect is "honor," which is displayed in the various ways men
indicate to one another "the value we set on one another" (*Lev.* 10.17). Men are
continually providing signs, large and small—from manifest subservience to
subtle shifts in the tones of our voices—of the respect or disdain we have for
one another's power. By observing the constant jostling of men for power and
our almost obsessive attention to its signs, Hobbes argues, one can discover
the underlying dynamics of what might otherwise be the incomprehensible
interactions among men (*Lev.* 10.17–47; see also *Elem.* 8.4–7, 9.21).

In his account of the nexus of relative power relationships, Hobbes allows
for the emergence of a certain sociality among men and even for a hierarchical structure of society that accords some men greater worth and dignity than
others (see especially *Lev.* 10.16–18). He could thus seem to be ceding some
ground to the Aristotelian view that he rejected at the beginning of *De Cive*.

But Hobbes insists, throughout his account, that the only important connections and distinctions among men are those that arise from the nexus of relative power relationships itself. Although he speaks of the unequal "worth" of men, Hobbes defines each man's worth in this way: "The *value* or WORTH of a man is, as of all other things, his price, that is to say, so much as would be given for the use of his power, and therefore is not absolute, but a thing dependent on the need and judgment of another" (*Lev.* 10.16). He puts the point even more starkly a few lines later: "As in other things, so in men, not the seller, but the buyer determines the price. For let a man (as most men do) rate themselves at the highest value they can; yet their true value is no more than it is esteemed by others" (10.16). In his denial that the worth of a man has any significance beyond the value determined by the collective judgments of other men—by "the market," as we would say—Hobbes presents an account of power, honor, and worth that is every bit as stripped of moral considerations as the earlier hedonistic strand of his analysis of human striving.[11] To grant some ground to the view that man is naturally social, then, is not to concede that men are naturally moved by morality. To the contrary, Hobbes suggests that his account of power, honor, and worth faithfully reproduces the significance—that is, the insignificance—that moral considerations naturally have for human beings. "Nor does it alter the case of honour," he writes, "whether an action (so it be great and difficult, and consequently a sign of much power) be just or unjust; for honour consisteth only in the opinion of power" (*Lev.* 10.48; see also 17.2, 28.23). The significance of power and the insignificance of justice in dictating the estimations of men can be seen, Hobbes contends, in the conviction of the ancient pagans that they were honoring their gods even as they portrayed them committing all manner of "unjust or unclean acts," in the respect that piracy and thievery once enjoyed "not only amongst the Greeks but also amongst all other nations," and in the persistence of private duels even after they have been outlawed (*Lev.* 10.48–49; see also *Beh.*, 176).

Hobbes's claim that power moves men far more than justice does is the moment in his account of human striving in which the debunking intention of his account is most obvious. That intention can also be seen by reflecting on the fact that, if one were to adopt Hobbes's outlook on power, honor, and worth, one could never reasonably become indignant over unrecognized worth or over honor that is deserved but not received; such notions lose their meaning in Hobbes's account. If Hobbes's account of human striving

<hr />

11. See Manent, *The City of Man*, 176; Macpherson, *The Political Theory of Possessive Individualism*, 36–40.

is debunking in these respects, it is so in another crucial respect as well. For Hobbes draws out its sobering implications for the question of happiness: What kind of satisfaction is possible for human beings, given our concerns and condition?

Hobbes makes two key statements on happiness in *Leviathan*.[12] The first comes at the end of his discussion of the passions in Chapter 6, and it reflects the emphasis placed there on the ceaseless motions that buffet us and the ever-flowing stream of desires they produce:

> *Continual success* in obtaining those things which a man from time to time desireth, that is to say, continual prospering, is that men call FELICITY. I mean the felicity of this life. For there is no such thing as perpetual tranquility of mind, while we live here,[13] because life itself is but motion, and can never be without desire, nor without fear, no more than without sense. What kind of felicity God hath ordained to them that devoutly honor him, a man shall no sooner know than enjoy—being joys that now are as incomprehensible as the word of schoolmen *Beatifical Vision* is unintelligible. (*Lev.* 6.58)

The audacity of this statement is matched in Hobbes's second statement on happiness. But the second statement is not a mere repetition of the first. Coming five chapters later, after Hobbes's treatment of power, worth, and honor, the second statement places more weight on the concern for power and the anxiety about the future on which the desire for power depends. Chapter 11 of *Leviathan* is devoted to "those qualities of mankind that concern their living together in peace and unity," and Hobbes indicates at its outset that it is with a view to that issue that he returns to the question of happiness (*Lev.* 11.1). He reasserts his view that "felicity in this life consisteth not in the repose of a mind satisfied," again denying the existence of a *"Finis ultimus* (utmost aim)" or *"Summum Bonum* (greatest good)" such as is "spoken of in the books of the old moral philosophers." But he now provides a deeper explanation of why happiness for human beings can consist in no more than the continual pursuit of one object of desire after another, without rest or repose.

---

12. These statements, *Lev.* 6.58 and 11.1–2, should be compared with *Elem.* 7.6–7, *De Hom.* 11.15, and *Anti-White* 38.5–8, which express essentially the same view as is expressed in *Leviathan*; see also *EW* IV, 231, 347. On Hobbes's view of happiness, see Bruell, "Happiness in the Perspective of Philosophy," 149–50; Ahrensdorf, "The Fear of Death and the Longing for Immortality," 584; Evrigenis, *Images of Anarchy*, 137; Oakeshott, *Hobbes on Civil Association*, 80–81, 152–53.

13. The word "here" in the phrase "while we live here" is omitted in the Latin *Leviathan*, which reads merely *dum vivimus* (while we live). If this makes the Latin version bolder (since it does not suggest that we might live elsewhere after death), Hobbes compensates by omitting from the Latin version the very bold sentence that follows this one in the English version.

"The cause" of this restlessness and of the limit it places on our happiness, he writes, "is that the object of man's desire is not to enjoy once only, and for one instant of time, but to assure forever the way of his future desire" (*Lev.* 11.1). "Therefore," he concludes, "the voluntary actions and inclinations of all men tend, not only to the procuring, but also to the assuring of a contented life" (11.1). This conclusion leads, in turn, to one of the most important statements in *Leviathan*, a statement that is in some respects the capstone of Hobbes's account of human striving:

> So that, in the first place, I put for a general inclination of all mankind a per-
> petual and restless desire of power after power, that ceaseth only in death. And
> the cause of this is not always that a man hopes for a more intensive delight
> than he has already attained to, or that he cannot be content with a moderate
> power, but because he cannot assure the power and means to live well, which
> he hath present, without the acquisition of more. (*Lev.* 11.2)

Perfect happiness is not possible for human beings, according to Hobbes, not only because we are perpetually buffeted by motions and desires, but also because our anxiety about the future makes us ever restless in the present. That men seek not just pleasure but also power is a response to this problem, but not a solution to it, for no amount of power can ever suffice to secure us fully against the twists and turns of fortune, to say nothing of the looming loss of all power that awaits us in death.

Hobbes's statement on happiness at the beginning of Chapter 11 is pivotal in more than one way. On the one hand, it spells out the decisive implications of his account of human striving for the kind of satisfaction that is available to us as human beings. In that respect, it is a conclusion. On the other hand, the statement, as already noted, introduces Hobbes's account of "those qualities of mankind that concern their living together in peace and unity." And it is in this connection that Hobbes goes on to indicate that different types of men react in different ways to the human condition and the yearnings to which it gives rise. The most important divide among men—which Hobbes sketches in the two paragraphs that immediately follow his statement on happiness (see *Lev.* 11.3–4)—is between those who become consumed with the desire for honor and those who are willing to content themselves with ease, sensual pleasures, and safety. The key bifurcation in human motives that we saw at the outset of *De Cive* thus appears in *Leviathan* as well (see pp. 196–97 above).[14] In *Leviathan*, both the desire for honor and the desire for pleasure and

14. It can be seen also in *The Elements of Law* (see, e.g., 8.2, 8.8, 9.1, 10.3, 14.2–3, 19.5) and *De Homine* (see, e.g., 11.6, 11.12–13, 12.6).

safety are presented as reactions to the exposed, needy, never-satisfied condition that all human beings confront. Yet, if each reaction is comprehensible on the basis of Hobbes's anthropology, that does not mean that Hobbes regards the two reactions as equally rational or equally benign.[15] Hobbes indicates that the desire for honor, when it becomes intense, "inclineth to contention, enmity, and war," whereas the desire for sensual pleasures and safety "disposeth men to obey a common power" (*Lev.* 11.3–4).

The political problem posed by the desire for honor is fairly straightforward. It can be summed up for present purposes by saying that the pursuit of honor drives men into competition rather than cooperation. But it is also important—and possible at this point—to understand the psychological roots of the problem and the path of its growth. The problem arises—the poisonous plant grows—in the following way. The concern for power and its signs in the honor received from other men begins, according to Hobbes, as an intelligible and even rational reaction to our needy condition, driven at first by the entirely sensible concern to ensure one's capacity to attain the goods one will want in the future. What begins as rational, however, can become pathological. Some men, especially those whose basic needs are met (see *Lev.* 11.2, 17.11; *De Cive* 12.10; *De Hom.* 13.5), become obsessed with the signs of power, that is, with honor and, in the most alluring case, with glory, the extreme of honor. Such men become so intoxicated by glory, so filled with pride or vanity, that their striving for power and its signs eventually becomes unmoored from its original basis and takes on a life of its own. Human beings, then, are not just rational power-seekers in Hobbes's view; some, at least, are also prone to intense, irrational pride, to a form of "excessive self-esteem" that, as Hobbes says in *De Homine*, "impedes reason" (12.9). Intense pride appears in Hobbes's analysis as a pathology, even as a form of "madness" (see *Lev.* 8.18–19), because the obsession with displaying one's superiority, although it arises from a sensible concern to secure one's future wherewithal, develops into something that threatens to destroy even the limited security that is possible for men—and to destroy it not just for those who hunger for glory, but for everyone. We have already encountered Hobbes's striking remark in *De Cive* that "no large or lasting society can be based on the passion for glory" (see p. 197 above). The same thought is central to *Leviathan*, as Hobbes confirms in his explanation of the title of the work: he borrowed the name "Leviathan"

---

15. See Strauss, *The Political Philosophy of Hobbes*, 10–19, 132–35, "Some Notes on the Political Science of Hobbes," 134–35; Ahrensdorf, "The Fear of Death and the Longing for Immortality," 581–82; Pettit, *Made with Words*, 102–3; Sullivan, *Machiavelli, Hobbes, and the Formation of a Liberal Republicanism in England*, 94–95; Oakeshott, *Hobbes on Civil Association*, 35–38, 63–64.

from the Bible, because in the Book of Job God calls the sea monster named Leviathan "king of the proud" (*Lev.* 28.27). If the biblical Leviathan is "a king over all the children of pride" (Job 41:34), so too is the Hobbesian Leviathan, the mighty sovereign, whose surpassing strength Hobbes wants to ensure precisely so that he can subdue the proud.

Of course, Hobbes does not leave the task of solving the problem of pride entirely to the sovereign. He also wages a rhetorical and educational struggle of his own against pride, attempting to purge it from those from whom it can be purged and to teach men the necessity of resisting it in the incorrigible few.[16] This is one of the chief purposes of Hobbes's state of nature teaching: to sober men up, and in particular to convince those who are capable of a sensible sobriety of the necessity of uniting in a rational commonwealth that can protect them against those who remain intoxicated by pride. Yet Hobbes teaches not just the *necessity* of resisting the proud by all necessary means, but also the *right* of doing so. As we turn to Hobbes's state of nature teaching, then, we will be brought back to one of the questions that emerged from our consideration of the opening pages of *De Cive*: Does the key bifurcation of human motives, which we have now seen in *Leviathan* as well as *De Cive*, carry moral significance for Hobbes? Is it a distinction, somehow, between what is good and what is evil in human beings? We can better understand from our consideration of Hobbes's account of human striving in *Leviathan* why that question is so puzzling and difficult to answer. For, in the central line of argument we have followed thus far, Hobbes has been making every effort to understand our humanity while denying the importance of morality. But he has also indicated that some forms of human striving are far more irrational and pernicious, especially to the prospects of a lasting peace, than others. Does Hobbes's condemnation of actions that are driven by the proud desire for glory point to a necessary qualification or modification of what would otherwise seem to be his view that, prior to the establishment of sovereign-made law, there are no rightful limits on what is permitted for human beings?

The State of Nature

The first impression one gets from Hobbes's state of nature teaching is that it continues his assault on traditional morality. That is not a false impression. Coming on the heels of Hobbes's argument in Chapter 12 that religion is

16. Compare Cooper, "Vainglory, Modesty, and Political Agency in the Political Theory of Thomas Hobbes," 250–63. See also Lloyd, *Ideals as Interests in Hobbes's Leviathan*, 46–47, 207–12, *et passim*.

rooted in anxiety and ignorance, Chapter 13 of *Leviathan*, "Of the NATURAL CONDITION of Mankind, as Concerning their Felicity and Misery," presents Hobbes's most direct answer to the question of whether there is any natural or divine support for justice. The answer is a rather clear and blunt *no*. Our natural condition, prior to the establishment of government—that is, prior to human authority backed by the sword (see *Lev.* 17.1–2)—is not a state of "felicity," but one of "misery." The state of nature[17] is a war of all against all in which each man is so endangered that there is no telling what he might have to do in order to survive. In such a state, force and fraud are the cardinal virtues, and "the life of man" is, in Hobbes's famous phrase, "solitary, poor, nasty, brutish, and short" (*Lev.* 13.13, 13.9).

If Hobbes's state of nature teaching is his most vivid portrait of the forlorn and endangered condition of mankind outside of civil society, it also is his most direct application to political philosophy of the resolutive–compositive method—the method that he would have replace the approach of Aristotle and his heirs in the classical tradition. Hobbes does not take his bearings here by common opinions as they are expressed in the fully developed political life of a healthy community; rather, he views the political community as taken apart, "dissolved," into its key elements. It is true that, insofar as the elements in question are not so much individual men as their natural passions, Hobbes's state of nature teaching depends on his prior account of human nature and human striving; in this sense, it does not stand alone (consider especially *Lev.* 13.6–7, 13.10; see also *De Cive* 1.1; *Elem.*, 14.1–2). But it works out the consequences of the prior account of man for our natural situation—the consequences, as the focus now becomes, for us less as individuals beset by ever-flowing streams of desires than as human beings who must live together amid the dangers we pose to one another. Hobbes's state of nature teaching, in other words, is an account of our collective misery, caused by the natural passions we share. The thesis of the account is that nature "dissociates" men by making us natural enemies to one another (see *Lev.* 13.8–10). Of course, this is the thesis of Hobbes's account only insofar as it is a statement of a terrible problem. Hobbes also wants to point the way to the solution: our natural passions—or, at any rate, *some* of them, if well assisted by reason—can guide us to our salvation from the problem that nature poses for us. Hobbes's state

---

17. In Chapter 13 of *Leviathan* Hobbes does not use the exact phrase "the state of nature," preferring instead the phrase "the natural condition of mankind." But the title of the corresponding chapter of *The Elements of Law* (Chapter 14) is "Of the Estate and Right of Nature," and Hobbes speaks of the "state of nature" in *De Cive* (see, e.g., section 14 of the preface: *quam conditionem appellare liceat statum naturae*).

of nature teaching, then, is meant not only to induce a much-needed sobriety by dispelling the illusions that fuel men's most destructive passions, but also to instruct men as to the best means of escaping the natural horrors we face. The picture is bleak; but it is meant as a call to arms, not a counsel of despair.

Hobbes departs from the classical tradition—from Aristotle, in particular—in the very act of turning to the state of nature. There is nothing in classical thought that quite corresponds to the state of nature as Hobbes conceives of it. It would be going too far to say that reflections on the origins of the political community play no role in classical thought. But when Aristotle, for instance, turns to examine the origins of the political community, it is not to draw his most decisive conclusions about the status of justice by nature, but rather to develop the suggestion that human nature reaches its full potential only in established political communities (see *Politics* 1.2). Aristotle's discussion of the origins of the political community is merely a preliminary stage of his argument in the *Politics*; it prepares the way for the more important investigation of the question of justice that comes later, when Aristotle turns to arbitrate between the claims of the various partisans as they are expressed in actual political life (compare *Politics* 1.2 with 3.7–18). In pondering this difference between Aristotle and Hobbes, the methodological question cannot be separated entirely from substantive considerations. For the relatively minor role that reflections on the origins of the political community play in Aristotle's thought is closely connected to his view that man is a political animal whose nature is best seen in its full development in the political community. If one contemplates men prior to or outside of the political community, one will see, according to Aristotle, only a primitive and impoverished form of human nature—a mere potentiality, like a bud that has not yet blossomed into the flower it can become. Thus, even when Aristotle examines the origins of the political community, he does so primarily to trace the development of human nature from its low beginnings to its higher ends.[18] Now, of course, Hobbes too, in his own way, affirms that human beings are better off in political communities. If anything, he is even more emphatic about that point than Aristotle is. But a key difference remains, because Hobbes does not suggest that nature benevolently directs men to unite in communities. His thesis, to repeat, is that nature "dissociates" men. Hobbes differs from Aristotle, then,

---

18. That is not to say that Aristotle is oblivious to the difficulties involved in the emergence of political communities or to the problems that beset even fully formed communities. For an examination of Aristotle's account of the origins of the political community that is attentive to these difficulties, see Ambler, "Aristotle's Understanding of the Naturalness of the City."

insofar as his concern is not to capture the stages by which a beautiful flower begins to bloom, but to infer from the passions of men—especially from our greed, fear, and pride (see *Lev.* 13.6–7 with 13.10)—the dangers we pose to one another and the obstacles that stand in the way of establishing a stable political order. Whereas Aristotle contends that man is by nature a political animal, which is to say that by nature man is a fellow citizen to man, Hobbes contends that by nature "man is a wolf to man" (*De Cive*, Ep. Ded.).

Few would deny that the picture of human nature that Hobbes paints in his description of the state of nature is darker than anything comparable in Aristotle. Some would trace this difference to the influence of Christianity on Hobbes's thought. Was it not Christianity that taught the world about the depths of man's sinfulness? Those who regard Hobbes as a sincere Christian are quick to embrace such an explanation of Hobbes's pessimism. Glover, for example, contends that "Hobbes's picture of man, 'solitary but not alone,' given to pride and a ceaseless striving after power over others, is very close to the Christian understanding of sinful man."[19] Glover shows some awareness, however, that one position may be "very close to" and yet decisively different from another when he expresses his dismay at "the failure of Hobbes to identify as sin that extreme egocentricity that sets every man against every other man unless restrained by the awe of some power competent to enforce natural law."[20] Glover is compelled to acknowledge that insofar as Hobbes presents the violence in the state of nature as a necessary consequence of man's natural passions, "the anthropology of Hobbes is not at this point Christian."[21] But Glover and others who regard Hobbes as a sincere Christian do not fathom the depth of the chasm between Hobbes's teaching and any plausibly Christian view. In fact, far from showing the influence of Christianity on his thought, Hobbes's description of men in the state of nature shows as starkly as anything does his break with Christianity. Hobbes's state of nature, after all, is a state of *nature*; its most important premise is expressed in the

19. "God and Thomas Hobbes," 293–94. See also Martinich, *The Two Gods of Leviathan*, 49–50, 74–75; compare Spragens, *The Politics of Motion*, 104.

20. "God and Thomas Hobbes," 293. Martinich, *The Two Gods of Leviathan*, 75–79, wrestles with the same difficulty confronting his claim that Hobbes held a "Calvinistic view of humans" (75). To resolve the difficulty that Hobbes does not speak of sin, law, or even God's existence in his account of the state of nature, Martinich draws a distinction between the "primary state of nature" (in which there is no law, no sin, and no divine authority) and the "secondary state of nature" (in which there is law, sin, and divine authority); but this distinction is imported into Hobbes's account, where it cannot be found.

21. "God and Thomas Hobbes," 293.

first four words of Chapter 13 of *Leviathan*: "Nature hath made men . . ." (13.1; see also 13.13).[22] It is true that the notion of a "state of nature" was not unheard of in Christian theology prior to Hobbes. But the traditional distinction was between the state of nature and the state of grace, with the state of nature itself split into the state of pure nature and the state of fallen or corrupt nature.[23] The key distinction for Hobbes, by contrast, is between the state of nature (as such or undivided) and civil society. Hobbes does not—*cannot*—juxtapose the state of nature with the state of grace, because grace presupposes sin, and Hobbes denies that there is sin in the state of nature. As many commentators have observed, Hobbes does not speak of mankind in the state of nature as having lost, through sin, a prior state of perfection and innocence. There is no reference to the Fall in Hobbes's account, and he gives no indication of believing that a pristine condition preceded the miseries of the state of nature. As he tells it, those miseries are due, not to God's punishment of man's transgression, but to the brutality of nature itself.[24]

Hobbes presents men in the state of nature "as if they had suddenly sprung up from the earth, like mushrooms, and reached maturity without any obligation to one another" (*De Cive* 8.1). In the state of nature, "nothing can be unjust," for "the notions of right and wrong, justice and injustice, have there no place" (*Lev.* 13.13). Men in Hobbes's state of nature, then, are not only nasty and dangerous to one another; they are also free of all moral restrictions. But why are men so radically free by nature, in Hobbes's view? The most direct explanation he offers as to why justice has no place in the state of nature is that there is no law there. Justice, according to Hobbes, has no meaning prior to law, and law depends for its existence on a "common power," but a common power is precisely what is missing in the state of nature (*Lev.* 13.13, 15.2–3).[25] If

22. See Owen, *Making Religion Safe for Democracy*, 37. See also *De Hom.* 1.1, the relevance of which to the question of creation was discussed on p. 76 above. Compare *Elem.* 14.2.

23. See Strauss, *Natural Right and History*, 184. In n. 23 on pp. 184–85, Strauss cites some of the earlier authors, including Aquinas, Suarez, Grotius, and Wycliffe, who spoke of a state of nature, or something akin to it, but in a sense different from what Hobbes means by the term. Helpful, too, on the history of the notion of a state of nature in Christian theology is Hoekstra, "Hobbes on the Natural Condition of Mankind," 112.

24. Among those who note the absence of the Fall in Hobbes's account are Owen, *Making Religion Safe for Democracy*, 37; Cooke, *Hobbes and Christianity*, 105–8; Hoekstra, "Hobbes on the Natural Condition of Mankind," 111–12; Strauss, *The Political Philosophy of Hobbes*, 123, *Natural Right and History*, 184 (see also 215–16); Manent, *An Intellectual History of Liberalism*, 24; Milner, "Hobbes on Religion," 404; Evrigenis, "The State of Nature," 233–34.

25. Hobbes argues for the dependence of justice on law in many places. Besides the passages cited, see, e.g., *Lev.* 15.2–3, 27.3; *De Cive* 3.4, 6.16, 12.1, 14.9; *EW* IV, 253, 369–70; *EW* V, 233–34; *A Dialogue*, 72–73. Regarding Hobbes's claim that there is no common power in the state of nature,

this is Hobbes's simplest and most direct argument as to why justice has no place in the state of nature, he makes another—related, but distinguishable— argument to explain why there is no sin or evil in the state of nature, even though there is plenty of violence. The violent actions of men in the state of nature, he argues, proceed from their passions, but men's natural passions, precisely as *natural* passions, that is, as woven into the fabric of our "animal nature" (*De Cive*, Pref.), are no more sinful or evil than the aggressive impulses nature has implanted in other animals. Like wolves or tigers, human beings in the state of nature are dangerous but not culpable for their destructive ways (see *Lev.* 13.10, 27.18; *De Cive*, Pref.). On the basis of these arguments—the argument from the absence of law, and the argument from the innocence of men's natural passions—Hobbes denies that morality has any significance in the state of nature. This denial, which amounts to the claim that by nature everything is permitted for human beings, is in keeping with the general spirit of his message to men about our natural condition: the fitting response to our natural condition is not reverence, gratitude, or guilt, but the earnest resolve to get to work asserting ourselves against a natural world that cares not what we do or how much we suffer.

Such is the moral situation of men in Hobbes's state of nature: radically free, obligated to no one and by nothing, bound by no law other than the "law" that superior force and fraud usually prevail. But is this Hobbes's last word? Is it true that everything is permitted in the state of nature? Are men, in Hobbes's view, simply in a state of radical freedom in which nothing is forbidden? Although the line of argument just summarized would seem to present such a picture of the moral situation of men in the state of nature—if "moral situation" is an apt term for a state in which morality has no meaning—we cannot leave matters at that. For there is the crucial complication that we have already noted but that we must now try to understand, namely, that Hobbes speaks of a *right* in the state of nature. As he puts it in the passage in which he

---

it is worth considering an addition Hobbes makes to 13.11 in the Latin *Leviathan*: "But there never was—someone may say—a war of all against all. What? Did not Cain kill his own brother Abel out of envy, a deed so terrible that he would not have dared it if there had then existed a common power capable of punishing him?" In a note on this passage, Curley remarks: "The Biblically alert reader might object that Cain *was* living under a power able to punish his misdeed. (Genesis 4:6–16 relates that God punished him immediately.)" Curley further suggests that this omission by Hobbes is "perhaps" what prompted Leibniz to write to Hobbes "offering him the following defense against charges of license and impiety: assuming God's existence as ruler of the world, there can be no purely natural state of man, nor does Hobbes really think there is." As Curley wryly notes, however, "If Hobbes replied, we do not have his letter." See also Evrigenis, *Images of Anarchy*, 161, 177–78, "The State of Nature," 234.

describes his use of the resolutive-compositive method, what is revealed by
the thought experiment of the state of nature is not just the fact that men in
the state of nature "necessarily will" fear and distrust one another, but also the
principle that each man "*rightly may*" protect himself by any means necessary
(*De Cive*, Pref., emphasis added). But what are the grounds, the meaning, and
the limits—if there are any limits—of the right that Hobbes proclaims? This
is a thorny bramble of questions, because Hobbes offers more than one argument on the matter, and his position is not free from ambiguity.

Hobbes's claim that there is a right in the state of nature is clearer in his
earlier presentations of his state of nature doctrine than it is in *Leviathan*.
Although Hobbes speaks of a "right of nature" in the chapter that follows his
account of the state of nature in *Leviathan* (see 14.1, 14.4), he does not use the
term in Chapter 13 itself. He does use it, however, in the parallel chapters of
The Elements of Law and *De Cive*. And more important than the mere use of
the term is that in those earlier works he presents a direct argument to establish the right that he proclaims. The line of argument, if not the key term, that
Hobbes presents in *The Elements of Law* and *De Cive* reappears in Chapter 13
of *Leviathan* in a partial and modified form. Thus, before we consider the
argument in its amended form in *Leviathan*, let us examine the critical passages in the earlier works.

In *The Elements of Law*, after describing the natural passions that lead to
perpetual war in the state of nature, Hobbes argues that men in such straits
have a right to use all of their powers to preserve themselves. His argument
runs as follows:

> And forasmuch as necessity of nature maketh men to will and desire *bonum
> sibi*, that which is good for themselves, and to avoid that which is hurtful—but
> most of all that terrible enemy of nature, death, from whom we expect both
> the loss of all power and the greatest of bodily pains in the losing—it is not
> against reason that a man doth all he can to preserve his own body and limbs,
> both from death and pain. And that which is not against reason, men call
> RIGHT, or *jus*, or blameless liberty of using our own natural power and ability.
> It is therefore a *right of nature*: that every man may preserve his own life and
> limbs, with all the power he hath. (*Elem.* 14.6)

The "necessity of nature" that Hobbes asserts in this passage—the necessity that drives each man to seek his own good, and especially to avoid "that
terrible enemy of nature, death"—is asserted even more emphatically in the
parallel passage of *De Cive*, where Hobbes restates and expands the same argument. In *De Cive*, too, Hobbes describes the dangers of the state of nature;
then comes perhaps the most important paragraph of the entire work:

Therefore, in the midst of so many dangers that arise every day from men's natural desires and threaten each man, one is not to be blamed for looking out for himself, because we cannot will to do otherwise. For each man is drawn to desire what is good for him and to flee what is bad for him, but most of all that greatest of natural evils, which is death; and this, by a certain necessity of nature, no weaker than that by which a stone is impelled downwards. Therefore it is not absurd, nor reprehensible, nor against right reason, if one does all that he can to defend his body and limbs from death and pain, and to preserve them. And that which is not against right reason, all men say is done justly and *by right*. For by the term *right* nothing else is signified than the liberty each man has of using all of his natural faculties in accordance with right reason. Thus, the first foundation of natural *right* is that *each man may protect his life and limbs as much as he can.* (De Cive 1.7)

After each of these two passages, Hobbes goes on to argue that, having established a right to the end of self-preservation, it is but a short step to the further conclusion that there is a right to the means to that end. Because "a right to an end is in vain if the necessary means are denied," men who have the right to preserve themselves must also have the right to use any means necessary to that end; and because each man is left to his own devices in the state of nature, each man must be the judge of the means necessary to his preservation (*De Cive* 1.8–9; *Elem.* 14.7–9). Although it follows from this extension of the argument that each man in the state of nature has a right to do anything he deems necessary for his own preservation—and hence that two sides in a violent struggle can each have right on its side in a way that hardly helps the weaker party (see *Elem.* 14.10–13; *De Cive* 1.10–11)—Hobbes is clearly on solid ground in arguing that an unqualified right to an end implies a right to use any available means to that end. Let us dwell, then, on the prior, more fundamental line of argument about the right to the end, as it is presented in the two passages quoted above.

Hobbes's argument is more complicated than it first appears, because it unfolds in two stages. The argument begins from the claim that all men are driven to seek what is good for them, and especially to avoid the terrible evil of death, by a natural necessity that is "no weaker than that by which a stone is impelled downwards." But the argument then moves, albeit not without retaining a connection to the claim about the compulsory power of natural necessity, to an argument about "right reason": if it is not against right reason to pursue the preservation of one's body and limbs, then one has a right to do it, for "all men say" that what is done in accordance with right reason is done justly and by right. Now, this second stage of the argument is connected to the first by the suggestion that men cannot reasonably be blamed for doing what their natures compel them to do because "it is not absurd, nor reprehensible, nor against right reason" to act as one is compelled by nature to act. But one could question this (combined) argument in several ways. First, is it really true that men are driven to seek what is good for them, and especially to avoid death, by an irresistible natural necessity? Hobbes's argument depends on the truth of that claim, but the argument itself does not establish it. And the claim could well be challenged by those who would point to instances in which men appear to be willing to sacrifice their lives out of devotion to an end higher than their own self-interest.[26] Very different from that challenge is another question that one could raise about Hobbes's argument. For even if it is true that men are driven by a natural necessity to seek what they regard as good for themselves, and especially to avoid death, why does that mean that they have a *right* to preserve themselves? To use Hobbes's own analogy: we would never say of a stone that falls downward that it is has a *right* to do so, even though it is obvious that it could not have done otherwise.[27] In response to this difficulty, Hobbes would presumably argue—as we can infer from the second stage of his argument—that stones do not have rights because they are not capable of reason and choice. Natural necessity has a different significance for rational beings who make decisions: if we are not so compelled by the primary natural necessities that press upon us that our irrational passions, acting as competing compulsions, cannot sometimes override them—this is presumably how Hobbes would explain the fact that men sometimes sacrifice their lives—we can also learn to take our bearings by those necessities that are rooted in our true needs, as opposed to our irrational desires (consider *De Cive*, Pref., 1.4, 1.12, 3.9, 3.25–26, 3.30; *Elem.* 16.10, 17.14, 19.2). Moreover, not only are we capable of rational behavior, but we are to be commended, or at least not to be blamed, for acting in a rational way. This is the fuller, if not fully expressed, connection between the argument from natural necessity and the argument regarding right reason. But does it adequately answer the question about *right*? Even if one grants that some actions are more rational and more necessary than others because they are rooted in genuine needs

---

26. Bramhall's objection that "Moses, St. Paul, and the Decii" did not share Hobbes's view that every voluntary act is performed for the sake of the actor's own good (see n. 8 above) is relevant in this connection, as is his complaint that Hobbes's principles cannot account for martyrs (see *The Catching of Leviathan*, 543, 545).

27. See Bolotin, "Is There a Right to Live as We Please?" 323. I am indebted to Bolotin, not only for this point, but also for shaping many of the other thoughts expressed in this paragraph and in the rest of this section. I will note the places where my analysis is especially close to his.

rather than spurious desires, there remains the question of whether Hobbes has established that self-preservation is our deepest need, and, beyond that, the question of why acting in accordance with our deepest need, even if it is rational, is acting in accordance with right. Why do we have a *right* to make our deepest need the guiding principle of our actions?

When Hobbes returns to the state of nature in *Leviathan*, he develops an argument that echoes some aspects of the argument just considered, but without the same emphasis on the compulsory power of a natural necessity.[28] He also, as already noted, does not speak explicitly in Chapter 13 of *Leviathan* of a "right" to self-preservation. Now, this latter difference between Chapter 13 of *Leviathan* and the passages from the earlier works is ultimately not as important as it appears at first glance. For not only does Hobbes go on to speak of a right to self-preservation in the chapter that follows his account of the state of nature, but the absence of the term "right" in Chapter 13 does not entail the absence of the notion. The continued presence of the notion of a right can be seen in the passage in which Hobbes repeats and expands some aspects of his earlier line of argument, even as he no longer speaks of a natural necessity compelling men to seek their preservation. The passage in question, like the earlier ones, comes in the wake of a description of the dangers that arise from men's mutual fear and distrust of one another in the state of nature. After an initial account of those dangers, Hobbes writes:

> And from this diffidence[29] of another, there is no way for any man to secure himself so reasonable as anticipation—that is, by force or wiles to master the persons of all men he can, so long till he see no other power great enough to endanger him. And this is no more than his own conservation requireth, and is generally allowed. Also, because there be some that take pleasure in contemplating their own power in the acts of conquest, which they pursue farther than their security requires, if others, that otherwise would be glad to be at ease within modest bounds, should not by invasion increase their power, they would not be able, long time, by standing only on their defense, to subsist. And by consequence, such augmentation of dominion over men, being necessary to a man's conservation, it ought to be allowed him. (*Lev.* 13.4)

Hobbes does not use the word "right" in this passage, but he speaks of what "is generally allowed" and of what "ought to be allowed." To speak especially of the latter is to speak of a right by another name, for by a right we mean

---

28. On this shift, see Malcolm, *Leviathan, Vol. 1: Introduction*, 19; Bolotin, "Is There a Right to Live as We Please," 324.

29. Latin *Lev.*: *tanto . . . metu* (such great fear).

something that "ought to be allowed."[30] What is Hobbes's argument here for the very broad right whose existence he again proclaims?

If Hobbes does not use the term "right" in this key passage but preserves the notion, the same may be said of his appeal to right reason. He does not use that term either, but he relies on the notion by referring to what is reasonable and necessary for a man faced with the dangers of the state of nature. In such threatening circumstances, Hobbes argues, "there is no way for any man to secure himself so reasonable as anticipation." And even if "anticipation" means using "force or wiles" to dominate other men before one is dominated by them, "such augmentation of dominion over men, being necessary to a man's conservation, it ought to be allowed him." Now, it might seem here—because he refers to what is "necessary"—that Hobbes is still basing his argument on a natural necessity that acts as a compulsion. The necessity in question in this passage, however, concerns only the means to the end of self-preservation—an end whose pursuit Hobbes continues to describe as reasonable and legitimate but no longer as compulsory. The argument from the compulsion by a natural necessity is replaced now with a fuller version of the argument that it is reasonable, and therefore not blameworthy or forbidden, to do everything one can to preserve oneself, even if that entails aggressive preemptive actions.

By stretching the realm of allowable or legitimate actions as far as he does here—so that it includes even attempts to master other men until no threats remain—Hobbes is expanding that realm well beyond its ordinary limits, as those limits would be judged by most men. And this poses a problem for his argument, for in trying to establish what "ought to be allowed," Hobbes appeals to what "is generally allowed."[31] It is doubtful, to say the least, that all men would agree that the concern for self-defense, which most would concede justifies violent resistance in extreme cases in which one is facing imminent death, extends so far as to justify the preemptive "mastery" of all men who might be considered threats.[32] To address this difficulty of the gap between what is (in fact) "generally allowed" and what he claims "ought to be allowed," Hobbes might respond by arguing that those who grant that self-defense is legitimate in extreme cases have already granted, in principle, his

---

30. Bolotin, "Is There a Right to Live as We Please?" 325; see also Burns, "Modernity's Irrationalism," 146.

31. In the Latin *Lev.*, Hobbes replaces "is generally allowed" with *ab omnibus concedi solet* (tends to be allowed by all).

32. See Bolotin, "Is There a Right to Live as We Please?" 325: "Although self-defense is indeed generally accepted as a legitimate reason for the use of violence, is it thought to justify an attempt to master the persons of others until all possible threats are removed? It doesn't seem so to me."

argument for a much more expansive right; they merely fail to see that, in the state of nature, the essential features of the extreme cases apply continually. After all, Hobbes himself denies that it is legitimate to strike out against others, even against aggressors, when one can rely on a sovereign power to keep order and punish transgressions (see *Lev.* 27.20). But in the absence of such a power—in a situation in which one cannot depend on any authority, civil or divine, to provide for one's defense—a man's life depends on taking matters into his own hands and acting with preemptive aggression. To claim otherwise is to underestimate the dangers of the state of nature and to consign those who seek only their self-preservation to be the prey of those who delight in conquest.

Hobbes is well aware, of course, that his argument that men "ought to be allowed" to seek their self-preservation by any means necessary is of no help to men in the state of nature, who must face other men with the same right, as well as those who pursue the pleasures of conquest "farther than their security requires." Hobbes's argument for the existence of a right in the state of nature is fully consistent with his view of that state as a brutal war of all against all. But is it fully consistent with his claim that right and wrong, justice and injustice, have no place in the state of nature? The difficulty of answering this question can be seen by considering another one: Does Hobbes's argument for a right justify *all actions* in the state of nature, or only those that are undertaken for the sake of self-preservation? To that question, Hobbes does not provide an unambiguous answer. Insofar as he goes on in *Leviathan* (as in his earlier works) to define "the right of nature" as a mere liberty that consists—as he contends liberty, "according to the proper signification of the word," must consist—merely in "the absence of external impediments," he would seem to be laying down a principle that does not depend on the motives of men's actions (see *Lev.* 14.1–2; see also *Lev.* 21.1–2; *Elem.* 14.10, 29.5; *De Cive* 1.10, 3.4, 2.18, 14.3). Are not those who pursue ends beyond self-preservation just as free from impediments in the state of nature as those who are more moderate or more fearful? The answer to that question is surely yes. But just as surely that cannot be Hobbes's final word on the question of right. For even in the passages in which he speaks of the right of nature as a mere liberty, he goes on to restrict that right—or, at any rate, to speak of it as extending—only to the pursuit of self-preservation (consider *Lev.* 14.1, 14.4, 26.44; *Elem.* 14.6–10; *De Cive* 1.7–10). If that restriction or limit is left somewhat ambiguous in the passages in question, Hobbes asserts it with greater emphasis and clarity elsewhere. For instance, in *De Cive*, he denies that a modest man, aggressive though he may be forced to be to defend himself in the state of nature, acts "with equal culpability" as a bolder man who harms others out of a vainglorious desire to demonstrate his superiority (1.4). The same thought is conveyed even more starkly in *The Elements of Law* when Hobbes declares that "nothing but fear can justify the taking away of another's life" (19.2).[33]

The distinction Hobbes draws between aggressive actions undertaken for the sake of self-preservation and similar actions undertaken for the sake of glory should be regarded as a moral distinction, tied to a view of right as a notion with moral significance.[34] It may be true that, to an observer in the state of nature, there would often be no discernible difference between the two kinds of actions; and it is certainly true that, in Hobbes's view, there is nothing that a man in the state of nature may not do in order to defend himself. But the distinction on the level of intentions retains its importance. Hobbes's affirmation that men in the state of nature may rightly do anything in order to survive should not be understood as an affirmation that they may do anything simply, or for any reason whatsoever. To clarify Hobbes's position in this way, however, is not to remove the difficulty in it. For it is hard to see how such a distinction as Hobbes draws can be maintained without the assumption—perhaps unacknowledged, but nevertheless necessary—of a moral law that rightfully binds men even in the state of nature.[35] How else could it make sense to say that there is a right to act for some reasons but not for others? Indeed, by speaking of the right in question as a *right*, Hobbes implies not only that the pursuit of self-preservation creates exceptions to a rule that otherwise binds, but also that such exceptions are *justified* in the sense that their legitimacy is recognized by a moral law that permits aggressive actions only if they are undertaken for the right reasons. When Hobbes declares that such actions "ought to be allowed," does he not mean, or at least imply, that they "ought to be allowed" by the moral law itself? By whom or by what else ought they to be allowed? This implication is problematic, of

33. The passages cited in the paragraph above are not the only ones in which Hobbes restricts the right of nature to the pursuit of self-preservation or draws a distinction between actions undertaken for the sake of self-preservation and those undertaken for the sake of glory in a way that exonerates the former but not the latter. For other examples, see *Elem.* 16.4, 16.10, 19.1; *De Cive*, Ep. Ded., 3.5–6, 3.9, 3.11, 3.27–30, 6.13, 6.16, 14.8; *Lev.* 15.17, 15.19, 17.2, 27.3, 27.20–24; *EW* IV, 253.

34. Compare Strauss, *The Political Philosophy of Hobbes*, 14–15, 23–27, 116, "On the Basis of Hobbes's Political Philosophy," 192, *Spinoza's Critique of Religion*, 233; Tuck, *Hobbes*, 60, "Optics and Skeptics," 260, *Natural Rights Theories*, 125, 129, 140–42; Malcolm, *Aspects of Hobbes*, 33; Bolotin, "Is There a Right to Live as We Please?" 324, 327; Burns, "John Courtney Murray, Religious Liberty, and Modernity," 26–27, "Modernity's Irrationalism," 146–47. Contrast Martinich, "Leo Strauss's Olympian Interpretation," 80–81, 86–91.

35. See Bolotin, "Is There a Right to Live as We Please?" 327–28. My analysis in this paragraph is indebted to Bolotin's essay.

course, because Hobbes flatly denies that there is any such binding moral law in the state of nature. As we have seen, he denies that right and wrong, justice and injustice, have any meaning prior to the establishment of a human sovereign who can enforce agreements and make laws. In fact, Hobbes's very argument for a right to self-preservation, insofar as it is meant as a critique of any position that would place limits on what men may do to survive in the state of nature, plays a role in his broader critique of the traditional understanding of morality as rooted in the primacy of a moral law. Hobbes argues that the right of each man to seek his own good is prior to any duties he may subsequently come to have to others. Yet, by restricting the good that each man may rightly seek at the expense of others to self-preservation, Hobbes affirms the existence of the kind of moral law that it is his primary intention to deny. If this means that his position is not entirely consistent, it also suggests that he was unaware of the inconsistency.

This line of reflection leads one to think that Hobbes was unaware of an inconsistency in his position because he did not see the role that considerations of justice continued to play in his own thinking about right in the state of nature. It is therefore tempting to counter it with the suggestion that Hobbes's talk of right as something with moral significance and his distinction between legitimate and illegitimate motives are merely rhetorical ways of cloaking an essentially amoral position.[36] Might not Hobbes, rather than being in any way confused in his own thinking, simply have realized that a nakedly amoral account, even of our natural condition, would be too harsh to be accepted by most men? After all, he himself says of his argument that there is no injustice in the state of nature that "the harshness of the conclusion can expel the memory of the premises" (*De Cive* 1.10). Perhaps Hobbes, without genuinely believing that there is any moral difference between motives in the state of nature, merely thought that it was necessary for the success of his doctrine to validate the pursuit of self-preservation and vilify the pursuit of glory. Because the one motive can be made the foundation of a lasting order whereas the other cannot, there are good prudential reasons, beyond softening a harsh argument, for speaking of only one of the two motives as in accordance with natural right. If Hobbes let himself be guided by such considerations, he would be following the same advice he gives to the sovereign, whom he counsels to judge crimes by their effects and to magnify the culpability of those criminals who are most harmful to the commonwealth while showing greater lenience toward those who are less detrimental

---

36. For an excellent presentation of this suggestion, see Zuckert, "Hobbes on Right and Obligation," 298–99, together with *Natural Rights and the New Republicanism*, 275–78.

(see *Lev.* 27.35–36). Yet the suggestion that the moral aspects of Hobbes's position are merely features of a rhetorical cloak covering a view that is amoral at its core, although it is not without some plausibility, is ultimately unpersuasive. For if Hobbes were guided entirely by a prudential concern to conceal the inner amorality of his position and to make his argument more palatable and politically effective, why would he so openly deny the significance of justice and morality in the state of nature? Hobbes's rhetoric would be more compelling, precisely as rhetoric, if he did not boldly and bluntly deny that justice and injustice, right and wrong, have any place in the state of nature. The very audacity and severity of that denial—which would make his rhetoric, if it were merely rhetoric, clumsy and self-defeating—speak against the suggestion that the statements that cut in the other direction are merely rhetorical. To state the matter another way, the fact that Hobbes's position on right in the state of nature is inconsistent *in the way that it is inconsistent*—with its amoral aspects bold and explicit, its moral ones subtle and implicit—is indicative, not of his rhetorical guile, but of his failure to see the inconsistency in his position.

Instead of dismissing the moral character of Hobbes's position as mere rhetoric, it is better to try to understand the basis of the moral judgment that Hobbes passes and to consider what may have kept him from recognizing it as a moral judgment. Now, on the question of the basis of the judgment, we may begin from a point that is sometimes summoned in support of the suggestion that the moral distinction Hobbes draws is merely rhetorical: Hobbes obviously regarded the pursuit of glory as destructive, not only of peace in the state of nature, but of the order that becomes possible with the rise of civil society. His conviction that the pursuit of glory poses a continual danger to the commonwealth gives him ample incentive to denounce it. Yet, rather than regarding that conviction as merely a prudential concern with no moral significance, we should see it as playing an important role in the moral judgment that Hobbes passes. For to believe, as Hobbes does, that only the fearful yearning for security can lead men out of the state of nature and into a lasting order (see *Lev.* 13.14) is to regard the desire for self-preservation as the bedrock of a potential common good that can be realized if the obstacles to it are removed. And the largest obstacle, in Hobbes's view, is the desire for glory, which obscures men's vision of their need for security and leads them to act in ways that are destructive of the potential common good. Moreover, not only does the pursuit of glory lead men to destroy the potential common good, but it does so for the sake of an end that they do not really need: the pursuit of glory is driven by a "lust of the mind" for an empty pleasure that arises from a vain sense of exaltation, not from the satisfaction of a genuine need (see *De Cive* 1.4, 1.12, 3.11–13; *Elem.* 14.3–5, 16.10; *Lev.* 27.13, 27.19–20, 27.30). Because the pursuit of glory is based on a deluded belief in one's superiority and a desire to triumph over others for no good reason, it can claim neither the necessity nor the rationality that makes the unrestrained pursuit of self-preservation permissible in Hobbes's view. Whereas aggressive actions for the sake of self-preservation "ought to be allowed" because they are necessary and reasonable means to the most important end that we naturally seek, such considerations cannot exculpate similarly aggressive actions when they are for the sake of glory. Unnecessary and unreasonable actions that destroy the potential common good are unjust—even in the state of nature.[37]

To be sure, Hobbes never quite states his views in this way. The question remains, then, of why Hobbes did not recognize the moral judgment at the basis of his own position. To address this question, it is essential to specify the sense in which it is true that he did not grasp the character of his own position. It is true in the sense that Hobbes remained unaware that his position implies the existence of a binding moral law even in the state of nature. That does *not* mean that he was unaware, even or precisely as he denied the existence of a binding moral law in the state of nature, that he was already looking ahead to another kind of moral law that could be based on the premise that the fundamental moral fact about our condition is a natural right. Hobbes was well aware, of course, that his account of the state of nature prepares the way for a new moral teaching, or a new doctrine of morality, of the sort that follows his account of the state of nature in each of his presentations of his political philosophy (see *Lev.*, Chaps. 14–15; *Elem.*, Chaps. 15–17; *De Cive*, Chaps. 2–3). Could it have been the very anticipation of that new moral teaching that kept him from seeing that his position had a moral basis from the very beginning, that is, even in his thinking about the state of nature? There is a more obvious explanation: the original, pre-civic moral law in which Hobbes continued to believe is so lenient or loose, allowing as it does even preemptive murder and enslavement when such actions are deemed necessary for self-preservation, that it is difficult to see that it remains a moral law in any meaningful sense.[38] But that explanation may be true and yet still not give us the complete picture. For even if it is true, it may also be the case— the two suggestions are not incompatible—that Hobbes's very confidence that a rational morality can be built on amoral premises kept him from probing the question of the true character of his premises, and thus from seeing that they are not in fact amoral. In other words, Hobbes may not have felt gripped by the need to confront squarely the question of the morality or amorality of the foundation of his position precisely because he was captivated by the rational moral teaching that he thought could be built on that foundation. The vision of that new moral teaching may not so much have distracted him as made it seem less essential to concern himself with the moral problem at the basis of his position. But even if this explanation, together with the more obvious one, accounts for Hobbes's failure to grasp a crucial aspect of his own position, it does not entirely excuse it. For the character of the foundation is not without a bearing on the integrity of the building, and the moral judgment that guided Hobbes more than he knew deserves a more critical analysis than he seems ever to have given it.

Hobbes's Moral Teaching

Hobbes opens each of his presentations of his moral teaching proper—his doctrine of the laws of nature—by indicating its novelty (see *Lev.* 14.1–3; *De Cive* 2.1; *Elem.* 15.1). These indications should be kept in mind because, for two very different reasons, the novelty of Hobbes's teaching can be difficult to appreciate. The first reason applies to us only as latter-day readers of Hobbes: because we have been so deeply influenced by the moral revolution that Hobbes helped to launch, it is easy for us to lose sight of the radical transformation that was required at its outset. The second reason, however, would apply at least as much to readers in Hobbes's own day: Hobbes disguises the revolutionary character of his moral teaching by presenting it in the terminology of the long-standing tradition of moral philosophy that began with classical thought and culminated in scholasticism. Hobbes presents his teaching as an account of moral virtue and a doctrine of natural law. Yet, although Hobbes's use of this traditional terminology obscures his break with the dominant tradition, it does not contradict that break. In fact, Hobbes's use—or usurpation—of the traditional terminology can be explained not only by his concern to conceal his own radicalism but also by his desire to occupy the fortress of the enemy. In this regard, Hobbes applies to moral philosophy a lesson that Machiavelli teaches about politics: if a prince wants to keep a firm hold of conquered territory, he should go live there, or at least establish colonies.[39]

But what is new about the moral teaching that Hobbes installs in the old fortresses? We have already encountered and considered the most important point: the fundamental moral fact, according to Hobbes, is a right, not a duty.

---

39. *The Prince*, Chap. 3.

This is the core of Hobbes's new teaching whether or not it is fully coherent to speak of a right that is prior to any moral law. But what are the implications of this point? It is sometimes said that Hobbes makes duty derivative from right. It is more precise to say that he makes duty derivative from the end whose unrestrained pursuit right validates and from agreements that men freely enter into in order to secure that end. The end in question, of course, is self-preservation, and if the right of nature tells us that we may preserve ourselves by any means necessary, the fundamental law of nature—from which all the others follow, according to Hobbes—tells us that we ought to seek peace as the essential means of self-preservation. The right of nature and the first law of nature, then, take their bearings from the same end. They are two branches of the same rule by which reason enjoins us to seek peace if it can be achieved and to resort to war only if peace is impossible (see *Lev.* 14.4; see also *De Cive* 2.2–3; *Elem.* 15.1–2). Yet, although this understanding of the relationship between right and duty might seem to accord them equal status, it has a crucial implication that transforms the meaning of duty: whereas the fundamental importance of self-preservation means that the most basic right of nature can never be relinquished, all duties, according to Hobbes, are instrumental and conditional upon their service to an end that precedes and determines them (consider *Lev.* 14.8, 14.29). Hobbes's laws of nature are not unconditionally binding imperatives. In fact, they are not really laws at all, as Hobbes frankly acknowledges at the end of his discussion of them in *Leviathan*: "These dictates of reason men use[40] to call by the name of laws, but improperly: for they are but conclusions or theorems concerning what conduceth to the conservation and defense of themselves, whereas law, properly, is the word of him that by right hath command over others" (*Lev.* 15.41).

Now, Hobbes adds to this statement a remark that has been the source of much controversy among Hobbes scholars, because it has led some scholars to interpret his position in a very different way from that just sketched. After indicating that he does not regard the laws of nature as genuine laws, Hobbes writes: "But yet if we consider the same theorems as delivered in the word of God, that by right commandeth all things, then are they properly called laws" (*Lev.* 15.41). This statement has been taken by some scholars as decisive evidence that Hobbes did indeed regard the laws of nature as unconditionally binding imperatives, and that he did so because he believed them to be

---

40. "Use" is not a typo here, even though it might seem that it should be "used." Hobbes is using "use" as a present tense verb with the meaning of "are wont" or "are accustomed." See Curley, "Religion and Morality in Hobbes," 118n52; contrast, Martinich, *The Two Gods of Leviathan*, 123–24.

commandments of God. According to this interpretation, which has come to be known as the Taylor-Warrender thesis, named after its original exponents A. E. Taylor and Howard Warrender, Hobbes's last word on the laws of nature— the remark quoted is literally the last sentence of the discussion of the laws of nature in *Leviathan*—reveals the basis on which his entire moral teaching rests. The foundation of Hobbes's moral teaching, and thus of all of the laws of nature that he outlines, is not the rightful pursuit of self-preservation by free individuals, but the unconditional commands of God. These alone, Taylor and Warrender argue, can supply the "transcendent obligatoriness" that Hobbes, with his "almost overwhelming sense of duty," regarded as essential to morality.[41] According to Taylor and Warrender, then, there is a perfectly straightforward explanation of why Hobbes calls the laws of nature "laws": he calls them laws because he thought that they *are laws*, and when he says that they are laws only if they are commands of God, that is an indication, not of why they should not be regarded as laws, but precisely of what makes them laws in his eyes.

The Taylor-Warrender thesis and other similar interpretations[42] have going for them the undeniable fact that Hobbes makes the remark in question (see also *Elem.* 17.12; *De Cive* 3.33). But how should the remark be taken? Does Hobbes mean for it to reveal the true basis of his position or merely to clarify the condition that would have to obtain for the laws of nature to be genuine laws and thus to underscore his declaration that they are not really laws? To reject the Taylor-Warrender thesis it is not necessary to insist on Hobbes's atheism. It suffices to observe, as many others have, that throughout his dis-

41. See Taylor, "The Ethical Doctrine of Hobbes," 410–11, 418–22; Warrender, *The Political Philosophy of Hobbes*, 97–100, 272–77. The quotations are from Taylor, 422; compare Warrender, 275–77.

42. See, e.g., Martinich, *The Two Gods of Leviathan*, 71–99, 120–35, "Leo Strauss's Olympian Interpretation," 91–92; Hood, *The Divine Politics of Thomas Hobbes*, 5–10, 83–99; Gillespie, *The Theological Origins of Modernity*, 240–46. Lloyd, *Morality in the Philosophy of Thomas Hobbes*, 97–260, defends a complex position that shares some aspects with what she calls the "divine command interpretations." She agrees with such interpretations insofar as she, too, believes that Hobbes regarded the laws of nature as God's laws—a point that, in her view, "it would be silly to deny" (*Morality in the Philosophy of Thomas Hobbes*, 183; see also "Natural Law," 283). But she does not believe that the "normativity" of the laws of nature consists, for Hobbes, in their being God's laws, nor that Hobbes derives them from divine commands (see especially *Morality in the Philosophy of Thomas Hobbes*, 182–85, 232n32, 249). Rather, she argues that Hobbes's laws of nature are derived from the rational principle of reciprocity and that the "only end *reliably* served by the Laws of Nature is *the common good, or the good of humanity generally*, and not the preservation or profit of the individual agent who is to follow those laws" (*Morality in the Philosophy of Thomas Hobbes*, 98; see also "Natural Law," 265–72). Hers is thus a middle position between the Taylor-Warrender thesis and the view that I will defend.

cussion of the laws of nature in *Leviathan*, Hobbes treats them, not as commands of God, but as maxims discovered by human reason in its search for
a path to peace, which itself is sought as the essential precondition of self-
preservation (see, in particular, *Lev.* 13.14, 14.8, 15.40, 26.8, 31.1; see also *De
Cive* 2.1, 3.1, 3.26; *Elem.* 15.1–2, 17.10).[43] Far from basing his account of the laws
of nature on the premise of divine legislation, Hobbes barely mentions God
in the course of his extensive discussion of the laws of nature. He mentions
him only to cast doubt on whether it is possible to make a covenant with him
(see *Lev.* 14.13 with 18.3), to deny that oaths add anything to the obligation
already involved in promises or covenants (*Lev.* 14.31–33), and to argue that
adherence to the laws of nature is rational even "taking away the fear of God"
(*Lev.* 15.4–5). Hobbes's laws of nature do not mandate any service to God,
nor do they aim at salvation.[44] The view that the aim of the laws of nature is
"the attaining of an eternal felicity after death" is not Hobbes's own view; it is
the view of "some that proceed further, and will not have the laws of nature
to be those rules which conduce to the preservation of man's life on earth"

43. See Curley, *"Religion and Morality in Hobbes,"* 103–5; Spragens, *The Politics of Motion*,
30–31, 118–24; Sommerville, *Thomas Hobbes: Political Ideas in Historical Context*, 77–79; Tuck,
Natural Rights Theories, 120, 130–32; Darwall, Review of *Ideals as Interests in Hobbes's Leviathan*
and *The Two Gods of Leviathan*, 751–52; Watkins, *Hobbes's System of Ideas*, 55–61; Kavka, *Hobbesian Moral and Political Theory*, 360–63.

See also Oakeshott, *Hobbes on Civil Association*, 37, 64–67, 90–91, 100, 103–19. In the last of
these passages, Oakeshott presents his most direct and extensive critique of Warrender's interpretation. Although he acknowledges that some of Hobbes's explicit statements on the laws of
nature are equivocal and that the evidence is thus mixed (see 115–17), Oakeshott argues that
Hobbes's equivocation is best seen as "artful" and that the features of Hobbes's statements on
which Warrender bases his interpretation should be regarded as aspects of an exoteric doctrine
that Hobbes constructed to appease readers who were unprepared to accept his more radical
position (see 117–19).

For an argument against the Taylor-Warrender thesis that is more historical than textual,
see Skinner, "The Context of Hobbes's Theory of Political Obligation," 136–42, "The Ideological
Context of Hobbes's Political Thought," 313–17.

44. These features of Hobbes's account did not go unnoticed by Bramhall: "Yet, to let us see
how inconsistent and irreconcilable [Hobbes] is with himself, elsewhere, reckoning up all the
laws of nature at large, even twenty in number, he hath not one word that concerneth religion, or
that hath the least relation in the world to God. As if a man were like the colt of a wild ass in the
wilderness, without any owner or obligation. Thus, in describing the laws of nature, this great
clerk forgetteth the God of nature, and the main and principal laws of nature, which contain a
man's duty to his God, and the principal end of his creation . . . Among [Hobbes's] laws he inser-
teth 'gratitude' to man, as 'the third precept of the law of nature'; but of the gratitude of mankind
to their Creator, there is a deep silence" (*The Catching of Leviathan*, 520–21).

(*Lev.* 15.8). Hobbes treats that view, moreover, as a threat to civil stability, combating it with the argument that we have no natural knowledge of "men's estate after death" but "only a belief grounded upon other men's saying that they know it supernaturally, or that they know those that knew them that knew others that knew it supernaturally" (*Lev.* 15.8.). It is also difficult to square the Taylor-Warrender thesis with Hobbes's blunt denial that there is any binding law or any common power in the state of nature (see again *Lev.* 13.13, 15.3) or with his assertion that there can be "no obligation on any man which ariseth not from some act of his own" (see *Lev.* 21.10; see also *EW* V, 180). The same is true of Hobbes's repeated insistence that the laws of nature ought to be followed only when they are backed up by a power—that is, a *human* power—who can enforce them (see, e.g., *Lev.* 14.5, 14.18–19, 15.3, 26.8, 26.22; *De Cive* 2.11, 3.27; *Elem.* 15.10, 17.10; *De Hom.* 15.4). Finally, it is worth noting that the key sentence on which so much hangs for the Taylor-Warrender thesis is omitted from the Latin *Leviathan*. Had Hobbes intended for that sentence to reveal the genuine basis of his entire moral teaching, it would have been very strange for him to drop it from the Latin text.[45]

If Hobbes's laws of nature are not commands of God and hence not laws in the strict sense, what are they? They are maxims of prudence by which men can attain what they most need: self-preservation (individually) and thus peace (collectively). That Hobbes understands them in this way—that is, as precepts of rational self-interest, rather than as binding laws—is confirmed by a consideration of their character. It is not necessary here to examine all nineteen of Hobbes's laws of nature. We may confine our focus to the basic structure of his doctrine and the moral spirit that he seeks to cultivate by it. Hobbes's "first and fundamental" law of nature, as we have already seen, advises men to seek peace when it is attainable. In telling men not only to seek peace but also to "follow it" (see *Lev.* 14.4), the first law leads immediately to the second: "*that a man be willing, when others are so too, as far-forth as for peace and defense of himself he shall think it necessary, to lay down [his] right to all things, and be contented with so much liberty against other men as he would allow other men against himself*" (*Lev.* 14.5). Hobbes's second law of nature points the way to the all-important contract by which men agree to limit them-

---

45. Consider also what Hobbes says when he revisits the conclusion of his discussion of the laws of nature in a later chapter of *Leviathan*: "The law of nature and the civil law contain each other and are of equal extent. For the laws of nature, which consist in equity, justice, gratitude, and other moral virtues on these depending, in the condition of mere nature (as I have said before in the end of the 15th chapter) are not properly laws, but qualities that dispose men to peace and to obedience" (*Lev.* 26.8; see also 26.22).

selves through the creation of a sovereign to rule over them; but the second law is directly derived—as Hobbes himself stresses (see *Lev.* 14.5)—from the more basic "command" that each man should seek a lasting peace in order to preserve himself. And from these first two laws of nature follow all the others, both because Hobbes conceives of all the other laws of nature as various means by which men can live peacefully with one another and because it becomes a crucial dictate of Hobbesian natural law that men obey the commands of the sovereign to whom they promise their obedience. The natural law, according to Hobbes, mandates adherence to the civil law, once it has been created (*Lev.* 15.3, 26.8; see also *De Cive* 14.9–10; *De Hom.* 13.9, 15.4).

As important as it is to grasp the role of this legal conception in Hobbesian natural law, it is even more important to appreciate the attitude that Hobbes seeks to cultivate through his natural law teaching. Hobbes wants to convince men that it is in their long-term self-interest to be as modest, accommodating, and tolerant as circumstances permit. Reasonable men, he advises, should take care not to resemble that jagged stone that "by the asperity and irregularity of its figure" cannot be easily fit into a structure with other stones and therefore is likely to be "cast away as unprofitable and troublesome" (*Lev.* 15.17; see also *De Cive* 3.9). Hobbesian morality is a morality of compliant civility.[46] Although it requires some restraint of one's passions, it does not make severe demands or call for devotion to high principles. The moral tone of Hobbes's message can be seen, for example, in his insistence that men should not seek revenge out of a proud desire to avenge past wrongs, but only, if at all, out of a prudent concern to deter future transgressions (*Lev.* 15.19; *Elem.* 16.10; *De Cive* 3.11). In the same vein, Hobbes teaches that virtue does not demand that men conquer their fears. In his most rigorous statements, he either omits courage from his list of virtues or explicitly denies that it should be considered a moral virtue (see *Lev.* 15.40; *De Hom.* 13.9; cf. *Elem.* 18.14; *De Cive* 3.32). Perhaps most revealing of the spirit of Hobbesian morality is the maxim by which Hobbes sums up his teaching for those who find it "too subtle a deduction" to follow his derivation of nineteen separate rules from the need for peace. That maxim—meant to make the Hobbesian teaching intelligible "even to the meanest capacity"—is *"Do not that to another which thou wouldst not have done to thyself"* (*Lev.* 15.35). Hobbes sometimes pretends that this revised, negative version of the Golden Rule is equivalent to the original, positive version. Yet, by encouraging his readers to compare the two, he lets us see the difference for ourselves. The difference may seem slight;

---

46. Oakeshott, *Hobbes on Civil Association*, 120, calls Hobbesian morality "the morality of the tame man."

in fact, it is vast. Whereas the Golden Rule of Christian morality calls on men to put the good of others before their own welfare and to sacrifice themselves even for their enemies, the Silver Rule of Hobbesian morality asks only that they not cause each other needless harm. Adherence to the Hobbesian rule may require a modicum of self-restraint, but it does not require serious self-sacrifice. And it is in keeping with this relaxation of the demands of morality that the collective aim of the followers of Hobbes's laws of nature is nothing more than peaceful coexistence in this world.[47]

Hobbes's effort to transform morality is not only an effort to relax its demands and lower its aims; it is also an effort to simplify and clarify what for so long had been left complex and obscure.[48] This aspect of his ambition can be seen especially in those passages in which Hobbes directly contrasts his moral teaching not so much with Christian morality as with the teaching of the classical tradition rooted in Aristotle. These passages include, not coincidentally, some of Hobbes's most emphatic proclamations of his success in raising moral philosophy at long last to the rank of a science (see especially *Lev.* 15.40; *De Cive* 3.31–32; *Elem.* 17.14). As we saw in our earlier consideration of Hobbes's critique of Aristotle, the key difference, in Hobbes's view, between his own clear and precise teaching and Aristotle's obscure one is that, whereas Aristotle praised the virtues while failing to see "wherein consisted their goodness," Hobbes identifies peace as the unambiguous end from which the virtues should take their bearings. Hobbes faults Aristotle for defining the virtues as means between extremes of various passions, rather than as means in the simpler sense of means to an end the virtues should serve. Aristotle proceeded "as if not the cause, but the degree" of the virtues, or of the passions they govern, made them virtues (see p. 20 above; see again *Lev.* 15.40, *De Cive* 3.32). Now, one could well ask—a question we refrained from asking earlier—whether this criticism is entirely fair to Aristotle. For

---

47. Hobbes's modification of the Golden Rule can be seen, e.g., in *Lev.* 14.5, 15.35, 26.13, 42.11; *Elem.* 17.9; *De Cive* 3.26, 4.23; consider also *Beh.*, 54. That Hobbes is well aware of the difference his modification makes is indicated by the fact that he refers to the original Golden Rule as the "law of the Gospel" and the Silver Rule (*quod tibi fieri non vis, alteri ne feceris*) as the "law of all men" (*Lev.* 14.5). See also his wry remark in *De Cive* that the Silver Rule is "proclaimed in pretty much the same words by our Savior" in Matthew 7:12 (4.23). On the difference between the Golden Rule and Hobbes's Silver Rule, see Owen, "The Tolerant Leviathan," 145; Mansfield, "Hobbes and the Science of Indirect Government," 101; Pangle and Burns, *The Key Texts of Political Philosophy*, 265, 269; Green, *Hobbes and Human Nature*, 84; Sullivan, *Machiavelli, Hobbes, and the Formation of a Liberal Republicanism in England*, 85; Vaughan, *Behemoth Teaches Leviathan*, 50–53.

48. Compare Skinner, *Visions of Politics, Vol. III*, 135–38.

Aristotle does, in certain key passages, identify an end served by the virtues.[49] That end is the noble, or the virtues themselves, insofar as virtuous actions are for their own sake (see, e.g., *Nicomachean Ethics* 1115b10–13, 1115b20–24). Moreover, the virtues get their specification as means, according to Aristotle, not by merely standing in the middle of a spectrum from excess to deficiency, but by being defined by right reason as the prudent man exercises it (see *Nicomachean Ethics* 1103b31–34, 1106b36–1107a2). Yet Hobbes's point still holds at least in one important respect, for Aristotle himself indicates that his explicit or official account of virtue's end and its specification is not fully satisfactory, and he goes on to treat the matter as a mystery or a problem to which he never gives a perfectly clear resolution (see, in particular, *Nicomachean Ethics* 1138b18–34, 1144a6–1145a11). It remains true, then—if in a somewhat more complicated way than Hobbes suggests—that a key difference between Hobbes and Aristotle is that the former seeks to bring simplicity and clarity to a realm the latter was willing to leave in something of a mist.

As for the argument by which Hobbes would establish the end that promises to give virtue its long-overdue simplicity and clarity, it is the following. Although men's appetites and aversions are so diverse and variable that men can never agree on what deserves to be called good, that very disagreement contributes to a state of conflict that clarifies the one thing on which they can agree, namely, that war is bad and therefore, by implication or inversion, that peace is good. The goodness of peace, Hobbes contends, is easily recognized and universally granted when men contemplate the state of anarchy that results from their otherwise irresolvable disagreements about good and evil (see *Lev.* 15.40; *De Cive* 3.31).

Hobbes's argument for the supreme importance of peace is not beyond challenge. It may be true that all reasonable men would readily agree that peace is good, especially when confronted by the horrors of war. It does not follow that all reasonable men—to say nothing of others—would agree that peace is the supreme good before which all other goods should bow and hence the unrivaled polestar of virtue. Is preserving one's life on earth, even if it is the precondition of all other pursuits in this world, obviously our most important concern, or are there other, higher tasks for which we ought to be willing to fight and die? Rather than press this difficulty at this point, let us postpone it until we can consider it as part of a broader assessment of Hobbes's moral teaching. It is better for present purposes—in part because it will prepare the way for such

---

49. Sorell, "Hobbes's Moral Philosophy," 134, makes a similar point, although he gives a description of Aristotle's position that differs from the one I give in what follows. See also Sorell, *Hobbes*, 106–8, "Hobbes and Aristotle," 374–75, 378–79.

an assessment—to complete our examination of Hobbes's moral teaching by taking up an important passage that can help us to understand what pulled Hobbes toward a simplified teaching of the sort he offers. The passage in question comes in the wake of, and as a kind of response to, Hobbes's unveiling of an aspect of his teaching that we have not yet considered: his doctrine of justice.

Hobbes's doctrine of justice is conveyed by his third law of nature: "*that men perform their covenants made*" (*Lev.* 15.1). This law of nature contains "the fountain and original of justice" in Hobbes's account, both because Hobbes denies that any action can be unjust prior to the making of covenants and because he affirms that, once covenants are made, injustice consists precisely in breaking them, and justice in keeping them (*Lev.* 15.2; see also *De Cive* 3.4; *Elem.* 16.2). Of course, Hobbes is quick to point out that "covenants without the sword are but words" (*Lev.* 27.2). Thus, for justice and injustice to have any real significance among men, he argues, the most important of all covenants—that establishing the authority of the sovereign—must be in place to secure all the others (*Lev.* 15.3). The erection of a commonwealth ruled by a sovereign is essential to the emergence of justice, according to Hobbes, not only because the sovereign's sword is necessary to ensure that private men will hold (or be held) to their covenants with one another, but also because the sovereign has the ultimate say in determining what belongs to whom and in making the laws and issuing the decrees that his subjects are obligated, by their fundamental covenant, to obey (*Lev.* 15.3; see also 26.8).

In Hobbes's account of the emergence of justice through the making of covenants and the creation of the sovereign, we can see with particular clarity two apparently competing tendencies that run throughout Hobbes's moral teaching as a whole. On the one hand, there is the simplifying, reductionistic, even debunking thrust of his argument: there is no justice prior to the creation of the commonwealth, and justice means nothing more than sticking to covenants, especially the decisive covenant to obey the sovereign's laws and other dictates. Hobbes reduces justice to mere promise keeping, respect for property, and obedience to civil law—all of which, by his account, are versions of essentially the same form of fidelity. On the other hand, having stripped justice of any exalted or pre-contractual meaning and reduced it to something so simple, Hobbes is then very much concerned to defend the rationality of justice so understood. This further step, however, is not so much a contradiction of the prior one, or a contrary tendency in his argument, as it is the other side of a single coin. The tension between the two tendencies is merely apparent, and in fact their cooperation is necessary to Hobbes's full argument, which may be summarized as follows: *if* justice is radically simplified, *then* it is rational.

Hobbes's defense of the rationality of justice is presented most fully and clearly in the passage that immediately follows his explanation of his doctrine of justice through his elaboration of his third law of nature. This crucial passage is Hobbes's confrontation with "the Fool." The Fool—Hobbes's Fool—is a descendant of the original fool of the Psalms, the fool who "hath said in his heart, 'There is no God'" (see Ps. 14:1). Hobbes's Fool differs from his biblical forebear insofar as he rejects justice more conspicuously than he rejects God. Hobbes's Fool "hath said in his heart, 'There is no such thing as Justice'" (*Lev.* 15.4). It is true that Hobbes's Fool no more believes in God than does the fool of the Psalms; but the atheism of Hobbes's Fool becomes an issue only because it bears on his critique of justice. Hobbes's Fool is brought on stage, or into the text, because he has a critique of justice—one that he does not always keep confined to his heart, but expresses "sometimes also with his tongue." The Fool's critique of justice, as Hobbes presents it, rests on the view that each of us is on his own in the world: "every man's conservation and contentment" is "committed to his own care," and it is of no use looking to God in hope or fear, for (in the Fool's view) God does not exist (15.4). Living as we do in such a forsaken condition, there is no reason, the Fool argues, for each man not to seek his own good by hook or by crook, and in particular there is no reason not to approach covenants in this spirit. The Fool grants something to Hobbes in making this argument: "He does not therein deny that there be covenants, and that they are sometimes broken, sometimes kept, and that such breach of them may be called injustice, and the observance of them justice" (15.4). Yet, if the Fool is ready to grant the existence of covenants and their centrality to the meaning of justice, he denies that it is always rational to keep them: "he questioneth whether injustice, taking away the fear of God (for the same Fool hath said in his heart there is no God), may not sometimes stand with that reason which dictateth to every man his own good." In the Fool's view, the reasonable course of action is always to seek one's own good, wherever it might lie. Sometimes it lies in fidelity to covenants, but other times it does not. And in the latter instances—especially when they allow one to gain "such a benefit as shall put a man in a condition to neglect not only the dispraise and revilings, but also the power of other men"—reason itself dictates that justice be abandoned and injustice embraced (15.4).

What is Hobbes's response to the Fool's argument? To appreciate the character of Hobbes's counterargument, it is important to take note of the considerable common ground between Hobbes and the Fool. We have just seen that the Fool grants something to Hobbes: not only the existence of covenants (which is obvious), but the centrality of covenants to the meaning of justice. The Fool accepts Hobbes's view of what justice and injustice consist in; he merely denies—although it is hardly just a quibble—that justice is always more beneficial than injustice. If the Fool thus makes a concession to Hobbes, Hobbes in turn grants something of importance to the Fool. He accepts the premise that the decisive question for determining the rationality of justice is whether justice is always in one's own interest. Hobbes accepts, in other words, the legitimacy and supremacy of the perspective of self-seeking prudence, or what the Fool calls "that reason which dictateth to every man his own good." One is tempted to say that Hobbes also shares the Fool's atheism. Since that is such a contested question, however, let us not take a firm position here on what Hobbes says in his own heart about God; we can limit ourselves to the less disputable claim that Hobbes's response to the Fool does not rely on any divine sanctions for injustice. To that extent at least, Hobbes follows the Fool in "taking away the fear of God." Hobbes, then, concedes quite a bit to the Fool—even more than the Fool concedes to him.[50]

Still, for all of their common ground, Hobbes rejects the Fool's critique of justice. The Fool's "specious reasoning," he declares, "is nevertheless false" (*Lev.* 15.4). According to Hobbes's counterargument, the Fool errs—and thereby earns his name—first by mistaking the occasional successes of unjust men as confirmation of their wisdom. Hobbes does not deny that it may turn out from time to time that men profit from injustice. Yet, even if one benefits from breaking a covenant and manages to escape punishment, that success does not make the original breech reasonable or wise, because the success could not have been known before the event; at that point, which was the critical moment of decision, the unjust man should have realized that he was running a terrible risk. That disaster did not strike does not mean that it was prudent to have tempted it to (*Lev.* 15.5). The Fool's second mistake is his failure to appreciate the vulnerability of individual human beings. As individuals, Hobbes argues, we are too weak to fend entirely for ourselves. We need "the help of confederates," and especially of that greatest of all confederations: the commonwealth. But confederations, and commonwealths in particular, reasonably demand fidelity of their members. The Fool would have the unjust man declare—if not necessarily with his tongue, then by his actions—that he thinks deception is sometimes reasonable. Such a man, however, "can in reason expect no other means of safety than what can be had from his own single power" (15.5). If he is received into society, it is only because other men fail to understand the kind of person they are dealing with; and if he continues

50. On the extensive common ground between Hobbes and the Fool, see Owen, *Making Religion Safe for Democracy*, 29; Hoekstra, "Hobbes and the Foole," 622, 627, 633, 637–68; Curley, "Religion and Morality in Hobbes," 111–13.

to be "retained" in society rather than being cast out, it is only because the ignorance of his confederates persists. To build one's life on the ignorance of others, Hobbes argues, is to build on sand, for the errors of others are "errors a man cannot reasonably reckon upon as the means of his security" (15.5).

Because the Fool is his own creation, Hobbes is able to give himself the last word in their quarrel. Yet one wonders how a Fool who was not merely conjured up for Hobbes's purposes might respond to Hobbes's counterargument. A Fool who was well instructed by some of the classical critics of justice whom he resembles[51] might respond by arguing that the ignorance and errors of others are not so unfathomable as Hobbes suggests. Not only is it possible to evade the detection of most men, but, by studying men's natures and cultivating the art of deception, one can take steps to increase one's chances of success. It is true that there are always risks involved in deception or any other form of injustice. But the rewards to be reaped often make those risks worth running, and one needs courage, or at least a certain boldness, to live well in a world that is there for the taking by those who are audacious enough to seize it. So might the Fool respond.

To this extension of the Fool's argument, Hobbes would reply in turn—as we can infer from his response to the Fool's explicit argument—that the good to be gained from injustice is not in fact worth the risks involved, nor do those who regard themselves as clever and bold enough to get away with their crimes usually prove to be as superior to other men as they suppose they are. Hobbes's argument against the Fool rests on more than a disagreement about the likelihood of success in unjust schemes. His more important contentions are that what is to be lost when injustice fails is much weightier than what is to be gained when it succeeds, and that some men's awareness of this point is obscured by a kind of vanity that keeps them from seeing clearly their own vulnerability and neediness. The Fool and his partners in crime fail to grasp that, in the endangered condition in which we find ourselves, it is far more important to avoid the *summum malum* of violent death than it is to maximize the less consequential goods that injustice can reap. Those who continue to regard fraud and audacity as virtues even after the state of nature has been replaced by civil society are not a rare breed of wise wolves; they are fools blinded by their pride, and they are liable to end up with an early death rather than the prosperity they envision.[52] Now, whatever one may think of

51. See, e.g., Plato, *Republic* 343b1–344c8, 358e1–361d3, 365a4–366b2.

52. Compare the following passage from later in *Leviathan* on "wisdom" as a source of crime: "And [it happeneth commonly] that such as have a great and false opinion of their own wisdom take upon them to reprehend the actions, and call in question the authority, of them

the strength of Hobbes's argument so elaborated,[53] this much is clear and more important for present purposes: Hobbes gives every indication that *he thinks* that he has a solid counterargument against the Fool. And that means that Hobbes thinks that he can show that justice, at least if its meaning is sufficiently pared down, is entirely reasonable. The heading he gives to the whole section that includes his exchange with the Fool is "Justice not Contrary to Reason" (see also *Lev.* 15.7, 15.35–36, 27.10, 30.5). Moreover, Hobbes's confidence that he can meet the challenge of the Fool has a crucial implication, because he thinks that he can meet that challenge, as we have seen, without denying the Fool's key premise about the primacy of self-interest and while abiding by his insistence that the fear of God be "taken away." Justice is

---

that govern, and so to unsettle the laws with their public discourse, as that nothing shall be a crime but what their own designs require should be so. It happeneth also to the same men to be prone to all such crimes as consist in craft and in deceiving of their neighbors, because they think their designs are too subtle to be perceived. These, I say, are effects of a false presumption of their own wisdom. For of them that are the first movers in the disturbance of [a] commonwealth (which can never happen without a civil war), very few are left alive long enough to see their new designs established, so that the benefit of their crimes redoundeth to posterity, and such as would least have wished it—which argues they were not so wise as they thought they were. And those that deceive upon hope of not being observed do commonly deceive themselves (the darkness in which they believe they lie hidden being nothing else but their own blindness), and are no wiser than children, that think all hid by hiding their own eyes" (27.16). See also Sullivan, *Machiavelli, Hobbes, and the Formation of a Liberal Republicanism in England*, 89–92.

53. On the much-discussed question of whether Hobbes's argument is sound, see, among many other sources, Hoekstra, "Hobbes and the Foole," 620–31; Curley, "Religion and Morality in Hobbes," 111–13; Zaitchik, "Hobbes's Reply to the Fool," 246–47; Hampton, *Hobbes and the Social Contract Tradition*, 64–81; Gauthier, *The Logic of Leviathan*, 76–89, "Thomas Hobbes: Moral Theorist," 553–58; Kavka, *Hobbesian Moral and Political Theory*, 136–56, "The Rationality of Rule-Following," 5–34; Nunan, "Hobbes on Morality, Rationality, and Foolishness," 40–64; Rhodes, "Hobbes's unReasonable Fool," 93–102. In comparing the wide-ranging positions of these scholars, one must also pay due attention to their sometimes divergent views of the character of Hobbes's argument. That is especially true when it comes to Hoekstra, who argues that Hobbes's argument is much stronger if it is seen as directed against "the Explicit Foole" (that is, a Fool who expresses his position publicly) than against "the Silent Foole" (that is, a Fool who has the good sense to keep his mouth shut). Hoekstra's analysis is insightful in many respects, and I have profited from it more than from any other discussion of Hobbes's exchange with the Fool. But I do not find his central argument convincing, because Hobbes's Fool (whom Hoekstra calls "the Explicit Foole") expresses his position openly or explicitly—that is, "with his tongue"— only "sometimes," and, more important, Hobbes's purpose in his exchange with the Fool is not just to warn against the public expression of a critique of justice but to vindicate the rationality of his third law of nature (see *Lev.* 15.7).

rational, in Hobbes's view, precisely in terms of the individual's self-interest, even if justice does not have divine support.[54]

Hobbes's exchange with the Fool can help us finally answer a question that arose in our earlier consideration of Hobbes's account of human nature and human striving: Why does Hobbes so bluntly and openly proclaim the primacy of self-interest as the dominant force in human motivations by declaring that every man, in everything he does, seeks his own good? Hobbes's assertion in this regard, as we noted earlier, amounts to what most people would see as an offensive or at least unsettling claim about the inescapability of human selfishness—the kind of thing one might expect from the Fool, but not from a man of the humanity of Hobbes (see p. 196 above). But we can now understand why Hobbes is so blunt. There is more than one reason. First, Hobbes did not see the pursuit of self-interest as necessarily inimical to justice. In his view, there is a basic coincidence of interests among human beings once they have come together in a commonwealth, at least if they understand their deepest interests correctly. The moral problem, then, can be solved, and the solution does not require that men overcome their self-concern, but only that they be taught to see what their true interests are. Prudent selfishness, far from being the principle of injustice or immorality that many take it to be, is, according to Hobbes, so compatible with a rational morality that it can be its very foundation. Furthermore, the rational morality that is possible on such a basis is not to be scorned, in Hobbes's view, for resting on self-interest, because it is superior to all earlier, muddled alternatives, which kept morality from attaining the clarity and efficacy that are possible on the new foundation. We have already considered the ways in which Hobbes differentiates his own teaching from Aristotle's in particular. It is in keeping with what we have seen that Hobbes would regard his frank

54. See Owen, *Making Religion Safe for Democracy*, 29. In contrast to Owen, Warrender distorts Hobbes's argument when he claims that the "discrepancy between the duty and the interest of the individual, and again between private and public interest . . . is overcome only if divine rewards and punishments are posited, and without the sanction of salvation (or ultimate destruction) Hobbes's theory is incomplete" (*The Political Philosophy of Hobbes*, 274). It is striking that Warrender must add to Hobbes's reply to the Fool an argument that Hobbes himself does not make—namely, that a rebellious subject "prejudices his salvation"—in order to ascribe to Hobbes the view that "only the punishments of God, whose wrath cannot be escaped, are capable of providing an adequate sanction, and of effecting a reconciliation between duty and interest" (276). Similar to Owen's view (and my own) are Johnston, *The Rhetoric of Leviathan*, 129–30, and Macpherson, *The Political Theory of Possessive Individualism*, 73; similar to Warrender's is Gillespie, *The Theological Origins of Modernity*, 241.

acceptance of self-interest as essential to his effort to succeed where Aristotle and his heirs failed, by at last clarifying morality and making it truly effective. And finally, there is the consideration—already raised, but relevant in this connection—that Hobbes's doctrine of justice and his moral teaching more broadly do not require that morality be supported by the threats or promises of a providential God. The simplest reason this is so we have just seen in the exchange with the Fool: Hobbes thought that it was possible to vindicate the rationality of justice without relying on the fear of God. To that point, however, we can add another. Hobbesian morality, because it rests on enlightened self-interest, does not summon men to profound devotion or demand great sacrifices. Thus, not only does it not need divine support, but it also is unlikely to prepare the way for piety by inspiring the hopes and expectations that arise with noble dedication to exalted principles. Hobbesian moralists, moral though they may be, will not find in morality an inducement to believe.[55]

✷

That Hobbes develops a moral teaching that does not depend on religious support and is more likely to draw men away from belief than toward it gives us reason to suspect that his desire to undermine religion contributed to his zeal to transform men's understanding of morality. It is also worth considering, in this connection, a point that we have not yet had occasion to consider, in part because Hobbes puts so much emphasis on peace as the sole end from which virtue ought to take its bearings: once peace has been secured, Hobbes suggests, the end of virtue can expand to include "commodious living" as well (see *Lev.* 13.14, 14.8, 15.40; *De Cive* 13.14). It is true that the pursuit of commodious living—that is, of the comforts and pleasures of prosperity—must always remain subordinate, in Hobbes's scheme, to the demands of peace, since prosperity is impossible without peace. But it is nevertheless wholly in keeping with the spirit, as well as the letter, of Hobbes's moral teaching that men should feel no compunction about striving to make their lives ever more comfortable. And that bears, too, on the question of religious belief, for the more comfortable men become in their lives in this world, the less likely they are to direct their hopes and concerns to another world.[56]

55. Compare Strauss, "The Law of Reason in the *Kuzari*," 140. Contrast Taylor, "The Ethical Doctrine of Hobbes," 422; Warrender, *The Political Philosophy of Hobbes*, 272–77.

56. See Bolotin, "Is There a Right to Live as We Please?" 331. Compare Montesquieu, *The Spirit of the Laws* 25.12.

But why would Hobbes have been drawn to a moral teaching that would help to undermine religious belief? The most straightforward answer, of course, is that he thought that a society in which religious zealotry had been defanged would be more stable and more conducive to meeting men's genuine needs, as he understood those needs. Hobbes's experience of the horrors of civil war arising from chaotic religious forces gave him an obvious incentive to address that political problem at its religious source. But there is also the further possibility that we raised earlier: Hobbes may also have been guided in some measure by a more theoretical intention, that is, by his desire to vindicate his conviction that there are no genuine miracles and that purported experiences of miracles, as well as other purported religious experiences, are rooted, not in genuine communication between God and man, but in anxiety and ignorance working in tandem with flawed political arrangements and unreasonable moral convictions (see pp. 182–83 and 193–94 above). Perhaps Hobbes, aware of the limits of his direct efforts to meet the challenge that claims of miracles and other religious experiences posed to his fundamental convictions, was moved by the hope that those claims could be consigned to history, such that educated men would cease to take them seriously and they would fade away as the influence of his doctrines spread. If such a hope were realized, Hobbes might well have believed, it would help to show that he was correct in dismissing such claims as dependent on remediable deficiencies in men's circumstances and convictions.

Now, as we noted earlier, even if Hobbes was drawn in such a direction by his awareness of the limits of his direct efforts to settle the question that most concerned him, it is difficult to know in what way he pursued this further strategy (see pp. 193–94 above). Was it a venture that he worked out with full awareness and clarity in his own mind, or was it a hope that moved him without his being wholly conscious of it? That question must remain unanswered, for even if our consideration of Hobbes's moral teaching gives us reason to think that he did indeed conceive of that teaching as contributing to a broader effort to undermine religious belief, it does not tell us exactly why he wanted to accomplish that—that is, whether the reasons of which he was aware went beyond the obvious practical ones. And there are further complications to be considered, some of which we have already touched on (see pp. 182–83 above). Most important are these: not only could Hobbes not have expected to live long enough to witness the full effects of the moral revolution he was trying to launch, but even if that success—which he could have anticipated in his mind's eye—were to be achieved, it would be in need of interpretation. It may well be true that a change in people's moral convictions, especially when coupled with the progress of science and the erection of a rational society devoted to secular ends, could bring about a sharp decline, perhaps even a disappearance, of religious zeal and claimed religious experiences. So, too, could men build Babel, at least for a time. But how could one know that the transition, even at its completion, would deserve to be understood as a movement from darkness into the light, rather than as the arrival of a new night? Would not the venture just sketched, resting as it does on an atheistic premise, presuppose what it needs to prove?

Hobbes might respond to this last difficulty by arguing that the success of the new order would be such that no reasonable person would be able to deny that it constituted a moral and political advance, and therefore any further changes in men's convictions and experiences that accompanied it would reasonably be interpreted as signs of health rather than as symptoms of a new kind of sickness. Who could reasonably deny that it is better for a society to be based on a rational morality than on one that makes all sorts of needless, irrational demands? And if a society were based on a rational morality and men there lived lives whose evident happiness bespoke the greatest possible satisfaction of their most important needs, would it not be only the bitterness of the dying remnants of the defeated Kingdom of Darkness that would continue to produce objections to the new order? In response to this imagined rejoinder from Hobbes, however, we must ask whether it is true that Hobbes's moral teaching is as rational as he claims it is. Let us conclude this chapter by raising and considering three questions about it.

The first is a question about the political wisdom of Hobbes's moral teaching: Is it reasonable to think that a successful commonwealth can be built on the basis of an unmitigated endorsement of self-interest and a stark assertion of man's natural asociality? The difficulty is whether such a teaching does not make it even harder than it already is for the commonwealth to ask its citizens to sacrifice their self-interest when such sacrifices are necessary for the common good.[57] This problem is most acute in times of war. As if recognizing the difficulty at the last minute, Hobbes goes out of his way, near the end of *Leviathan*, to offer the following addendum to his laws of nature: "To the laws of nature declared in the 15th Chapter, I would have this added: *That every man is bound by nature, as much as in him lieth, to protect in war the authority by which he is himself protected in time of peace*" (Review and Conclusion, 5). Yet, not only does Hobbes fail to mount an argument to show that adherence to this additional law is always in each individual's self-interest, but he grants

---

57. See Bolotin, "Is There a Right to Live as We Please?" 332; Strauss, *Natural Right and History*, 197; Mara, "Hobbes's Counsel to Sovereigns," 408–9; Kavka, *Hobbesian Moral and Political Theory*, 424–27.

elsewhere that men who are afraid to fight may refuse or even flee when they are ordered into battle without thereby committing an injustice. Fearful deserters may be dishonorable cowards, but because they act out of "natural timorousness," Hobbes argues, they should not be regarded as unjust (*Lev.* 21.16). This exoneration of desertion is, on one level, an admirable display of Hobbes's commitment to working out the implications of his principles with rigorous consistency. But his consistency in this case exposes the weakness of his principles as a foundation for sound politics. If a commonwealth could avoid ever going to war, the problem of inducing fearful soldiers to fight might never arise. It is not reasonable, however, to expect the need for war to disappear entirely, nor is war the only time when a commonwealth must ask sacrifices of its citizens.

Second is a less directly political problem, although it is ultimately not without political consequences of its own: Can people fully embrace a doctrine that tells them that they should subordinate all other concerns to peace and security? Hobbes's argument that peace is the end from which all the virtues should take their bearings can be questioned in two different but related ways: Does he offer a compelling argument? And are there not human longings that make it difficult for people to accept the conclusion to which his argument leads? On the former question, the chief difficulty with Hobbes's direct argument for the supremacy of peace has already been raised: even if all men, when confronted by the horrors of war, would agree that peace is good, that does not mean that they would agree—nor that they necessarily *should* agree—that peace is a good of such importance that all other goods ought to bow down before it (see p. 229 above). To this difficulty, Hobbes might respond by insisting that his case for the supreme importance of peace consists not only in his direct argument regarding what all men would acknowledge under the right conditions but also in his claim that self-preservation, the avoidance of death, is our most powerful desire by nature, even if it can be obscured by deluded opinions and irrational passions (see again, e.g., *Elem.* 14.6, 14.13, 17.14; *De Cive* 1.7, 2.18; *Lev.* 14.29, 15.17; *De Hom.* 11.6). But that is a claim—an *assertion*—that Hobbes does not show to be true. And it is not so obviously true as not to need further argument. Moreover, there is an important question that must be asked about Hobbes's claim: Is it *death as such* that nature makes us so concerned to avoid, or is it only *violent death*?[58] After all, the attainment of peace in a secure commonwealth can protect us from the latter, but it can merely delay the former. In order for Hobbes's moral teaching to be fully welcomed in people's hearts and

---

58. See Bruell, "Der Tod aus der Sicht der Philosophie," 210; Ahrensdorf, "The Fear of Death and the Longing for Immortality," 584–85.

minds, he has to try to convince people that their longing to overcome death as such is not so important, that they can recognize and accept the futility of that longing and commit themselves entirely to avoiding the kind of death that is avoidable. Hobbes does make such an effort (see again, e.g., *Lev.* 6.58, 11.1–2, 12.5–6, 15.8, 29.15; *Elem.* 7.6–7, 14.6; *De Hom.* 11.6). But was it reasonable of him to think that it could succeed? If nature has implanted in us a powerful aversion to death—"that terrible enemy of nature" (*Elem.* 14.6)—can we be satisfied merely to ward off premature death at the hands of other human beings and thereby postpone our inevitable demise? This problem bears on Hobbes's teaching about the virtues. For Hobbes's account of the virtues depends on the thought that it is entirely reasonable to fear violent death and to avoid it at all costs. Thus, not only does Hobbes refuse to hold out any promise that virtuous actions will enable men to overcome death as such, but he also demotes those virtues, such as courage, that require a willingness to risk one's life. Hobbes's teaching in this regard may well have led to a lowering of the esteem in which such virtues were held by many modern men who were influenced by Hobbes and his heirs—an effect that is still visible today. But it is striking that the late modern revolt against the Hobbesian outlook included a passionate, almost fanatical, attempt to restore the virtues that Hobbes had denigrated. It suffices here to think of Nietzsche's celebration of courage and of the frustrated yearnings to which it spoke.[59]

Hobbes repeatedly praises his own moral teaching for its simplicity and clarity; it is therefore reasonable to assume that he would point to those qualities to defend it against our critical questions. But the third and final question we should consider is whether the simplicity and clarity of his teaching are not, in some sense, specious, and whether their appearance does not come at a high cost. The fuller version of Hobbes's claim, as we have seen, is that, unlike prior moral philosophers, who took their bearings from men's passion-soaked opinions and failed even by innovations such as the Aristotelian doctrine of the mean to dispel the fog of common opinions, he has achieved a clear and rigorous deduction of morality from a single end (see pp. 20–21 and 228–29 above). Yet, to turn away from common opinions as Hobbes does—to substitute a clear answer to the question of virtue's end for older answers that, in their very murkiness, were more faithful to the muddled convictions that prevail in men's ordinary moral lives—is to break much more radically with men's

---

59. See Strauss, *The Political Philosophy of Hobbes*, 164–65, "German Nihilism," 370–72; Manent, *The City of Man*, 175. Consider the sequence of speeches "On War and Warriors" and "On the New Idol" in Nietzsche's *Thus Spoke Zarathustra*; see also *Beyond Good and Evil*, aphs. 252–53.

everyday opinions than Aristotle and other traditional moral philosophers did. Hobbes, of course, would not quarrel with this description of the difference between him and his predecessors. To the contrary, he would embrace it as capturing one of the great advantages of his approach, even its decisive superiority. But, in response to that assessment, we may ask whether the effect of Hobbes's approach, in drawing men away from their original opinions, is in fact a simplification leading to clarity and not rather the introduction of a new kind of obfuscation. The new obfuscation is one in which men's admittedly ambiguous prescientific moral convictions become hidden, even in their own minds, behind the screen created by a purportedly clear and scientific teaching. For instance, is it reasonable to expect the common conviction that virtuous actions are noble, and that the noble itself is the end of virtue, simply to disappear because Hobbes's "rational" teaching has no place for such a thought and would replace it with something simpler and clearer? Is it not more likely that that conviction and others like it will come to live underground lives, as buried and thus poorly understood aspects of an outlook whose new surface features are in tension with them? It is worth considering, in this regard, even the case of Hobbes himself, since his own understanding of right in the state of nature proved upon close examination to be confused and contradictory on the crucial question of whether right has any pre-civic moral significance. Hobbes's own thinking proved to lack the simplicity and clarity of which he boasts, and not on a minor matter but on the question of whether justice is simply meaningless in the state of nature or whether human beings always live under at least some binding moral restrictions. That we do always live under some moral restrictions is implied in Hobbes's assertion of a right that allows any and all actions only when they are for the sake of self-preservation, even as it is denied in his explicit statements (see pp. 217–22 above). The confusion that we saw in Hobbes's understanding of what he regards as each man's fundamental right—and thus as the basis, in a certain respect, of his entire moral teaching—persists in the modern moral outlook that he did so much to shape. That outlook, which regards the rights of each individual as prior to his duties, claims to have achieved not only a welcome liberation from oppressive obligations but also a rational clarity in moral matters that earlier ages lacked. Yet, by failing to take sufficiently seriously the conviction that men are bound by duties that precede their rights—a conviction that its adherents tend, like Hobbes, to retain without being aware of it—the modern moral outlook mistakes as signs of unprecedented enlightenment what are in fact its own confusions and blind spots.

7

Hobbes's Political Philosophy II:
The Hobbesian Commonwealth

In the course of our consideration of Hobbes's moral teaching, I referred from time to time, as was all but inevitable, to the political transformation that Hobbes hoped would accompany the moral revolution he sought to initiate. Hobbes's political vision, his conception of the commonwealth as the mighty Leviathan, is that for which he is most famous. And one could well think, from his reputation as a political philosopher and from a glance at his political works, that, for Hobbes, the moral is entirely in the service of the political: Hobbes wanted to initiate a moral revolution so that men would be better, more obedient citizens of the new kind of commonwealth he envisioned.[1] We need not regard that as an adequate account of the relationship between Hobbes's moral argument and his political argument to agree that the two travel together and that, to understand Hobbes's venture, it is necessary to consider his account of sovereignty and the commonwealth. The need for such a consideration is especially obvious in a study of Hobbes that focuses on his struggle with religion, for Hobbes regarded religion as a political problem as well as a theoretical challenge—to say nothing now of the possibility we have considered that his moral-political project was part of his response to the theoretical challenge posed by religion. This final chapter, then, will examine Hobbes's account of sovereignty and the commonwealth, not with the aim of delving into its many details, but with the aim of highlighting its most novel and important features, especially those that bear on the problem of religion.

If it is misleading to explain the relationship between Hobbes's moral argument and his political argument by describing the former as a mere hand-

---

1. See, e.g., Laird, *Hobbes*, 174–88; Willey, *The Seventeenth Century Background*, 100–101.

maid of the latter, how should we conceive of that relationship? We can begin to answer that question by observing that in each of his main political works, by the time Hobbes turns to his political argument proper, he has already presented his moral teaching. This is clearest in *Leviathan*, where Part I, which includes the state of nature chapter as well as the chapters on the laws of nature, is entitled "Of Man," and Part II is entitled "Of Commonwealth"; but it is true of *De Cive* and *The Elements of Law* as well. That the moral argument precedes the political argument is not merely a reflection of Hobbes's view that, because man is both the matter and the artificer of the commonwealth, an account of human nature must precede an account of the commonwealth (see *Lev.*, Intro.; *Elem.* 20.1). Nor—what is perhaps to say the same thing in a different way—is it merely an implication of Hobbes's resolutive-compositive method, according to which the commonwealth must be viewed as dissolved into its elements before it can be reconstituted as a complex whole (see again *De Cive*, Pref.). The further and ultimately more important implication of the priority of Hobbes's moral argument is that by the time he turns to his account of the commonwealth, the question of the end of the commonwealth has already been answered. The commonwealth's essential purpose, according to Hobbes, is to provide peace and thereby to secure the preservation of the individuals who make it up. But this is established in Part I of *Leviathan* (and in the corresponding parts of *De Cive* and *The Elements of Law*) such that it can be presented as a premise at the outset of Part II (see *Lev.* 17.1). Hobbes's moral argument, then, is so far from being a mere handmaid of his political argument that the chief purpose of the Hobbesian commonwealth is to secure an end whose primacy is established before Hobbes's direct discussion of the commonwealth even begins. To put the point in Hobbes's own, more substantive terms: what men most need and the rules of conduct by which they can get it are established by reflection on the state of nature and the laws of nature; if men could secure what they most need and live safely by the laws of nature without the power of the sovereign to ensure the keeping of covenants, there would be no need for the commonwealth; it is only because the laws of nature are not self-enforcing and "covenants without the sword are but words" that the commonwealth is necessary at all (*Lev.* 17.1–2).

This simple argument with which Hobbes begins his discussion of the commonwealth determines his account throughout. And this fact is an aspect of a broader paradox that runs throughout Hobbes's discussion of the commonwealth. As infamous as is Hobbes's advocacy of a mighty sovereign—of a power so strong that Hobbes compares it to the biblical sea monster that no man can subdue and portrays it, in the unforgettable image from the title page of *Leviathan*, as a towering figure so immense as to incorporate all of his subjects within his body—Hobbes's sovereign is in fact the creation and servant of a collection of individuals who are radically free by nature and who unite merely for the sake of their own preservation as individuals. Hobbes denies that there is any meaningful unity among men before they form commonwealths (see *Lev.* 16.13–14; *De Cive* 6.1, 7.7; *Elem.* 21.11). And he denies that the sovereign—any sovereign—has a natural or God-given title to rule that precedes or supersedes the covenant by which he comes into being as a sovereign. In contrast to Aristotle, who approaches the central questions of politics—Who should rule? and, To what end or ends?—by looking at matters as they stand within already established and stratified political orders with various parties making arguments for their claims to rule, Hobbes rejects out of hand the notion that any person or party is naturally more deserving of rule than any other.[2] This is another way in which his moral argument determines his political argument: by arguing that men are free and equal by nature, Hobbes implies that no man has natural authority over any other man, just as no man by nature owes obedience to another. The absence or meaninglessness of pre-civic claims to unity, authority, and obligation pertains, in Hobbes's account, most obviously to men considered as individuals, reaffirming as it does his view that men are by nature free individuals; but it extends also to man as such, since it implies the unrestricted freedom of man to remake his world so as to make it more hospitable for human habitation. In other words, not only is each individual, according to Hobbes, free by nature to enter for reasons of his own self-interest into any commonwealth that will have him, but human beings as such are free to form groups and build commonwealths as they see fit, with a view to nothing but the advantages of such political orders for meeting human needs.[3] Of course, since most men are bad judges of how to secure what is good for them and how to avoid what is ruinous to the commonwealth, they need a "very able architect" to advise them in building a solid and lasting structure (*Lev.* 29.1). Hobbes regarded himself as the first architect up to the task (with *Lev.* 29.1, see 30.5; *De Cive* 13.9).

Sovereignty

Why did Hobbes choose not to follow Aristotle's approach of immersing himself in the arguments, opinions, and claims to rule that political partisans express in everyday political life? Why did he conclude instead that theoreti-

---

2. See Mansfield, "Hobbes and the Science of Indirect Government," 98–100; Orwin, "On the Sovereign Authorization," 32; Pettit, *Made with Words*, 122.

3. See Kraynak, *History and Modernity in the Thought of Thomas Hobbes*, 168, 179, 190.

cally, if emphatically not practically, the whole edifice of rule or sovereignty needed to be torn down and rebuilt on a new foundation? Our earlier examination of Hobbes's critique of classical thought provides us with some of the reasons: the opinions expressed in the disputes in ordinary political life are hopelessly diverse and contested; the rival partisans cannot agree about who should rule, and their various arguments, far from pointing upward to an adequate resolution of the matter, point downward to the divergent interests in which they are rooted; the realm of political opinions is more fundamentally a realm of passions seeking justification than a realm of prephilosophic attempts to grasp the truth (see pp. 19–20 above). These reflections surely guided Hobbes in his abandonment of Aristotle's course and his effort to chart a very different one. But there was also another reason. For Hobbes had to contend with a force and a set of doctrines that Aristotle had to confront only in much tamer pagan forms. The force and doctrines in question had, in the long interim between Aristotle and Hobbes, unnaturally intervened in the ordinary operation of political life, whether by the work of divine providence, or, as Hobbes saw it, through a complex and protracted power grab by the Kingdom of Darkness. The clearest example of Hobbes's opposition to one such doctrine, which emerged later than some others but had risen to prominence in his time, can be seen in this simple yet revealing fact: as firm an advocate as Hobbes was of absolute monarchy, he was not a proponent of the doctrine of the divine right of kings. By stressing that he was giving a *new* account of the basis of sovereignty and remaining silent about the divine right of kings, Hobbes indicated with sufficient clarity his rejection of the doctrine on which the Stuart monarchy, in particular, based its claim to rule (see *Lev.* 19.3, 20.19, 31.41, Review and Conclusion, 13).[4]

Hobbes's effort to replace the traditional doctrine of the divine right of kings with a novel doctrine reveals the revolutionary character of his account of sovereignty. In one sense, of course, it is strange to describe Hobbes's account as revolutionary, since nothing is more anathema to Hobbes than rebellion against established sovereigns. Yet, if we have already taken note of one paradox that runs throughout his account of sovereignty—the paradox of basing the absolute authority of the mighty sovereign on the freely given consent of his subjects—another, related paradox is that Hobbes is at once

---

4. On Hobbes's rejection of the divine right of kings, see Malcolm, *Leviathan, Vol. 1: Introduction*, 50; Skinner, *Visions of Politics*, 3:203–4; Pettit, *Made with Words*, 122; Lilla, *The Stillborn God*, 85–90; Hoekstra, "Disarming the Prophets," 128–29; Schmitt, *The Leviathan in the State Theory of Thomas Hobbes*, 32–34, 46, 53, 67; Jackson, *Hobbes, Bramhall and the Politics of Liberty and Necessity*, 17–18.

history's least and one of its most revolutionary political philosophers, especially on the question of sovereignty. He is antirevolutionary in the obvious sense that he urges men to submit, in almost all cases, to whatever sovereign they have, and he portrays insurrection against an established order as the height of folly. But he is revolutionary in the sense that he would have men radically reconceive of their relationship to the sovereign and of the basis of his authority. In contrast to the doctrine of the divine right of kings, or any other doctrine according to which authority flows down to the sovereign from a source above man, Hobbes's new doctrine holds that the sovereign derives his authority from below, from a collective act of individual human beings each of whom acts on his own behalf and voluntarily relinquishes his own rights. Even if the sovereign is an absolute monarch—as Hobbes hopes he will be—his authority is a human creation flowing from a democratic source.[5]

In what way is the sovereign's authority a human creation? And how does it flow from a democratic source? Although the essential elements of Hobbes's account are present in *The Elements of Law* and *De Cive*, the classic expression of his vision of the generation of the sovereign and the commonwealth comes near the beginning of Part II of *Leviathan*.[6] It does not come at the very beginning, because Hobbes first reaffirms his view that there is no meaningful pre-civic unity among men as well as his denial that men are naturally political such that nature alone can lead them to union and agreement (see *Lev.* 17.1–12). Lasting agreement among men is "by covenant only, which is artificial" (*Lev.* 17.12). Yet, even if the political community is not natural, in Hobbes's view, it can emerge in the following way:

> The only way to erect such a common power as may be able to defend them [*sc.*, a multitude of men] from the invasion of foreigners and the injuries of one another, and thereby to secure them in such sort as that by their own industry, and by the fruits of the earth, they may nourish themselves and live contentedly, is to confer all their power and strength upon one man, or upon one assembly of men, that may reduce all their wills by plurality of voices unto

5. On the democratic basis of even absolute monarchy in Hobbes's account, see *Elem.* 21.6–9; *De Cive* 7.5–11; Sommerville, *Thomas Hobbes: Political Ideas in Historical Context*, 59; Orwin, "On the Sovereign Authorization," 32; Kraynak, *History and Modernity in the Thought of Thomas Hobbes*, 179; Malcolm, *Aspects of Hobbes*, 543; Watkins, *Hobbes's System of Ideas*, 48–49; Garsten, "Religion and Representation in Hobbes," 522–27.

6. On the consistency between the account of sovereign authorization in *Leviathan* and the somewhat less fully or perfectly developed accounts in *The Elements of Law* and *De Cive*, see Orwin, "On the Sovereign Authorization," 26–32, *contra*, among others, Pitkin, "Hobbes's Concept of Representation," 903–12, and Gauthier, *The Logic of Leviathan*, 101–12.

one will, which is as much as to say, to appoint one man or assembly of men to bear their person, and every one to own and acknowledge himself to be author of whatsoever he that beareth their person shall act or cause to be acted, in those things which concern the common peace and safety, and therein to submit their wills, every one to his will, and their judgments, to his judgment. (*Lev.* 17.13)

Hobbes describes here a quasi-democratic moment, before democracy (so he hopes) disappears into the sovereign, which may be an assembly, but will not be if the "authors" of the sovereign's existence are sensible. More important than the practical matter of Hobbes's preference for monarchy is the theoretical conception here. According to Hobbes, many men are able to confer their power on one man or on an assembly of men by agreeing among themselves to relinquish their rights as individuals to resist the sovereign's decrees and henceforth to regard the newly created sovereign as their representative (with *Lev.* 17.13, see *Lev.* 14.5–6, 16.4, 16.13–14; *De Cive* 5.7–11; *Elem.* 19.7–10). By this agreement with one another, they "authorize" the sovereign, giving him an artificial authority constructed out of the transferred natural rights of the multitude of individuals who consent to his rule. In the process, the newly minted subjects also transform themselves into a united commonwealth, given its unity precisely by their collective submission to their new representative. As Hobbes describes it:

> This is more than consent or concord; it is a real unity of them all in one and the same person, made by covenant of every man with every man in such a manner as if every man should say to every man, *I authorize and give up my right of governing myself to this man, or to this assembly of men, on this condition, that thou give up thy right to him and authorize all his actions in like manner.* This done, the multitude so united in one person is called a COMMON-WEALTH, in Latin, CIVITAS. This is the generation of that great LEVIATHAN, or rather (to speak more reverently) of that *Mortal God,* to which we owe, under the *Immortal God,* our peace and defense. (*Lev.* 17.13)

The Leviathan, the new mortal god made by men, is at once the sovereign and the commonwealth, for in the sovereign, according to Hobbes, "consisteth the essence of the commonwealth," defined as *"one person, of whose acts a great multitude, by mutual covenants one with another, have made themselves every one the author, to the end that he may use the strength and means of them all as he shall think expedient for their peace and common defense"* (*Lev.* 17.13).

It is hard to read Hobbes's account of the generation of the sovereign and the commonwealth without wondering what in that account is intended as fact and what as fiction. There seems to be something too magical about the way in which "the larval multitude" transforms itself into "a corporate butterfly."[7] Consider Hobbes's claim that, as previously unconnected men become fellow subjects of the sovereign, what emerges "is more than consent or concord; it is a real unity of them all." In what sense is mere consent transcended and a "real unity" created? Hobbes suggests that the unity consists in the new artificial being that emerges as a multitude of natural beings take on a shared artificial identity. And it is, of course, not just any artificial being that emerges, but one so important to the lives of men that Hobbes named his greatest work after it.[8] Hobbes's emphasis, then, on the artificiality of the commonwealth—on its emergence as an unnatural human creation—is by no means meant as a critique or criticism of it. Still, that does not fully resolve the question of whether there is not something, not only artificial, but also fictitious about the unified commonwealth as Hobbes describes it. Hobbes is well aware that even in commonwealths that emerge "by institution," some men do not get the sovereign they want (see, e.g., *Lev.* 18.1). Are not those who lose out compelled to regard as "their own" the actions and decrees of a sovereign who, given the inevitable divisions among men, may oppose many of their wishes and interests? And then there is the more basic difficulty—of which Hobbes is also well aware—that many, if not most, commonwealths do not emerge by "institution" at all, but rather by "acquisition," that is, by conquest or violent domination of some other sort (see, e.g., *Lev.* 17.15, 20.1–2; *De Cive* 8.1; *Elem.* 22.1–2).[9] By quietly granting this point, but then arguing that it makes no difference to the rights of sovereigns, which are established by reflection on commonwealths by institution, does not Hobbes use his account of the generation of the commonwealth as a kind of theoretical construct that, in its pristine simplicity, obscures the messy realities of actual political life? Hobbes intends, to be sure, to give men a new lens through which they

7. Pettit, *Made with Words*, 72. See also Watkins, *Hobbes's Systems of Ideas*, 116–17; Martinich, "Authorization and Representation in Hobbes's *Leviathan*," 332–36.

8. It is noteworthy that Hobbes acknowledges in the passage under consideration that there is something irreverent about the title of *Leviathan*. Why is it irreverent to call the commonwealth ruled by the sovereign the "Leviathan"? The answer, I believe, is that in the primary biblical passage from which Hobbes takes that name (Job 41), God speaks of the mighty sea monster called the Leviathan as an example of something that he alone can create and men cannot subdue. Hobbes, however, uses the name for the commonwealth, thereby suggesting that men, too, *can* create a Leviathan—and more than that, that it is the *humanly created Leviathan*, not God or his monsters, that provides for our deepest needs.

9. See *Lev.* Review and Conclusion, 8: "there is scarce a commonwealth in the world whose beginnings can in conscience be justified." Consider also *Lev.* 20.19, 31.41. See Macpherson, *The Political Theory of Possessive Individualism*, 20; Craig, *The Platonian Leviathan*, 378–83, 492.

can look at actual political life and see its foundation. But is his account not also a kind of myth or a newfangled noble lie that distorts as much as it clarifies the true origins and character of politics?

Hobbes would probably reply to those inclined to press such questions by urging them to recognize the value of his account in getting people to accept the legitimacy of the sovereign and therefore the importance of preserving what he might well grant is at least an embellishment of the truth about politics. If, as he says, "the power of the mighty hath no foundation but in the opinion and belief of the people" (*Beh.*, 16), that is reason not to insist too strenuously that fact be separated from fiction. Nevertheless, since our interest is more in understanding Hobbes's account than in perpetuating it, we should take note of two further difficulties that make his account more complicated and tension-ridden than it first appears. Hobbes, of course, wants people to give their undivided allegiance to the sovereign they already have. Even if he teaches men to look at the sovereign in a new light, that does not mean that they should regard themselves as any less obligated to obey him. To the contrary, Hobbes's expectation is that, by severing the connection between the rights of the sovereign and any higher principles, not only can he free the sovereign from restraint by such principles, but he can also sap challenges to the sovereign's authority of their strength by cutting them off from their traditional sources. Insurrectionists can be deprived of their power if they have no principles left to appeal to in their rallying cries. But Hobbes cannot entirely iron out two wrinkles that remain even in the new fabric. First, he too, as much as any earlier thinker, gives men *a reason* that they should obey the sovereign; and even if the reason he gives allows for the derivation of the rights of the sovereign from a lower source rather than a higher one, it nevertheless means that the duties of subjects are ultimately contingent in his account as well.[10] If men submit to the sovereign for the sake of their own preservation, then they are freed from their obligation to obey the sovereign when he either threatens their preservation or can no longer reliably provide for it. And it is ultimately the natural individuals themselves—the only beings in Hobbes's account whose most fundamental rights can never vanish—who must judge when such a point has been reached. This difficulty displays itself most clearly in Hobbes's frank acknowledgment that nobody, innocent or guilty, is obligated to submit to capital punishment (see *Lev.* 21.12–17). But more important are situations of foreign invasion and civil strife, in which the sovereign's power can deteriorate to the point that he can no longer protect his subjects and hence can no longer reasonably insist on their obedience

10. See Strauss, "On the Basis of Hobbes's Political Philosophy," 193–94.

(see *Lev.* 21.21–25, Review and Conclusion, 6–7; *De Cive* 6.13, 7.18). It is a mark of Hobbes's consistency that he acknowledges these dilemmas; but they reveal that the natural rights of individuals are so far from being wholly absorbed in the artificial person of the sovereign that they can trump or invalidate the duties of subjects in instances of direct conflict.[11] The second difficulty is simpler. Hobbes is well aware that, even if all sovereigns are somehow creations of their subjects, all sovereigns are not created equal. In short, as much as he wants men to respect and obey the sovereign they have, Hobbes cannot deny that some sovereigns are better than others.

"Better" does not mean more just, according to Hobbes. Hobbes denies that it is possible to distinguish between sovereigns on the grounds of justice and injustice, because no sovereign is a party to the contract by which men relinquish their rights to all things: the sovereign, as a natural man (or assembly of men), remains in the state of nature, where no actions are unjust, and, as an artificial man, he is the font of justice in the commonwealth and therefore not bound by it (see, e.g., *Lev.* 18.6, 18.10, 26.2–10, 28.2, 30.20; *De Cive* 6.14–18, 7.12–14). Yet, although Hobbes argues that it is both theoretically incoherent and practically dangerous for private men to sit in judgment on the justice of the sovereign's actions, he himself *does* distinguish between better and worse sovereigns, if not in terms of justice, then in terms of their efficacy in providing peace and stability (see, e.g., *Lev.* 19.4). Hobbes expresses his preferences with regard to types of sovereigns—that is, different forms of government—as well as individual instantiations of the types. His preference on the former level is obvious, because he so clearly argues that monarchy is superior to other forms of government. He does not claim that monarchy is the only legitimate form of government; but he does argue that it is the best. Or rather, since he is not oblivious to its drawbacks, such as the problem of succession, it is better to say that he regards monarchy as the least problematic of the alternatives. Hobbes's defense of monarchy reminds one, as a kind of inversion, of Churchill's famous dictum that democracy is the worst form of government, except for all the others. But why did Hobbes regard the others, including democracy, as even worse than monarchy? His main line of argument against government by "assemblies," which may be more or less democratic, is that assemblies allow pernicious divisions and factional interests to penetrate the sovereign power itself, and thus they are more apt to become forums of factional conflict than solutions to it. The instability of assemblies is exacerbated by their susceptibility to seduction by glory-loving orators and captivation by angry demagogues, who can turn them into hot-

---

11. See Jaume, "Hobbes and the Philosophical Sources of Liberalism," 208–13.

beds of intense partisanship and perpetual infighting. Monarchy is better because it is simpler and more unified, and its simplicity and unity conduce to greater constancy and protect the commonwealth from the winds that blow in stormy assemblies (see *Lev.* 19.4–9, 10.1–19; *Elem.* 24.3–4; see also *Beh.*, 68–69; *On Thucydides*, 572).[12]

The ideal Hobbesian sovereign, then, would be a monarch. (That is why it is customary and reasonable to follow Hobbes in referring to the sovereign as "he" rather than "they," although it should be noted that Hobbes has no objection if "he" should happen to be "she.")[13] Of greater interest and importance, however, than the well-known fact that Hobbes was a proponent of monarchy is the advice he gives to individual monarchs to make them better sovereigns. As Jeffrey Collins has argued, this is an underappreciated aspect of Hobbes's political project: his effort to counsel sovereigns in the prudent use of their sovereignty.[14] The neglect of this aspect of Hobbes's project is despite his own indications of its importance. On more than one occasion in *Leviathan*, Hobbes calls attention to his role as an advisor or teacher of the sovereign (see, e.g., Intro., 25.23, 29.1, 30.5, 31.41, Review and Conclusion, 14). In fact, one of Hobbes's chief aims in presenting his new doctrine of sovereignty is to forge a new alliance between philosophy and the sovereign power—a new alliance from which each party has something to gain. The sovereign can make his power more secure by following Hobbes's new teaching, while Hobbes himself, the "very able architect," needs a sympathetic sovereign to build the structure he has designed, or, as he puts it, to "convert this truth of speculation into the utility of practice" (*Lev.* 31.41). In addition to the sovereign and Hobbes himself, there is a third party to the new alliance. The third party is the people, whom Hobbes also instructs so that they will come to see that their own interests are in harmony with those of a reasonable sovereign who, like them, wants nothing so much as a strong and secure commonwealth (see *Lev.* 19.4, 30.21, 30.29; *De Cive* 13.2–4; *Elem.* 28.1; *A Dialogue*, 76). The inclusion of the people in the new alliance does not mean, however, that *everyone* is included. Before we consider who is excluded and opposed by the new

12. For a fuller account of Hobbes's preference for monarchy as the regime that best avoids the perils of demagogic rhetoric in public deliberation, see Burns, "Hobbes and Dionysius of Halicarnassus on Thucydides, Rhetoric and Political Life," 411–13.

13. Regarding Hobbes's openness to female sovereigns, see the exchange between Pateman and Skinner in "Hobbes, History, Politics, and Gender," 26–29.

14. Collins, *The Allegiance of Thomas Hobbes*, 128, see also 34. The major exception is Mara, "Hobbes's Counsel to Sovereigns," 390–410. Compare Malcolm, *Leviathan, Vol. 1: Introduction*, 56–57; Craig, *The Platonian Leviathan*, 338–40, 471–78.

alliance, let us consider some of the more striking aspects of Hobbes's advice to the sovereign.

Perhaps the most surprising aspect of that advice is Hobbes's recommendation that the sovereign limit his subjects' freedom no more than is necessary for peace and security. Hobbes's entire conception of the role and rights of the sovereign is based, as we have seen, on the premise of the natural liberty of men as individuals in the state of nature. Of course, Hobbes would have neither the sovereign nor his subjects ever forget that the original, precivic state of liberty was a disaster, and therefore the sovereign should feel no compunction and his subjects should voice no complaints about the measures that must be taken to prevent a return to that wretched condition. There can be no doubt that Hobbes wants to relieve the sovereign of any qualms he may have in this regard, just as he wants to keep the principle of liberty from ever becoming a beacon for resistance by the subjects.[15] Still, Hobbes urges the sovereign to bear in mind that it is only for the sake of peace and security that he should ever restrict liberty, and that this limited end does not generally require extreme oppression.[16] In *Leviathan*, Hobbes advises the sovereign to avoid making unnecessary laws and to regard those laws he does make, not as rigid restraints that "bind the people from all voluntary actions," but as hedges put in place "not to stop travellers, but to keep them in their way" (*Lev.* 30.20–21). In *De Cive*, the analogy is different, but the point is the same: the sovereign should bear in mind that just as standing water stagnates and spoils when it is tightly enclosed, so can the vital energies of the people be destroyed by laws that are too numerous or too onerous (*De Cive* 13.15; see also *Elem.* 28.4). An enlightened Hobbesian sovereign, then, will keep his laws as minimal and mild as is compatible with his primary task of securing order in the commonwealth. And in those matters in which the law is silent— that is, in those affairs "praetermitted" by the sovereign's decrees (*Lev.* 21.6)— the subjects are free to do as they please. This is the "liberty of subjects" in Hobbes's conception, a sphere of freedoms that is determined in its scope by the discretion of the sovereign but that is not for that reason inconsequential. In an inversion of the classical principle that what the law does not command it forbids, Hobbes teaches that what the law does not forbid it allows

---

15. The latter point is a major theme of Skinner's *Hobbes and Republican Liberty*. See, e.g., 120–23, 140–49, 173–77, 208–10.

16. See Owen, "The Tolerant Leviathan," 134–40; Jaume, "Hobbes and the Philosophical Sources of Liberalism," 209–10; Ryan, "A More Tolerant Hobbes?" 50–51, 56–57; Tuck, *Hobbes*, 72–74, *Philosophy and Government, 1572–1651*, 333; Skinner, *Hobbes and Republican Liberty*, 166–67.

(compare *Lev.* 21.6, 21.18, and *De Cive* 13.15 with Aristotle, *Nicomachean Ethics* 1138a7 and 1129b14–25).[17]

There are four realms in particular in which Hobbes advises the sovereign to show greater leniency than is commonly appreciated by those who regard the Hobbesian sovereign as a totalitarian tyrant. The first is the realm of private opinions or inner thoughts. Hobbes is notorious for declaring that the sovereign has the right to regulate, even to the point of complete suppression, the expression of any doctrine or opinion that he regards as a threat to the peace of the commonwealth. His argument in this regard is well known, if not well liked: because opinions are the sparks of actions, it is not enough merely to control their effects by putting out the fires they cause; at least in some cases, one must stop the blaze from ever igniting by smothering its sources (see *Lev.* 18.8–9; *De Cive* 6.11). Hobbes not only gives the sovereign the right to regulate opinions and doctrines; he urges him to use that right aggressively to censor dangerous opinions before they cause trouble in the commonwealth. Less appreciated, however, is the limit that Hobbes places, as a matter not of principle but of prudence, on the extent to which he would have the sovereign attempt to reach into the minds of his subjects.[18] According to Hobbes, it is a mistake—a long-standing error of "civil philosophy" with biblical roots, not classical ones—to extend the power of the law beyond the regulation of actions into "the very thoughts and consciences of men" (*Lev.* 46.37). It is true that the expression of a thought is itself a kind of action, and such an "action," in Hobbes's view, may well need to be regulated or even prevented when it threatens the peace. But the silent holding of an opinion is a different matter. It would be unduly oppressive for the sovereign to attempt the futile task of forbidding the very thinking of certain thoughts (with *Lev.* 46.37, see 26.41, 40.2, 42.43; Latin *Lev.*, Appendix, 1203; *Elem.* 25.3; *Beh.*, 62; *EW* IV, 339).[19]

17. Cf. Owen, "The Tolerant Leviathan," 139; Oakeshott, *Hobbes on Civil Association*, 48; Mara, "Hobbes's Counsel to Sovereigns," 406; Skinner, *Hobbes and Republican Liberty*, 167–68.

18. Although this point is not widely appreciated, it has not gone entirely unnoticed. Among those who have called attention to it are Collins, *The Allegiance of Thomas Hobbes*, 124; Owen, "The Tolerant Leviathan," 141; Milner, "Hobbes on Religion," 418; Curley, "Hobbes and the Cause of Religious Toleration," 312; Ryan, "Hobbes, Toleration, and the Inner Life," 206–8, "A More Tolerant Hobbes?" 50–51, 56–58.

19. In light of Hobbes's indication that the extension of law to the (attempted) regulation of men's inner thoughts was "never learned of Aristotle, nor Cicero, nor any other of the Heathen" (*Lev.* 46.37), it is notable that Hobbes's sovereign, in his moderation in this regard, will differ not only from rulers shaped by the biblical tradition but also from the biblical God himself. Hobbes points in *Leviathan* 20.17 to the biblical God's punishment of unexpressed thoughts—

The second realm in which Hobbes would have the sovereign allow men greater liberty than is often recognized is more mundane. He advises the sovereign to leave his subjects generally unencumbered in their commercial activities, so as not to destroy the commercial energies of the commonwealth.[20] Making use of his image of the commonwealth as an enormous body, Hobbes tells the sovereign to remember that money is the blood of the commonwealth. The Hobbesian sovereign has the right to regulate commerce and property as he sees fit. But Hobbes advises him to use a light hand in order to keep the commonwealth's blood flowing vigorously and thereby to keep up the body's strength (see *Lev.* 24.1–14; see also 21.6, 30.19; *De Cive* 13.4, 13.6, 13.10, 13.14–15).

Third is the realm of crime and punishment. Here, too, Hobbes declares that the sovereign's right is unlimited: he may punish whomever he wants, whenever he wants, as severely as he wants. But Hobbes indicates that the sovereign would be foolish to use this right wantonly or cruelly. A prudent sovereign should punish in accordance with penalties that have been clearly announced before the relevant crimes have been committed, for, as Hobbes tells him, "a great part of the liberty that is harmless to the commonwealth, and necessary for the citizens to live happily, is that there be no punishments to fear but those that can be foreseen or expected" (*De Cive* 13.16). Moreover, the sovereign should judge criminals and their crimes by the damage they do and the threats they pose to the preservation of order in the commonwealth. He should go easy on those whose crimes stem from relatively harmless forms of weakness and deal more harshly with arrogant criminals who pose a more serious danger (see *Lev.* 27.21–36). In urging the sovereign to keep his attention fixed on the goal of preserving order in the commonwealth, Hobbes is urging him to take what Hobbes himself regards as the only rational approach to punishment. Hobbes displays no sympathy for the indignant desire for retribution or revenge, which he variously describes as arising from cruelty, irrational zeal, and hardness of heart (see, e.g., *Lev.* 15.19, Review and Conclusion, 10). If the sovereign came to share Hobbes's outlook, he would never use punishment to vent his anger at past wrongs, but would look only to the future consequences of his punitive actions (see *Lev.* 28.1, 28.10, 28.20, 30.23; Latin *Lev.*, 1203; *De Cive* 13.16). Hobbes must have hoped that the spirit

---

the thoughts, in that case, implicit in Adam and Eve's shame at their nakedness, "wherein it was God's will to create them." See also *Elements* 18.10, where Hobbes, after pointing to the declaration in *Romans* 14:23 that doubt will be punished with damnation, writes: "And in innumerable places both in the Old and New Testament, God Almighty declareth, that he taketh the will for the deed, both in good and evil actions. By all which it plainly appears, that the divine law is dictated to the conscience."

20. See Mara, "Hobbes's Counsel to Sovereigns," 397–98.

of calm rationalism with which his enlightened sovereign would punish would come to permeate the commonwealth as a whole, making the Hobbesian commonwealth very different in its attitude from earlier orders, including the old kingdom of the Israelites, in which the zeal for retribution ran rampant (see *Lev.*, Review and Conclusion, 10–11).

It is likely that Hobbes anticipated a similar effect in the fourth realm in which he counsels the sovereign to be more lenient than is often supposed: the realm of sexual morality. Hobbes's own attitude on matters of sexual morality is indicated by his willingness to leave to the determination of the sovereign such questions as the very meaning of marriage and adultery, even if that should entail opening the way to such things as divorce and polygamy (see *Lev.* 20.4, 21.18; *De Cive* 6.16, 14.10).[21] Hobbes's sovereign is unbound by any pre-civic restrictions regarding sexual morality for essentially the same reason that, in Hobbes's view, all sexual unions are licit in the state of nature (see *De Cive* 14.9).[22] But here, too, not only does Hobbes want to teach the sovereign about the extent of his rights—in this case, about his right to determine questions of sexual morality, if he sees fit, entirely by secular political considerations—but he also wants to educate him in the prudent exercise of his rights. And what lesson is the sovereign likely to draw from Hobbes's argument that those who deem even men's animal passions sinful are naïve in their expectations and too severe in their demands (see *Lev.* 27.21, 42.21, 46.33)? When Hobbes wryly remarks that the delight that one man takes in the imagination of possessing another's wife is "no breech of that law that saith *Thou shalt not covet*" (*Lev.* 27.21), must he not be hoping that the sovereign, among others, will come to share his cynicism toward older, sterner attitudes about human sexuality? That telling quip comes at the beginning of the chapter of *Leviathan* entitled "Of Crimes, Excuses, and Extenuations,"

21. Hobbes's latitudinarian attitude toward the family is an important theme in some recent feminist interpretations of Hobbes. For instance, Hirschmann, "Hobbes on the Family," 242–63, argues that Hobbes was not an unambiguous advocate of a patriarchal structure of the family. According to Hirschmann, before the sovereign issues his or her decrees, "We have no idea ahead of time whether he or she will decree mother-right or father-right, monogamy or polygamy, or even any family structure at all" (258). Hirschmann argues that this indeterminacy or flexibility is one of the aspects of Hobbes's thought that has at least protofeminist implications, if not feminist intentions. Without fully intending to, according to Hirschmann, "Hobbes seems to have set the stage for the egalitarian marriage that later feminists like John Stuart Mill were to advocate" (244). See also Lloyd, "Power and Sexual Subordination in Hobbes's Political Theory," 47–62; Jaquette, "Defending Liberal Feminism," 63–82; Sreedhar, "Toward a Hobbesian Theory of Sexuality," 260–79.

22. See Sreedhar, "Toward a Hobbesian Theory of Sexuality," 266–67.

throughout which Hobbes gently nudges the sovereign toward a more realistic view of man's fallibility and a more lenient view of his culpability.

Hobbes's efforts in these four realms reveal something of the broader moral spirit that he hoped would come to prevail in the enlightened commonwealth he envisioned. We have already considered the various ways in which Hobbes sought, in his own moral teaching, to simplify the aims of morality and relax its demands. What is important in the present context—and may now be added to our earlier reflections—is that Hobbes hoped to recruit a well-instructed sovereign to his project of moral reform. The Hobbesian sovereign, precisely for reasons of his own interest—that is, because he could anticipate that the spread of the new moral outlook would make for tamer, more peaceable subjects—could and should act as a conduit of Hobbesian morality. Even if he might risk losing something of his subjects' devotion to him as they come to see their commitment to the commonwealth he represents as "nothing but the price they pay to purchase peace" (De Cive 13.10), the sovereign should bear in mind the Machiavellian lesson that it is better to be feared than loved as well as the Hobbesian modification that it is best if the subjects' fear can be tempered by a rational appreciation of the benefits that a powerful sovereign can provide. It may be true that Hobbes does not quite encourage the people to view the sovereign with fully disenchanted clarity, insofar as his doctrine of the sovereign's creation and character retains something of the character of a noble lie (see pp. 247–49 above). Yet, even if Hobbes would grant that his doctrine is a cloak concealing the naked truth about politics, he would surely insist that the new Hobbesian cloak is a much thinner garment than older ones, such as the divine right of kings, and that it is compatible with a society that can become ever more sober and tolerant in its moral spirit as Hobbes's principles spread their influence.

How could an enlightened sovereign help to promote Hobbesian morality? In several ways: by following Hobbes's advice in the four realms just considered, by teaching it directly, and by exemplifying it in his own conduct, at least to the extent compatible with the demands of his unique role. The assistance that Hobbes most explicitly requests, however, is in reforming the universities. According to Hobbes, "the universities are the fountains of civil and moral doctrine," and for far too long, he thought, the fountains had been pouring forth putrid water that flowed to the pulpits and down from there to the people (Lev., Review and Conclusion, 16; see also 30.14; De Cive 12.13, 13.9; Elem. 28.8; Beh., 56–59, 90; EW VII, 345). The source of the problem, however, can also provide the solution, for if putrid water can flow down to the people, so can pure. In fact, if the universities had long been promulgating doctrines that are "false and no more intelligible than if someone pulled random words

from an urn and strung them together" (*De Cive* 13.9), that is a further reason
for optimism—for "how much more would men imbibe true doctrines?" (*De
Cive* 13.9; see also *Lev.* 30.6). Hobbes makes it abundantly clear that a major
goal of his own ambition was to transform the universities such that his own
doctrines would prevail in them.[23] In a striking passage on the universities
in *Leviathan*, he poses to himself two questions: whether the universities in
England are already "learned enough" to teach a new generation of young
men sound doctrines, which could then spread to the pulpits and the people,
and whether he himself is undertaking to teach the universities. "Hard questions," he replies. After answering the first question by pointing to the long-
standing errors still plaguing the universities, Hobbes gives a nice answer to
the second: "But to the latter question, it is not fit, nor needful, for me to say
either Aye or No; for any man that sees what I am doing may easily perceive
what I think" (*Lev.* 30.14). The one man whom Hobbes most certainly wanted
to see what he was doing was the sovereign, for Hobbes's goal of reforming
the universities could not be accomplished by Hobbes alone.

The New Alliance and the Question of Religion

The universities were a major target in Hobbes's struggle not only because
they were fountains of pernicious doctrines, but also because they had long
served as training grounds and fortresses from which his opponents regularly
sent forth new waves of troops. But which opponents in particular, and what
kind of troops? In suggesting that Hobbes was proposing a new alliance with
the sovereign and the people, I indicated that the alliance excludes certain
groups in the commonwealth. In a word, "the people" does not mean every-
body, and there are enemy forces to be defeated or at least marginalized in the
Hobbesian scheme. Who are they?

To address this question, let us start from a remark of Hobbes that has
puzzled many readers, because it seems inconsistent with his absolutism. In
the Epistle Dedicatory of *Leviathan*, Hobbes says that he sought to find a
middle path between the extremes of "those that contend, on one side for too
great liberty, and on the other side for too much authority." How can Hobbes
have regarded himself as a moderate on the question of liberty and authority
when he endeavored, as he indicates in the very same letter, "to advance the

---

23. On the importance of this goal for Hobbes's broader project, compare Malcolm, *Levia-
than, Vol. 1: Introduction*, 56–57, *Aspects of Hobbes*, 544; Ahrensdorf, "The Fear of Death and the
Longing for Immortality," 583; Lloyd, *Ideals as Interests in Hobbes's Leviathan*, 207–12; Garsten,
"Religion and Representation in Hobbes," 520.

civil power" as much as possible (see also *Lev.* 18.20, 20.18)? The answer is provided only in part by the consideration that Hobbes's ideal sovereign is a gentler, more lenient ruler than is often supposed. The further consideration that completes the answer is that there are figures and groups outside of "the civil power" that nevertheless seek authority, claim special privileges, and desire to oppress. One such group is the proud—those ambitious, contentious men, usually leisured aristocrats, who resent the dimming of their own stars by the light of the sovereign's sun and who yearn to expand their authority whenever they can. Hobbes advises the sovereign to break their resistance by removing all uncertainty as to whether they are his subordinates and by ensuring that all honors, offices, and titles flow through him.[24] Since some spirited men cannot easily be mollified, they must be reined in with a firm hand, and hence it is essential that the sovereign augment his power and preempt any would-be Caesars by monopolizing popular support. Like Machiavelli, Hobbes advises his prince to side with the people against "the great."[25] But "the great" in the sense of the traditional aristocracy, even when they are politically ambitious, are not Hobbes's most serious foes. Much more threatening to the very foundation of a Hobbesian commonwealth are those who claim a spiritual authority that flows from its own separate sources.

It is not a new revelation to disclose that Hobbes was concerned about the challenge posed to the civil sovereign by those who claim a separate spiritual authority; we have encountered this concern already (see, e.g., pp. 24–25 and 136–37 above). But we need to think through the issue more directly and adequately than we have thus far. For it raises a broad question about Hobbes's political project as a whole. There can be little doubt that Hobbes was worried about the danger that religious claims can pose to stable politics, and it is reasonable to suppose that Hobbes's "starting-point" in this regard, as Malcolm has put it, was "the hope that he could persuade a future absolute king to deal with religion in the way he recommended."[26] But in what way is that? If it is obvious that the political problem of religion was central to Hobbes's concerns, it is much harder to say how he thought it should be addressed.

Let us approach the matter by reviewing the roots and character of the problem as Hobbes saw it. As we have already noted, Hobbes's entire political

---

24. See Cooper, "Vainglory, Modesty, and Political Agency in the Political Theory of Thomas Hobbes," 258–61; Mara, "Hobbes's Counsel to Sovereigns," 398–99.

25. Compare Machiavelli, *Prince*, Chap. 9, with *Lev.* 18.15–19, 27.13–18, 29.20, 30.6, 30.25, 30.29; *De Cive* 12.10–12, 13.12; *Elem.* 27.3, 28.7. See Sullivan, *Machiavelli, Hobbes, and the Formation of a Liberal Republicanism in England*, 82–83, 98–101.

26. Malcolm, *Leviathan, Vol. 1: Introduction*, 80.

teaching depends on the supreme importance of sovereign-enforced peace as the means by which each individual can secure his own preservation. The desire for self-preservation draws men into the commonwealth, or, stated more negatively but more instructively, the fear of violent death makes men flee the state of nature and seek the security that only the commonwealth can provide. The sovereign, moreover, can ensure the obedience of his subjects by freeing them from the fear of violent death at the hands of other men while instilling the fear of punishment by his own sword. Thus, "the passion to be reckoned upon is fear" (*Lev.* 14.31), for fear supplies the foundation on which Hobbes builds his political structure, the basic goal of which is to replace anarchic fear with orderly or order-producing fear. But this simple solution to the problem of anarchy is threatened by the fact that the fear of other men in the state of nature and the fear of punishment by the sovereign in the civil state are not the only significant kinds of fear. There is also the fear of the power of "spirits invisible." Even if most men, according to Hobbes, are not often swayed by this fear because invisible spirits are not so manifestly threatening as the visible officers of the sovereign (see *Lev.* 14.31), that is not true in all cases. At least for some men, "the fear of darkness and ghosts is greater than other fears" (*Lev.* 29.15). And these men, superstitious though they may be, are not simply crazy. They have a powerful reason for fearing invisible powers more than visible ones, for only the former can threaten men with eternal punishments and entice them with eternal rewards. Precisely because spirits belong—or are believed to belong—not to the visible, temporal realm of bodies, but to a higher, more mysterious realm, they can induce fears and make promises that trump those of the civil sovereign. But the "spirits" in question, in Hobbes's view at least, do not speak to men directly. The true sources of the problem are the men who claim to represent them and who claim a special authority as the spokesmen of a realm to which other men do not have access. In Hobbes's view, there is no greater threat to the commonwealth than the influence of these "ghostly authorities." For they induce men to believe that they should serve two masters, one temporal, the other spiritual, and to fear for their eternal souls more than for their temporal bodies. Where such beliefs and fears prevail, "the commonwealth is destroyed from inside" (*De Cive* 6.11), because "it is impossible a commonwealth should stand where any other than the sovereign hath the power of giving greater rewards than life, and of inflicting greater punishments than death" (*Lev.* 38.1).[27]

---

27. The elements of Hobbes's analysis of the problem sketched in this paragraph can be found scattered throughout his works. The fullest accounts of the problem as a whole are *De Cive* 6.11 and *Leviathan* 29.15—the first, the classic "two masters" statement, the second, the

Given the character of the problem just sketched, the solution to it would seem to be straightforward: the sovereign should assert his superiority and exert firm control over the religious authorities in the commonwealth. But through what ecclesiastical arrangement should the sovereign establish his supremacy? There are some who have argued that the traditional Anglican episcopacy was entirely acceptable to Hobbes.[28] They can appeal to the testimony of Hobbes himself, who certainly portrayed himself as a loyal and consistent supporter of the Church of England. Not only does his friend and biographer Aubrey report that, in a private moment, Hobbes "declared that he liked the Church of England best of all other,"[29] but Hobbes himself claims to have written even *Leviathan*, the work most suspect in this regard, "without any word against episcopacy, or against any bishop, or against the public doctrine of the church" (*EW* IV, 407).[30] Without dwelling here on whether that is true—that is, on whether Hobbes did not suffer from selective amnesia when it comes to certain passages of *Leviathan* (see, e.g., 12.32, 42.71, 47.3, 47.20)—let us take note of the three most obvious ways in which Hobbes departs from traditional Anglicanism. Two of them concern ecclesiology.[31] First, Hobbes declares that the sovereign should be regarded as the chief pastor of the church, on the grounds that the church in a Christian common-

---

description of the "epilepsy" caused in the commonwealth by the "ghostly authorities." But see also *Lev.* 18.6, 38.1, 39.5, 42.67; *De Cive* 12.5, 17.25–27; *Elem.* 26.1, 26.10; *De Hom.* 13.6–7; *Beh.*, 8, 49–50, 94–95; *EW* V, 289. Helpful discussions of Hobbes's view of the problem are Orwin, "On the Sovereign Authorization," 35–36; Owen, *Making Religion Safe for Democracy*, 23, 27, 30–31; Strauss, *Natural Right and History*, 198; Johnston, *The Rhetoric of Leviathan*, 100–101, 121, 149–50, 201; Ahrensdorf, "The Fear of Death and the Longing for Immortality," 583; Lloyd, *Ideals as Interests in Hobbes's Leviathan*, 37–38, *et passim*.

28. See, e.g., Martinich, *The Two Gods of Leviathan*, 280–85, *Hobbes: A Biography*, 172; Eisenach, "Hobbes on Church, State, and Religion," 226–36; Glover, "God and Thomas Hobbes," 275–97. Compare the more qualified account of Lessay, "Hobbes's Protestantism," 265–94.

29. *Aubrey's Brief Lives*, 156.

30. For similar statements, see Latin *Lev.*, 1127; *Vita* [prose], xvi–vii; *EW* IV, 364, 428, 432; *EW* V, 453–54; *EW* VII, 5, 351–54. What Hobbes says in the last of these passages indicates the grain of salt with which all of them must be taken. He claims there that he wrote *Leviathan* for "the vindication of the Church of England from the power of the Roman clergy." Yet he then goes on, not only to criticize "the clergy here" for aiming "of late" at ecclesiastical power, but to respond to his critics (John Wallis and Seth Ward) with this double-edged remark about his (supposed) lack of criticism of the Anglican bishops in *Leviathan*: "Fifthly, when I had in my *Leviathan* suffered the clergy of the Church of England to escape, you did imprudently in bringing any of them in again. An Ulysses upon so light an occasion would not have ventured to return again into the cave of Polyphemus."

31. On the following two points, see Lessay, "Hobbes's Protestantism," 274–75; Collins, *The Allegiance of Thomas Hobbes*, 26, 66–67. Malcolm, *Leviathan, Vol. 1: Introduction*, 36–37.

wealth is nothing distinct from the commonwealth itself (see *Lev.* 39.4–5, 42.67–72, 42.79–80; Latin *Lev.*, 1197; *EW* IV, 337, 345; *EW* V, 444–47). Second, in keeping with this conception of the church as a mere arm of the state, Hobbes argues that the bishops ought to be in no way independent of the sovereign. The bishops, who in the past used the claim of authority by divine right to "slyly slip off the collar of their civil subjection" (*Lev.* 42.71), should be regarded as subordinate ministers whose authority is entirely derivative from the sovereign's (see *Lev.* 23.6, 42.71; *Elem.* 26.11; *Beh.*, 46–47; *EW* IV, 364; *Correspondence*, Letter 37). The third way in which Hobbes departs from traditional Anglicanism is even more radical, and it goes beyond matters of ecclesiology. For, as we have seen, Hobbes declares that the very authority of Scripture as binding law and even (in its various parts) as genuine revelation ought to be dependent on the sovereign's decrees (see pp. 161–62 above; see again *Lev.* 26.41, 33.24, 38.5; *De Cive* 17.27; *Beh.*, 46). Indeed, the various attributes that should be ascribed to God himself in the public worship of him should depend on the sovereign's decrees (*Lev.* 31.38)! If this is Anglicanism, it is an Anglicanism that is so radically "Erastian," that is, state-controlled, that it is no wonder that proponents of the traditional form, including the leading Anglican bishops, were among Hobbes's fiercest critics. Hobbes's position, however, is in keeping with his message to the sovereign himself, whom he repeatedly warns of the dangers of clerical power and exhorts to make sure that the hands on the reins of that power are always his own (see, e.g., *Lev.* 29.3). We seem to have an answer, then, to the question of Hobbes's proposed solution to the problem of the "ghostly authorities": the modification of traditional Anglicanism in a radically Erastian direction. As Rousseau put it in a famous remark in his *Social Contract*, "Of all Christian authors, the philosopher Hobbes is the only one who correctly saw the evil and the remedy, who dared to propose the reunification of the two heads of the eagle, and the complete return to political unity."[32]

But we cannot leave matters at saying that Hobbes proposed a modification of Anglicanism in a radically Erastian direction. For Hobbes's Erastianism, as the scholar who has most emphasized it has argued, is so "extreme," so "strident," so "beyond the pale" of any authentically Protestant Erastianism, that it cannot be seen as a mere modification of the sort that earlier writers, including Erastus himself, proposed to prior Protestant ecclesiology.[33] The most immediate difficulty is this: an Erastianism as radical, not to say as

32. *Social Contract* 4.8. Cf. Boyd, "Thomas Hobbes and the Perils of Pluralism," 406; Boyd quotes the same remark of Rousseau.

33. See Collins, *The Allegiance of Thomas Hobbes*, 11, 24–26, 35–36, 56.

cynical, as Hobbes's requires as a precondition of its acceptance the conviction on the part of both the sovereign and the people that secular considerations—peace and civic stability—are so decisive that they justify uniting authority in the sovereign and granting him the right to govern religion for political ends. Who, after all, has ever looked at the famous title page of *Leviathan*—with the sovereign towering over the commonwealth, holding a sword in one hand and a crozier in the other[34]—and been moved by the profound piety of the image? It is doubtful, to say the least, that Hobbes would have expected all of his readers to embrace his Erastian vision. He could have expected that his skeptical arguments about the reliability of the claims of religious authorities to be genuine conduits of God's commands would sway some of his readers, especially those already inclined to doubt; and he could have expected a wider group of readers to be influenced by his more direct arguments for his Erastianism, which, by stressing the dangers of civil strife when temporal and spiritual authority are divided, remind them of the practical stakes involved in his attempt to unify authority in the sovereign. But these latter arguments can—and did—have the opposite effect of intensifying the resistance of other readers and prompting their protest against such a nakedly political approach to religion.[35] At this point, we can see the harsh side of Hobbesian Erastianism. For Hobbes was well aware that it was not to be expected that the "ghostly authorities" and their most zealous followers would simply relinquish their weapons and submit to the subordination that his scheme demands of them. One of the main reasons that Hobbes was at such pains to alert the sovereign to the dangers of independent clerical power, and to turn as many people as possible against it, was that he knew that the power of those who refused to surrender on the proposed terms would have to be broken. Such an asser-

34. See Appendix.

35. As in so many other instances, the responses of Bishop Bramhall are instructive: "All other men distinguish between the Church and the commonwealth; only T.H. maketh them to be one and the same" (*The Catching of Leviathan*, 531); "[Hobbes's] fifth conclusion may be, that the sharpest and most successful sword, in any war whatsoever, doth give sovereign power and authority to him that hath it, to approve or reject all sorts of theological doctrines concerning the kingdom of God, not according to their truth or falsehood, but according to that influence which they have upon political affairs . . . This doctrine may be plausible to those who desire to fish in troubled waters; but it is justly hated by those which are in authority, and all those who are lovers of peace and tranquility" (*The Catching of Leviathan*, 540–41). See also Bramhall's objections on pp. 520, 533–34, 543–44; compare Jackson, *Hobbes, Bramhall and the Politics of Liberty and Necessity*, 245–46. As Mintz, *The Hunting of Leviathan*, 28–29, 53–54, indicates, Bramhall was not alone in his hostility to Hobbes's "ultra-Erastian" position. Compare, for instance, Ross, *Leviathan Drawn out with a Hook*, 63–64; Hyde, *A Brief View and Survey*, 165, 187–88, 205–8, 234–35, 270–74. See also Parkin, *Taming the Leviathan*, 168, 189, 231, 259, *et passim*.

tion of the necessity for the sovereign to reinforce his supremacy by using his sword to keep down those who would reclaim the crozier can be defended in the name of liberty and peace; but that defense requires the acknowledgment that liberty for most citizens may require imposing the yoke on a few, and that peace sometimes depends on the threat and use of force.[36]

These considerations would seem to mean no more than that Hobbes's Erastianism is too starkly and aggressively secular to be well understood as just another variant of Protestant ecclesiology. There is a further difficulty, however, that cuts in a different direction and makes Hobbes's ultimate position much harder to pin down. For in some passages at least, Hobbes urges the sovereign to consider actually *loosening* his grip on religion in the commonwealth. The passages in question are not only those in which Hobbes advises the sovereign not to punish men for their beliefs but only for their actions. Nor are they only these together with those in which he warns the sovereign that, in combating entrenched forces, one must proceed carefully lest one cause a backlash, as did those impatient princes whose efforts to resist the encroachment of clerical power "before their subjects' eyes were opened" only bolstered the power they resisted (*Lev.* 47.18). The even more striking passages are those in which Hobbes praises a kind of religious freedom and seems to suggest that the commonwealth would be better off if men were free to worship as they wish.

The most important passage in this regard comes near the end of *Leviathan*. It is a passage that has drawn the attention of many scholars.[37] In what has

36. In a digression in *Behemoth* that reads as if Hobbes momentarily handed his pen to Machiavelli (94–95), Hobbes describes the situation in ancient Ethiopia, where the priests had so mastered the kings by manipulation of their superstition that the kings would commit suicide at the priests' command. This terrible custom was abolished by a certain King Ergamenes who, "having had his breeding in philosophy after the manner of the Greeks," was the first "that durst despise" the power of the priests. Ergamenes, writes Hobbes, "took heart as befitted a King; came with soldiers to a place called Abaton, where there was then the golden temple of the Aethiopians; killed all the priests, abolished the custom, and rectified the kingdom according to his will." Of course, from his telling of this bloody story from ancient history, one should not infer that Hobbes would ever sanction such a thing in Christian times. But he does go on, after excusing the cruelty of Ergamenes' act by describing the much more pernicious cruelty of the Ethiopian priests, to suggest that if the seditious Presbyterian ministers most responsible for the English Civil War had been killed before they could preach, the killing of "not perhaps 1,000" would indeed have been "a great massacre," but it could have prevented the far greater massacre of "near 100,000 persons." Compare *Lev.* 42.127.

37. For other discussions of the passage considered in this paragraph, see Collins, *The Allegiance of Thomas Hobbes*, 129–30; Owen, *Making Religion Safe for Democracy*, 51–52, "The Tolerant Leviathan," 142–43; Lessay, "Hobbes's Protestantism," 290–91; Malcolm, *Leviathan,*

come to be known as the "knots" passage, Hobbes gives an account of how the "knots" on "Christian liberty" that were tied through a long historical process have finally come unraveled (*Lev.* 47.19–20). Just as he suggested in Chapter 12 that an examination of the growth of religion helps to shed light on the process of its "resolution" into its first seeds or principles (see again 12.23), so here in Chapter 47 Hobbes describes the tying of the knots on Christian liberty with a view to explaining their undoing. As he puts it with his signature clarity: "as the inventions of men are woven, so also are they raveled out; the way is the same, but the order is inverted" (*Lev.* 47.19). Now, the binding of Christian liberty, in Hobbes's account, involved the tying of three knots. The first came with the movement in the minds of the early Christians from the belief that they followed the apostles of their own accord, "out of reverence, not by obligation," to the acceptance that later decrees of assemblies of presbyters were obligatory and legitimately enforced by excommunication. The second knot was tied when the presbyters appropriated the name and authority of bishops. And the third was tied by the concentration of authority and power in the hands of the most oppressive of all bishops, the "Bishop of Rome," whose ascension completed "the whole *synthesis* and *construction* of the Pontifical Power" (*Lev.* 47.19). More significant than Hobbes's brief account of the tying of these knots is what he goes on to say about how they have been undone. The first step in this process of liberation, which "beginneth with the knot that was last tied," was "the dissolution of the praeterpolitical Church government in England," that is, the rejection of the authority of the Pope and the subordination of the bishops to Queen Elizabeth and her successors. If that step is unsurprising, the next is more striking, because in describing it Hobbes makes one of his rare remarks openly hostile to Anglicanism. "After this," he writes, "the Presbyterians lately in England obtained the putting down of episcopacy, and so was the second knot dissolved." More striking still is his account of the final step:

> And almost at the same time, the power was taken from the Presbyterians. And so we are reduced to the Independency of the primitive Christians to follow Paul, or Cephas, or Apollos, every man as he liketh best, which, if it be without contention, and without measuring the doctrine of Christ by our affection to the person of his minister (the fault which the Apostle reprehended in the Corinthians), is perhaps the best. (*Lev.* 47.20)

Vol. 1: Introduction, 61–65; Sommerville, "Hobbes and Independency," 155–73; Curley, "Hobbes and the Cause of Religious Toleration," 324–26; Johnston, *The Rhetoric of Leviathan*, 204–5; Tuck, *Hobbes*, 87–88, "Hobbes and Locke on Toleration," 163–64; Hood, *The Divine Politics of Thomas Hobbes*, 248; Pocock, "Time, History and Eschatology in the Thought of Thomas Hobbes," 197–98.

Hobbes goes on to give two reasons why "Independency" is "perhaps the best": the only power over the consciences of men should be that of "the Word itself," and it is unreasonable for religious authorities, "who teach there is such danger in every little error," to demand that men relinquish the use of their own reason and stake their salvation on the judgment of others (*Lev.* 47.20).

What are we to make of this remarkable passage? Some have taken it as evidence of Hobbes's ultimate preference for religious toleration. Curley, for instance, remarks that "at moments like this Hobbes does indeed sound like a saint of liberalism."[38] Others have taken the passage as Hobbes's decisive endorsement of Independency, that is, of the movement for congregational independence that defeated the mid-seventeenth-century Presbyterian efforts to establish a uniform and compulsory national church.[39] The Independents had risen to dominance among the various religious factions in England by the time Hobbes wrote *Leviathan*, and there can be no doubt that Hobbes welcomed their success in defeating the only faction that rivaled the Catholics in his disdain. Any group that "plucked out the sting of Presbytery" (*Beh.*, 169) cannot have been wholly bad in Hobbes's eyes. To describe the "knots" passage as an unambiguous endorsement of Independency, however, is to go too far, and not only because Hobbes omitted the passage entirely from the Latin *Leviathan*. It is true that the omission of the passage from the Latin text, published after the Restoration, can be explained by the drastic changes in the political and ecclesiological circumstances in England. Yet cannot Hobbes's praise of Independency in the English text of 1651 be explained, at least in part, on similar grounds? Rapid transformations in political circumstances, especially when they create common enemies, can make for strange bedfellows. And Hobbes and the Independents, a group of fiery Puritans committed to religious purity and the rights of conscience, were strange bedfellows indeed.[40] After all, the Independents were a faction that Hobbes himself would later describe, in his Restoration retrospective on the Civil War, as a band of ambitious and murderous fanatics (see *Beh.*, 2–3, 136, 155, 159, 165,

38. Curley, "Hobbes and the Cause of Religious Toleration," 325–26; see also Owen, "The Tolerant Leviathan," 142–43; Flathman, *Thomas Hobbes: Skepticism, Individuality, and Chastened Politics*, 154.

39. See Collins, *The Allegiance of Thomas Hobbes*, 102, 129–30, 136, 275; see also Tuck, *Hobbes*, 87–88, "Hobbes and Locke on Toleration," 163–65, *Philosophy and Government, 1572–1651*, 333–35, "Hobbes, Conscience, and Christianity," 496–98.

40. The differences between Hobbes and the Independents are stressed by Sommerville, "Hobbes and Independency," 160–70, and Kow, "Hobbes's Critique of Miltonian Independency," 39–40, 45–50. See also Malcolm, *Leviathan, Vol. 1: Introduction*, 63.

169, 181). Even Collins, the most vigorous defender of the view that Hobbes endorsed Independency, is ultimately compelled to acknowledge the gulf between Hobbes's concerns and theirs.[41] Something of that gulf, or at least a hint of Hobbes's reservations about Independency, is evident in the knots passage itself, if one looks closely at Hobbes's "endorsement": a return to "the Independency of the primitive Christians," he says, "*if it be without contention*, and without measuring the doctrine of Christ by our affection to the person of his minister . . . is *perhaps* the best" (emphasis added).[42]

How should these qualifications be taken? Perhaps they merely express Hobbes's doubts that the movement of Independency, even if it had a quasi-Erastian bent insofar as most Independents were willing to cede jurisdictional control over religion to the state,[43] would ultimately prove compatible with his own far more radical vision of an Erastianism guided by secular concerns. But Hobbes's doubts may well have extended beyond the question of whether mid-century Independency in England was likely to lead to a lasting settlement that he could endorse. The key phrase with which Hobbes expresses his doubts—"*if it be without contention*"—points to a broader problem with religious toleration as such. By allowing a multiplicity of religious sects to coexist in the hope that their coexistence will be peaceful, Independency, or any other form of religious toleration, supplies the battlefield on which that hope can die a painful death. And if the hope were to die, its death would not be accidental in Hobbes's view, for there is something in the nature of strongly held religious convictions, or those who hold them, that seeks not just toleration but domination (see *Lev.* 22.32, 44.1–2; *Elem.* 25.13; *De Cive* 6.11, 17.27; *De Hom.* 13.3; *Beh.*, 16, 22–24, 52, 62–63; *EW* V, 290).[44] Those who strive for an oppressive spiritual authority can sometimes be forced into a temporary retreat or truce; but that does not guarantee their permanent defeat. They may be merely biding their time for new offensives. Hobbes concludes Chapter 47 of *Leviathan*, the final chapter of the main text, by expressing precisely that

41. See, e.g., Collins, *The Allegiance of Thomas Hobbes*, 252–53: "Hobbes and the Cromwellian Independents operated from different premises: . . . Independency sought to destroy clerical authority in the interests of individual congregations, while Erastians sought to glorify the state"; 241: "The affinity between Hobbes and the Cromwellian Independents should not be exaggerated." See also 87, 207, 278.

42. Compare Garsten, *Saving Persuasion*, 39.

43. See Collins, *The Allegiance of Thomas Hobbes*, 102, 109–110, 228; see also Malcolm, *Leviathan, Vol. 1: Introduction*, 63.

44. Since Hobbes praises "the Independency of the primitive Christians" in the knots passage, it is worth noting that he indicates elsewhere that the freedom of the independent congregations among the early Christians did not always lead to peace (see *Lev.* 42.56–57).

concern. After praising Henry VIII and Elizabeth for their success in banishing the Pope and his minions from English politics, he makes the following statement in the final paragraph:

> But who knows that this Spirit of Rome—now gone out, and walking by missions through the dry places of China, Japan, and the Indies, that yield him little fruit—may not return, or rather an assembly of spirits worse than he, enter, and inhabit this clean swept house, and make the end thereof worse than the beginning? For it is not the Roman clergy only that pretends the Kingdom of God to be of this world, and thereby to have a power therein distinct from that of the civil state. (47.34; cf. Latin *Lev.*, 1125; Matt. 12:43–45)

Does not toleration, by propping open the door, make a return of the "Spirit of Rome," or the entrance of "an assembly of spirits worse than he," more likely?

The answer to this question is not an obvious yes, and Hobbes's indications of the dangers of toleration should not lead us to conclude that he was opposed to it under all circumstances. Hobbes's official position, so to speak, is that the sovereign may decide for himself whether or not to insist upon a uniform worship in the commonwealth.[45] Whether the sovereign chooses uniformity or toleration is a matter of prudence rather than principle, at least if he takes his bearing from Hobbes.[46] If the sovereign opts not to establish a single worship, then the commonwealth would not have a "public worship," nor would the commonwealth itself, in Hobbes's formulation, be "of any religion at all" (*Lev.* 31.37). Now, it is true that no well-advised Hobbesian sovereign is likely to think that toleration alone would be the best answer in most situations. For a form of simple toleration that leaves the coals of intense religious passions and convictions still smoldering risks new fires whenever strong winds blow. Mere toleration alone, therefore, is insufficient to provide the lasting security from religious challenges and conflicts that the Hobbesian sovereign ought to be concerned to achieve. But what if the convictions themselves were transformed, such that they became less intense and

---

45. In a key passage of the English *Leviathan*, which is in some tension with the knots passage, Hobbes writes that the commonwealth, as "but one person," "ought also to exhibit to God but one worship" (31.37). In the Latin version, however, the "ought" is replaced by "may" (*potest*). It is clear even from the passage in the English text that the sovereign, according to Hobbes, has the *right*, if he wishes to use it, not to institute or support any uniform public worship. On the passage in the English text, compare Waldron, "Hobbes on Public Worship," 41–42, who reads the passage as an unambiguous endorsement of a national church.

46. See Boyd, "Thomas Hobbes and the Perils of Pluralism," 409; Ryan, "Hobbes, Toleration, and the Inner Life," 217, "A More Tolerant Hobbes?" 57–58.

threatening, or even faded away? Hobbes was aware of the danger posed by intense religious convictions and thus the risks of toleration; but he was also aware that men's religiosity is not a static matter.[47] The much-disputed question of what ecclesiastical arrangement he regarded as best in the immediate, highly fraught circumstances of mid-century England, then, is not the same as the question of what he might have thought possible and best over time, especially if a well-disposed sovereign should help to broaden the influence of his own teaching. When Hobbes raises the possibility of a commonwealth that is not "of any religion at all," might he be pointing, not only to a situation in which there is no established public worship, but also to the possibility of a society in which religion as such had faded away? Is that the ultimate destination of the transformation that he hoped a well-disposed sovereign could help him to set in motion? After all, a perceptive sovereign might well draw the conclusion from Hobbes's treatment of the political problem of religion that only such an extreme solution would truly end the problem by no longer leaving smoldering coals but instead removing, once and for all, the most serious and persistent challenge to the supremacy of civil authority.

There are reasons to accept what Malcolm has called the "radical interpretation" that Hobbes's ultimate preference was for a commonwealth that would be "in the fullest sense of the term" not "of any religion at all."[48] Although Malcolm himself is noncommittal as to whether he regards that interpretation as correct, he is certainly right to point out that "it would be hard to maintain that promoting the religion of the Independents in England—a set of fervent biblicist Puritan Protestants—was the best way to produce such an end-result."[49] But that is why it is essential to separate the question of what Hobbes regarded as best in the immediate circumstances of mid-century England from the question of his ultimate hopes, and to give greater attention to the latter question. That question is more important not only because it is not confined to a specific historical situation, but also because, whereas Hobbes had little power to affect the prospects of the Independency in England, he could—and did—do much to shape the thinking about the character and trajectory of the modern state, not only in England but throughout

---

47. This point is stressed by Owen, *Making Religion Safe for Democracy*, 31, 39–40, 52–56, "The Tolerant Leviathan," 141–44; Strauss, *Natural Right and History*, 198–99; and Johnston, *The Rhetoric of Leviathan*, 112–13, 120–33, 183–84. Consider also the remark of Milner, "Hobbes on Religion," 421, that "religion evanesces as enlightenment advances."

48. *Leviathan*, Vol. 1: *Introduction*, 63.

49. *Leviathan*, Vol. 1: *Introduction*, 63.

early modern Europe. Yet why should one even entertain, much less accept, what is admittedly a "radical interpretation"?[50]

The primary reason arises from the same consideration that could lead a sovereign to conclude from Hobbes's treatment of the political problem of religion that the only adequate solution would be to eliminate the very sources of the problem. The danger of the persistence of religion is not just that smoldering coals can reignite; it is also that, so long as men remain religious, the fear of violent death at the hands of other men can always be challenged in their souls by the fear of damnation and the hope for salvation. Only with the fading away of religion—that is, only in a society that is "in the fullest sense of the term" not "of any religion at all"—would the fear of violent death gain unambiguous primacy and stand unrivaled as the pillar of the civic structure. To be sure, the sovereign could try instead merely to exert a firm control over the effects of the fear of damnation and the hope for salvation, either through a policy of limited and watchful toleration or through a more rigorously Erastian insistence on uniformity. Yet, insofar as men would remain in the grips of religious passions, or, to put the matter in Hobbes's terms, insofar as they would remain superstitious, they would always be susceptible to being swayed by those who claim to have special access to the workings and wishes of invisible powers. The sovereign would thus need to remain always on guard against the diverse and dangerous surges of a force that is too arbitrary and variable in its manifestations to be brought under complete control. Would it not therefore be preferable to remove the need for such constant vigilance by treating the problem at its source? If Hobbes says of himself that he cannot be "made to believe that the safety of a state depends upon the safety of the Church," nor that "a clergy is essential to a commonwealth" (*EW* IV, 433), does he not suggest that his system would function most smoothly if those unnecessary and frequently obstructive elements of the traditional commonwealth were removed entirely?

---

50. One reason, even if it is not the most important one, nor one that I will discuss in the text below, is that the "radical interpretation" has been advanced by some of the most perceptive and thoughtful scholars of Hobbes. Malcolm, as I noted above, mentions it as a possible interpretation, but he does not commit himself one way or the other (in addition to *Leviathan, Vol. 1: Introduction*, 63, consider also 80, *Aspects of Hobbes*, 544–45, *Reason of State, Propaganda, and the Thirty Years' War*, 121–22). Stronger advocates of the interpretation are Strauss, *Natural Right and History*, 198–99 (see also 169–75, "On the Basis of Hobbes's Political Philosophy," 186), and Owen, *Making Religion Safe for Democracy*, 31, 35–36, 39–56. Owen's version of the interpretation is more qualified and hesitant than Strauss's. My discussion below is indebted to both. Compare also Johnston, *The Rhetoric of Leviathan*, 210–13.

Even a sympathetic sovereign might well regard that as a step too far, and many scholars would agree with him if he did. A prudent sovereign, these scholars would argue, would see it as a mistake to destroy a tool that he can use for his own purposes. According to a common interpretation of Hobbes's position on sovereignty and religion, Hobbes advocated a "neo-pagan" use of religion as an instrument of prudent politics.[51] And *prima facie*, this suggestion seems eminently sensible: Why should the Hobbesian sovereign not do as the ancient pagan legislators did and use religion to buttress his authority by adding the force of superstitious fear to the rational fear of human punishment? Is not "superstition" too powerful a weapon for a sovereign not to use it himself once he has taken it from the hands of his competitors? Yet the suggestion that Hobbes was a neo-pagan on the question of sovereignty and religion is far less compelling than it seems on first consideration. It is true that Hobbes calls attention to the pagan legislators' use of religion, and even that he points to the political benefits of their manipulation of religion, which he contrasts with the problematic "divine politics" that emerged with biblical religion (see pp. 107–8 above). But he does not hold up the pagan legislators as models to be imitated.[52] Simply put, Hobbes does not in fact urge the sovereign to use superstition for his own ends. The occasional passages that could be taken to suggest such a thing are tepid and equivocal (see, e.g., *Lev.* 11.27, 12.20–22, 14.31–33, 30.7–10; Latin *Lev.*, Appendix, 1207); they pale in comparison to Hobbes's vehement warnings about the dangers that superstition poses to the commonwealth (compare, e.g., *Lev.* 29.15, 38.1; *De Cive* 6.11). And more important than the tone of competing passages is this consideration: if Hobbes thought that superstition was politically useful—or, better, that its benefits outweighed its dangers—then it would be very hard to understand his own manifest efforts to undermine it. As he himself puts it, if "[the] superstitious fear of spirits were *taken away*"—that is, *not* if it were put to a more prudent use—"men would be much more fitted than they are for civil obedience" (*Lev.* 2.8, emphasis added). Hobbes follows this striking re-

51. For the best presentation of this interpretation, see Collins, *The Allegiance of Thomas Hobbes*, 36–57, 87, 278. See also Oakeshott, *Hobbes on Civil Association*, 73–76; Tuck, *Hobbes*, 79–80, 89–90 (cf., however, "Hobbes, Conscience, and Christianity," 489–99, especially 498 and n. 49); Mortimer, "Christianity and Civil Religion in Hobbes's *Leviathan*," 504–9, 515–17; Tarlton, "The Creation and Maintenance of Government," 327; Holmes, "Political Psychology in Hobbes's *Behemoth*," 142. Compare Beiner, "Machiavelli, Hobbes, and Rousseau on Civil Religion," 624–31, 635–36; Garsten, "Religion and Representation in Hobbes," 534–35.

52. See Malcolm, *Reason of State, Propaganda, and the Thirty Years War*, 121–22; Owen, *Making Religion Safe for Democracy*, 35–36, 52–53. See also Glover, "God and Thomas Hobbes," 282; Hoekstra, "Disarming the Prophets," 142, 147–51.

mark, as we saw earlier, by saying that the destruction of superstition "ought to be the work of the schools" (*Lev.* 2.8; see also 27.20, 45.30; *De Hom.* 13.3; *EW* VII, 79; pp. 40, 91–92 above). These remarks hardly sound like the thoughts of a neo-pagan. They are, however, very much in keeping with the spirit of an author who mocks pagan religion mercilessly (see again *Lev.* 12.13–19). Finally, in addition to the obvious reason that Hobbes would have resisted a neo-pagan approach—namely, that it would keep superstition alive and thus risk its proliferation and use by men other than the sovereign—there is this further problem: whatever the virtues of the pagan ways in Hobbes's view, the "human politics" of pagan religion ultimately proved an inadequate bulwark against the emergence of the more dangerous "divine politics" of biblical religion. Would not a neo-pagan resurgence of the old approach, then, merely invite a return to the beginning of what long ago proved to be a bad development, in which the civil powers were eventually overwhelmed by the very forces they had summoned to their cause?

Even if Hobbes was not a neo-pagan in the sense of encouraging the political use of superstition, he might have thought that a simplified version of Christianity, stripped as much as possible of its encrusted (and original) superstition, could provide a solid support to the commonwealth. Is not the primary purpose of Parts III and IV of *Leviathan*, many scholars would ask, to reinterpret Christianity in just such a way? Yes, to some extent, and if the suggestion that Hobbes was a neo-pagan is modified in this way, there is surely some truth to it. Hobbes's reinterpretation of Christianity *is* intended, on some level, to remake it into a religion that would be politically salutary rather than politically destructive. But to leave it at that would be to forget Hobbes's more radical intention in Parts III and IV of *Leviathan*, which, as we saw earlier, is to sketch the lineaments of a thoroughgoing critique of the Bible and Christianity. Hobbes's deepest intention is not to convince his most perceptive readers that the Bible teaches what he teaches, but rather to reveal the gulf separating the authentic biblical teachings from his own rational doctrines and thereby to sow the seeds of doubt. If some of Hobbes's contemporary readers, like many latter-day scholars, were to grasp only Hobbes's more obvious intention and not his deeper one, that would have been acceptable to Hobbes. For not only does the acceptance of an obviously politically driven reinterpretation of Christianity sow the seeds of doubt in its own less direct way—by fostering in its readers the kind of cynicism it presupposes in its author—but Hobbes may well have thought that it was necessary to proceed by stages and that it would take time for the influence of those who were moved by his deeper teaching to spread. After all, one of Hobbes's messages to any sovereign who would join him in the fight against the forces of darkness is that patience is necessary to succeed where earlier, hastier efforts against the same foe failed (see again *Lev.* 47.18).[53]

This last point can be stated more broadly: Hobbes's ultimate aim, as I believe our study of his writings has shown, was not just to tame and "rationalize" Christianity by purging it as much as possible of superstition, but to spread a far-reaching and comprehensive enlightenment. We have seen the many fronts on which Hobbes launched his attacks. His forthright presentation of his debunking mechanistic materialism; his thinly veiled critique of religion in general and of the Bible and Christianity in particular; his efforts to bring about a revolution in men's understanding of morality; his secularizing political teaching—all of these are battles in Hobbes's broader war against the Kingdom of Darkness. And the ultimate goal of that war was to replace the Kingdom of Darkness with a new Kingdom of Light. To focus only on his rationalizing modifications of Christianity, then, is to miss the breadth of Hobbes's venture. Finally, let us not forget that Hobbes ended his most direct discussion of religion as such by pointing toward its "resolution" back into "its first seeds or principles." To be sure, he declared that these seeds or principles "can never be so abolished out of human nature, but that new religions may again be made to spring out of them by the culture of such men as for such purpose are in reputation" (*Lev.* 12.23). But that key formulation, as we noted earlier, is more radical than it first appears. For not only does it remind us that religions can die, but it leaves open the possibility that under the right conditions the very seeds themselves could be, if not entirely abolished from human nature, at least so depleted, and the cultivators of them so marginalized, that they would not grow into a new religion. Hobbes, I submit, was seeking the sovereign's help in bringing about precisely those conditions.[54]

*

A reader still unconvinced by the "radical interpretation" just defended might turn from the second half of *Leviathan*—that is, from Hobbes's reinterpretation of Christianity—to the very beginning: the title page.[55] Does not Hobbes there, in "perhaps the most famous visual image in the history of political

---

53. See also *De Hom.* 14.13: *Paulatim eruditur vulgus* (Gradually the common people are educated), a phrase quoted also by Strauss, *Natural Right and History*, 200; Owen, *Making Religion Safe for Democracy*, 51; and Tönnies, *Thomas Hobbes: Leben und Lehre*, 195.

54. See p. 112 above, especially n40, on the replacement in the Latin *Leviathan* of "by the culture of such men as for such purpose are in reputation" with *si Cultores accesserint idonei* (if suitable cultivators exist).

55. See Appendix below.

philosophy,"[56] show the sovereign holding a crozier as well as a sword? If that is a symbol of Hobbes's radical Erastianism (see p. 262 above), is it not also an indication that the Hobbesian sovereign would use religion to bolster his power, and thus that religion would persist even in an ideal Hobbesian commonwealth? Perhaps. But there is another feature of Hobbes's famous image that makes its ultimate message more of a question. It is not—what others have noted—that many of the symbols of religion in the image (for instance, the two double-spired churches, the split–top bishop's miter, or the horns of a theological dilemma) are indicative of division and dispute.[57] Those features are striking and telling; but more important is something else. The sovereign in Hobbes's image famously towers over a walled city with a church in it, and his body is made up of the figures of many human beings, symbolizing the natural people who as subjects constitute the artificial sovereign. What frequently goes unnoticed, however, is that Hobbes's sovereign stands behind a range of mountains, separating him from the walled city itself, and that the people who make up his body have their backs turned toward that city. Does that not suggest that they have left the walled city, the city dominated by the church, to cleave to the new sovereign? The image is at least ambiguous: Is Hobbes's sovereign ruling over the city pictured, or is he leading an exodus from it? And if it is the latter, might it not be possible for him, once the exodus is complete, to put down the crozier, which in the image remains closer to the walled city than does the sword in his other hand?

That Hobbes also uses the biblical sea monster named Leviathan as an image of the commonwealth is not evidence against this suggestion, even though that image comes from the Bible. For, as we noted earlier, Hobbes turns the message of that biblical image on its head, transforming the Leviathan from a symbol of man's weakness and God's power into nearly the opposite: a call to a great act of collective human self-assertion through the creation of a "mortal God" to save us from ourselves (see pp. 205–6 above and note 8 to this chapter). Nor, certainly, does it cut against the suggestion in question that Hobbes must have been aware that there was a tradition of

56. Malcolm, *Leviathan, Vol. 1: Introduction*, 128. Malcolm, 128–41, offers an extensive account of the production of the title page, the artistic design of which can be attributed "with reasonable certainty" to the French etcher Abraham Bosse. Despite Bosse's likely role as the artist, it "cannot be doubted," according to Malcolm, "that Hobbes was closely involved in the development of the whole design." Malcolm explains the grounds for this reasonable assumption: "no artist, on his own, would have been sufficiently familiar with the contents of the book to come up with such an elaborate, apt, and powerful representation of its argument."

57. See, e.g., Malcolm, *Leviathan, Vol. 1: Introduction*, 130; Skinner, *Hobbes and Republican Liberty*, 194–96.

regarding the Leviathan as a symbol of the Devil.[58] No one can know for sure what Hobbes had in mind in naming his greatest work after what earlier authors had taken to be a symbol of the biblical God's greatest enemy; but that decision does not speak against the "radical interpretation."

Let us not dwell on matters that admit only of speculation. Rather than trying to decipher Hobbes's ultimate intentions from the images he uses, it is better here at the end simply to appreciate the audacity of his undertaking. In setting out to establish the new alliance that we have considered, Hobbes was attempting to forge a union, not just between himself and a sympathetic sovereign, but between philosophy as such and civil authority as such. It is true that Hobbes urged all of his prospective allies, including any sovereigns who would join the cause, to be patient and cautious in advancing against the common enemy (see p. 263 above). But Hobbes's own patience and caution extended only so far, for at some point they gave way to the greater force of his boldness and impetuosity. Hobbes's boldness is one of his most attractive traits, because it gave him a disdain for obscurity and an irrepressible desire to go to the heart of things. His boldness, however, was not only an aspect of his natural character. It was also a consequence of his confidence in the ultimate success of his venture. The basis of Hobbes's confidence was, in part, his appraisal of the forces that philosophy and the civil power could muster once they united and began to win the people to their cause. But deeper than that—and the source of his conviction that the people could be won over—was Hobbes's belief in the superior rationality of his doctrines to all that had come before. In a remarkable moment, Hobbes drops his guard almost entirely and allows himself to pose this question:

> Shall whole nations be brought to acquiesce in the great mysteries of the Christian religion, which are above reason, and millions of men be made believe that the same body may be in innumerable places at one and the same time, which is against reason, and shall not men be able, by their teaching and preaching, protected by the law, to make that received which is so consonant to reason that any unprejudiced man needs no more to learn it than to hear it? (*Lev.* 30.6)

What is most striking about this remark is not its cynicism in suggesting that if masses of men can be brought to believe Christian doctrines, they can be made to believe almost anything. Rather, it is its optimism about the prospects of Hobbes's own doctrines coming to be accepted precisely because

---

58. See Malcolm, *Leviathan, Vol. 1: Introduction,* 116–18; Curley, "'I Durst not Write so Boldly,'" 571–72; Schmitt, *The Leviathan in the State Theory of Thomas Hobbes,* 6–8, 22–23.

they are "consonant to reason."[59] To be sure, Hobbes acknowledges that the immediate acceptance of his doctrines would require an "unprejudicated" audience, and he was surely well aware that most men are not blank slates in that sense. That is the most important reason why he also issued the reminder that it is necessary to proceed gradually in educating the people. Still, the problem, in Hobbes's view, lies in obstacles that thwarted the builders of the past only because they failed to remove them, or, as he himself puts it, when speaking of why so many commonwealths have perished from "internal diseases," "the fault is not in men as they are the *matter*, but as they are the *makers* and orderers of them" (*Lev.* 29.1). In Hobbes's estimation, then, there is no reason in principle that a rational structure cannot be erected using the blueprints of a "very able architect." The stability of the new structure will be guaranteed precisely by its rationality. Thus we see on the political plane the same thing we saw on the moral plane: Hobbes's revolutionary efforts rested on the bedrock of his belief that he was bringing the light of reason to a world that had lived for too long in the dark.

It is not hard to appreciate the power and allure of this vision, both for Hobbes himself and for those who followed him. How could men who knew well the problems of the old order not be inspired by the prospect of liberating philosophy from its enslavement in the Kingdom of Darkness, dispelling the mists of superstition, and helping men at long last to construct a rational political order? Yet, just as we were compelled to ask whether Hobbes's moral teaching is as rational as he claims it is, the same question eventually arises with regard to his political teaching, too. The heart of Hobbes's political venture is his attempt to transform the commonwealth such that it would be at once of unquestioned supremacy and devoted to a much more limited end than it had been in the past. In reconceiving of the commonwealth in this way, Hobbes paved the way for the progressive centralizing, secularizing, and liberalizing of modern politics. But in the process of this transformation, the commonwealth—or the modern state, as it would become—turned into something that at least some of its most thoughtful inhabitants came to regard as a pale reflection of what it once had been. For the commonwealth had always promised more than the provision of security, freedom, and the conditions necessary for prosperity; it had claimed to be a greater whole that demanded devotion of its citizens as it also promised to perfect and complete them. In our earlier consideration of the limits of Hobbes's moral teaching, I alluded to Nietzsche's protest against Hobbes's demotion of courage (see p. 240 above).

---

59. This formulation is even stronger in the Latin *Leviathan*: *cum ratione naturali exquisitè congruunt* (perfectly consistent with natural reason).

Equally powerful is his protest against the modern state. Whereas "creators" once unified peoples by hanging "a faith and a love" over them, the modern state, Nietzsche declares, is the work of "annihilators" who have won over the masses by hanging "a sword and a hundred appetites" over them.[60] "A sword and a hundred appetites"—could there be a better expression for the ways and means of "the coldest of all cold monsters," the modern Leviathan state? And even if the modern state protects life, must one not at some point ask, with Nietzsche, what kind of life that is, and whether the life of a society cannot degenerate into something resembling "the slow suicide of all"?

To point to Nietzsche's protest, however, could seem to some readers—as it does to this author—to be at least a partial vindication of Hobbes. After all, Nietzsche is not exactly a paragon of sober political judgment. And if Hobbes prepared the way for the political transformation that would eventually give rise to the modern liberal state, whereas Nietzsche inspired the most virulent of all reactions against that transformation, that difference would hardly seem to reflect poorly on Hobbes. Is not Hobbes to be admired rather than despised for putting politics on a more sensible foundation and helping the modern world to move beyond the politics of peoples, fatherlands, and faiths? To that question, I would give the following answer. It is possible to admire Hobbes's audacity and humanity in attempting to design a new political order in which human beings could at last stand on their own feet; it is possible to admire his unrelenting fight against an enemy that had indeed been a source of chaos, suffering, and ignorance; it is possible to appreciate the security, freedom, and prosperity at which Hobbes aimed and which the modern state has, in con- siderable measure, achieved—it is possible to admire and appreciate Hobbes in all of these ways and yet still not accept his claim that he was leading men from the darkness to the light. For Nietzsche's protest is not just the howl- ing of a tormented soul; it also the voice of those aspects of human nature that cannot be satisfied by the modern state. Our longings are ultimately as important as our fears. And because, as human beings, we cannot but yearn for more than security, freedom, and prosperity, it is impossible for us to give ourselves wholeheartedly to a state that makes those its only goals.

This problem persists today. It manifests itself in the lingering discontent, even in the most advanced parts of the world, with modern politics, and in the shallow, frenzied ways in which modern men try to distract themselves from their own dissatisfaction. The dissatisfaction that modern men reveal even in their attempts to conceal it from themselves cuts to the core of Hobbes's claim

---

60. See Nietzsche, *Thus Spoke Zarathustra*, Part One, "On the New Idol." Compare Schmitt, *The Leviathan in the State Theory of Thomas Hobbes*, 62–63.

about the new order he sought to bring about, for it bespeaks the fact that the modern Hobbesian state, in telling us that we can and should be satisfied with the security, freedom, and prosperity attainable in this world, tells us something about ourselves that is not true. Hobbes's classical opponents—to say nothing further of Nietzsche—would have been amazed, not just by the immense optimism of Hobbes's hope to unite philosophy and politics such that these perennial rivals could finally stand arm-in-arm, but also by his belief that this venture could succeed by making both parties servants of man's lower needs. That such a thing could be done, they likely would have conceded. But that it could be done without a heavy cost, they would have denied. The cost is still being exacted in the discontent of modern men, whose political communities ask of them too little, and in the disappointment with reason, of which Hobbes taught the modern world to ask too much.

Appendix

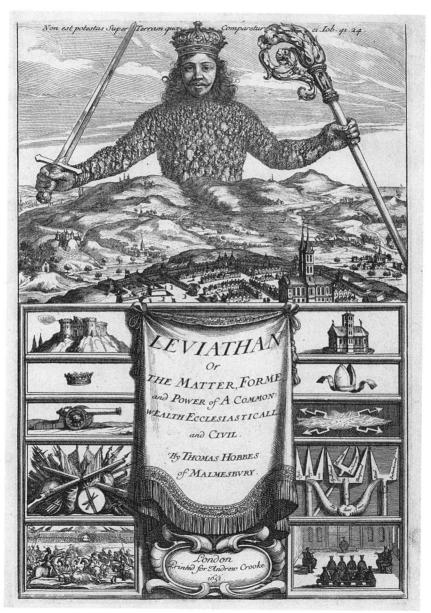

Leviathan, Head edition, engraved title page, reproduced by permission of the Harry Ransom Center, The University of Texas at Austin.

Bibliography

Ahrensdorf, Peter J. "The Fear of Death and the Longing for Immortality: Hobbes and Thucydides on Human Nature and the Problem of Anarchy." *American Political Science Review* 94 (2000): 579–93.

Ambler, Wayne H. "Aristotle's Understanding of the Naturalness of the City." *Review of Politics* 47 (1985): 163–85.

Aquinas, Saint Thomas. *Summa Theologica*. Trans. Fathers of the English Dominican Province. Vol. I. New York: Benziger Brothers, 1947.

Aubrey, John. *Aubrey's Brief Lives*. Ed. Oliver Lawson Dick. Jaffrey, NH: David Godine, 1996.

Bacon, Francis. *The Advancement of Learning*. Philadelphia: Paul Dry Books, 2001.

———. *The New Organon*. Ed. Lisa Jardine and Michael Silverthorne. Cambridge: Cambridge University Press, 2000.

Beiner, Ronald. "Machiavelli, Hobbes, and Rousseau on Civil Religion." *Review of Politics* 55 (1993): 617–38.

Berkowitz, Peter. "*Leviathan*, Then and Now." *Policy Review* 151 (2008).

Bolotin, David. "Is There a Right to Live as We Please? (So Long as We Respect the Right of Others to Do the Same)." In *Enlightening Revolutions: Essays in Honor of Ralph Lerner*, ed. Svetozar Minkov with the assistance of Stephane Douard. Lanham, MD: Lexington Books, 2007.

Boyd, Richard. "Thomas Hobbes and the Perils of Pluralism." *Journal of Politics* 63 (2001): 392–413.

Bramhall, John. *The Catching of Leviathan, or the Great Whale*. In *The Works of the Most Reverend Father in God, John Bramhall, D. D.*, Vol. 4. Oxford: John Henry Parker, 1844.

Brandt, Frithiof. *Thomas Hobbes' Mechanical Conception of Nature*. Copenhagen: Levin and Munksgaard, 1927.

Bruell, Christopher. *Aristotle as Teacher: His Introduction to a Philosophic Science*. South Bend, IN: St. Augustine's Press, 2014.

———. "Happiness in the Perspective of Philosophy." In *Recovering Reason: Essays in Honor of Thomas L. Pangle*, ed. Timothy Burns. Lanham, MD: Lexington Books, 2010.

———. "Der Tod aus der Sicht der Philosophie." In *Der Tod im Leben: Ein Symposion*, ed. Friedrich Wilhelm Graf and Heinrich Meier. Munich: Piper Verlag, 2010.

Burns, Timothy W. "Hobbes and Dionysius of Halicarnassus on Thucydides, Rhetoric and Political Life." *Polis* 31 (2014): 387–424.

———. "John Courtney Murray, Religious Liberty, and Modernity, Part I: Inalienable Rights." *Logos* 17 (2014): 13–38.

———. "Leo Strauss on the Origins of Hobbes's Natural Science." *Klēsis, Revue philosophique* 19 (2011): 102–28.

———. "Modernity's Irrationalism." In *After History? Francis Fukuyama and His Critics*, ed. Timothy Burns. Lanham, MD: Rowman and Littlefield, 1994.

Burtt, E. A. *The Metaphysical Foundations of Modern Physical Science*. London: Routledge and Kegan Paul, 1972.

Calvin, John. *Institutes of the Christian Religion*. Ed. John T. McNeill. Trans. Ford Lewis Battles. Vol. I. Philadelphia: Westminster Press, 1960.

Cassirer, Ernst. *The Philosophy of the Enlightenment*. Trans. Fritz Koelln and James Pettegrove. Boston: Beacon Press, 1955.

Collins, Jeffrey R. *The Allegiance of Thomas Hobbes*. Oxford: Oxford University Press, 2005.

Cooke, Paul D. *Hobbes and Christianity: Reassessing the Bible in Leviathan*. Lanham, MD: Rowman and Littlefield, 1996.

Cooper, Julie. "Vainglory, Modesty, and Political Agency in the Political Theory of Thomas Hobbes." *Review of Politics* 72 (2010): 241–69.

Craig, Leon. *The Platonian Leviathan*. Toronto: University of Toronto Press, 2010.

Cropsey, Joseph. "Hobbes and the Transition to Modernity." In *Ancients and Moderns: Essays on the Tradition of Political Philosophy in Honor of Leo Strauss*, ed. Joseph Cropsey. New York: Basic Books, 1964.

Curley, Edwin. "The Covenant with God in Hobbes's *Leviathan*." In *Leviathan after 350 Years*, ed. Tom Sorell and Luc Foisneau. Oxford: Clarendon Press, 2004.

———. "Hobbes and the Cause of Religious Toleration." In *A Critical Companion to Hobbes's Leviathan*, ed. Patricia Springborg. Cambridge: Cambridge University Press, 2007.

———. " 'I Durst not Write so Boldly,' or How to Read Hobbes' Theological-Political Treatise." In *Hobbes e Spinoza, Scienza e Politica*, ed. Daniela Bostrenghi. Naples: Bibliopolis, 1992.

———. "Religion and Morality in Hobbes." In *Rational Commitment and Social Justice*, ed. Jules Coleman and Christopher Morris. Cambridge: Cambridge University Press, 1998.

Darwall, Stephen. Review of S. A. Lloyd, *Ideals as Interests in Hobbes's Leviathan*, and A. P. Martinich, *The Two Gods of Leviathan*. *Philosophical Review* 103 (1994): 748–52.

Descartes, René. *Discourse on Method and Meditations on First Philosophy*. Ed. David Weissman. New Haven: Yale University Press, 1996.

———. *Meditations on First Philosophy*. In *The Philosophical Writings of Descartes*, trans. John Cottingham, Robert Stoothoff, and Dugald Murdoch. Vol. II. Cambridge: Cambridge University Press, 1985.

———. Preface to the French edition of *Principles of Philosophy*. In *The Philosophical Writings of Descartes*, trans. John Cottingham, Robert Stoothoff, and Dugald Murdoch. Vol. I. Cambridge: Cambridge University Press, 1985.

———. *Principles of Philosophy*. In *The Philosophical Writings of Descartes*, trans. John Cottingham, Robert Stoothoff, and Dugald Murdoch. Vol. I. Cambridge: Cambridge University Press, 1985.

———. *The World*. In *The Philosophical Writings of Descartes*, trans. John Cottingham, Robert Stoothoff, and Dugald Murdoch. Vol. I. Cambridge: Cambridge University Press, 1985.

Dunlop, Katherine. "Hobbes's Mathematical Thought." In *The Oxford Handbook of Hobbes*, ed. A. P. Martinich and Kinch Hoekstra. New York: Oxford University Press, 2016.

Eisenach, Eldon J. "Hobbes on Church, State, and Religion." *History of Political Thought* 3 (1982): 215–43.

Evrigenis, Ioannis D. *Images of Anarchy: The Rhetoric and Science in Hobbes's State of Nature.* New York: Cambridge University Press, 2014.

———. "The State of Nature." In *The Oxford Handbook of Hobbes*, ed. A. P. Martinich and Kinch Hoekstra. New York: Oxford University Press, 2016.

Farneti, Roberto. "Hobbes on Salvation." In *The Cambridge Companion to Hobbes's Leviathan*, ed. Patricia Springborg. Cambridge: Cambridge University Press, 2007.

Flathman, Richard. *Thomas Hobbes: Skepticism, Individuality, and Chastened Politics.* Newbury Park, CA: Sage, 1993.

———. *Willful Liberalism: Voluntarism and Individuality in Political Theory and Practice.* Ithaca, NY: Cornell University Press, 1992.

Foisneau, Luc. "Omnipotence, Necessity and Sovereignty: Hobbes on the Absolute and Ordinary Powers of God and King." In *The Cambridge Companion to Hobbes's Leviathan*, ed. Patricia Springborg. Cambridge: Cambridge University Press, 2007.

Forde, Steven. *Locke, Science and Politics.* New York: Cambridge University Press, 2013.

Frost, Samantha. *Lessons from a Materialist Thinker: Hobbesian Reflections on Ethics and Politics.* Stanford, CA: Stanford University Press, 2008.

Galileo. *Le Opere di Galileo Galilei.* Ed. Antonio Favaro. Vol. VI. Florence: G. Barbera, 1896.

Garber, Daniel. "Natural Philosophy in Seventeenth Century Context." In *The Oxford Handbook of Hobbes*, ed. A. P. Martinich and Kinch Hoekstra. New York: Oxford University Press, 2016.

Garsten, Bryan. "Religion and Representation in Hobbes." In Thomas Hobbes, *Leviathan*, ed. Ian Shapiro. New Haven: Yale University Press, 2010.

———. *Saving Persuasion: A Defense of Rhetoric and Judgment.* Cambridge, MA: Harvard University Press, 2006.

Gassendi, Pierre. "Fifth Set of Objections." In *The Philosophical Writings of Descartes*, trans. John Cottingham, Robert Stoothoff, and Dugald Murdoch. Vol. II. Cambridge: Cambridge University Press, 1985.

Gauthier, David P. *The Logic of Leviathan: The Moral and Political Theory of Thomas Hobbes.* London: Oxford University Press, 1969.

———. "Thomas Hobbes: Moral Theorist." *Journal of Philosophy* 76 (1979): 547–59.

Gert, Bernard. "Hobbes on Language, Metaphysics, and Epistemology." *Hobbes Studies* 14 (2001): 40–58.

Gillespie, Michael Allen. *The Theological Origins of Modernity.* Chicago: University of Chicago Press, 2008.

Glover, Willis B. "God and Thomas Hobbes." *Church History* 29 (1960): 275–97.

Goethe, J. W. von. *Maximen und Reflexionen.* In *Goethe Werke, Hamburger Ausgabe*, Vol. 12. Munich: C. H. Beck, 2008.

Goldsmith, M. M. *Hobbes's Science of Politics.* New York: Columbia University Press, 1966.

Green, Arnold W. *Hobbes and Human Nature.* New Brunswick: Transaction, 1993.

Habermas, Jürgen. *An Awareness of What Is Missing: Faith and Reason in a Post-Secular Age.* Cambridge: Polity Press, 2010.

———. *Between Naturalism and Religion: Philosophical Essays.* Cambridge: Polity Press, 2008.

———, with Joseph Ratzinger. *The Dialectics of Secularization: On Reason and Religion*. San Francisco: Ignatius Press, 2006.

———. *The Future of Human Nature*. Cambridge: Polity Press, 2003.

Hampton, Jean. *Hobbes and the Social Contract Tradition*. Cambridge: Cambridge University Press, 1988.

Hanson, Donald W. "Reconsidering Hobbes's Conventionalism." *Review of Politics* 53 (1991): 627–51.

———. "Science, Prudence, and Folly in Hobbes's Political Theory." *Political Theory* 21 (1993): 643–64.

Hepburn, Ronald. "Hobbes on the Knowledge of God." In *Hobbes and Rousseau: A Collection of Critical Essays*, ed. Maurice Cranston and Richard S. Peters. New York: Anchor Books, 1972.

Herbert, Gary B. *Thomas Hobbes: The Unity of Scientific and Moral Wisdom*. Vancouver: University of British Columbia Press, 1989.

Hirschman, Albert O. *The Passions and the Interests*. Princeton: Princeton University Press, 1977.

Hirschmann, Nancy J. "Hobbes on the Family." In *The Oxford Handbook of Hobbes*, ed. A. P. Martinich and Kinch Hoekstra. New York: Oxford University Press, 2016.

Hoekstra, Kinch. "The *De Facto* Turn in Hobbes's Political Philosophy." In *Leviathan after 350 Years*, ed. Tom Sorell and Luc Foisneau. Oxford: Clarendon Press, 2004.

———. "Disarming the Prophets: Thomas Hobbes and the Predictive Power." *Rivista di storia della filosofia* 59 (2004): 97–153.

———. "The End of Philosophy (The Case of Hobbes)." *Proceedings of the Aristotelian Society* 106 (2006): 25–62.

———. "Hobbes and the Foole." *Political Theory* 25 (1997): 620–54.

———. "Hobbes on the Natural Condition of Mankind." In *The Cambridge Companion to Hobbes's Leviathan*, ed. Patricia Springborg. Cambridge: Cambridge University Press, 2007.

———. "A Lion in the House: Hobbes and Democracy." In *Rethinking the Foundations of Modern Political Thought*, ed. Annabel Brett and James Tully with Holly Hamilton-Bleakley. Cambridge: Cambridge University Press, 2006.

Holmes, Stephen. "Political Psychology in Hobbes's *Behemoth*." In *Thomas Hobbes and Political Theory*, ed. Mary Dietz. Lawrence: University Press of Kansas, 1990.

Hood, F. C. *The Divine Politics of Thomas Hobbes*. London: Oxford University Press, 1964.

Hyde, Edward. *A Brief View and Survey of the Dangerous and Pernicious Errors to Church and State, in Mr. Hobbes's Book, Entitled Leviathan*. London: Routledge/Thoemmes Press, 1996.

Jackson, Nicholas D. *Hobbes, Bramhall, and the Politics of Liberty and Necessity*. Cambridge: Cambridge University Press, 2007.

Jaquette, Jane S. "Defending Liberal Feminism: Insights from Hobbes." In *Feminist Interpretations of Thomas Hobbes*, ed. Nancy J. Hirschmann and Joanne H. Wright. University Park, PA: Pennsylvania State University Press, 2012.

Jaume, Lucien. "Hobbes and the Philosophical Sources of Liberalism." In *The Cambridge Companion to Hobbes's Leviathan*, ed. Patricia Springborg. Cambridge: Cambridge University Press, 2007.

Jesseph, Douglas M. "Hobbes on the Foundations of Natural Philosophy." In *The Oxford Handbook of Hobbes*, ed. A. P. Martinich and Kinch Hoekstra. New York: Oxford University Press, 2016.

Johnson Bagby, Laurie. *Thomas Hobbes: Turning Point for Honor*. Lanham, MD: Lexington Books, 2009.

Johnston, David. *The Rhetoric of Leviathan: Thomas Hobbes and the Politics of Cultural Transformation.* Princeton: Princeton University Press, 1986.

Kant, Immanuel. "An Answer to the Question: 'What is Enlightenment?' " In *Political Writings,* trans. H. B. Nisbet. Ed. Hans Reiss. Cambridge: Cambridge University Press, 1991.

Kavka, Gregory S. *Hobbesian Moral and Political Theory.* Princeton: Princeton University Press, 1986.

———. "The Rationality of Rule-Following: Hobbes's Dispute with the Foole." *Law and Philosophy* 14 (1995): 5–34.

Kennington, Richard. *On Modern Origins: Essays in Early Modern Philosophy.* Ed. Pamela Kraus and Frank Hunt. Lanham, MD: Lexington Books, 2004.

Kow, Simon. "Hobbes's Critique of Miltonian Independency." *Animus* (2004): 37–51.

Kraynak, Robert P. *History and Modernity in the Thought of Thomas Hobbes.* Ithaca, NY: Cornell University Press, 1990.

Krüger, Gerhard. "The Origin of Philosophical Self-Consciousness." *New Yearbook for Phenomenology and Phenomenological Philosophy* 7 (2007): 209–59.

Laird, John. *Hobbes.* New York: Russell and Russell, 1934.

Leijenhorst, Cees. "Hobbes's Theory of Causality and Its Aristotelian Background." *Monist* 79 (1991): 426–47.

———. *The Mechanisation of Aristotelianism: The Late Aristotelian Setting of Thomas Hobbes's Natural Philosophy.* Leiden: Brill, 2002.

———. "Sense and Nonsense about Sense: Hobbes and the Aristotelians on Sense Perception and Imagination." In *The Cambridge Companion to Hobbes's Leviathan,* ed. Patricia Springborg. Cambridge: Cambridge University Press, 2007.

Lessay, Franck. "Hobbes's Covenant Theology and Its Political Implications." In *The Cambridge Companion to Hobbes's Leviathan,* ed. Patricia Springborg. Cambridge: Cambridge University Press, 2007.

———. "Hobbes's Protestantism." In *Leviathan after 350 Years,* ed. Tom Sorell and Luc Foisneau. Oxford: Clarendon Press, 2004.

Lilla, Mark. *The Stillborn God: Religion, Politics, and the Modern West.* New York: Knopf, 2007.

Lloyd, S. A. *Ideals as Interests in Hobbes's Leviathan: The Power of Mind over Matter.* New York: Cambridge University Press, 1992.

———. *Morality in the Philosophy of Thomas Hobbes: Cases in the Law of Nature.* New York: Cambridge University Press, 2009.

———. "Natural Law." In *The Oxford Handbook of Hobbes,* ed. A. P. Martinich and Kinch Hoekstra. New York: Oxford University Press, 2016.

———. "Power and Sexual Subordination in Hobbes's Political Theory." In *Feminist Interpretations of Thomas Hobbes,* ed. Nancy J. Hirschmann and Joanne H. Wright. University Park: Pennsylvania State University Press, 2012.

Lubienski, Zbigniew. *Die Grundlagen des ethisch-politischen Systems von Hobbes.* Munich: E. Reinhardt, 1932.

Lupoli, Agostino. "Hobbes and Religion without Theology." In *The Oxford Handbook of Hobbes,* ed. A. P. Martinich and Kinch Hoekstra. New York: Oxford University Press, 2016.

Machiavelli, Niccolò. *Discourses on Livy.* Trans. Harvey C. Mansfield and Nathan Tarcov. Chicago: University of Chicago Press, 1998.

———. *The Prince.* Trans. Harvey C. Mansfield. 2nd ed. Chicago: University of Chicago Press, 1998.

Macpherson, C. B. *The Political Theory of Possessive Individualism.* Oxford: Oxford University Press, 1962.

Maimonides, Moses. *The Guide of the Perplexed.* Trans. Shlomo Pines. Chicago: University of Chicago Press, 1974.

Malcolm, Noel. *Aspects of Hobbes.* Oxford: Clarendon Press, 2002.

———. *Leviathan, Vol. 1: Introduction.* Oxford: Clarendon Press, 2012.

———. *Reason of State, Propaganda, and the Thirty Years' War: An Unknown Translation by Thomas Hobbes.* Oxford: Oxford University Press, 2007.

Manent, Pierre. *The City of Man.* Princeton: Princeton University Press, 1998.

———. *An Intellectual History of Liberalism.* Princeton: Princeton University Press, 1994.

Mansfield, Harvey C. "Hobbes and the Science of Indirect Government." *American Political Science Review* 65 (1971): 97–110.

Mara, Gerald M. "Hobbes's Counsel to Sovereigns." *Journal of Politics* 50 (1988): 390–411.

Martinich, A. P. "Authorization and Representation in Hobbes's *Leviathan.*" In *The Oxford Handbook of Hobbes,* ed. A. P. Martinich and Kinch Hoekstra. New York: Oxford University Press, 2016.

———. *Hobbes: A Biography.* Cambridge: Cambridge University Press, 1999.

———. "Leo Strauss's Olympian Interpretation: Right, Self-Preservation, and Law in the Political Philosophy of Hobbes." In *Reading between the Lines: Leo Strauss and the History of Early Modern Philosophy,* ed. Winfried Schröder. Berlin: De Gruyter, 2015.

———. *The Two Gods of Leviathan.* Cambridge: Cambridge University Press, 1992.

McClure, Christopher Scott. "Hell and Anxiety in Hobbes's *Leviathan.*" *Review of Politics* 73 (2011): 1–27.

Milner, Benjamin. "Hobbes on Religion." *Political Theory* 16 (1988): 400–425.

Mintz, Samuel. *The Hunting of Leviathan.* Bristol: Thoemmes Press, 1996.

Mitchell, Joshua. "Religion and the Fable of Liberalism: The Case of Hobbes." *Theoria* 115 (2008): 1–15.

Montesquieu. *The Spirit of the Laws.* Trans. and ed. Anne M. Cohler, Basia Carolyn Miller, Harold Samuel Stone. Cambridge: Cambridge University Press, 1989.

Mortimer, Sarah. "Christianity and Civil Religion in Hobbes's *Leviathan.*" In *The Oxford Handbook of Hobbes,* ed. A. P. Martinich and Kinch Hoekstra. New York: Oxford University Press, 2016.

Nietzsche, Friedrich. *Beyond Good and Evil: Prelude to a Philosophy of the Future.* Trans. Walter Kaufmann. New York: Random House, 1989.

———. *Thus Spoke Zarathustra: A Book for None and All.* Trans. Walter Kaufmann. New York: Penguin Books, 1978.

Nunan, Richard. "Hobbes on Morality, Rationality, and Foolishness." *Hobbes Studies* 2 (1989): 40–64.

Oakeshott, Michael. *Hobbes on Civil Association.* Indianapolis, IN: Liberty Fund, 1975.

———. "Introduction." In Thomas Hobbes, *Leviathan,* ed. Michael Oakeshott. Oxford: Blackwell, 1946.

Orwin, Clifford. "On the Sovereign Authorization." *Political Theory* 3 (1975): 26–44.

Owen, J. Judd. *Making Religion Safe for Democracy: Transformation from Hobbes to Tocqueville.* New York: Cambridge University Press, 2015.

———. "The Tolerant Leviathan: Hobbes and the Paradox of Liberalism." *Polity* 37 (2005): 130–48.

Paganini, Gianni. "Hobbes's Critique of the Doctrine of Essences and Its Sources." In *The Cambridge Companion to Hobbes's Leviathan,* ed. Patricia Springborg. Cambridge: Cambridge University Press, 2007.

Pangle, Thomas L. "A Critique of Hobbes's Critique of Biblical and Natural Religion in *Leviathan*." *Jewish Political Studies Review* 4 (1992): 25–27.

———. "The Hebrew Bible's Challenge to Political Philosophy: Some Preliminary Reflections." In *Political Philosophy and the Human Soul: Essays in Memory of Allan Bloom,* ed. Michael Palmer and Thomas Pangle. Lanham, MD: Rowman and Littlefield, 1995.

———. *The Theological Basis of Liberal Modernity in Montesquieu's Spirit of the Laws.* Chicago: University of Chicago Press, 2010.

Pangle, Thomas L., and Timothy W. Burns. *The Key Texts of Political Philosophy: An Introduction.* New York: Cambridge University Press, 2015.

Parkin, Jon. *Taming the Leviathan: The Reception of the Political and Religious Ideas of Thomas Hobbes in England, 1640–1700.* Cambridge: Cambridge University Press, 2007.

Pateman, Carole, and Quentin Skinner. "Hobbes, History, Politics, and Gender: A Conversation with Carole Pateman and Quentin Skinner, Conducted by Nancy J. Hirschmann and Joanne H. Wright." In *Feminist Interpretations of Thomas Hobbes,* ed. Nancy J. Hirschmann and Joanne H. Wright. University Park: Pennsylvania State University Press, 2012.

Peters, Richard. *Hobbes.* London: Penguin Books, 1967.

Pettit, Philip. *Made with Words: Hobbes on Language, Mind, and Politics.* Princeton: Princeton University Press, 2008.

Pitkin, Hanna. "Hobbes's Concept of Representation." *American Political Science Review* 58 (1964): 328–40.

Plutarch. *Moralia.* Vol. III. Trans. Frank Cole Babbitt. Cambridge, MA: Loeb Classical Library, 1931.

Pocock, J. G. A. "Time, History, and Eschatology in the Thought of Thomas Hobbes." In *Politics, Language, and Time.* New York: Atheneum, 1971.

Polin, Raymond. *Politique et philosophie chez Thomas Hobbes.* Paris: Vrin, 1977.

Raylor, Timothy. "Hobbes, Payne, and *A Short Tract on First Principles*." *Historical Journal* 44 (2001): 29–58.

Rhodes, Rosamond. "Hobbes's unReasonable Fool." *Southern Journal of Philosophy* 30 (1992): 93–102.

Ross, Alexander. *Leviathan Drawn out with a Hook, or, Animadversions upon Mr. Hobbes his Leviathan.* London: Thomas Newcomb, for Richard Royston, 1653.

Rousseau, Jean-Jacques. *On the Social Contract, with Geneva Manuscript and Political Economy.* Ed. Roger D. Masters. Trans. Judith R. Masters. New York: St. Martin's Press, 1978.

Ryan, Alan. "Hobbes, Toleration, and the Inner Life." In *The Nature of Political Theory,* ed. David Miller and Larry Siedentop. Oxford: Oxford University Press, 1983.

———. "A More Tolerant Hobbes?" In *Justifying Toleration: Conceptual and Historical Perspectives,* ed. Susan Mendus. Cambridge: Cambridge University Press, 1988.

———. *The Philosophy of the Social Sciences.* London: Palgrave Macmillan, 1970.

Saxonhouse, Arlene W. "Hobbes and the Beginnings of Modern Political Thought." In *Three Discourses: A Critical Modern Edition of Newly Identified Work of the Young Hobbes,* ed. Noel B. Reynolds and Arlene W. Saxonhouse. Chicago: University of Chicago Press, 1995.

Schmitt, Carl. *The Leviathan in the State Theory of Thomas Hobbes: Meaning and Failure of a Political Symbol.* Westport, CT: Greenwood Press, 1996.

Schotte, Dietrich. *Die Entmachtung Gottes durch den Leviathan: Thomas Hobbes über Religion.* Stuttgart: Frommann-Holzboog, 2013.

Schuhmann, Karl. "Hobbes and the Political Thought of Plato and Aristotle." In *Selected Papers on Renaissance Philosophy and on Thomas Hobbes,* ed. Piet Steenbakers and Karl Schuhmann. New York: Springer-Verlag, 2004.

Schwartz, Joel. "Hobbes and the Two Kingdoms of God." *Polity* 18 (1985): 7–24.

Shapin, Steven, and Simon Schaffer. *Leviathan and the Air-Pump: Hobbes, Boyle, and the Experimental Life.* Princeton: Princeton University Press, 2011.

Sherlock, Richard. "The Theology of *Leviathan*: Hobbes on Religion." *Interpretation* 10 (1982): 43–60.

Skinner, Quentin. "Classical Liberty and the Coming of the English Civil War." In *Republicanism: A Shared European Heritage, Vol. II: The Values of Republicanism in Early Modern Europe,* ed. Martin van Gelderen and Quentin Skinner. Cambridge: Cambridge University Press, 2002.

———. "Consent and Conquest: Hobbes and the Engagement Controversy." In *The Interregnum: The Quest for Settlement,* ed. G. E. Aylmer. London: Macmillan, 1972.

———. "The Context of Hobbes's Theory of Political Obligation." In *Hobbes and Rousseau: A Collection of Critical Essays,* ed. Maurice Cranston and Richard Peters. New York: Anchor Books, 1972.

———. "History and Ideology in the English Revolution." *Historical Journal* 8 (1965): 151–78.

———. *Hobbes and Republican Liberty.* Cambridge: Cambridge University Press, 2008.

———. "The Ideological Context of Hobbes's Political Thought." *Historical Journal* 9 (1966): 286–317.

———. *Reason and Rhetoric in the Philosophy of Hobbes.* Cambridge: Cambridge University Press, 1996.

———. *Visions of Politics, Vol. III: Hobbes and Civil Science.* Cambridge: Cambridge University Press, 2002.

Solzhenitsyn, Aleksandr. "A World Split Apart." In *Solzhenitsyn at Harvard: The Address, Twelve Early Responses, and Six Later Reflections,* ed. Ronald Berman. Washington, DC: Ethics and Public Policy Center, 1980.

Sommerville, Johann P. "Hobbes and Independency." *Rivista di storia della filosofia* 21 (2004): 155–73.

———. *Thomas Hobbes: Political Ideas in Historical Context.* New York: Palgrave Macmillan, 1992.

Sorell, Tom. *Hobbes.* London: Routledge and Kegan Paul, 1986.

———. "Hobbes and Aristotle." In *Philosophy in the Sixteenth and Seventeenth Centuries: Conversations with Aristotle,* ed. Constance Blackwell and Sachiko Kusukawa. Aldershot-Brookfield, UK: Ashgate, 1999.

———. "Hobbes's Moral Philosophy." In *The Cambridge Companion to Hobbes's Leviathan,* ed. Patricia Springborg. Cambridge: Cambridge University Press, 2007.

Spinoza, Benedict. *Theological-Political Treatise.* Ed. Jonathan Israel. Cambridge: Cambridge University Press, 2007.

Spragens, Thomas A. *The Politics of Motion: The World of Thomas Hobbes.* Lexington: University of Kentucky Press, 1973.

Springborg, Patricia. "The Enlightenment of Thomas Hobbes." Review of Noel Malcolm, *Aspects of Hobbes. British Journal for the History of Philosophy* 12 (2002): 513–34.

Sreedhar, Susanne. "Toward a Hobbesian Theory of Sexuality." In *Feminist Interpretations of Thomas Hobbes*, ed. Nancy J. Hirschmann and Joanne H. Wright. University Park, PA: Pennsylvania State University Press, 2012.

Strauss, Leo. "German Nihilism." *Interpretation* 26 (1999): 353–78.

———. *Hobbes's Critique of Religion and Related Writings*. Trans. and ed. Gabriel Bartlett and Svetozar Minkov. Chicago: University of Chicago Press, 2011.

———. "The Law of Reason in the *Kuzari*." In *Persecution and the Art of Writing*. Chicago: University of Chicago Press, 1988.

———. *Natural Right and History*. Chicago: University of Chicago Press, 1953.

———. "Notes on Carl Schmitt, *The Concept of the Political*." In Heinrich Meier, *Carl Schmitt and Leo Strauss: The Hidden Dialogue*, trans. J. Harvey Lomax. Chicago: University of Chicago Press, 2006.

———. "On the Basis of Hobbes's Political Philosophy." In *What Is Political Philosophy? And Other Studies*. Chicago: University of Chicago Press, 1988.

———. *The Political Philosophy of Hobbes: Its Basis and Its Genesis*. Trans. Elsa M. Sinclair. Chicago: University of Chicago Press, 1963.

———. "Some Notes on the Political Philosophy of Hobbes." In *Hobbes's Critique of Religion and Related Writings*, trans. and ed. Gabriel Bartlett and Svetozar Minkov. Chicago: University of Chicago Press, 2011.

———. *Spinoza's Critique of Religion*. Chicago: University of Chicago Press, 1991.

———. *Thoughts on Machiavelli*. Chicago: University of Chicago Press, 1995.

———. "What Is Political Philosophy?" In *What Is Political Philosophy? And Other Studies*. Chicago: University of Chicago Press, 1988.

Suárez, Francisco. *Opera Omnia*, Vol. III. Ed. Michel André. Paris: Ludovicum Vives, 1856.

Sullivan, Vickie B. *Machiavelli, Hobbes, and the Formation of a Liberal Republicanism in England*. New York: Cambridge University Press, 2004.

Sutherland, Stewart R. "God and Religion in *Leviathan*." *Journal of Theological Studies* 25 (1974): 373–80.

Tarlton, Charles D. "The Creation and Maintenance of Government: A Neglected Dimension of Hobbes's *Leviathan*." *Political Studies* 29 (1978): 307–27.

Taylor, A. E. "The Ethical Doctrine of Hobbes." In *Hobbes Studies*, ed. K. C. Brown. Cambridge, MA: Harvard University Press, 1965.

Tönnies, Ferdinand. *Thomas Hobbes: Leben und Lehre*. Stuttgart: Friedrich Fromman Verlag, 1971.

Tuck, Richard. "The Civil Religion of Thomas Hobbes." In *Political Discourse in Early Modern Britain*, ed. Nicholas Phillipson and Quentin Skinner. Cambridge: Cambridge University Press, 2010.

———. *Hobbes*. Oxford: Oxford University Press, 1989.

———. "Hobbes and Descartes." In *Perspectives on Thomas Hobbes*, ed. G. A. J. Rogers and Alan Ryan. Oxford: Oxford University Press, 1988.

———. "Hobbes and Locke on Toleration." In *Thomas Hobbes and Political Theory*, ed. Mary Dietz. Lawrence: University Press of Kansas, 1990.

———. "Hobbes, Conscience, and Christianity." In *The Oxford Handbook of Hobbes*, ed. A. P. Martinich and Kinch Hoekstra. New York: Oxford University Press, 2016.

———. *Natural Rights Theories: Their Origin and Development*. Cambridge: Cambridge University Press, 1979.

———. "Optics and Skeptics: The Philosophical Foundation of Hobbes's Political Thought." In *Conscience and Casuistry in Early Modern Thought*, ed. Edmund Leites. Cambridge: Cambridge University Press, 1988.

———. *Philosophy and Government, 1572–1651*. Cambridge: Cambridge University Press, 1993.

Vaughan, Geoffrey M. *Behemoth Teaches Leviathan: Thomas Hobbes on Political Education*. Lanham, MD: Lexington Books, 2002.

Waldron, Jeremy. "Hobbes on Public Worship." *Nomos* 48 (2008): 31–53.

Wallis, John. *Elenchus Geometriae Hobbianae*. Oxford: H. Hall, 1655.

———. *Hobbius Heauton-timorumenos, or, A Consideration of Mr. Hobbes his Dialogues*. Oxford: A. and L. Lichfield, 1662.

Warner, D. H. J. "Hobbes's Interpretation of the Doctrine of the Trinity." *Religious History* 5 (1969): 299–313.

Warrender, Howard. *The Political Philosophy of Hobbes: His Theory of Obligation*. Oxford: Oxford University Press, 1957.

Watkins, J. W. N. *Hobbes's System of Ideas: A Study in the Political Significance of Philosophical Theories*. London: Hutchinson University Library, 1973.

———. "Philosophy and Politics in Hobbes." *Philosophical Quarterly* 19 (1955): 125–46.

Weinberger, J. "Hobbes's Doctrine of Method." *American Political Science Review* 69 (1975): 1336–53.

Willey, Basil. *The Seventeenth Century Background*. Garden City, NY: Anchor Books, 1953.

Wolin, Sheldon. "Hobbes and the Culture of Despotism." In *Thomas Hobbes and Political Theory*, ed. Mary Dietz. Lawrence: University Press of Kansas, 1990.

Zaitchik, A. "Hobbes's Reply to the Fool: The Problem of Consent and Obligation." *Political Theory* 10 (1982): 245–66.

Zuckert, Michael P. "Hobbes on Right and Obligation." A review essay on *Hobbes and Locke: The Politics of Freedom and Obligation* by W. Von Leyden. *Review of Politics* 46 (1984): 295–301.

———. *Launching Liberalism: On Lockean Political Philosophy*. Lawrence: University Press of Kansas, 2002.

———. *Natural Rights and the New Republicanism*. Princeton: Princeton University Press, 1994.

Index